The World of the Urban Working Class

Buildings early in the demolition of the West End.

The World of the Urban Working Class

by Marc Fried

with ELLEN FITZGERALD
PEGGY GLEICHER
CHESTER HARTMAN
and James Blose
Charles Ippolito
Edwina Nary Bentz

Harvard University Press
Cambridge, Massachusetts
1973

For
Erich Lindemann, M.D., Ph.D.
who spawned this research and created an
environment in which it could be fulfilled
and
The People of the West End of Boston
who provided the data for this study
most often willingly and even happily
despite their travails of those years

Acknowledgments

A great many people have been involved in this study and many have contributed to the final outcome of this and subsequent volumes. First and foremost, this study would not have been possible without the guidance and wisdom of Erich Lindemann. As Chief of Psychiatric Services at the Massachusetts General Hospital, he had the foresight to perceive the importance of studying the wide spectrum of responses to a crisis like relocation and the sensitivity to encourage a basic investigation of working-class life as an essential framework for interpreting the meaning of reactions to that crisis. Leonard Duhl was also a central person in every phase of the study. As a staff member of the Planning Branch of the National Institutes of Mental Health he encouraged the initial funding of the study and he was, throughout, a model for the effective facilitation of research. His vision of the possibilities of the study, his discussion of the issues in the study, and his ability to cope with complex, internal strains were invaluable contributions. Early in the planning phase, a number of additional people helped to make an exciting potentiality into a realistic investigation: Laura Morris, Peter Sifneos, Gerald Caplan, and Philip Kubzansky were among these, as were Herbert Gans, Lois Paul, Elliot Mishler, and Lucy Thoma. Herbert Gans, Elliot Mishler, Lois Paul, and Lucy Thoma further gave of their wide knowledge and understanding to the initial research and interview design. A small number of persons deserve special mention since they joined the staff quite early and continued to contribute to it throughout its life, often without pay and certainly beyond the call of duty: Peggy Gleicher, Ellen Fitzgerald, Chester Hartman, and Elaine Frieden were among the most determined and effective of this hardy group.

A number of people were involved in the study for shorter periods of time before the data were ready for final analysis: Edwina Nary Bentz, Joan Levin Ecklein, Margaret Mayr, Anthony Ruscio, Edward Ryan, David Scharff, and Hilda Perlitsch; Gustavo Iacono, Ivor Browne, Jason Aronson, and David Satin; and, in their secretarial responsibilities, Patricia McKenney Scovinski and Patricia Robertson. Many other staff members, interviewers, coders, and supervisors participated briefly and lent their aid. In the last few years, several others helped to see the study to completion: Cindy Aron, James Blose, Linda Brockington, Lorna Ferguson, John Havens, Charles Ippoliti, Frank Twiggs, and Nan Waldstein did useful analytic work; Elizabeth Jones, Gloria Bronstein, and Dori St. John converted several thousand pages into typescript. John Havens's extraordinary ability to communicate both with computers and with social scientists and his profound understanding of mathematics and its application to the social sciences gave this work a character it could not otherwise have had. For this first volume on working-class life, initial materials for chapters were prepared by Chester Hartman (chapter 4), Peggy Gleicher (chapter 5), Ellen Fitzgerald (chapter 6), Edwina Nary Bentz (part of chapter 7), James Blose (chapter 8), and Charles Ippolito (chapter 9). These analyses have all been replicated, carried further, often reinterpreted, and, for the most part, rewritten. The senior author, thus, is alone responsible for the final analysis, interpretation of the literature, and writing.

This study was conducted and the analyses and writing completed with the aid of several grants from the National Institutes of Mental Health. The data were initially collected and analyzed under a grant from the Professional Services Branch of NIMH and the analyses and writing completed under another smaller grant from the Center for the Study of Metropolitan Problems of NIMH. We are grateful not only for the funds that made this study possible but also for the constant sense of support and appreciation so many staff members of NIMH provided.

It is conventional also to thank the members of one's family for tolerance during the trying phases of work on a manuscript. My wife and children were certainly forebearing and helped, as well, as listeners, discussants, readers, and participants, in many of my struggles to understand some of the foundations of working-class life.

M.F.
Boston, Massachusetts
March 1973

Contents

Illustrations

Figures

Map

The World of the Urban Working Class

A street in the West End after a snowstorm.

Prologue: The West End and the World of Working-class People

This is the story of a working-class community on the eve of its destruction. But it is less than that and it is also more than that. It is less because it is not the full story of the community or of its destruction. And since it examines intricate patterns of social functioning, it presents a less vivid image of individual behavior and community life than would emerge in a purely descriptive account. But it is also more than the story of one community since it is an effort both to understand the West End of Boston and to compare it with similar communities in other urban, industrial working-class areas of the Western world. Fundamentally, therefore, it is an effort to understand the causal connections between economic and social conditions, the social order of the community and society in which working-class people live, and characteristic working-class attitudes and behaviors.

The West End of Boston was a tenement district of fifty acres near the core of the central city. For over one hundred years it was one of the main routes through which immigrants from all over the world traveled in the process of shedding an anachronistic identity in order to adapt, gradually, to the urban, industrial society of the United States. In April of 1958, the city took title to these fifty acres and their assorted dwellings, stores, and churches, and started a program of total demolition for the purpose of slum clearance and urban renewal. As our observations and analyses can evidence, it was not only a physical area that was destroyed. A community was, quite literally, demolished.

We will touch only briefly on the impact of the crisis of relocation on the lives of the displaced population.[1] Any attempt to clarify the meaning of dislocation and relocation in the West End and in similar neighborhoods is contingent on understanding the people and the community life of the working class. Such knowledge and understanding are essential, not only for anticipating the effects of urban renewal and residential relocation, but also for assimilating the burgeoning data from research about underprivileged people and for designing programs and policies that affect these population groups.

1

Although the primary data for this study come from the West End of Boston, wherever possible we will draw upon a wider set of working-class communities that have been investigated. Nonetheless there are important limitations due to the restricted population in the West End and to the relatively unsystematic distributions of other populations that have been described. Since the West End included very few blacks we have no empirical basis in these data for discussing the Negro working class. To the very limited extent that other data on the Negro working class exist, however, we shall take them into account. The fact that there were so few blacks in the West End is hardly accidental and implies resistance to residence by blacks and discriminatory attitudes as part of the orientations of working-class people. Nor was severe poverty widespread in the West End, although a substantial minority of the residents fell below any reasonable designation of the poverty line. Some of the discussion in the literature on poverty treats it as an issue of relatively pure economic deprivation. An increasing body of work carries it one step further in recognizing that many other social and psychological problems are associated with poverty either as causes or, more often, as consequences of economic deprivation. Relatively few studies go beyond this in viewing poverty or economic deprivation as one among a number of important aspects of the lowest positions in our stratification system. Those that do, fortunately, provide us with some systematic information about ways of life, social organization and disorganization, and psychological functioning of the most underprivileged members of our society.

There has been an increasing trend, in recent years, to designate these positions of lowest status, so closely linked to poverty, as lower class, distinguishing them from working-class statuses. But whether the term lower class or working class is used for the entire range of low status positions or mainly to differentiate subgroupings, they refer to continguous positions in a class hierarchy and have numerous similarities. The boundary between lower class and working class is often used to distinguish differences in social behavior, cultural patterns, and psychological characteristics but it is fundamentally associated with differences in income and employment. Thus, the boundary distinguishes those people in low status and low income occupations who are stably employed and live at a precarious but just adequate economic level from the more severely deprived who are unemployed, underemployed, or have no available wage earner in the household. For these reasons, the lower class are those people who live at the very margins of subsistence or below. Often they live at the very level of subsistence only by virtue of meager social and welfare benefits. The large minority of the West End population who would be categorized, by these definitions, as lower class provide us with an opportunity to examine the ways in which people in different lower social class positions maintain similar or different roles and relationships. While the grave and frequent deprivations and problems associated with lower-class status warrant fuller attention, they must be seen as deviations from working-class norms rather than as defections from middle-class models.[2]

Most people in the West End belonged to the stable working class and particular emphasis will be placed upon their characteristics and sources of stability. For a century and a half, the lowest status positions in occupation, income, and prestige have been dominated by the peasantries of Europe who migrated to the United States and by their second- and third-generation descendants. As more recent migrants from rural areas have moved into the urban, industrial environment, the former migrants have moved into higher status positions and into more stable employment opportunities. Whether the current lower class, dominated by Negroes, Puerto Ricans, and Mexican-Americans, will similarly be enabled to become a stable working-class population remains a matter of conjecture. The most recent data suggest that marked changes in education, occupation, and income have certainly taken place for the Negro, the Puerto Rican, and the Mexican-American populations (Fried, 1969). Whether the rates of upward social mobility will be similar to the slow but consistent progress of past, in-migrant populations and whether changes in social positions will give way to acceptance and assimilation remains to be seen. To the extent that the white, ethnic, working class experienced a long and difficult period of adjustment to rejection and continues to find both class and ethnic barriers to achievement, they represent a past transition which can provide some forecast of the processes, problems, and impediments to social achievement of all in-migrant populations in our society.

At the other end of the low status scale, the higher levels of working-class positions like those of skilled manual workers or some of the more modest nonmanual occupations (postman, fireman, taxicab driver, retail clerk) merge very gradually with the lower middle class. While skilled workers were fewer in number than the unskilled workers living in the West End, in many respects they were the core of community life in the area. The proportions of the West End population, however, who were middle class were moderately small. This group is diverse in type, in any case, and includes the small storekeeper, the people who have essentially moved out of skilled manual positions through supervisory responsibilities (foreman, inspector), and office workers (secretary, bookkeeper). There are a number of other levels represented, including students, nurses, and other professionals attracted by the convenience of the neighborhood to transportation and to the downtown area, its closeness to the Massachusetts General Hospital, its tolerance for deviants (but not for deviance), or its low rents. Although some of these people of higher status were "outsiders" and may well be deviants from their own class positions, lower-middle-class people were an integral part of the life of the West End. Their residence in the West End was quite natural, just as the residence of working-class people in middle-class areas is frequent. In both instances, however, there are often subtle segregations by subclass within neighborhoods that appear superficially homogeneous. The comparison of lower-middle-class people with several levels of working-class positions will help to clarify some of the similarities and differences within a narrow range of social statuses.

The data on the West End of Boston are based largely on extensive interviews with a random sample of the population living within the relocation area. Sampling was based on the files of the relocation office. Since these files were geographically arranged cards based on a total population survey with a return rate of 99 percent, our selection of every fifth card that met the sampling criteria was a systematic probability sample. These interviews covered a wide range of substantive issues: residential orientations and housing situation, community participation and commitments, marital roles and relationships, parental roles and conceptions, interpersonal relationships and social affiliations with kin and friends both within and outside the West End, occupational functioning and experiences, status orientations and mobility, and personality dispositions and characteristics.

A large part of the analysis is based on the responses of 486 women who received the full prerelocation interview in 1958 or 1959. Approximately two to three years after the residents had moved out of the area, we visited them in their new homes for follow-up interviews. We tried to see everyone in the original sample, whether they had granted us the first interview or not, and obtained postrelocation interviews with 503 women.[3] At the same time we interviewed the husbands of the female respondents and used extensive retrospective questions about the prerelocation experience comparable to those asked of the women before relocation. There remain, nonetheless, a number of gaps in these data. The sampling criteria were that there be a female head of household between the ages of twenty and sixty-five in the dwelling unit. Thus we have no systematic interview data for women under twenty, for those over sixty-five, or for men living in a household without a woman aged twenty to sixty-five. Several sources are available for correcting these deficits and for providing other supplementary data: (a) the extensive diary collected by Herbert Gans in the course of his observations in the West End and the descriptive and analytic material reported in the volume that was largely based on this diary (Gans, 1962); (b) extensive preliminary interviews obtained from selected small samples which provide a wealth of qualitative information; (c) interviews with elderly couples in the West End collected by Elaine Frieden under the auspices of the United Community Services and her reports on these data (Frieden, 1959, 1960, 1962); and (d) ethnographic observations and interviews, relatively unsystematic and fragmentary, collected by a number of observers.[4]

We must be careful to weigh the effect on the data of the fact that we sampled and studied a working-class population on the verge of what was widely conceived as an impending disaster. By the time we entered the field for observation and interviews, urban renewal, redevelopment, and relocation had become household words. The alternation of hope and despair for more than five years may have distorted certain facts and perceptions or may have provided a temporary bias to perspectives on West End experiences among the people we interviewed. Gans (1962) suggests that one such effect was a new sense of the West End as a single area rather than as a number of adjacent neighborhoods. However, challenges and crises create a self-consciousness about many aspects of life which have previously existed but have remained obscure and embedded in the patterns and routines of daily living and of familiar expectations. Thus, they may provide us with crystallized insights into processes of central importance which normally fall outside the purview of the observer. Moreover, comparisons of the West End with other working-class communities occasionally allow us to determine the likelihood that such biases have colored the responses of people from the West End. The most serious limitation due to the rapid influence of renewal expectations was that approximately one-third of the sample had voluntarily left their apartments in the area before we were able to interview them. These interviews generally took place several weeks or even several months after they had moved into housing outside the West End. Although we asked the same questions about housing retrospectively and have included these people in the study sample, the absence of interviewer observations of housing and the fact that this information was no longer so immediate have limited the analysis of housing data.

As in many large studies, there is an unwritten chapter concerning the means by which an impossible study was ever completed under impossible conditions. The technical problems of design, processing, and analysis in a large-scale study are considerable; they can, however, be resolved. But their implementation in the face of frustrations and impediments that seem disastrous place great burdens in the way of effective work. The administration and organization of a complex study and staff, the integration of diverse and often conflicting forces and interests, the efficient use of scarce resources, and the maintenance of high levels of morale and motivation over long and often discouraging periods of time present formidable difficulties. If there are models to be followed, we had not and have not found them. The enormity of the task is occasionally compensated by the value one anticipates in the product. But a research investigator and a research staff are too narcissistically involved and, at the same time, too self-critical to make such judgments comfortably. We are convinced that some of the major problems of our society can only be clarified by massive investment in large and ambitious studies. But it is an enormous task to undertake such a study and for long years an unrewarding one, a reality that should dissuade all but the most determined (and perhaps foolhardy) from confronting so arduous a challenge.

The systematic collection of the data for the West End study was completed early in 1962 except for several small-scale substudies. The data were largely coded and organized and several papers written by 1963. However, the completion of this study and of the several volumes about the people from the West End of Boston required more than a decade, with several intervening years during which little work was possible due to lack of funds and the fact that staff members had to make other commitments. Even while funds were available, numerous problems slowed analytic progress, not least of which was a premature effort to utilize electronic data processing equipment in the statistical analysis of the data. After more than a year devoted to transforming the data for this purpose, it became evident that available computer programs and personnel skills were inadequate to meet our needs. Even before 1965 when the grant ended, the analysis moved haltingly because of little time, reduced budget, and a cumbersome processing arrangement. Most of the work took place at the Massachusetts General Hospital until 1964. In that year, the senior investigator moved to Boston College and was able to use computer time and other opportunities provided by the university to facilitate the data processing and analysis. A computer program borrowed from the Department of Social Relations at Johns Hopkins was of great aid. By the winter of 1966–1967 we were able to move slowly forward and, with a grant from the Center for the Study of Metropolitan Problems of the National Institutes of Mental Health in 1968–1969, we could effectively reorganize the data for use with modern, high-speed data processing equipment. Increasing sophistication on our side during these early years of using equipment designed for purposes other than social science investigations as well as the increasing availability of appropriate computers, computer programs, and technically skilled programmers led to a successful effort.

The problems of developing the social organization and the human skills commensurate with technological capacity are familiar strains in our society and were most directly revealed to us during this period. A similar set of problems, although less dependent on technology alone, involves the use of mathematical and statistical knowledge in social science research. The most advanced ideas about research design, data collection, and, most particularly, data analysis have moved quite far since the West End study was undertaken. It has not been possible to take full advantage of these developments in a study initiated in 1958 but the extensive reorganization of the data provided an opportunity to take some account of newer potentialities. As a consequence, the analysis has proceeded more expeditiously and with greater precision and assurance than it might have previously. It is useful to compare earlier analyses with those based on more recent statistical evaluation. Basic interpretations and conclusions were generally similar. The results of more intricate statistical analysis bore out most of the findings that had previously been obtained. But the use of multiple regression techniques, particularly, and the conception of path analysis as well as the ready availability of more extensive sets of tabular data permitted a greater clarification of causal sequences and more effective integration of results than would have been possible at an earlier date.

A wooden structure in the West End demolished in 1926 for code violations.

1 Continuities in Working-class Experience

The Situation of the Urban Worker

For at least a century, the United States has reaped the benefits of an expanding economy, a rising standard of living, the development of a massive technological apparatus, and the emergence of vast realms of opportunity in education and occupation. Yet it remains a society with enormous inequalities of access to opportunity and large contrasts between deprivation and privilege in economic, political, and social life. Similar inequalities are quite characteristic for all the urban, industrial societies in the world today, regardless of differences in social class traditions or in egalitarian ideology.[1] We might expect that the countries of western Europe, with a long tradition of aristocratic prerogative and a history of legal distinctions which defined the rights and obligations of different social orders, would show a more marked or more rigid social class structure than the United States. Or we might anticipate that the communist societies of eastern Europe would have diminished drastically the inequalities of position and opportunity in pursuit of a socialist ideal. Neither of these appears to be true. While there are significant differences in the social class patterns of industrialized societies, they are differences largely in the sources and symbolisms of inequality and in paths to mobility rather than in the degree of inequality or in the importance of social class differentiation.

There is a striking, almost repetitive, quality in the concrete history, current experiences, and dilemmas of different working-class populations. Over the course of many centuries in Western history, there have been many changes in the actual conditions of working-class life. And many differences appear among different, contemporary working-class populations. But these are less frequent than the similarities and are less basic to the relative position of working-class people in the larger society. Broad generalizations about working-class populations, thus, have considerable justification in the available evidence and are as applicable to the United States as to European countries with a longer and more sharply defined working-class tradition. Indeed, the United States has developed a reputation in recent years among many European observers and even among ordinary foreign citizens of harboring among the most extreme forms of inequality in the Western world. Whether this reputation is justified or not, a matter that is difficult to assess precisely, the gradual diminution of severe under-privilege in much of western Europe has sharpened the contrast with the United States, a fabulously wealthy nation in which so many millions of persons bear the marks of poverty and discrimination.

In discussing the working class, we imply that the people we are describing and analyzing represent one segment or stratum in a structure that includes a number of different social classes and, by extension, that social class position is an important dimension of American life. Despite extensive work by social scientists on poverty and inequality, on the hierarchy of social classes in our society, and on the limitations of social opportunity and mobility, the idea of the United States as a highly stratified society seems strange to the popular American conception of our social structure. Except for short periods of heightened concern with social problems, social class has generally seemed irrelevant as a variable for analysis or as a subject for theoretical clarification even among many social and behavioral scientists. The American tradition has tended rather to ignore the significance of social class position and, in ignoring it, to allow its consequences to become compounded until they have periodically reached crisis proportions. Manifest inequalities that cannot be dismissed have frequently been encapsulated in oversimplified conceptions like "the problem of poverty," or, more recently, "the Negro problem." Poverty and the situation of the Negro in the United States are certainly matters that warrant immediate attention and action. But poverty is only part of the problem of social class differences. The situation of the black American, while integrally tied to the inequalities inherent in our social structure, is part of another broad (and related) problem of racial and ethnic segmentation, segregation, and discrimination embedded in the social orientations and practices of American life.

The many overt and subtle contrasts among social classes in the Western world are readily obscured by the general sense of affluence and by the cloak of invisibility between classes. This invisibility is due to real limitations of contact and to a widespread denial of inequalities in the midst of democratic ideals. Industrial workers as an occupational and interest group, unionized and vocal in our society, are an integral part of our conceptions of society. But workers as a segment of the population, as people who live in somewhat separate communities and maintain distinctive patterns of life that can be traced to their distinctive economic and social positions in society are less evident, less visible. The world of the urban working class remains a strange, encapsulated, and unfamiliar world within the larger, industrial society of the twentieth century. Despite common features of cultural experience, the social stratifications of our society are embedded in the ways of life of different social classes and enveloped within residential and social segregations. Many neighborhoods include people from slightly different social positions and, thus, through schools, common shopping places, occasional organizational activities, there is some exchange in relatively impersonal or formalistic situations. But opportunities for significant egalitarian interaction between people from markedly different social classes are infrequent, and we do not ordinarily have a chance to learn much about the public or private social behavior of social classes different from our own.

Upper- and upper-middle-class people generally become aware of the divergent patterns of working-class behavior and life experience only in peripheral ways. They drive past run-down tenements, congealed masses of three-deckers, dilapidated, shantytown shacks. They enter unfamiliar and ominous neighborhoods only to visit exotic stores or foreign restaurants. In transit they may see the noisy horseplay of teenagers, the anonymous laborer, the tough-looking, heavy-set man or the tired and drawn woman on the street. They may hear about the child in school whose learning difficulties pursue him in an inextricable cycle of antagonisms between teacher and child. Beyond these impersonal contacts and the frequently magnified problems of delinquency and crime, promiscuity and illegitimacy, riots, unemployment, and families on welfare, our society manages to isolate the world of the working class so that it intrudes minimally on the consciousness of other classes. Similarly, working-class people often misconstrue the characteristics of upper-class and upper-middle-class people. They overemphasize the striving for status, the affluence and luxury of living, the deliberate misuse of economic and political power, the freedom from hard work and stress, and the human indifference of people in all higher status positions. Thus, people in different strata readily depersonalize one another and either imagine a homogeneity that is unrealistic or interpret the great diversities in life situation and cultural patterns as mainly psychological or moral in origin. At the same time they are "blaming the victim," ascribing to individual motives social conditions that are properly located within the social system itself (Ryan, 1971).

Although much of the blame for social problems is often attributed to those people in the lowest status positions who are the most evident victims of social injustice, there is a sense in which people in all status positions are the victims of systems that sustain high levels of inequality. Much of the conflict and strain in modern industrial societies which affect the entire population can be traced to inordinate inequalities that are not warranted either by the large resources of the society or by differences in ability and performance. To maintain these, a vast array of economic, legal, social, and psychological mechanisms must be brought into play that occupy extensive resources and require constant vigilance on the part of public and private organizations and agencies. The barriers to ready confrontation and interaction between people in different social classes help to perpetuate misconceptions between classes and, thus, produce spurious justifications for a structure that has little intrinsic rationality.

There is a large gap between pointing to a problem and providing a basis for its solution. Indeed, the problems created by social class systems in modern, affluent, democratic societies are themselves implicit, rather than explicit, in studying the lives and situations of working-class people. But the study of people in lower status positions in industrial society does reveal the fundamental importance of social position as a crucial determinant of the ways in which people function. The influence of an individual's social position on his behavior is only one among the several ways in which the class structures of modern societies ramify through every aspect of institutional patterning and personal functioning. It may not even be the most crucial consequence of social class. But the extent to which social class position provides relatively narrow limits to human behavior and influences a wide array of social and psychological attributes discloses how powerful these forces are even in democratic societies.

The major theme of this study is that the patterns of working-class life represent adaptations to a number of historical and contemporary conditions and structural constraints. No one of these forces alone can adequately account either for the great similarities among working-class populations or for their manifest diversities and variations. The factors of greatest moment, we believe, are those that stem most directly from structured situations of inequality: differences in the range of options available for people in different social class positions and a general consequent expectation among working-class people that invidious distinctions will affect every aspect of life and most particularly the distribution of rewards and opportunities. These are given greater significance by virtue of the familiarity of these conditions in the past of working-class people, a past that has been fairly continuous for many centuries. Although the history of the working class is often neglected, some fundamental features of the social class structure of modern societies and of the position of low status people in the class structure are direct evolutionary products of the stratification systems of Europe since the Middle Ages. Under conditions of rapid and dramatic change during the eighteenth and nineteenth centuries, these class systems were markedly altered but, nonetheless, retained many characteristic features. Some of the vitality of social class experiences and perceptions in contemporary life stem from a historically-induced consciousness, no matter how vague and informal, of these endemic consequences of inequality.

To appreciate the ways in which the current class situation of low status people affect their wider social adaptations and to visualize the effects of social mobility on both the class system and on the situation of the working class, it is further essential to understand the major dimensions of social class in industrial democracies. The structure of social class as a system of relatively stabilized inequalities creates the economic, social, and political context for modern working-class life. The specific conditions, experiences, and dislocations of those people who have successively filled the ranks of the working class further influenced their orientations and adjustments to the urban, industrial environment. The vast majority of the people who entered the urban, industrial labor force at its lowest levels were from the peasantries and villages of Europe during the nineteenth and early twentieth centuries. They were followed, in subsequent decades, by former peasants from Mexico and Puerto Rico, and by blacks from the South living in near-peasant situations. The conditions of existence of these populations and the ways of life in their communities, as well as the processes and problems of migration and transition, form another important feature of the background of most working-class people. It is difficult to understand their tolerance for the intolerable circumstances of their new lives and their ready accommodation to American working-class life styles without some appreciation of the spare and fragmented economic and cultural environments from which they fled.

Many immigrants from Europe moved rapidly to the Midwest to perpetuate their former experiences as farmers. The majority of the immigrant populations, however, entered existing slums in the urban areas of our large cities. It was this experience, their incorporation into the occupational activities and community life of low status people in the new world that served to organize a different identity out of past deprivation and neglect, old cultural traditions, and a continuous sense of being victimized by their low status and their lack of resources. Although the social institutions and cultural patterns of these slums were more familiar and more comfortable to the newcomer than the totally alien institutions of the larger society, the new environment required many adaptations. The working-class slum might be an urban village, but it reflected a different social order and involved new orientations to family, kin, and neighbors, new conceptions of work, leisure, and geographical mobility, and new relationships to friends, strangers, authorities, and organizations.

The opportunity to adapt slowly to the new society under the relatively sympathetic and cohesive conditions of working-class community life has undoubtedly been a fundamental condition of effective transition for low status people in our society. As individuals became more fully assimilated within their working-class environments, they could also begin to absorb the norms and orientations of the larger society. This often brought them into confrontation with the wide gap between ideals and realities in the American opportunity structure, but it also meant a slow process of social mobility for a modest number of the transplanted workers. Often these achievements did not produce the automatic acceptance and the attrition of discriminatory attitudes they had expected, but this too they had to learn to recognize or to deny as part of the American complex. Many working-class men and women have, in fact, denied the full import of the limited opportunity structure and few have recognized it as one manifestation of a highly regulated system of social inequality. Whether or not such denial is simply a protective psychological mechanism to avoid a sense of helplessness and discouragement, the price of successful adaptation can often be found in many attitudes and personality characteristics of working-class people. The denial of the class stratifications of our society is supplemented by a host of other forces: a moderately high standard of living, available targets for displaced anger such as blacks and student radicals, and the intricacies of economics and social structure that readily obscure the foundations of inequality. Certainly, working-class people are not alone in their denial, for this is one of the more widely shared illusions of modern, industrial societies. The more closely one examines the data, however, the more difficult it is to sustain this illusion. To the extent that we believe that a realistic assessment of social organization and social behavior is the only basis for rational action, a careful consideration of the effects of social class position on the lives of people and the more general implications of a high degree of inequality in the United States and in other industrial nations are essential for recognizing ourselves and our society.

Social Progress and the Distribution of Rewards

Few contemporary workers can trace their origins to urban, working-class populations in the distant past. The peasantry rather than the urban labor force has been the continuous source of more recent working-class populations. While social mobility in industrial societies is not so marked or so perpetual as the image of a mobile society would suggest, over a period of several generations there have been large-scale shifts in social position affecting all social class levels.[2] Thus, continuities in the history of the working class are social phenomena that have affected different families over time. Recurrent elements in working-class history, however, readily become a part of the consciousness of new working-class generations. Repetitive experiences of deprivation, of oppression, and of inequality generate folk expectations and provide stable and persistent meanings to contemporary and seemingly transitory events. It is not only the influence of this history as part of the tradition of the working class that makes it relevant. Working-class history also merits attention because some of the recurrent events reveal the circular and compounding nature of inequalities in the midst of progressive changes that vitiate the foundation and justification for those former inequalities. Even a cursory consideration of major events in the history of low status people reveals the pattern of successive restructuring of inequalities and injustices.

One of the fascinating and not wholly comprehensible events that took place during the Middle Ages in Western Europe was the gradual debasement of a population of free peasant farmers who eventually emerged as a vast, servile laboring force, bound to their lands and their lords.[3] The great agricultural estates of the Roman Empire were based on slave labor. With the decline of the empire and the loss of conquered territories, the sources of slaves vanished. As the control of local life passed from a centralized state that had lost its authority into the hands of large landowners, the farming of the estates was increasingly dependent on local peasant populations. By the time of Charlemagne, slavery was infrequent in Europe. But the free peasantry was gradually becoming enserfed by large proprietors with enormous power stemming from their military prowess. Apart from the naked conquest of entire villages, the successive ravages of the invading Moslems, Magyars, and Norsemen provided the military aristocracy with an opportunity to provide "protective custody" for large peasant populations at the price of serfdom. Peasant lands were often destroyed by the invaders, nonetheless, and were even ravished by the lord and his military vassals in search of food so that the decimated lands frequently retreated to forest or desert.

The warrior nobility emerged from these struggles as a legally recognized estate with vast powers and privileges and, for the higher nobility, virtually unfettered control. An embracing system of vassalage that affected all levels of the population served their interest in luxurious living and in extending their power over wider domains. The peasants, on the other hand, returned to their former lands, not as free men but as serfs, only a mite less servile than the slaves had been. Thus, the Middle Ages saw a division of most of the population of western Europe into a very small number of great landowners living on vast estates and a large population of servile laborers supporting the leisure of their masters.

In theory the serf was the chattel of his lord who could dismiss or sell him at will. The serf could not voluntarily leave the land, he could own no property, and he had no hereditary rights since everything he held belonged to the lord to whom it reverted upon the death of the serf. However, in the absence of written law and natinal institutions, legally-recognized manorial customs developed that were more liberal in practice than were feudal principles. Moreover, whatever rights the serfs could wrest from manorial authorities, they did. When the rise of free cities made available potential havens for excape or when famine or epidemics reduced the size of the labor force, the bargaining power of the serf often improved. Under these conditions, peasants could force their lords to grant concessions and to offer improved tenurial arrangements.

Although the structure of social classes under feudalism was quite rigid, it was evidently neither as stark and unambiguous as formal definitions would imply nor as impervious to change as hereditary legal status suggests. Fluidity in position among the upper classes was an inevitable function of shifts in military power, in alliances, in the manipulation of advantage. The rise of burgher wealth meant that landed estates and titles of nobility might be purchased or parlayed from the king, a practice that proved extremely lucrative to the royal exchequer. At lower levels, serfs could escape from bondage and become outlaws, or hide away in towns, or seek improved conditions on another estate. Some serfs gained control over more extensive farmlands while others lost their proprietary rights entirely and became landless. Gradual manumission produced a larger number of free peasants. Thus, alongside the gross legal distinctions between estates, there were many finer variations in economic and social status and a social class system developed that was not entirely congruent with the formal divisions among the population.

More dramatic in retrospect than the slow attrition of the onerous burdens of serfdom, the rise of towns and cities represented a sharp break with feudal conceptions of status. During the tenth and eleventh centuries, the revival of long-distance trade reestablished contact between distant regions and countries. Stimulated by the needs of merchants for stable storage and commercial outlets, urban areas began to grow far beyond their ancient outlines. By the end of the thirteenth century, Milan, Venice, Florence, and Genoa had populations of more than 100,000 and Paris, London, and several cities in Flanders were rapidly becoming major urban centers. The continuing demand by merchants and craftsmen for limitations of feudal obligations and restrictions, for jurisdictional privileges, for rights to divide and sell land were contradictory to the very essence of feudal society, and the absence of legal differentiation among the citizens of a town were implicit denials of the hierarchical principles of feudalism.

The burgesses paid handsomely for these privileges but their returns were handsome as well. Urban growth was reinforced by the expansion of population that occurred throughout Europe beginning in the tenth or eleventh century. As the towns and cities grew, they too developed sharp distinctions between different social classes. These distinctions were largely based on occupation, economic status, and power and were not embedded in a legal structure. The serf who escaped from the land, who was willing to accept the jobs that nobody else wanted to do, whose family remained in the city for several generations might anticipate some social improvement over many decades. But the lowly peasant, born of servile parents, had many legal and practical impediments in his path and, despite the legal equality of the city, bore the marks of his origin within the urban social class hierarchy. Those serfs who remained on the estates of their masters found little improvement in their status or situation as a result of the urban challenge to feudal ideas.

In the long run of history, the gradual disappearance of slavery and of serfdom were events of great consequence. But legal freedom does not insure freedom of action, particularly when economic and social servitude persist and when the courts are reluctant to promote the realization of de jure rights. Eventually legal serfdom in Europe was bound to vanish. Throughout Europe, moving gradually from east to west and from north to south, the development of new potentialities and influences in agriculture, industry, trade, and urban agglomerations produced new conditions of work and new forms of social organization in work. Inevitably the practical advantages to landlords of a free labor force became evident and it was this, rather than any democratic ideology, that led to the decline of serfdom. The peasants paid heavily for their change in status and waited a long time for commensurate improvements in social and economic position.

The earliest, the most extensive, and the best documented changes in the position of the lower classes occurred in England. The agrarian economy of the Middle Ages was based on large estates held as proprietary domains by lords whose tenants, servile or free, provided agricultural and other services to the lord in exchange for the small tenures they held for their subsistence needs. The contractual relationship between lord and tenant was relatively permanent and only over long periods of time could the custom of the manor, which specified the size of holdings and the rent or services involved, be modified. The major service was ordinarily agricultural work on the demense lands of the lord. In addition to their own tenures, however, the peasants relied heavily on access to the common fields for pasturing their animals, for manure for their farms, and for other resources such as wood, fruit, berries. With the growth of trade, there were shifts in the relative importance of different agricultural products. Often, as in the increased value of wool compared to grains, these changes made a large, agricultural labor force superfluous. Moreover, international economic conditions affected the livelihood of great landlords in other ways. Thus, the widespread inflation of the sixteenth century resulted in a devaluation of currencies and a rise in prices. But the custom-determined stability of rents and services reduced the real rate of return from the land for the proprietor. The English landlords, progressive entrepreneurs that they were and more constrained by legal authority from trespassing on the rights of serfs than the French or German nobility, sought some means to increase their revenues from their lands.

In principle, many landlords worked to transform their estates into capitalist farms with wage laborers or with tenants on short leases. The means by which this was often achieved involved the enclosure of the common lands on their estates, abrogating the rights of use of the commons by their serfs and free peasants. Occasionally peasants were directly evicted from their holdings and the customary obligations owed by the lord were vitiated, but this could lead to court action and the Tudor monarchs opposed such evictions. Subtler approaches were therefore frequently employed, such as successive encroachments on the commons, rendering it gradually unavailable to the peasantry, or the rental of the entire estate to a large farmer who was less clearly bound by the traditional obligations of the proprietor. With the loss of common rights, the economic situation of the peasants deteriorated rapidly. Some managed to struggle along for awhile under these conditions. Many others became landless tenant farmers or left the land entirely, often wandering aimlessly to seek odd jobs, sometimes learning to rob and pillage in order to live.

These early enclosures, leading to the demise of serfdom, reveal some of the focal issues in the unequal distribution of the prices and profits of progress. As a matter of social organization, the enclosures of the sixteenth and subsequent centuries altered a restricted and traditional agrarian economy and adapted it to modern conditions of agriculture, expanding commerce, and developing industry. The feudal arrangement provided security to both lord and peasant under stable conditions, but it discouraged agricultural and commercial innovation or reform. In this sense, the enclosures were signs of economic and social progress. At the same time, they reveal a gross inequity. The great landlords did not own their properties in the modern sense but were tenants with proprietary rights. Even the overlord was a tenant-in-chief of the king and owed obligations to the king in exchange for these rights. A lord, moreover, had obligations to his vassals, whatever their status, in exchange for their tenurial obligations to him. With the gradual demise of feudalism and the emergence of more modern patterns of ownership, the lords gained a great deal but the peasants lost virtually everything. The lord who had been a proprietary tenant now became a property-owning landlord. His obligations to his overlord disappeared in the process and his obligations to his tenants similarly vanished. Thus, the enormous gains he achieved were cost-free. The peasant, on the other hand, paid dearly for his freedom. The rights he claimed of the lord were simply obliterated; his obligations for service to the lord were, at best, commuted to rents, taxes, and dues. At worst, of course, he was simply evicted from the land or became a wage laborer. Were we able to specify the monetary value of these transactions, it seems certain that much of the economic expansion that resulted from these agrarian changes was paid for by the capital investment of the rights lost by millions of peasants. In accordance with the principle of blaming the victim, the English Poor Laws were designed to punish the vast numbers of uprooted peasants who migrated from one place to another, without land, with few skills, and without industrial opportunities that might substitute for the loss of their tenures.

In the eighteenth century, new measures were developed to give legal foundation to the processes of enclosure. In England, thousands of private acts were passed granting rights to enclose specific properties. Many of them involved the most serious abuses and the denial of due process to the injured small farmers. While landowners amassed vast holdings, the consequences for the economic condition and morale of the lower classes were destructive. As the Hammonds (1911) point out, even when the small farmer received strict justice in the division of the common fields, he was often obliged to sell his property because he could not sustain his share of the legal costs and the additional expense of fencing his allotment. Enclosure was never so popular on the continent as in England. In most continental countries, serfdom persisted long after it had disappeared in the British Isles. But similar forms of agricultural reorganization took place, converting aristocratic estates into capitalist farms and reducing the status of the peasant to that of a wage laborer in exchange for slight gains in freedom from traditional bonds.

The impetus to change came from the great territorial and commercial competition that began to develop among the European powers in the sixteenth and seventeenth centuries. India, Africa, the West Indies, and the Americas were opened up to exploitation during these centuries. With new markets, industrial activity began to advance. The absolute monarchies of Europe, eager to enjoy the benefits of growth in manufacturing, heavy industry, and commerce increased their control over all forms of craft and industrial production. The reinforced power of the guilds and the development of new monopolies froze competition and impeded organizational or technical innovation. At the same time, they diminished the status and reduced the opportunities for social mobility of craftsmen. Apprentices and journeymen could no longer expect to become masters and many of the master craftsmen themselves had to accept the conditions of wage workers. It was the merchant, with control over markets and with extensive capital, who slowly gained control over the entire productive process. Little of the merchant's investment was in fixed capital or equipment so that he could expand or contract his operations depending on costs, prices, and demand. As a consequence, however, there was great job instability for the workmen who had become increasingly dependent on wages. At the same time, the vast expansion of enterprise saw the rise to wealth and prominence of a small number of mercantile and manufacturing entrepreneurs, some of whom eventually entered the ranks of the nobility. The grave inequalities in the distribution of costs and benefits, often attributed to the industrial revolution, long antedated that remarkable development and, in fact, were largely independent of industrialization per se.

Without historical distance, the contemporary poor and, more generally, people in the working class are often upbraided for lack of effort in extricating themselves from their condition. Over longer historical periods, however, it becomes evident that the circumstances of working-class life have been produced by large social processes that have often been further responsible for inducing profound demoralization along with economic deprivation. Certainly the degradation of skills and the loss of independence among peasants and craftsmen during the mercantile era affected people who had formerly attained modest levels of social status, economic stability, and psychological security.[4] Competition from factory production led to long struggles between handicraft producers and manufacturers. Craftsmen tried to resist the dominance of the factory with little hope of prolonged success. The emergence of a huge, underprivileged population of paupers, virtually outside the structure of society, was an even more devastating consequence of the development of industrial societies in the West. Contemporaries often denied the problem of poverty by defining it as vice. Alcoholism, robbery, begging, riots, mental and physical illness, and a host of social evils plagued the cities, towns, and even the countryside throughout western Europe. These conditions were most frequent among the poor who were, thus, seen as the source of the problem. There was little recognition of the fact that these were mainly the symptoms of poverty and hopelessness among people who had often been deprived of their former livelihoods by the very forces of progressive change.

To exacerbate these problems, Europe experienced a population explosion during the eighteenth century when the population grew from 120 million to more than 190 million. The new industrial towns and the cities became overburdened metropoli. London approached a population of one million, Paris went beyond half a million, and a great many cities housed more than 100,000 people. This was also a period of great economic growth and, for the entrepreneur, one of great affluence. Some of the profits of enterprise were reinvested in further expansion, but a considerable part of the new wealth was utilized for attaining princely standards of living, building palaces, amassing treasure from all of Europe, maintaining retinues of servants. For the skilled worker, the economic situation improved at first under conditions of relatively stable prices and a high level of demand for his services. But with rises in the cost of living and with competition from factory production, his position started to decline. For the mass of the population, living conditions appear to have deteriorated more consistently. In England, the total number of unemployed was probably as high as a third of the population and early in the nineteenth century at least 20 percent of the people were receiving poor relief. In France, indigence reached a fairly stable level of about 20 percent of the population during the eighteenth century and rose considerably during economic recessions. Real wages started to rise slowly in the manufacturing regions of England, France, and Germany in the early part of the nineteenth century, but the numbers of poor did not diminish.

The situation of the independent artisan in the eighteenth century may too often be idealized and romanticized as a contrast with the factory worker of later decades, but there is little doubt that early factory production introduced a new dimension of inhumanity and undermined the autonomy and even the hope of workers at all levels of skill. Those men and women who became factory laborers suffered from the rapacious struggle for profits, a struggle unbounded by legal restrictions or social traditions. Some historians claim that the horror stories of factory discipline, the cruelty toward children, and the desperate condition of pauper apprentices at the mercy of unscrupulous employers were exaggerated. But the problem of child labor was extremely serious and the hours and conditions of work were nothing less than abominable. In retrospect it is evident that this was one of the great eras of technological and social progress. Vast new potentialities were opened up by these advances. The workers who lived through this time, who worked seventy hours a week or more at difficult, dangerous, or incredibly monotonous, ill-paid jobs, who knew neither leisure nor security, bore a very large part of the cost for this progress.

The human tragedy of industrialization during the eighteenth and nineteenth centuries became most poignant in the long gap between potential and accomplishment, in the desperate search for a livelihood by many millions faced with the visible manifestation of concentrated wealth and power, in the economic and political powerlessness of a vast working class struggling to achieve a modicum of equity in the accelerating enterprise of industrial society. Progress was slow for the laborer and for a long period of time the gulf between propertied and propertyless classes widened. The growth of real wages, shifts in the occupational structure, the development of unions among industrial workers, and the extension of the suffrage gradually increased the bargaining power of the urban, industrial working class during the latter part of the nineteenth century. These were important accomplishments, but they did not abrogate the large differences in privilege and prerogative nor did they eliminate poverty and deprivation.

Slowly, inequitably, painfully, industrial workers reaped some benefits from the advances of the nineteenth century. But the low status agrarian population received virtually none of the rewards of technological and social development. After centuries of serfdom, extending well into the nineteenth century in many countries, the advancing economies of industrializing nations provided few improvements in income, in status, or in living conditions for the large peasant populations who farmed the great agricultural estates as day laborers, tenants, or sharecroppers, or worked their small plots as owners or leaseholders.[5] Even the bare subsistence levels of living among many rural populations could only be maintained through constant emigration from the countryside to the cities of Europe and the United States. For several centuries, in addition to the striking evictions, expulsions, and enclosures, the growth of population coupled with the failure to modernize farming practices led to a continuous decline in the conditions of peasant and village life. It was not merely the economic condition of agricultural workers on large estates or of freehold farmers trying to work plots that were too small for families that were too large that placed the peasantry at the low ebb of human existence. They suffered many social, cultural, and psychological deprivations as well. Traditional patterns of cooperation, integration, and village autonomy were undermined by the changes in tenurial arrangement. The economic base of family continuity all but disappeared both for agricultural laborers who owned no land and for small-scale farm owners whose lands could not tolerate subdivision among the children in a family. Constant migration out of the village fragmented the residues of cultural integrity and continuity and destroyed the significance of locally-based kinship and neighbor patterns.

In western Europe, some semblance of dignity was maintained in the integrity of village life and of neighbor relationships; in Ireland, in southern Italy, and in much of central Europe, the alternation between backbreaking, primitive labor and enforced idleness due to the intense competition for scarce resources and scarce jobs destroyed the significance of village life. There was neither leisure for neighboring nor money to spend in social and cultural activities. Even in the quasi-feudal societies of eastern Europe, where the village retained some communal meaning, it was largely a collectivity with few functions. Regions of small-scale ownership appear to have maintained greater social stability with persisting forms of communal cooperation, investments in cultural traditions, and less striking manifestations of psychological retrogression in spite of economic deprivation. By contrast, those regions dominated by large estates farmed by day laborers or tenant farmers on short leases seem to have lost all semblance of integrated social units even when they provided better economic conditions or more efficient administration. To some degree this may well have been a function of the extent to which the peasant could participate in decisions that affected his economic or political situation. This is suggested by the paradoxical example of the Jewish communities of eastern Europe in which the *shtetel,* the local village community, was forced to care for itself and its population because the authorities rejected this responsibility. These communities, as much as any in Europe, retained their social and cultural integrity despite severe economic deprivation and many forms of oppression that might have led to psychological degradation and cultural disintegration.

Such regional variations almost certainly produced differences in the rates of emigration and may also have entailed differences in the success of adaptation among those who migrated. But widespread poverty, subservience, and restrictions produced a characteristic peasant type of migrant and a set of expectations that could account for the ready acceptance of and even gratitude for the meager conditions of working-class life in the United States and in European cities. Within the peasant village, centuries of deprivation and loss created a strange mixture of clinging to the soil and massive migration, of traditional group commitments coupled with profound distrust of others, of stark individualism and ready subordination to others. Often the struggle to retain a fractured cultural identity served further to destroy the peasant society. Intensified support for shared values and group interdependence meant intolerance for deviance. As they grew less authentic, these traditions became more autarchic. Public opinion became a tyrannizing force, with gossip as the major medium of exchange. As communal functioning deteriorated and the outside world impinged more forcibly on the little community, localism became a territorial parochialism. Throughout the peasant lands, there was little improvement in economic condition to compensate for other losses and, in many areas, the economic situation deteriorated even further with population growth, subdivision of farms, and expanding agricultural estates competing for limited markets.

So brief a summary of some major changes in the social structure of western Europe that affected lower status populations across a millennium cannot reveal all the successive strains and crises. By the eighteenth century, similar events began to occur in the United States and the relatively stable organization of inequality soon became apparent in this new society. Many of the gains achieved by the lower classes, serfs and slaves, peasants and farmers, urban craftsmen and industrial workers involved conflict, tragedy, and even bloodshed: strikes, riots, rebellions, and other civil disorders as well as subtler battles in the ordinary course of daily work and political activity. Nonetheless, for all their struggles, one enduring feature of a thousand years of relatively continuous progress and economic advance has been the unequal distribution of costs and benefits for different social classes. Certainly this view is not universally accepted and for each of these great periods of change one can find historians who reflect a variety of opinions. However one may explain or justify the pattern and despite occasional variations, there is little doubt that the distribution of benefits, and probably of costs as well, followed quite closely the hierarchy of social positions. People in the lowest status positions paid an inordinate share of the price of progress and the benefits filtered down in successively smaller shares from the highest to the lowest classes. More recent historical events seem to reveal a similar phenomenon, although, close to these events as we are, they are more difficult to visualize with balance.

It is not possible to document the impact of past inequities in the allocation of costs and benefits on contemporary working-class attitudes and behaviors, but workers widely anticipate precisely such forms of maldistribution. This working-class view does not derive from an organized perception of the structure of social class but is a more informal, inbred sense of class relationships. Certainly the former peasant arriving in an urban area from situations of impoverishment, overwhelming constraints and limitations, and repetitive crises is least likely to perceive the structured forms of disadvantage in the urban, industrial environment. Even when he has become integrated within the urban work force and has incorporated a sense of that history and its consequences for workers, he is more likely to see these problems as part of the total situation and to take inequity for granted. Indeed, the attitudes and behaviors of urban workers are largely the adaptations of people acclimated to disaster, for whom the meager rewards of industrial work are experiences of comparative comfort and security, who have learned to tolerate situations they cannot readily change. Moreover, in societies with a modicum of opportunity for achievement, workers more often make a dimly-conscious choice of slight social and economic advancement rather than struggling to rectify injustices that are so large and so pervasive. The migration from rural to urban areas, however, and the process of transition form an integral component of these adaptations to urban, industrial life and of learning to be a member of the working class in a modern society. It is in this situation of transition, confronted by the realities of work, of community, and of class status, guided by peers who have already accommodated themselves to the manifold demands, pressures, and opportunities of their positions, that working-class life styles are established.

Poplar Street in the West End

2   Ethnic Origins of Working-class Communities

Immigration to the United States

One of the more important and distinctive features of social class differences in the United States has been the close association of social position with differences in ethnic background, racial origins, and assimilation status. This is hardly surprising since so large a proportion of the working class was of immigrant origin and came from low status positions in their many different native lands. In the early history of the new world, along with a small elite of military governors, aristocrats with large land grants, merchants, and craftsmen, there was a slow but continuous stream of migrants from the lowest social class positions: indentured servants, former convicts, peasants fleeing oppression or seeking a home after being dispossessed. The blacks, captured or purchased and forcibly transplanted as slaves, were particularly distinctive in color and origin as well as in status.

From the middle of the nineteenth century and even earlier many millions of immigrants arrived in the United States from countries and regions that formed a sharp cultural contrast with the familiar Anglo-Saxon style that had developed in this country. Cast up by misery and deprivation, they formed the lowest status segment of our society with the lowest occupations, the lowest incomes, and the poorest conditions of housing and human welfare. The fact that their language, their dress, their ways of perceiving and behaving were so foreign facilitated the association of class position and alien origin. Since the beginning of the twentieth century, as the technological development of the United States became an omnivorous force requiring huge resources of manpower, and as the immigration from Europe diminished because of restrictive legislation, vast new populations entered the urban industrial labor force: Negroes from the South, Mexican peasants, poverty-stricken Puerto Ricans, all of them marked by alien cultures and physical appearance.

Ethnic and cultural differences have often exacerbated seriously the inequalities suffered by incoming populations and have frequently become symbolic expessions of social class differentiation. Indeed, the ethnic character of low status populations in the United States has often helped to obscure the underlying structure of social class in this country. Certainly ethnic discrimination and rejection, particularly manifest toward those ethnic minorities who were most distinctively different from the white Anglo-Saxon prototype and thus expressed most powerfully against black Americans, have been forces of great importance in characterizing the American ethos. But ethnic discrimination has been superimposed on the inequalities stemming from social class differences. The structure of social inequality in our society antedated the arrival of each successive population and served to incorporate the migrant into the most menial and unrewarding positions. However, the excessive concentration on ethnic differences obliterated any consciousness of the profound significance of the social class structure in defining the conditions that confronted the newcomers.

Acceptance by other working-class people and incorporation within working-class communities has ordinarily been a major factor in the effective adjustment of millions of migrants who have found the larger society exclusive, rejecting, and demeaning. Thus, the displacement of frustrations and hostilities generated within the class structure onto new migrants, using their differences in ethnic origin and orientation as a focus for blame, has been a particularly unfortunate, even a catastrophic factor in the social class history of the United States. It has served to delay the assimilation of new working-class populations and to fragment the sparse elements of common working-class identity. In light of the vastness of migratory movements into the urban areas of the United States, the interplay between ethnicity and class status is a fundamental aspect of working-class life.

When we consider the size of these migratory movements to the United States and the impact of successive waves of millions of people from different countries and cultures, we can begin to understand the ostensible conflicts among low status people that led to alienation between the established working class and the new outsiders. During the century and a quarter between 1790 and 1914, an estimated 35 million immigrants arrived in this country from all over the world.[1] The gross immigration reported by the U.S. Bureau of Immigration for the period from 1819 to 1910 totals more than 25 million persons from Europe alone, but these calculations do not take into account the large number of immigrants who returned home after arriving here or those who went back and forth between Europe and the United States. Although these figures undoubtedly overestimate the net immigration into the United States during the century, perhaps by as much as one-third, it was clearly the greatest population redistribution the world had ever seen.

Figures that reveal the influence of this migration on the population of the United States are equally impressive. In 1790, there were half a million people of foreign birth in the United States among a total population of 3.9 million. These calculations, moreover, exclude nonwhites, who formed almost 20 percent of the American population in 1790. By 1850 the number of foreign born had grown to 2.2 million, a slight decrease in proportion since the total population had increased to 23.2 million by that date. After 1850, the proportion of foreign born began to increase again. By 1910 there were 13.5 million foreign born in a population of 92 million. Thereafter the number of foreign born rose only slightly and then began to drop after the restrictions on further immigration to the United States. Strikingly enough, however, the percent of foreign born did not vary greatly during the half century between 1870 and 1920, the peak years of immigration. The continuing influx of foreign born remained a fairly constant proportion of the native white population of the United States. But the total foreign stock, defined as the foreign born and the native children of foreign or mixed parentage, continued to expand in numbers and proportions. In 1870 the foreign stock was 32 percent of the population in the United States and by 1910 it had reached the enormous proportion of 39 percent. Thus, early in the twentieth century not very much less than half the people in the United States were either themselves of foreign birth or of immigrant origin.

These figures begin to indicate the extent to which the United States is a nation of immigrants. The social impact of the foreign born and their children is even more impressive if we take into account their distribution within the United States. Although there were extensive movements of immigrants to the farming areas of the Midwest, particularly Scandinavian and German, the majority of immigrants stayed within major urban and industrial centers (Carpenter, 1927). In many regions of the United States and in most of the great cities, the majority of the population in the latter half of the nineteenth century was either of foreign birth or the children of immigrants. In 1910, 61 percent of the population in New England was of foreign stock and only a slightly smaller percentage in the Middle Atlantic and Pacific states. On the other hand, few immigrants went to the South Atlantic or South Central states. The dominance of the foreign stock in large cities was even more dramatic. New York, Chicago, Cleveland, Boston, and Detroit all had populations in which more than 70 percent of the people were of foreign stock. While the immigrants and their children lacked economic, political, or social power, their very numbers meant that they inevitably exercised considerable influence on urban life.

In order to understand more clearly the background and context of immigrant life and the processes of adaptation among immigrants and their children, it is essential to know about the social origins and social destinations of this great immigration. The immigration statistics of the United States provide us with a record of more than a century and a half of population movement from all over the world. The first immigration data from 1819–1820 reveal that, even at that early date, Ireland was by far the largest source of movement to the United States with England and the German empire a distant second and third. During the great famine in Ireland the numbers from that devastated land grew astronomically for several years, but by 1853 the German immigration became the largest stream of movement to this country, a position it maintained until the early 1890s. The Irish immigration remained at a high level into the twentieth century. Starting in the last decade of the nineteenth century, the Jewish immigration from Russia and Poland, the southern Italian immigration, and the Polish, Austrian, and southern Slavic immigration streams expanded to vast size and continued to grow until the eve of World War I. These more recently arrived ethnic groups were derogatorily referred to as the "new immigration" to distinguish the newer and highly suspect arrivals from eastern and southern Europe from earlier immigrants. The immigration of distinctive ethnic groups from other continents was relatively small, although the Chinese arrived in moderately large numbers between 1860 and 1882.

The comparative numerical significance of different ethnic origins is evident in the United States Census of 1920, after the tide of migration had waned and shortly before the restrictive legislation of 1924 markedly diminished all subsequent immigration into the United States (table 2.1). The very large contribution to the population of the United States from German, east European, and south European sources is quite evident in the distributions. Nearly half of the Russian immigrants, however, were Jewish and although these figures do not distinguish people by ethnicity or religion apart from country of origin, immigration data reveal that foreign-born Jews were among the most numerous groups during this period.[2]

Determining the social class positions and conditions of migration of the immigrants is far more difficult than estimating national origins.[3] The great majority of the immigrants were from rural or semirural areas and

TABLE 2.1   Foreign-born population in the United States from countries with 500,000 or more foreign born in the United States Census of 1920

Country of origin	Number of foreign born
Germany	1,686,108
Italy	1,610,113
Russia (including Latvia, Estonia)	1,400,495
Poland	1,139,979
Canada (including French Canada)	1,124,925
Ireland (Irish Free State)	1,037,234
England	813,853
Sweden	625,585
Austria (Austro-Hungarian Empire)	525,627

Source: Adapted from Hutchinson, 1956.

represented the declining era of European peasantries. But they were not uniformly farmers or farm workers and often included moderately large proportions of both skilled and unskilled rural craftsmen and laborers. The earlier German migrations from the southwest were composed both of poverty-stricken peasants and nonagricultural workers and tradesmen from rural areas and villages. Toward the middle of the nineteenth century, with the decline in grain prices, migration from the great agricultural estates in the east increased and a larger number of propertyless day laborers were included in the German emigration. The English, Welsh, and Scottish emigrations also relied heavily on agricultural workers from rural and semi-rural areas, but between 30 and 50 percent of the British emigration comprised highly skilled workmen. These were the weavers, miners, metal workers, and other artisans who had been bypassed by British technological advances, men whose skills the growing and technologically undeveloped industries of the United States desperately needed. Many means were employed by American industry to attract them and these skilled craftsmen experienced altogether special conditions of transportation, contracts, and employment (Erickson, 1957).

By contrast, the movement from Ireland was predominantly a migration of unskilled peasants, farmers, farm laborers, and common laborers. The Polish and south Slavic migrations were perhaps most clearly movements of small-scale peasant farmers, although many agricultural laborers were included. The Jews, mainly from the small towns and villages of their restricted regions in Russia and Russian Poland, were predominantly semi-skilled workers specializing in the needle trades, with a moderately large proportion of unskilled laborers and petty tradesmen. The emigrants from Italy were mainly south Italian and Sicilian peasantry, although moderately large numbers of north Italian tenant farmers and small landholders also emigrated.

Thus, the emigrants from different European countries came from different occupational backgrounds and varied, as well, in literacy and in familiarity with industrialized forms of work, but they shared similar origins in agrarian, village, and small town life. The conditions that led to migration in different European countries also revealed many differences and certain underlying similarities. Not least among the similarities was the enormous increase in population in every country and region of Europe during the nineteenth century, hard on the heels of the population expansion of the eighteenth century. There was no hope of increasing farm productivity without capital investments beyond anything the peasant could effect or the landlords were willing to consider. The peasants, thus, confronted a true situation of overpopulation. The produce of the soil could not contain the number of people it had to support. Whatever economic deterioration the peasantries of Europe had experienced before, the threat of greater suffering was evident. The other factor of importance was the diminution in legal restrictions against emigration from most European countries. The pressures for migration had been building for a long time before the legitimization of such movement opened the channels to mass departures during the nineteenth century.

Along with these similarities there were also marked differences in conditions in different European countries. Germany, England, and some of the Scandinavian countries had suffered from the amalgamation of peasant properties into great, commercial agricultural estates and the small craftsman had found himself unable to compete with the factories. The situation of the earlier migrants from these countries, many of them skilled workers who refused factory employment, left them some modicum of choice. There can be little doubt that the pull of opportunity in the United States, well-paid factory work for skilled English or German craftsmen and cheap land for the asking in the vast Midwest, were extremely potent influences on decisions to migrate. However, in numerous instances the pressure of expulsive forces was so great that attractions and opportunities served merely to guide the direction of movement rather than to determine its occurrence or even its size.

Migratory movements may be conceived on a continuum ranging from the most highly selective and volitional movements to those which result from the virtual or actual exercise of force in producing population redistributions. The most massive migrations generally have a strong involuntary component which most drastically affects the lowest status members of a population.[4] Whether they are really prepared to leave or not, whether they have the youth, the skills, the tolerance to bear the strains of a drastic transition or not, the degradation that awaits them at home and the propulsion of a vast movement often leads them to migrate in spite of their debilities. While none of the population movements during the great European migrations was entirely volitional, those from the Scandinavian countries and from England occurred under conditions of less severe economic or social stress than those from Ireland, or from southern or eastern Europe. Those from Germany, varying considerably from one period of time to another, fell largely in between the more volitional and the more massive, virtually forced migrations.

One correlate of these differences in the degree of volition seems to be a difference in expectations. Many of the migrants from the north and west of Europe came to the United States, not merely escaping stressful conditions, but seeking the maximum benefits and opportunities they could find. Most of the migrants from the more massive and less voluntary movements, on the other hand, fled from entirely intolerable conditions hoping merely to escape disaster. Certainly the total number of English and German migrants who came to the United States in the course of a century was huge, but during any given year these migrants represented only a tiny percentage of the population in their regions of origin. By contrast, the long-term migration from Ireland involved the loss of approximately one-third of the population of Ireland during the second half of the nineteenth century and rose as high as 3 percent of the population during peak years. The rates of migration from the regions of greatest loss in Italy involved only slightly smaller proportions of people in those areas. The annual Jewish migration rate from Russia represented at least 1.5 percent of the indigenous Jewish population.

To what degree the differences in occupational and economic achievement of immigrants from different countries can be attributed to differences in prior skills, to expectations of modest status, and to some degree of freedom of choice in the decision to migrate is uncertain. The immigrants from northern and western Europe were relatively advantaged in all these respects compared to those who came from southern and eastern Europe. Those who were relatively skilled workers, with some degree of education, living in countries which were in the forefront of industrial development, had a wider range of options than the choice between emigration and disaster or even death that so often characterized Italian, Polish, or Jewish migrants. It is impossible to extricate the relative significance of these different forces as determinants of the differences in adaptive success among the different migrant streams. Nor, for our purposes, is the analysis of this issue crucial. In a more global sense, however, the evidence suggests that even among these generally underprivileged populations who sought to emigrate as a solution to strains in their native lands, modest differences in prior advantage produced rather considerable differences in their economic and occupational attainments after coming to the United States.

In spite of the manifold advantages of those migrants who came from northern and western Europe, however, it may well be that the *relative* difference in situation and opportunity between their countries of origin and their eventual destinations may have been smaller than for the migrants from southern and eastern Europe. Indeed, differences between potentialities in America and the conditions of their lives at home must have been enormous to affect the land-bound and traditional villagers who made up the immigrant populations from southern and eastern Europe, from Ireland, and from the Jewish Pale of Settlement in Russia and Poland. Most people are reluctant to move from one society to another. Preindustrial, lower status people are generally most fearful of leaving home. The evidence of resistance to leaving an area or a city in which one feels at home despite bombing during war, extreme persecution, or the possibility of relocation to superior dwellings and conditions is extensive and persistent. Massive migrations inevitably take place during and following intolerable conditions of economic or social deprivation and cultural disorganization. While the conditions precipitating mass migrations to the United States differed in intensity, they were uniformly severe economic crises or unremitting oppression. Even these crises do not adequately explain the massive outflows of people, many of whom had lived with endemic poverty or were acclimated to brutality, and who moved in spite of the dangers and difficulties of passage to and adjustment within the United States.

In view of the long experience of suffering, particularly among the Irish, Italians, Poles, and Jews, and considering the circumscribed world of tradition within which they lived, more ominous and pervasive destructive forces must have served to loosen their attachment to the lands of their birth. Only the gradual destruction of that social order which gave their poverty-stricken lives some semblance of meaning could have been a force profound enough to have uprooted so many millions.[5] The catastrophes of the nineteenth century must have contributed an important impetus. As the movement to migrate grew in strength, it further destroyed the society in which they lived. For those who stayed behind, these departures provided hope for the reestablishment of a viable peasant economy. But for those who left, fragments of data suggest that they were leaving behind the remains of a community that no longer had the capacity to provide a meaningful sense of social identity, not merely one that offered no hope of a decent livelihood.

Incorporation and Assimilation of Immigrants

Whatever the conditions that precipitated the large migrations of the nineteenth and early twentieth centuries and however modest the opportunities available to them in the United States, the new world clearly offered hope for improvement that few of the immigrants could anticipate in their homelands. With the wider opportunities of cheap land in the Midwest gone, with hardly enough money to make the Atlantic passage, often with labor contracts to fulfill, more of these immigrants remained in the great cities of the United States than had been the case a few decades earlier. In the cities, new problems faced them: derogation in the larger society, resentment by former immigrants, suspicion from organized labor, hovels for housing, inadequate jobs, and periodic depressions. Many returned home but the majority remained, determined to struggle. These were the conditions in which people moved into the West End of Boston, as they moved into so many other cities along the eastern seaboard.

The actual conditions of migration and the initial situations that met the immigrants on arrival were often among the most difficult challenges they had to face. The immigrants from southern and eastern Europe had to confront a particularly long and difficult period of adjustment and needed psychological strength to resist economic hardship and social abuse. Due to the intervention of government and private charitable organizations during the late nineteenth century, however, the worst features of the initial impact of arrival on the immigrant had been modified: the lures of swindlers offering the immigrant jobs that never existed, essential goods that could never be used, payment in advance for housing that the most destitute immigrant would shun, and even worse forms of robbery and extortion. In other respects, however, conditions of immigrant life grew more bitter.[6] Anti-immigration sentiment intensified, and almost every vice that manifested itself among the poor or in their dwelling areas was generalized to all the poor and magnified in conceptions of the foreign born. Immigrant experiences of isolation, exploitation, and exclusion were implemented by severe antagonism from labor, occasional lynchings, riots, and police suppression.[7] But the growth of industry created a continuing demand for heavy, unskilled, cheap labor in the iron and steel mills, in the mines and cotton mills, in the building trades, and in laying railroad track across the country. Few of these former peasants obtained better jobs than these and many of the men with experience suffered a demotion in status.

Despite the growing number of manual jobs, despite the fact that the newcomers were willing to work at these wretched jobs, the proportions who were unemployed for long periods during the year were very large. During periodic recessions, unemployment rates rose to tremendous heights among the foreign born and the rolls of public and private charities burgeoned. Moreover, the massive flow of laborers kept wages extremely low. Real wages for unskilled and semiskilled jobs actually declined for several decades after the 1880s. Most of the immigrant families were able to sustain themselves marginally only when the entire family, father, mother, and children, were working. Hours of labor were extremely long. Most wage earners worked a sixty to sixty-five hour week and a ninety hour work week was not uncommon. The health status of the poor and, most particularly, of the immigrants was extremely low, and frequent illness and work-incurred disabilities further disrupted the flow of wages in many families. Conditions in the sweat shops, in the mines, in the railroad camps, and even in the large factories were abominable and grew worse after efforts at unionization were defeated toward the end of the nineteenth century. The constant outcry from reformers who wanted regulatory legislation and inspection of work situations remained unheeded in the midst of congealing industrial power and profits.

The problems of poverty were grave and great, but for a long time the full extent of the problem was hidden by ignorance and prejudice. Booth's (1902-1903) monumental study of the working classes of London, using a most conservatively stringent criterion, revealed that more than 28 percent of the working people in that great city lived in dire poverty during a period of unexampled prosperity. Rowntree (1901) followed with a study of York and showed that 31 percent of the population fell below the same poverty line. There were no American estimates available, but Hunter's (1904) calculations indicated that the rates in this country were close to the English levels. An even more important contribution of these studies was the marshaling of evidence to show that only a very small proportion of the poor were degraded and reluctant to work because of alcoholism or other vices, although this was assumed to be typical. They were clearly distinct from the criminal classes. The large majority of the poor lived in poverty because of irregular employment coupled with low wages and their economic condition was often exacerbated by illness and other difficulties over which they had no control. However, efforts at labor reform ran into the concerted opposition of employers. At the beginning of the twentieth century, the United States remained one of the most backward of all the industrial nations in the control of those secondary conditions that contributed to the miseries of the poor: the untrammeled use of child labor, unregulated hours and work conditions, and entirely inadequate assistance or compensation for work-connected injuries or death.

Although the United States was also far behind in the establishment of public standards of housing and sanitation, the conditions of immigrant housing were more carefully studied, better documented, and more feasible targets for change than were working conditions. Perhaps they were worse than conditions of work or merely more visible and accessible. The earliest reports gave abundant evidence concerning housing conditions. Thus, one such report notes that:

Most of the houses are those which were formerly occupied by the wealthy who have removed up town, and now in their dilapidated state many of them are tenanted by miserably poor Irish and German emigrants. Large rooms have been divided by rough partitions into dwellings for two or three families (each, perhaps, taking boarders), where they wash, cook, eat, sleep, and die—many of them prematurely, for the circumstances in which they live make fearful havoc of health and life; and in addition, night lodgers consisting of homeless men, women, and children are not unfrequent, who for a trifling sum are allowed temporary shelter. There, huddled together like cattle in pens, the inmates are subjected to the most debasing influences. Many of the dwellings, moreover, are out of repair, and the yards, from neglect of the sinks, in so vile a condition they can scarcely be stepped into, without contracting filth of the most offensive kind.[8]

Bad as were housing conditions in the middle of the nineteenth century and despite wider use of brick instead of wood and of sewage disposal, conditions in the slums deteriorated further. New sources of immigration brought larger, poorer, and less skilled populations than the cities could successfully incorporate. Landlords, seeking higher rental incomes, continued to subdivide apartments and poured families into every conceivable space and into many inconceivable cellars and unlit rooms. The stable middle-class population, who viewed the immigrants as repugnant and vicious influences, moved to the suburbs. Naturally there was no open space in the slums. Even the alleys teemed with hazardous wooden structures. Despite ostensible improvements in plumbing, an entire tenement was often dependent on a single privy in the courtyard which readily overflowed its container forcing the tenants to use cellars, roofs, and hallways instead. Little water supply was available in any of the houses. And rates of disease and death confirmed the worst expectations of health officials.[9] In spite of these deplorable conditions, numerous studies reveal that slum inhabitants paid extraordinarily high rents for the space and facilities they held.

As knowledge and public awareness of contagion grew, the sanitary menace of slum conditions turned many public health officials, legislative commissions, social workers, and journalists toward reform. Boston and New York were among the leaders in housing reform and in new housing legislation. In the West End, as in other slum areas, many of the oldest houses in the rear alleys and courtyards were torn down, often to be replaced by brick tenements. While the tenements did little to decrease areal densities, they often gave families ampler dwelling space, some meager opportunities to obtain light and air, and improved water and toilet facilities. With the development of more stringent building regulations and inspection procedures at the beginning of the twentieth century in the most progressive cities and a decade or two later throughout most of the country, the urban slums began to take on the physical appearance they bore until recently. But the changes were sporadic and met continued resistance from landlords. While legislative intervention created improved contidions and newly constructed buildings were superior to the former hovels, neglect and abuse left the urban ethnic slum little better than it had been.[10]

With hindsight, it is evident that most of the abused and neglected immigrants who lived through the era of transition and remained in this country moved very slowly on to improved work and living conditions. At closer hand, however, the immigrants were more often seen as incorrigible incompetents, reveling in their own morass. Occasional observers attributed the miseries of the slums and of their residents to environmental circumstance, but none could entirely free themselves from the damning images of almost bestial, illiterate, amoral individuals who comprised the immigrant slum population.[11] Indeed, the immigration of the period 1870 to 1914, dominated by streams of movement from southern and eastern Europe, confronted resistances that deterrred substantial progress. The gap between the immigrants and the native white population in economic and cultural status was great and persisted for a long time.

Despite the fact that the Irish started migrating to the United States relatively early, they had a difficult time getting jobs, education, or respect. The second generation of Irish advanced somewhat and entered lower level white collar jobs and public service occupations, but parity in occupational status with the native white population was only achieved in the 1950s, a

full century after the great migration had begun.[12] The Italians were markedly underrepresented in high status occupations as late as 1950 and the
second generation moved very slowly toward modest achievements. The
Slavs also served a long and difficult apprenticeship. In the steel mills of
Pittsburgh and the Midwest, they encountered barriers to progress and only
after several decades did the many different Slav populations begin to
move into more skilled positions. Although second-generation Jews made
dramatic advances in occupational status, they suffered severely under the
sweating system of garment production for many years. Moreover, exclu-
sionary policies toward Jews gave way slowly and, in attenuated form,
continued to affect subsequent generations of high status Jews.

   Although obstacles to stable employment and occupational achievement
touch the economic core of any in-migrant population, many ethnic groups
encountered other forms of discrimination and rejection as well. Despite
extensive descriptive evidence revealing the intensity of hostility toward
the immigrants and their children, neither the degree of discrimination nor
its effects are easily measured and, thus, the attrition of these attitudes and
behaviors over time can only be conjectured. One measure that allows for
estimates of ethnic discrimination and separation is the residential distribution and segregation of people from different ethnic origins. During the
period of great influx, ethnic concentrations existed in all the urban slums
of great American cities and ethnic homogeneity in the early phase of
in-migration is hardly surprising. Their long-term persistence suggests external barriers to assimilation manifested as either voluntary or involuntary
segregation. As late as 1950, indices of residential segregation reveal the
perpetuation of many ethnic enclaves, and unassimilated minorities and
areas containing an array of different working-class ethnic groups are undoubtedly even more frequent. The level of segregation of Negroes remains
higher than that of any other ethnic group, but remarkably high rates of
residential segregation for other ethnic groups persist as reminders of the
restrictions to assimilation in an open society (Lieberson, 1963).

   While ethnic concentrations in slum areas are largely due to the low
status of immigrant populations and to derogatory discrimination which
produce or intensify barriers to social mobility and assimilation, the segregated slums of the urban United States have performed important functions for in-migrant populations. The profound attachments people had to
the urban slums in which they lived have been amply documented.[13] Despite the disgraceful condition of slum housing, all efforts to displace slum
populations or to destroy slum housing have met great resistance. This
resistance was often seen as evidence that the inhabitants wallowed in their

obloquy. Little attention was paid to the fact that, although the residents of urban slums could do little to alter their physical environment, they were able to create fragments of community, of viable forms of social organization out of the conditions of chaos, and they developed great interpersonal commitments within the neighborhood. It is possible that reasonable forms of immigrant adjustment could occur only because the slum developed its own social and cultural processes and provided a smaller, more intimate, and more meaningful environment within the larger society. Certainly the adjustments of low status immigrants to the opportunities and resistances of the larger environment can only be understood in the context provided by the protective and supportive functions of the urban, ethnic slum.

Social Functions of the Urban Ethnic Slum

Most low status immigrants arrived in the large cities of the United States only to retreat into these smaller enclaves of the urban, ethnic slum. The lingering image of the city as a bewildering array of movement, of isolated individuals caught in a tissue of casual and impersonal activities and relationships, of easy vice and easy virtue that lead to social disorganization and anomic morality is most acutely challenged by the cultural integrity and social cohesiveness of these residential slums. The urban environment includes an enormous variety of cultural styles and patterns of social organization that evade any simple classification. But working-class ethnic areas, whether located in the core of the city or in its outer rings, are particularly notable for the development of closeknit neighborhoods with a high degree of social solidarity and communal involvement. For most immigrants, this urban, ethnic, working-class community was the only city they knew. It was the city in which they lived and from which they drew social sustenance. Only this tolerant city within the impersonal and hostile society made possible the adjustment of many bewildered and downtrodden peasant immigrants.[14]

The slums of large cities had been the habitat of the disreputable and deviant long before the industrial revolution created larger slums with a mass population base. But earlier conceptions of the slum, fostered by interest in the depraved and forbidden, still persist.[15] The skid-row type of slum, which caters to the skidders from all walks of life, has colored popular conceptions of slums out of all proportion to the numerical or social significance of such flophouse areas. Skid rows are occasionally adjacent to working-class homes, but they differ in almost all fundamental social and cultural respects and share only the signs of impoverishment and deterioration. In contrast to skid row, the working-class slum represents the stable residence of families living within a highly localized and socially organized community.[16]

The urban ethnic slum was both a harbor and haven for the working class of foreign birth. It was a residue of immigrant passage, receiving and supporting new migrants in a complex, threatening, ambiguous, and frequently hostile industrial society. It offered low status strangers the possibility of developing a sense of identity with peers, a feeling of social commitment, and some dim hope of future prospects shared with others in the struggle for economic and social benefits. Acculturation and assimilation to the small society of the slum was facilitated by the fairly benevolent response of the residents to deprived newcomers. Indeed, the much slower process of acculturation and assimilation to the larger society occurred, to a considerable degree, through the infiltration of American values, expectations, and role conceptions into the culture and social structure of the local community. Thus, the urban, ethnic slum served as a processing mechanism, protecting the immigrant from the more dangerous and undermining onslaughts of the larger industrial society and, at the same time, prepared him for fuller adjustment to this society. Once acclimated to the new environment, a few immigrants and many more of their children, eager to garner the ostensible rewards of their long struggle, moved on to less poverty-stricken, more heterogeneous areas beyond the urban core. As they moved out, their places were rapidly filled by newer recruits who might repeat again the long and painful process.

The class or ethnic homogeneity of the residential slum, its continuities with village life, the familiarity of working-class behavioral styles and of the transmuted forms of traditional peasant views partially cushioned the shock of transition. The primordial function of the slum as a low-cost residential area had to be supplemented in order to fulfill the human and social needs of migrants. Often the immigrants found their way to a particular city and a particular neighborhood through relatives or friends who had already settled there, who could offer them a bed or a room during their first encounters with the job market. Chain migration formed a link between the old world and the new and has continued to mediate between rural and urban areas for more recent migrants, black and white. And an essential link it has been, leading the migrant into the few areas which might receive him with decency and offer him a contrast less sharp and strange.[17] Ethnic organizations and associations often served to maintain greater continuity with the past and provided benevolent services during the transition (Lopata, 1964). Ethnic newspapers were widely read and provided a temporary sense of shared identity with other people of the same ethnic origin (Park, 1920; Park et al., 1925).

The social necessity of the urban slum was particularly crucial while the immigrant tried to cope with the strange demands of an industrial labor market. The newcomer had to work in order to survive, but the process of job hunting was often a humiliating and discouraging experience. The meager jobs available were little compensation for the strains of migration, and the ethnic and cultural discrimination provoked degrading self-conceptions and reinforced a long history of alienation. These conditions necessarily forced the immigrant back upon his community for maintaining a modicum of self-esteen and a sense of support. Through kinship, friendship, community participation, and local involvements in casual conversation, shopping, or entertainment, all within a bounded residential region, the urban slum enveloped and sustained the immigrant. Interpersonal conflict and ethnic rivalries might arise and recede. Neighbors and kin were often physically inescapable and their moral judgments ineluctable decisions. But for all these limitations, local social relationships provided some of the sense of support, esteem, and interpersonal responsiveness all human beings require. The urban, working-class slum became the small and private world which in-migrants could invest with all the sentiment and symbolism of home. In the process of adapting to the urban slum, however, most immigrants gradually acquired American cultural patterns and wider social contacts, and developed greater comfort outside the protective environment in which they lived. Thus, each at his own pace, these deprived immigrants came to experience an expanded sense of options and either they or their children or grandchildren could slowly become absorbed, even if only partially, in the larger society.

For all the resistance of our society to the in-migrants who performed tasks that others were unwilling to fulfill, the meager conditions of their new lives were often better than the frugal, fragmented, and oppressive circumstances from which the migrant had fled. The physical environment of the slums was inexcusable by civilized standards, but many immigrants had lived in far worse, more densely packed hovels in Europe and were, thus, more tolerant of their American dwellings than the reformers who wanted to destroy their homes. The economic situation of the immigrant in the United States was precarious, but standards of living and the availability of charity in emergency provided greater hope than they had known in their European villages. The derogation and humiliation they experienced within the industrial society were probably no worse and perhaps less debasing than the characteristic attitudes toward the peasantry among the European aristocracy and middle class. There was little enough to support human dignity, but the encompassing environment of the ethnic community offered a more integrated opportunity for living within a relatively traditional ethos than did the European peasant village during its social and cultural decline. Thus, for many of the newcomers, the scant rewards of the land of plenty were only dimly perceived until they had attained enough stability to confront the inequalities of their opportunities. Even then the local community offered many compensations which sustained people during the stages of transition and helped to obliterate any keen awareness of injustice.

There were also many problems associated with changing economic conditions, with the phase of in-migration, and with the diverse origins of the in-migrant populations. Ethnic conflict within the local area has occasionally been a serious threat to in-migrants. There is evidence of great variation from situations of generous and harmonious integration of different nationalities within the same neighborhood to cautious tolerance of strangers and, at the other extreme, of overt hostility between ethnic groups occupying adjacent territories. The most severe conflicts have frequently arisen during the height of in-migration of new ethnic populations. These conflicts have accompanied very high densities, housing deterioration, segregation, and widespread deviant behavior. As rates of in-migration diminished, and particularly during periods of prosperity, the poorest housing often went begging for tenants, levels of segregation decreased, and the stable, working-class people began to sort themselves out from the poverty-stricken, dependent, or deviant population. Ethnic enclaves, however, have frequently persisted for some time during periods of residential invasion and succession and have been most marked among pariah populations like the Chinese, Jews, Japanese, and Negroes. These restraints to residential dispersion reflect oppressive forces of discrimination and segregation which intensify the attractive forces within the community. While evaluations of the social esteem of different ethnic groups within the larger society led the way, the working class itself readily mirrored these patterns of differential derogation toward various ethnic minorities. Only at a distance of decades can we surmise that working-class dissatisfactions with the larger society were often displaced onto adjacent and innocent ethnic groups, particularly during periods of economic and social strain, just as, at other times, these dissatisfactions were denied and submerged within a common, multiethnic, working-class identity.[18]

Thus, while the conditions for the successful assimilation, acculturation, and absorption of immigrants into the urban, industrial society of the United States have varied considerably from time to time and for different ethnic minorities, the broad outlines of transition have remained remarkably consistent. The working-class slum has been the fundamental unit for the processing of immigrants, the major source for facilitating the transition from one society to another. In this respect, the transitional functions of the working-class community have been among its most important contributions to American life. But working-class slums also can serve other functions. Thus, working-class areas can provide a relatively high degree of sheltering anonymity for other slum inhabitants.[19] For many low status residents, authority signifies impersonal, impervious, and graft-ridden power and the local neighborhood provides protection from vague but not entirely unwarranted fears of invasion and persecution from these sources. The community also offers some protection for the various forms of minor illicit behavior that are widespread: small-scale betting and gambling, playing the numbers, and the purchase of low-cost stolen goods among them.[20] Communal reciprocities provide security against detection although they also afford opportunistic criminals a degree of invisibility. Another type of anonymity is also available for those who seek a temporary or permanent moratorium from the demands of society: higher status persons who want relief from intolerable work or family pressures, individuals with psychiatric, social, or sexual difficulties, or bohemians who find the suspicious tolerance of the slum more acceptable than the deprecatory sympathy of the urban middle class. While the working-class slum serves numerous populations and functions, it remains primarily a transitional community, helping to absorb low status migrants who are economically necessary but socially neglected participants in urban, industrial life.

Large-scale migration to the urban areas of the United States has become an internal rather than an international movement during the past half century. Old ethnic groups have begun to disappear and those that have persisted reveal a wide array of social class positions and of levels of assimilation. In some of the older ethnic communities we see arrayed the results of a series of transitions that have gone on slowly and arduously for more than half a century. But the processes of migration and transition of low status people are endlessly recapitulated throughout the world. Newer in-migrant populations reveal similar strains, similar dilemmas, and similar crises. The conflicts provoked among black Americans by continued discrimination and inequality under conditions of affluence that sharpen the contrast may be more evident and more costly than those of the past but are not unique. Processes of absorption and integration of blacks, of Puerto Ricans, and of Mexican minorities may be slower than the incorporation of former immigrants, but the sequences of transition are likely to repeat both the difficulties and achievements of the past. Certainly the world of the urban working class, the small environing community which makes life tolerable and the larger, inhospitable society which erects barriers to success, is perpetuated through the generations and across differences in ethnicity and history.

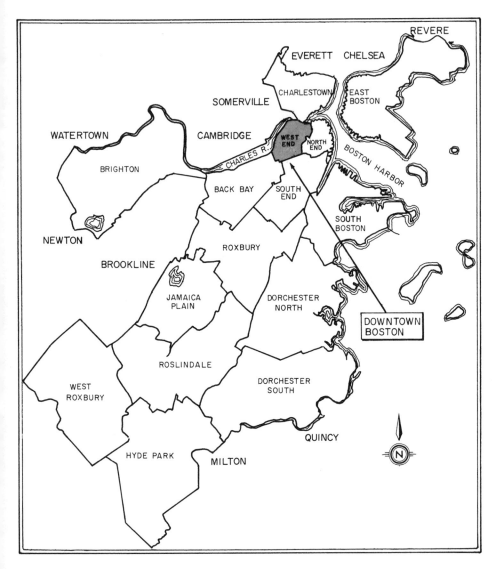

Map of areas of city of Boston, with adjacent cities and towns.

3 The Population of the West End

Stability and Change in Population

Ethnic slums and the people who inhabit them vary in their histories, in ethnic origins, and in the occupations, statuses, and age distributions of the population. Although the United States was the major immigrant-receiving country for several centuries, other countries have also had ethnic, working-class slums. Another source of possible variation, therefore, is the place of the working class and of ethnic minorities in the larger society. Yet it is striking that there are so many common features among different ethnic, working-class communities. These consistencies in the face of apparent diversity provide considerable assurance that broad generalizations are reasonable and cannot be traced simply to specific and limited sets of conditions or situations. But rarely do available reports allow precise comparisons among working-class populations, or careful contrasts between people of different statuses, or substantial conclusions about causal relationships. The data from the West End of Boston, because of their extensive detail and the relatively wide range of social class positions represented, often permit us to make essential comparisons and to reconsider the implications of these findings in their support for (or contradiction of) other sources of information. However, conclusions drawn from the population of a single community must be tempered by the realization that selective factors may have led people of moderately high status to live in a working-class neighborhood. In fact, selective preferences may have determined the continued residence of working-class people who had sufficient incomes to purchase better housing. A closer view of the population of the West End, the attributes of its residents, and some of the population changes that occurred over time provide some perspective on the people whose lives and life situations are the primary sources of information.

The West End of Boston was a receiving station for successive waves of immigrants for over a hundred years. Close to the core of the central city, hemmed in by natural and manmade barriers and divisions, it still included many people of foreign birth as well as their second- and third-generation descendants as late as 1958. The history of the West End is quite typical of urban ethnic slums throughout the new world and of many in the old world. Before it was demolished in 1958, its fifty acres of tenements, interspersed with many local stores and settlement houses, contained approximately 2,500 families and a total population of 7,500 people from many different ethnic origins. Like most other immigrant areas, the population had declined gradually from its peak densities around the turn of the century. In many respects, however, the area had changed relatively little during more than half a century since it had been a vital node in the process of immigrant adjustment to the United States. If it differed from other family-based ethnic slums, the differences resulted from its function as an area of second settlement for the overflow from the older and adjacent North End.

During colonial days, the North End, planted directly on the harbor, had been the seat of government and the receiving station for newcomers. Despite the central location of the West End, it remained suburban in character for a long time. In the middle of the eighteenth century, its farm-lands and pastures were subdivided into substantial house lots for the upper middle class. As urbanization persisted, as the central city expanded into nearby regions, and as part of the river basin was filled with the rock and soil from the decapitation of Beacon Hill, the area of the West End was extended and its suburban homes converted to lodging and rooming houses.[1] The government moved out of the North End into a beautiful Bullfinch mansion on top of Beacon Hill and the former seat of new world glory became a true harbor for the immigrants. But the demands of an uninterrupted stream of Irish immigrants and of a swelling number of East European Jews, Slavs, and Italians overran the capacity of the North End.

The slightly newer tenements in the West End, with bathrooms in most apartments, served to attract many of the immigrants from the North End who had already made an initial adjustment to the city and its job market. Gradually the West End came to share the immigrant population with the North End and by 1900 it was almost entirely devoted to their residential and community needs. The Irish were still in possession of major segments of the area, but the Jews were rapidly achieving numerical predominance, and the Italians and Poles and Ukranians slowly drifted in. The West End was, thus, ethnically more diverse than the dilapidated areas of first settlement. At any one time, there were residues of earlier streams of immigrants, a small number of the most recent newcomers, and vast proportions of the populations that had dominated the immigration of the previous few decades.

This ethnic diversity, however, was neither entirely unique nor a manifest of ethnic integration. Most slums in the United States became ethnically homogeneous during periods of enormous in-migration by a single foreign group and, subsequently, grew more heterogeneous as the neighborhoods either became stabilized or were invaded by new waves of immigrants.[2] In recent years the different ethnic groups in the West End were minimally segregated from one another and people from different ethnic backgrounds interacted extensively with one another. But "ethnic maps" of the area from 1900 show considerable separation of subareas by the national origin of their residents. Although an ethos of tolerance had developed gradually during the twentieth century, the intermixture of these working-class populations did not include Negroes. Earlier in the century, in fact, the West End had housed a moderately large number of blacks. But the large-scale migration of Negroes into Boston after 1940 was directed to other areas beyond the central city district, areas which had become the major segregated harbors and ghettos for the Negro population.

Discrimination or overcrowding has occasionally led to the development of new slum areas or the expansion of existing areas. But in spite of continuous migration to the cities and in spite of periodic, short-term increases, the decrease in the densities of urban slums shows up as a long-term trend (Frieden, 1964). This has largely been due to the slow outward movement, increasingly in the direction of modest suburban life, of established working-class people. As workers have achieved some degree of social mobility, of economic security, and as more housing has become available at competitive rental prices, this process of residential mobility has made the old slums available to new migrants and has led to diminished crowding within those areas. Nor is this process only a recent development in the changing patterns of urban life. It dates back clearly to the beginning of the twentieth century and is manifest in the population history of the West End of Boston. The West End experienced a marked decrease in population after reaching a height of overcrowding toward the end of the nineteenth or the beginning of the twentieth centuries. Between 1910 and 1950, the last census date prior to the taking of land by the city of Boston, the population declined as follows:[3]

| 1910 | 23,000 |
| 1920 | 18,500 |

1930	13,000
1940	13,000
1950	12,000

The periods of greatest diminution were the relatively prosperous decades of World War I and the 1920s, while the depression of the 1930s resulted in a static population size. The decade of the 1940s saw an increase in net movement out of the area, and an accelerated decline of population occurred during the following decade while redevelopment plans were under discussion. By 1958, the total population for the comparable area (including some blocks that were not part of the renewal plan) had diminished to only 7,900.[4]

Urban neighborhoods change even during relatively stable conditions, and in the face of momentous events like the emergence of plans for the demolition of an entire area, they are bound to change more rapidly. Nonetheless, people continued to move into the West End while others continued to move out until the very eve of redevelopment. Public knowledge about plans for an urban renewal program in the West End began to filter through early in the 1950s and by 1952 the residents in the area realized that definite plans were in process. Inevitably, as the discussions between the city of Boston and Washington continued and seemed ever more likely to become a reality, more people began seeking other housing. What became apparent to people in the local area was a gradual decrease in population in the West End. In fact, between 1952 and 1953 the decline of population accelerated to the point it had reached during the decade between 1910 and 1920; and between 1953 and 1954 it began to exceed the average annual rate of decline of the decade between 1920 and 1930. By 1955, when tensions and tempers concerning the redevelopment plans flourished, the decline of population became quite striking.

At first sight the decline in population appeared to be a direct result of markedly increased movement out of the area due to the threat of demolition. Closer analysis, however, revealed that the gross number of people moving out of the West End had not increased a great deal compared with the previous decade. Outward movement was an endemic phenomenon that had occurred during most decades and continued, relatively unmodified, during this period. The unnoticed fact that largely accounted for the net population decline was a sharp diminution in movement into the West End after 1953. Thus, in 1947 approximately ninety-six people had moved into the West End for every one hundred persons who had moved out and in 1948 inward and outward movement had almost reached parity. As late as 1952, when people were just becoming fully aware of demolition plans for the West End, ninety-one persons had moved into the West End for every one hundred persons who moved out. While the number of persons moving out of the area increased very slowly, the number of persons moving into the West End dropped off quite sharply. In 1955 only fifty-four people moved into the West End for every one hundred who moved out and in 1956 the ratio was sixty-nine in to one-hundred out. The widespread impression, therefore, that movement out of the West End was reaching exodus proportions, an impression supported by the increased number of empty apartments, was erroneous. West Enders, quite determined to retain their community, continued to follow the pattern of slow, long-term residential mobility out of the area. But as knowledge of renewal plans spread throughout the metropolitan region, people were increasingly reluctant to move into an area that faced imminent annihilation.

The residential dynamics associated with expected demolition was only one of several features of population change in the West End. We have already seen that there was a decline in population during the relatively affluent decades of 1910–1920 and 1920–1930, while the decade of the great depression saw little change in population size. We have also observed that urban slums have ordinarily decreased in population density after periods of heightened in-migration. These facts support the general view of the gradual residential mobility of those inhabitants of urban slums who have been socially mobile. It is fair to assume that, at any point in time, some proportion of the population is residual in the sense that they have failed to achieve that degree of economic status that has enabled some of their neighbors to seek better housing. Certainly this is not the complete picture since people move into and out of urban slum areas for a variety of reasons. Indeed, some people move out for the very opposite reasons: they cannot maintain a stable income and seek housing in more deteriorated areas or, unable to pay the rent, they move to neighborhoods where their credit standing is unknown. Moreover, many people remain in these working-class communities despite the fact that they have already achieved higher status but are unwilling to relinquish their community attachments to people or places. Despite the diversity of slum populations and the manifold reasons for which people move into, out of, or remain in low status working-class communities, however, we must take account of the possibility that a disproportionate number of the inhabitants may have been left behind by their more successful neighbors. Although this does not seriously limit the conclusions we can draw about people living in an urban, working-class slum at any given time, we must recognize the fact

that excessive weight may be given to those working-class people who have
had the greatest difficulty in attaining the modest status rewards of the
working class as a whole.

Some of the flow of different types of people into and out of the community is revealed by a closer examination of the changing composition of
the West End in the five-year period immediately prior to urban renewal.
During this period, the ethnic composition changed, but this appears to
have been part of a long-term trend rather than a mere response to the
emergency situation. Thus, the proportions of Italians, Slavs, and Irish
increased during these years, while people of Anglo-Saxon origin and Jews
decreased in proportions. In particular, the Italians and Slavs had been
expanding in the West End during the previous decade while the Jews were
a slowly diminishing population. Another trend, less clearly traceable in
previous years, was an increase in the proportions of people over sixty and
a decrease in the twenty to twenty-nine year age group. This change may
well have been a product of the immediate situation and there is other
evidence to indicate the great reluctance among the older people to move
out. The shift in occupational composition during the years immediately
prior to redevelopment is particularly striking since it seems to reveal
some characteristics of the populaton dynamics of the West End over
longer periods of time. During these years, there was a slight proportionate
increase in the numbers of people of highest occupational status, a fact that
is commensurate with their frequent use of the West End as an area of
temporary residence for reasons of convenience. Conversely, the skilled
manual workers showed the largest decrease in proportion during these
years, implying that they had a number of options that allowed them either
to move out in greater numbers or to find other housing rather than moving into an area slated for demolition. On the other hand, the proportions
of semiskilled and unskilled manual workers remained unchanged. While
these movements undoubtedly comprise both long-term and short-term
trends, the larger picture that emerges and is consistent with other evidence
is one of a slowly shifting population: some residents who remained in the
area with great stability, a slow influx composed both of incoming populations and of transitory people, and a slow attrition of those populations
with broader options due either to youth, occupational status, or cultural
assimilation.

Population Composition of the West End

The long-term and short-term changes that produced the dynamics of
population in the West End provide a meaningful context for seeing the

composition of the recent population as one among several forms of ethnic and class segmentation in a changing, industrial society. The West End of Boston was most clearly a multiethnic community. We have already indicated that there was a sequence of populations that reflected the larger immigration into Boston. The Irish were the first working-class population to dominate the area, succeeded by the Jews late in the nineteenth century and by Italian, Polish, and other Slavic immigrants shortly thereafter. By 1958, the Italians were the predominant ethnic group in the midst of a wide and scattered array of other ethnic minorities. At that time, the Italians comprised 46 percent of the West End households; the Poles and the Jews each accounted for another 11 and 10 percent respectively; there were a small number (6 percent) of people of older American ancestry; and the Irish were only 5 percent of the households. The rest of the people were from diverse ethnic backgrounds and no other group represented more than a tiny minority. Apart from the period between 1948 and 1958, it is difficult to date the periods of domination by different ethnic groups. It seems evident that the Jews were the largest minority in the West End around the turn of the century (Woods, 1902) and their numerical preponderance was probably maintained for several decades. However, the continued in-migration of Italians, Poles, and other Slavs led to the increased prominence of these ethnic groups for at least several of the previous decades.

Although we refer to the West End as a multiethnic community and it was generally considered to be one of the foreign enclaves of Boston, most of the adults and even more of the children were of American birth. Fully 67 percent of the adult men and women and 95 percent of the children were born in the United States. Of course the vast majority of West Enders (83 percent) could trace their ancestry to recent origins in foreign countries and often identified themselves as Italian, Polish, or Jewish. Indeed, few of the adults were born in the United States of native-born parents (17 percent). The largest proportion of the adults sixty-five years of age or under were second generation (50 percent), the American-born offspring of foreign-born parents. Exactly one-third of the adults were born in a foreign country. Among people sixty-five years old or more, 88 percent were born in a foreign country (Frieden, 1959, 1960, 1962). Clearly the proportions of people in the West End who would be classified as foreign stock, the foreign born and the native born of foreign parents, were large (65 percent), and a considerably higher proportion than the foreign stock in the city of Boston (46 percent in 1960).

For a variety of reasons, the relative proportions of foreign and native

residents differed among the different ethnic groups. The largest proportion of foreign born (61 percent) were among the people of central
European origin, many of them refugees from the devastation of World
War II. Many Poles and a number of people from other Slavic regions
came to the United States under similar circumstances, swelling the number of foreign-born Poles (51 percent) and other Slavs (45 percent). On
the other hand, the relatively large number of foreign-born Jews (48
percent) were residues of earlier immigrations. They were so large a proportion of the total Jewish population in the community because of the
exodus of second- and third-generation Jews to other neighborhoods and
the failure of the area to attract younger Jewish residents during recent
years. The Italians, whose numbers were little influenced by recent
migrations from Europe, included relatively few people (28 percent) of
foreign birth. Only a small proportion (25 percent) of the Irish were
foreign born. The large number of adults born in the United States of
foreign parents among the larger ethnic groups (ranging between 46
percent among the Jews to 64 percent of the Italians) points up the
function of the community as a residential area for second-generation
people of low status.

The majority of the adults in the West End were not only second-
generation Americans but were also predominantly in their middle years
of life. The age distributions varied from one ethnic group to another.
The youngest group by far were the Americans whose foreign ancestry is
lost in history. With almost a third of their members between twenty-
five and twenty-nine years of age and a median age of twenty-nine, they
differed from the rest of the population in the area. At the other extreme, those of British-Canadian and, even more strikingly, of Jewish and
Irish origin had the oldest membership: the median age of the British-
Canadians was forty-seven, of the Jews, fifty-two, and of the Irish, fifty-
six. Moreover, 31 percent of the Jews and 46 percent of the Irish were
between sixty and sixty-five years old. They were typically the residual
ethnic populations of the West End, people who represented a former
ethnic era and who were left behind by changing patterns of residence.
The age composition of most of the other groups falls in between the
Americans and the Jewish and Irish extremes. Among the largest ethnic
clusters, the median age for the Italians and for the Poles was forty, and
for the other Slavs it was thirty-eight. Most of the ethnic groups in the
West End were, thus, represented by a second-generation, early middle-
aged majority.

A clearer picture of the ethnic patterns in the West End emerges when

we add information about length of residence to the data we have
already considered. The ethnic clusters with the longest average tenure in
the area were those people who arrived in massive numbers during the
earlier part of the twentieth century: Italians, Poles, other Slavs, and Jews.
Approximately one-third of the people from each of these ethnic origins
had lived in the West End for all or most of their lives. With few recent
arrivals, the Jews had the longest average tenure; 86 percent had lived in
the West End for a long time. The Italians were also stable in their neighborhood residence but a larger proportion were relatively recent arrivals. The
Poles and the Slavs from other regions had even larger proportions of post-
World War II arrivals. Few of the Irish in the West End had been born
there, but they were generally long-term residents. Most of the people of
other ethnic origins had come to the West End only within the previous
few years.

   Studies of urban ethnic slums and of ethnic segregation and concentration present two discrepant images: an impression of extremely homogeneous ethnic enclaves or a total intermingling among people from different ethnic backgrounds. Both impressions are almost certainly exaggerated
and result from differences in the scale of observation as well as from differences in the period during which the observations were made. The
more detailed examination of ethnic distributions within slum areas suggests that ethnic concentrations existed, even in apparently heterogeneous
areas, at the micro-level of houses or blocks and that larger units such as
neighborhoods have almost invariably included people from diverse ethnic
origins.[5] Changes in levels of segregation of individual ethnic groups over
time also suggest a very high degree of concentration is associated with
periods of large-scale in-migration which tend to diminish when the rates
of ethnic movement into urban areas fall off. As an area largely of second
settlement, the West End contained an extremely heterogeneous mixture
of ethnic groups for a long time. Nevertheless, small ethnic clusters existed
within the larger neighborhood (Woods, 1902). Even in 1958 the different
ethnic groups were not uniformly distributed throughout the West End but
showed a mild tendency toward residential clustering. The proportions of
the different ethnic groups living in three distinguishable sectors of the
area reveal these patterns. All the ethnic groups show quite a wide dispersion, but some sectors were clearly preferred residential areas for one or
more ethnic populations. Thus, the sector of highest status, bordering the
outside world, included a relatively large proportoin of the most recent
residents (Americans, British-Canadians, and a miscellaneous group of
diverse Latin origins) and the Jews. The sector which was intermediate in

status contained a disproportionate number of Poles, Slavs, central Europeans, and Irish. The lowest status sector was the residence for a majority
of the Italians (51 percent) and for moderately large proportions of the
Irish, Poles, and Slavs.

In contrasting stable, organized areas of poor housing with skid-row
slums, the familistic character of the residential slum appeared as one of
its more distinctive features. Certainly the West End was a family area and
was dominated by the sense of family life. However, the relatively high
divorce and separation rates found among low status people in our society
were also evident in the West End and were only partly counteracted by
the predominant religious commitment of the population to Roman
Catholicism. Most of the people in the area (70 percent) were married and
living with a spouse. But almost a third of the households (30 percent)
were female-based, only a slightly smaller proportion than the rates
reported for lower status Negro populations.[6] A large minority (10 percent)
had never been married. Almost as many (9 percent) were widowed. The
remainder (11 percent) were either divorced or separated and were not
living with a spouse. These distributions of marital status do not vary much
among ethnic groups, among people of different assimilation levels, or
even among those of different social class position. A few noteworthy
variations do stand out and enrich the picture of the West End population.

Three ethnic groups, the Americans, the British-Canadians, and the Jews,
included a moderately large number of people who had never been married
(21 percent, 22 percent, and 20 percent respectively). Among the Americans and the British-Canadians, who were not truly integrated within the
life of the community, the convenience of the area was particularly attractive for single people. By contrast, the great majority of the dominant
Catholic groups were married and living with their spouses: the Italians
(85 percent), the Poles (83 percent), and the other Slavs (80 percent).
Most of the households in the community included children who were an
essential part of daily life in the West End both statistically and visually.
But the families were relatively small. Most households contained between
one and three children and only a small proportion (8 percent) had four or
more children. There were few three-generation households but a moderately large minority (17 percent) of the households included some relative
beyond the conjugal family unit. Most of the families in the West End (57
percent) had had relatives living in the area within recent years and a substantial number (11 percent) had a great many kin living nearby, imple-
menting the sense of the area as a family neighborhood.

Thus, although the population varied in ethnic origin, assimilation status,

age, length of residence, and family status, it was dominated by multiethnic, second-generation family households with long-term residence.
Similarly, despite a wide range of social class characteristics, the West End
was primarily a neighborhood of relatively poor but stably employed
working-class people. While there were a few people of high occupational
status, the vast majority were in low-status occupational positions (table
3.1). Most of the men (79 percent) were blue collar workers and there
were more unskilled (25 percent) and semiskilled manual laborers (37 percent) than skilled manual workers (17 percent). Many people had the
impression that the area included a large number of students and professionals associated with the adjacent Massachusetts General Hospital or
with other nearby academic and professional institutions, but the total of
professional, semiprofessional, and business people other than local shopkeepers was only 6 percent. If we include the small local business people
and the skilled clerical workers and public service employees, the total of
moderate or higher status occupational positions rises to only 21 percent.
Compared to the distribution of occupations in the United States, in 1960,
these figures stress the working-class character of the area. Moreover,

TABLE 3.1   Occupational distribution of male heads of household

Occupational status	Percent	N^a
Professional	3	13
Business and executive	1	4
Semiprofessional	2	8
Small business	4	16
Clerical and public service	5	18
Skilled manual	17	68
Semiskilled clerical	6	25
Semiskilled manual	37	148
Unskilled manual	25	101
Totals[b]	100	401

[a]N in this and subsequent tables refers to the number of cases in sub-
categories excluding those cases in which the relevant information is missing.
[b]There were 151 uncodeable cases due mainly to the absence of any
male head of household. The total N of 552 includes the 486 respondents
interviewed before relocation as well as 66 cases interviewed only with the
postrelocation schedule for whom this information was available.

despite a large proportion of stably-employed men, many of the men were unemployed or irregularly employed. Thus, only 54 percent of the households included a male who was regularly employed or, considering only those households in which a husband was present, 78 percent of the male heads of household were regular wage earners. The proportion actually unemployed (6 percent) was a little higher than the national average in 1958 (5 percent), but, in addition, a strikingly large proportion (12 percent) worked only part time or from time to time.

Levels of education and of income were also very low. Only 6 percent of the male heads of household had completed college or had gone on to graduate or professional schools and another 6 percent had some college education (table 3.2). Conversely, fully 46 percent of the men had eight years of schooling or less. The educational levels of the women were somewhat lower. Thus, as with occupation, there was considerable diversity, but the majority of the population were of very low educational attainment. Incomes and financial condition were also meager. Although the income of the husbands was supplemented by the moderately large proportion of wives who worked full-time or part-time (42 percent), the incomes of the men were extremely low. Altogether, the majority of the men (54 percent) for whom information was available earned less than $75 a week and few (16 percent) earned $100 a week or more. According to conservative criteria of poverty and omitting people over sixty-five years of age, 23 percent of the households in the West End fell below the minimum standards of family finances and an additional 32 percent were of marginal financial status.[7]

Differences in status among the people of various ethnic backgrounds and of different assimilation levels were minor. There was a strong relationship between assimilation status and educational attainment but little variation in occupational level and even less in income level among the first-, second-, and third-generation people. Variations in indicators of social class position among the different ethnic groups were small and scattered. The largest proportion of the heads of household in each ethnic group were semiskilled manual workers. Only the Americans and people of central European origin included large proportions in high status occupations (24 percent and 29 percent respectively), a fact that is certainly associated with the convenience of the area for students, young physicians, and nurses or other hospital personnel. At the other extreme, less than 1 percent of the Italians, about 6 percent of the Poles, and 10 percent or less of the Slavs, Irish, and Jews, the groups for whom the West End had once been a major area of residence, were in these high status occupational categories. The

TABLE 3.2 Educational distribution of male and female heads of household

Education completed	Male		Female		Total	
	Percent	N	Percent	N	Percent	N
No formal schooling	9	35	7	36	7	71
1–4 years	9	37	8	43	8	80
5–8 years	29	118	27	146	28	264
9–11 years	24	101	29	155	27	256
Completed high school	18	76	18	100	19	176
Some college, technical-professional school	5	22	7	36	6	58
Completed college, technical-professional school	3	11	3	16	3	27
Graduate or professional school	3	13	1	5	2	18
Totals[a]	100	413	100	537	100	950

[a]There were 139 uncodeable male cases and 15 uncodeable female cases. For further explanation see footnote to table 3.1.

small proportion of highly skilled (professional, semiprofessional, and business) people in the West End were predominantly recent residents who had lived in the area two years or less in contrast to the long-term residence that characterized the people of lower occupational status levels.

Many features of ethnic distribution and assimilation, of family status and length of residence, and of socioeconomic and employment status are quite similar from one working-class slum community to another.[8] The multiethnic character of the West End with its small-scale ethnic concentrations was more characteristic of slum areas in the United States than the specific distribution of ethnic backgrounds, but even the ethnic origins of the West End population were typical of the European immigration from 1880 to 1910. Earlier in the century the West End, like other working-class slums in major cities, had a far higher proportion of foreign born than it did by the middle of the twentieth century, but with the attrition of the European migration the population remaining in these areas represented, to an ever greater extent, the second-generation children of immigrants. Long-term residence within the same area is a fairly consistent feature of ethnic residential slums. The quality of the area as a family-based community with many local kinship ties is also characteristic of other low status neighborhoods. The predominance of people with low levels of education, occupation, and income along with small proportions of people with fairly high status achievements seems to characterize the ethnic slum community. But the moderately high rates of poverty and of unemployment, in the West End as in other working-class slum communities, point up the precarious economic situation in which large proportions of the populations have been living. Despite half a century of reform and rising standards of living that have affected the entire population, the urban residential slum reveals in most concentrated form the large, residual deficits in economic and social status, in opportunity and integration that continue to define the life situations of many minorities long after their replacement in the lowest ranks by new and more severely underprivileged populations.

Distributions of social characteristics provide a background for understanding the patterns of social roles, social relationships, and psychological orientations in a population or community. They delineate some of the objective bases for examining the ways in which housing, interpersonal interaction, and family relationships are integrally linked to the life styles of people in different social positions. They will serve to guide us in understanding differences in occupational behavior, in social achievement and deprivation, and in personality among people from different social backgrounds within the same slum community. In examining the life experiences, social roles and relationships, and personal orientations of people in the West End, we can more adequately compare the people in this community with other working-class populations and communities in order to assess the situation of the working class and some of the most prominent forms of adaptation to this situation in our society.

4 Residential Experiences and Orientations

Working-class Housing Areas

Working-class dwelling areas in the very large cities of the Western world have a monotonously similar character. During the nineteenth century multistoried, low-rent housing spread far and wide through many urban, working-class districts to create a distinctive type of residential section, the tenement slum.[1] Some cities retained more traditional types of semi-detached and constricted wooden houses or three-deckers endlessly arrayed, frequently in the most serious states of dilapidation and disrepair. But the tenement became the prototype of working-class housing and many of the smaller wooden structures were subdivided and took on some of the characteristics of tenements. Even the massive and institutionalized public housing developments of brick and concrete are dominated by the same principle of agglomerating large populations in small areas of ground space with little attention to needs other than primitive forms of shelter and household functions.

During recent decades, mass suburbanization has produced lower-middle-income suburbs that deviate markedly from traditional working-class housing, a trend that may represent the slow decline of familiar patterns of ethnic, slum residence. But even if we consider these improvements for some of the more affluent workers, most low-rent housing areas share the burdens of economic constraint in physical appearance and facilities. These are due partly to the unhappy realities of the housing and real estate markets in our society and partly to a derogatory estimate of the housing needs and standards of low status populations. Building lots are filled to capacity with dwelling space in the slum. The only areas immediately available for leisure are the streets and sidewalks. Buildings and streets are often severely neglected by landlords and urban administrations alike. In new housing developments, with an increasing number of working-class home owners, there are opportunities for improvements and amenities unknown in rental housing. But the constraints are visible even in privately owned working-class homes. The majority of low-income families, even with the growth of suburbanization and home ownership, continue to live in rental housing in highly urbanized areas (Frieden and Newman, 1970).

Most tenements whether erected initially to house a mass of low status immigrants or transformed from old and well-worn town houses by new brick fronts and internal subdivision, are quite uniform within any single area. Because of this similarity and their close attachment to one another, they give the impression of a barely differentiated mass rather than of individual buildings. The sense of crowding is usually reinforced by the narrow streets and sidewalks pushed to their very limits to accommodate cars that are parked, cars trying to move, children playing ball, people standing in small knots talking and almost oblivious to local traffic. Many of the houses have alleys leading into the basement and into small, con-crete backyards, alleys which alone fulfill an essential function of provid-ing opportunities for seclusion and mystery for games the children play. The total tenement façade is sometimes broken by older and smaller build-ings which bear testimony to an affluent past. Storefronts often spread along the street, their provisions or services readily visible and accessible to the local population. This would be an affront to most middle-class neigh-borhoods, many of which are protected from such mixed uses by zoning codes. But for the working class the local stores are an important part of the total life space of the community, an extension of the household economy. No matter where the slum is located and which particular types of housing the area contains, regardless of differences in ethnic origin of the people or the relationship of the neighborhood to other parts of the city, characteristically the slum represents a unique blending of social and physical space. More than other neighborhoods, the urban slum is a circum-scribed and distinguishable segment of the world in the midst of the metropolis, an alien and alienated segment that encompasses a small and self-contained unit of working-class society.

Although the housing of working-class people in the slums is a widely deplored feature of working-class life, the close integration of physical and social space makes it difficult to understand either housing or residential behavior without talking about people, about social relationships, and about social organization. People are everywhere almost all the time. Build-ings are visibly peopled. The streets are filled with people standing, people moving, people being, people doing. Only late at night or on winter evenings are the streets silent and even then it is a less total silence than occurs in areas inhabited by the upper middle class. The sense of people and of human processes is given greater vitality by the ebb and flow of functions: diurnal changes in the age composition of the streetscape and in motility patterns, seasonal changes in the numbers of people and the size of clusters. During the spring and summer months, the contrast between high levels of activity and interaction in working-class communities and the absence of people from the streets in higher status neighborhoods is particularly remarkable. In the late morning or the early afternoon, adult women and smaller children are everywhere to be seen in many working-class areas. By late afternoon, as the women begin to filter back into their apartments, the clusters of teenagers become more apparent, clearly separated by sex but often covering a fairly wide age range. After supper the teenagers emerge again; the younger adult men congregate near the corner or just outside a favorite store or bar. The stoops of the houses and the sidewalks nearby are often crowded with older people and middle-aged adults, especially women. The hallways of the buildings also serve a social function. The many and varied audible sounds, the array of diverse odors, the activity in stores and shops and on the street, and the faces at the windows create an almost ceaseless sense of a population living in, investing a physical area.[2]

The Quality of Housing in the West End

The housing experiences and residential orientations of people in the West End revealed these characteristics vividly and tell us a great deal about the meaning of housing quality and residential behavior for housing satisfaction. The West End of Boston was largely a neighborhood of tenements with three to six apartments in a building, although quite a few buildings had a larger number of apartments. Nearly two-thirds of the buildings were constructed before 1900 and most of the others were completed before 1910. Within these fifty acres there were 2,700 household units containing more than 7,500 people in 798 residential buildings.[3] Most of the buildings occupied almost every inch of the lots on which they were situated (Hartman, 1967). It was one of the most densely populated areas in the city of Boston with 368.7 persons per inhabited acre (in 1940) compared with a citywide average of 94.5 persons per inhabited acre. Thus, the areal density was high even when compared with the vast overcrowding in other contemporary or earlier slums. In Boston, only the North End had a higher areal density with 924.3 persons per inhabited acre (Hartman, 1967). Despite the high density of people living in the area, the average

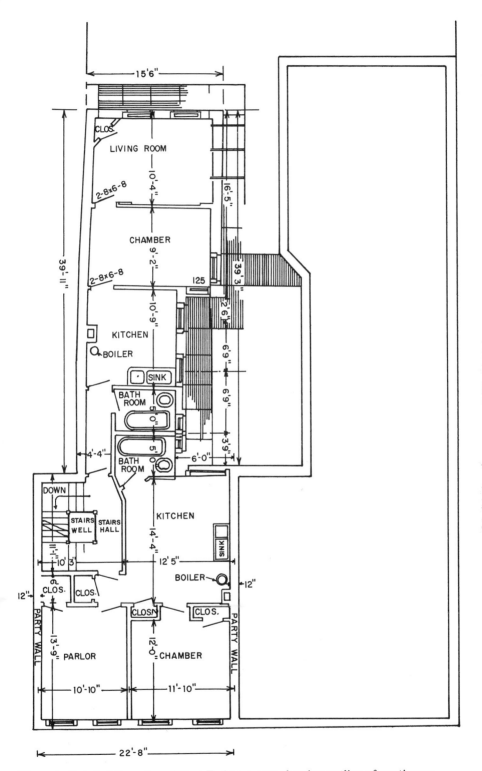

Figure 1. Detailed floorplan of West End tenement showing outline of contiguous building.

household density based on number of persons per room was relatively low for reasons related to life cycle changes and widespread reluctance to give up familiar apartments. Using the U.S. Cenus Bureau's criterion of severe overcrowding as 1.5 persons per room or more, only 4.5 percent of the households in the West End showed such excessive densities in 1940. By 1958, just prior to the redevelopment of the area, 16 percent of the house-holds had densities higher than 1.0 person per room, a moderately low level of overcrowding.

Other features of housing quality were far more variable and ranged from the most miserable slum conditions to remarkably fine apartments. The buildings were quite narrow, a characteristic of tenement construction in the late nineteenth and early twentieth centuries. Frequently they were built on lots of 20 by 100 feet to maximize the number of rooms one could put into a single building. In most instances, 90 percent of the lot was occupied by the tenement and the very small spaces between the buildings allowed little light to reach those rooms that did not look out directly toward the front or rear. During daylight hours, these rooms were sufficiently dark to prevent close observation of the apartments of neigh-bors which were often little more than ten feet away and, thus, easily visible at night when the lights were lit. Compared to other slum areas that have been investigated, the number of rooms per apartment was fairly ample: only 3 percent of the apartments had two rooms or less and 46 percent had five rooms or more.[4] But the rooms were usually quite small and frequently opened upon one another without hallways in between. The saving grace was that the small size of the rooms made the apartments easier and cheaper to heat, a matter of considerable importance since only 43 percent of the dwelling units were centrally heated. A large proportion (21 percent) of the apartments lacked a parlor or living room and a modest number (10 percent) lacked a separate bathroom in the apartment or some other major resource. Even if we ignore the absence of central heating, almost a third of the apartments were seriously deprived of living space and housing utilities.

Compared to housing built for more affluent populations, the average apartment in the West End was, thus, clearly disadvantaged, with inade-quate light, inadequate heating arrangements, inadequate space, the frequent absence of major facilities, and an excess of dirt and dust. Al-though numerous apartments suffered few of these disadvantages, the buildings themselves were often seriously deteriorated. More than a third of the buildings (36 percent) were in poor or very poor condition. Only a modest proportion (24 percent) of the buildings were rated as good or excellent. Although these ratings indicate that the widespread impression of entirely uniform conditions of severe dilapidation in working-class slums is erroneous or, at least, exaggerated, many of the buildings were in sad need of rehabilitation and some of them were beyond such minor surgery. In fact, these figures may underestimate the poor condition of the buildings. The ratings themselves, like most such ratings, were based on judgments by middle-class interviewers.[5] Their prior expectations were often worse than the conditions they found. As a consequence, they may reflect a frequent reaction of pleasant surprise. But it is evident that while these evaluations reveal a wide range of variability in the condition of the buildings, few of them would have met middle-class criteria of excellence or even of minimal acceptability.

While the buildings themselves were old and the majority were maintained in barely adequate condition, the apartments were remarkably well kept. They often lacked many of the essentials of decent housing, but many of the tenants exercised great ingenuity in creating a pleasant and effective housing environment. Contrasted with the condition of the buildings, only a quarter (26 percent) of the dwelling units were in poor or very poor condition and a considerable proportion (41 percent) were in good to excellent condition (table 4.1).[6] The remarkable cleanliness and excellent state of repair of the apartments was a major accomplishment which often required the full investment of working-class compulsiveness and concern about beautiful surroundings. The tasks included frequent

TABLE 4.1   Distributions of housing attributes (in percentages)

Quality	Building condition	Dwelling-unit condition	Apartment furnishings
Excellent–good	24	41	46
Fair	40	33	34
Poor–very poor	36	26	20
N[a]	314	314	308

[a]The basic sample size for all tables based on West End information is 486. However, information about housing that required interviewer ratings, as in this table and in all those using the index of housing quality, is available for a maximum of 328 cases. The remaining cases were interviewed shortly after leaving the West End and are, thus, uncodeable for these measures. In addition, there were 14 cases that were uncodeable for building condition and dwelling-unit condition and 20 for apartment furnishings because no interviewer ratings were done.

washing of walls and scrubbing of floors, annual or semiannual painting of the apartment, efforts to retrieve declining furniture and curtains, and perpetual vigilance as well to prevent excessive use or abuse of the apartment by the children. By virtue of these efforts the condition of apartments, which the tenant could repair and improve, were superior to the condition of the buildings, over which the resident had little control. The condition of the furniture, which was even more completely subject to tenant control, was least often old, dilapidated, or in disrepair. The image of slum residents as people largely incapable of maintaining decent conditions of housing is manifestly at variance with the great care and attention lavished upon the dwelling units by many of these working-class tenants.[7]

The effect of the qualitative differences in the apartments on observers was often dramatic. Many of the comments of the interviewers captured these extremes and the impact of pleasure or disgust was often evident in their descriptions. Some apartments were a delight to the observers who could scarcely suppress their surprise:

This is one of the most cheerful, neat, modern apartments I've seen so far in the West End.
The apartment was all neatly decorated—hardwood floors—from what little I saw, it appears to be in excellent condition.
Very cosy looking—child's room completely done in circus motif with many stuffed clowns, pictures of clowns, circus drapes, and so forth. Early American furniture in bedroom of R, also guest room—neat, cheerful, and pleasant.
Well furnished, elaborately decorated, kitchen has all modern utilities and conveniences.
Respondent's apartment was immaculate and beautifully furnished with Dutch cabinets, beautiful china in the corner of the kitchen.

The majority were simply reasonably livable and revealed the effort to convert inadequate housing conditions into satisfactory apartments:

Apartment dark, kitchen clean and well kept up, tiled (husband fixed place up). Sturdy-looking apartment although quite drab-looking.
Furnishings are about seven years old but have been worn through use. R works hard to keep apartment clean and stylish.
Apartment was kept clean and tidy although it is an old apartment with fairly old furniture and furnishings.
The apartment is an old one . . . Sparsely furnished but well cared for, R had all sorts of handwork, laces, tablecloths, and so forth around that she had made by herself.
Her apartment was very nice and reflected the pride she has in it.

At the other extreme, some of the apartments were in the utmost and even offensive states of neglect.

This is one of the most depressing homes visited. The cold, the rundown condition inside and outside of the building, the lack of facilities, and the poverty of the furnishings all added to this. Though R herself was not unclean, there was little attempt made to make the best of things. She, the furnishings, the building, and the lot were all depressing.

Filthy, dirty apartment. Food littered all over kitchen, dirty pots and pans on top of old, black, rusty stove.

This is the worst apartment I have been in—it smells of urine and dog feces—there is very little furniture and that in hopeless repair, and the place has not been cleaned in perhaps months.

The house was terribly dirty; it had a dank odor and was horrible, dark and cluttered.

The apartment was incredibly filthy. Junk piled up in the kitchen practically to the ceiling. There were two dogs on leashes in this small apartment along with a mangy, half-dead chicken in a fruit basket with a cover on it.

It has often been observed that the cost of working-class housing and, particularly, of slum housing is disproportionately high for the space and the facilities it commands. However, housing in the West End was unusually inexpensive and the rents were surprisingly uniform. While there was a linear increase in rental costs for apartments in better buildings and for better dwelling unit conditions, average rentals extended over only a narrow range from $38 a month for housing in a poor dwelling unit and a poor building to $51 for housing in a good dwelling unit and a good building. Thus, many families with very low incomes were able to live in decent housing. But within this relatively homogeneous local community, dominated by a population of low status and low income, differences in the quality of housing and in the status of various subsections reflected many of the same inequalities and class-determined influences that characterize our society as a whole.

Using a composite index of housing quality, we can take account of a number of different housing characteristics in determining the conditions that lead to variations in the overall quality of the dwelling unit.[8] Differences in family income clearly made a difference in the quality of housing of people in the West End. Among low-income families, 26 percent lived in poor housing while only 5 percent of the families with higher incomes (incomes that were, nonetheless, quite modest by wider standards) lived in equally poor housing. But family income is a relatively weak indicator of economic status since it neglects the number of persons who have to be housed and clothed and fed within a given budget. A preferable measure of economic position is the per capita income of the family. We find much larger differences in the effects on housing quality of this finer assessment of the economic situation of the family.[9] Among those families in poverty, whose per capita income was below a relatively conservative criterion of minimal subsistence, 32 percent lived in poor housing while hardly any of those in more adequate financial circumstances (4 percent) lived in poor housing.[10]

Within the relatively narrow range of West End statuses as well as in the population as a whole, people of low education or low occupation are more often than not in poor financial circumstances as well. The major determinants of differences in housing quality derive from the interactive effects of these different aspects of social class position. Each dimension of social class position independently contributes to these differences in housing quality. When we examine the effect of per capita income on housing quality among people of relatively homogeneous social class positions, we can see how each facet affects these differences in housing quality (Appendix table 4.1). (1) The incidence of good housing increased markedly among West Enders both with higher social class position and with increased per capita income. (2) By and large, social class position was a more potent and general influence on housing quality than family per capita income. (3) Most strikingly, differences in per capita income had a particularly potent effect on the housing quality of people in the higher and moderate social class positions while among those lowest on the social class scale, there was virtually no variation in housing with different levels of per capita income. Thus, while people of higher and moderate status generally obtained decent housing, increased incomes led to commensurate improvements in their housing situations. The housing of people in low status positions, however, was dominated by their social class status and improved little or showed little deterioration with differences in their economic situation. Whether this was due to status-striving through housing among people with more education and better occupational positions, to differences in expectation of future income, or to a high degree of tolerance for poor housing quality among people of lower education and occupation remains uncertain.

That status alone and differences in aspirations and strivings implied by status lead to demands for better housing, however, is quite evident from a number of sources. Housing aspirations, as we shall see, are closely tied to other forms of desire for social mobility and of expectations that improved housing is realistic. But the diverse status-linked attributes that influence the quality of housing can be traced to the socioeconomic status of a person's parents as well. It is unfortunate but not unusual to find that the sins of the fathers are visited upon their guiltless children in housing as in other respects. Duncan and Duncan (1955) report that the occupation of the fathers of heads of households are quite powerfully associated with the residential location of Chicago families. A similar relationship obtained in the West End: among those people who were themselves of high status, the proportions who lived in good housing diminished from 56 percent of those with relatively high status origins to 47 percent of those with moderate social class origins to 27 percent of the people whose parents were of low status (Appendix table 4.2). People of low socioeconomic status origins, however, varied little in the quality of their housing regardless of their own social class position.

Differences in quality of housing, however, are not limited to direct manifestations of status but result from a number of other characteristics that are influenced by economic, social, and cultural position. One important intervening factor, related to both aspirations and origins on the one hand, and to housing behavior on the other was the general standard of living that people maintained. The standard of living, expressed in such forms as owning a car, having a telephone, the proportion of income devoted to rent, and the freedom to indulge in social activities outside the home, was itself markedly affected by economic and social status and by past experience and future expectations. Even within the narrow range of options among people in poverty or in marginal economic conditions, differences in standard of living produced large variations in housing quality. Thus, among those in the poorest financial circumstances, 40 percent of the people with a very low standard of living also had poor housing, while only 16 percent of the poor people who maintained a higher standard of living had equally poor housing. Among people in better economic circumstances, differences in their standard of living had little effect on the quality of their housing. It seems likely that little special effort was required to obtain decent housing among those who were in a relatively comfortable financial position, while the strivings implicit in a moderately high standard of living were critical in order for poorer people to obtain better dwellings.

The summation or even the cumulation of diverse aspects of social class position, economic status, social class origins, class-linked aspirations and expectations, and class-influenced standards of living provided a powerful imprint to differences in housing quality. However, other realities and circumstances further influenced the quality of housing in which people in the West End lived. The length of time a person lives in an area is an important factor in residential behavior, but the effects of long-term residence on the quality of housing people obtained varied considerably with their social class positions. Among people of relatively high status, new-

comers more often lived in good housing (61 percent) than did long-term
West Enders (41 percent). On the other hand, people of low status, who
less frequently lived in good housing than those of higher status no matter
how long they remained in the neighborhood, improved their housing considerably if they stayed within the local area. Among those of low status,
30 percent of the long-term residents, 19 percent of those who had lived in
the West End for a moderately long time, and none of the recent inhabitants lived in good housing. The dynamics of the process are difficult to
verify, but many comments and relationships suggest that low status
people who wanted good housing remained in the West End and sought
every opportunity to get better apartments within their limited means by
trying to find decent dwelling units as they became available nearby, by
making arrangements with friends or relatives who owned West End tenements, and by upgrading the apartments they had.

   A number of household or family characteristics were also associated
with differences in housing quality. With considerable regularity, the larger
the size of the household or the more children in the household, the poorer
was the quality of housing.[11] At one extreme, single people and families
with no children most often lived in the best housing in the West End.
Even beyond this, however, the more children there were in the household,
the poorer was the housing. Nor was this simply due to the added financial
burden of a larger number of children since the same pattern held even
among people with equivalent per capita incomes. However, the poorer the
economic circumstances of a family, the more readily did an increase in
family size lead to poor housing. For people in poverty, the proportion
living in good housing dropped markedly (from 33 percent to 13 percent)
with two or more children. Among people with marginal incomes, an
equivalent decrease in housing quality (from 29 percent to 12 percent in
good housing) did not occur until there were at least three children. Among
those who were better off financially, there was no marked drop in housing quality although there was a gradual decrease in the proportion of
households living in good housing with each successive increase in family
size.

   The reason for the effect of family size on housing quality remains
obscure. It is at least possible, however, that the explanation lies in an increase of strain and greater difficulty in managing the household with
expanding family size, particularly in families with meager or modest incomes. Certainly it is the case that overt manifestations of household or
family strain were also linked to poor housing. The level of marital satisfaction, as a reflection of numerous household and family relationships,

had an important, independent influence on housing quality, unmodified by differences in social class position. Although there was little difference in the housing of people who were highly or moderately satisfied with their marriages, people who were maritally dissatisfied far less often lived in good housing. It is also noteworthy that in maritally satisfied families at all social class levels, an increase in family size had relatively little influence on the quality of housing.

It is, of course, difficult to disentangle cause and effect in many of these findings. We have given implicit causal priority to marital dissatisfaction as a determinant of poor housing for several reasons. Those characteristics of housing that were subject to improvement or neglect (for example, the appearance of the apartment) were more strongly linked to marital satisfaction than were housing attributes that a tenant could least alter (for example, the condition of the building). Moreover, other sources of household strain like an alcoholic member of the family or marital values that stressed distance and compromise rather than sharing and positive affects also were associated with poorer housing. Indeed, when we put a number of measures of household social problems together into a composite index, the effect is quite powerful.[12] Relatively few people (13 percent) with minimal social problems lived in poor housing, only a somewhat larger proportion (26 percent) with moderate social problems lived in poor housing, while almost half (45 percent) of those with severe social problems had poor housing. With social problems as with most instances of household or family strain, the effects on housing were quite consistent at all social class levels. Not only was the level of social problems, along with discrete sources of marital strain, a major influence on housing quality, but when we take simultaneous account of a wide range of factors that might affect the quality of housing in which people lived, severity of social problems remains the major, independent determinant of housing quality.[13]

As a general result, it is not surprising to find that housing quality is associated with social class position, income, and other status-linked attributes.[14] However, that the inequalities of housing opportunity that so sharply segment the life chances and experiences of people in the larger society are visible within the small compass of a single and relatively homogeneous working-class neighborhood is itself a striking indication of the pervasive nature of class distinctions in our society. Social class influences, however, are supplemented by other factors and, particularly, by strains in family relationships as determinants of the quality of housing. Some of these strains are themselves indirect products of low social position or may lead to declining status. Others are more distantly or more tenuously related to social class position, but their effects are most striking among the people of lowest status who rarely have decent housing under conditions of strain or situational difficulties. In fact, few of the forces that influence housing quality are entirely free of social class implications. Thus, the impact of social class position on housing quality gains further significance by virtue of the summating and circularly-reinforcing processes through which economic and social status directly influence housing quality and have further consequences for a wide range of other behaviors and experiences that also affect the quality of housing in which people reside. However, it is of some importance that, while there are direct and fairly strong effects of overt social class differences on the quality of housing, the main sequences of influence on housing are indirectly linked to or modified by social class. They occur through strains and problems that are themselves partly the product of social class position or through conditions, situations, and experiences that differentially affect people in different social class positions and, most frequently, lead to poor housing among those of lowest status.

Residential Satisfaction: The Apartment

Most people in the United States, at all social class levels, appear quite satisfied with their housing and their residential neighborhoods.[15] By conventional, middle-class standards, however, many working-class people live in housing that falls below acceptable criteria and, as we have seen, this was also true in the West End. Regardless of middle-class standards, a basic sense of residential satisfaction was characteristic for people in the West End as it is in other urban slum areas and in areas of middle-class residence. Observations among working-class people have particularly stressed the deep commitment of most residents of these areas to their housing and residential situations. While they may express many dissatisfactions with the limitations of their dwellings, they tend to remain long-term residents and to resist any possibility of change.[16]

In assessing the attitudes of working-class people toward their homes and communities, it is difficult to distinguish the effects of limited housing alternatives and resistances due to overt and subtle discrimination from intrinsic, attractive forces within the working-class neighborhood. Certainly there are severe economic and social constraints on the open market in housing. Apart from actual discriminatory rental policies, realistic differences in life circumstances and expectations tied to social class position have considerable significance for housing decisions. For blacks and other recently urbanized minorities, unambiguous discriminatory practices by landlords and real estate agents are too dramatic to be overlooked (Stern-lieb, 1966). It is less widely recognized that similar, if less severe, discriminatory practices affect white ethnic groups of working-class status. Working-class communities have themselves often discriminated against newcomers from divergent ethnic origins. Within the West End, overt ethnic discrimination was mainly evident toward blacks since the majority of the population held broadly ethnospansive attitudes, signifying their acceptance of people from other ethnic origins.[17] Indeed, there was little ethnic clustering within buildings or streets and, despite some social class differentiation of subneighborhoods, a considerable dispersion of people from different status positions throughout the West End.

Overt ethnic or class discrimination are only two forms of housing restriction among many. With the exception of public housing, new construction is rarely available to any but the most affluent workers and even lower-middle-income housing is often beyond the budget of working-class people. In the past, the filtering down of older housing vacated by people of higher status provided an important source of dwellings for low status populations.[18] But a combination of forces has reduced the competitive position of low-income families for such housing. Slum clearance, rehabilitation of moderate cost housing, and pressures from other subgroups have reduced the supply; movement to the suburbs and outlying urban regions has reduced the concentrated and effective demand of such populations. Thus, most working-class people operate in a very tight housing market in which economic, social, and psychological forces converge to place them in a weak bargaining position. By and large, they must accept what is available and learn to make the best of it. That they have often, in fact, made the best of it is a striking manifestation of adaptive achievement.

Whether these constraints on the housing choices of low-income and low status families contribute to the housing stability of working-class families or not, it is essential to recognize the very high degree of such stability of residence. One of the most extraordinary and persistent observations about working-class slums in many parts of the world, an observation that contrasts sharply with conventional conceptions about extensive transience, is that the majority of residents in these areas have lived there much of their lives and had planned to continue living there.[19] The patterns of housing and community stability in the West End were strikingly similar to those in other working-class slums. Almost a quarter of the women (23 percent) and half as many of the men (12 percent) had been born in the West End. The majority of both the women and the men (67 percent of the women,

69 percent of the men) had lived there ten years or more. Remarkably enough, as we have shown, there was only a slight increase in rates of movement out of the area during the five years prior to urban renewal when the threat of relocation hung over the heads of the residents. Rates of turnover in apartments were, quite naturally, somewhat greater but these were also surprisingly low. Thus, 30 percent of the people had lived in their present apartments for ten years or more and 59 percent had lived in the same apartment for at least five years.

Other factors also point to a keen desire on the part of most of the population to live and remain in the West End. Only 13 percent of the people had been planning to move apart from the forced relocation entailed by urban renewal; an additional 14 percent had been thinking about moving; and the remaining 73 percent had planned to stay on in the West End. Certainly the relatively low rents in the West End were themselves attractive. The rent-income ratio in the West End, with an average of 13.6 percent of income allocated to rental costs, already indicates the housing bargain of West End living (Hartman, 1967). But this was rarely offered as a major feature of the attractiveness of the area. The low rents may have enabled people to divert larger expenditures for improving and decorating their apartments. If this were so, it clearly implies that residents preferred such expenditures to moving into better housing. Indeed, the high degree of uniformity in West End housing, even in the size of apartments, and the low turnover rates meant that most people who wanted to stay in the West End had to make this choice in spite of the many restrictions entailed: relatively meager apartments in spite of increasing incomes, and marked discrepancies between family needs and apartment space.[20]

We need not rely only on circumstantial evidence to support the view that the great majority of West Enders were pleased with their apartments. More than three-quarters of them (78 percent) said they liked their apartments. Even if we use a more restrictive criterion, 74 percent liked most of the features of their apartments. The main sources of satisfaction were both realistic and modest: light, disposition of rooms, facilities, space. Pressed to give attributes of the apartment they disliked, on the other hand, 31 percent could mention nothing while, at the other end of the scale, only 3 percent were totally dissatisfied. The major specific objections to the apartment were the lack of space or specific types of space like closets (19 percent), general atmosphere like the cold, noise, or darkness (15 percent), specific inconveniences ranging from lack of a toilet or hot water to the number of steps the tenant had to walk to reach the apartment (15 percent), and housing deterioration, disrepair, insects, or rats

(14 percent). While the full range of housing aspirations of West End residents may not have been met by the actual conditions of the apartments, as is evident in these complaints, other factors seemed to compensate for their dissatisfactions with their housing.

One of the more remarkable features of housing in the West End, indeed, was the relatively modest effect of housing quality on the feelings people had about their apartments. Most people who lived in good housing liked their apartments (89 percent), but the majority of those who lived in poor housing also liked their apartments (65 percent). At the other end of the housing quality scale, the pattern was similar. Few people (6 percent) who lived in good housing disliked their apartments, but not very many of those living in poor housing expressed serious dissatisfaction (22 percent). From a quantitative point of view these differences are not inconsequential but, in view of our general expectation that housing quality should have a major effect on apartment satisfaction, the proportion of people in poor housing who liked their apartments was surprisingly large.

The apparent contradiction between moderately low levels of housing quality, evidence of fairly high standards coupled with widespread, realistic complaints, and a strikingly high degree of apartment satisfaction poses a basic question. To what degree does satisfaction with the apartment reflect attitudes of tolerance or a recognition of limited alternatives or do positive feelings about the larger residential environment override such specific considerations about housing? Interestingly enough, when asked about their apartments, a large number of people (32 percent) referred to the neighborhood as a major source of satisfaction. By contrast, when people were asked about the features of the neighborhood they liked, the apartment was rarely given as a source of satisfaction.

While involvement and participation in the local area and satisfaction with the West End did not entirely vitiate the effects of poor housing on the feelings people had about their apartments, apartment satisfaction was a resultant of forces stemming from different components of life in the West End.[21] Thus, 28 percent of the people who had good housing but disliked the West End were highly satisfied with their apartments; and a very similar proportion, 33 percent, of those who had poor housing but liked the West End were highly satisfied with their apartments (Appendix table 4.3). If we use a more objective measure of residential behavior, the use of local resources, and compare its effects with those of housing quality on apartment satisfaction, we find that similar interactive effects influenced the feelings people had about their dwelling units. People who made extensive use of local resources were little affected by the quality of their housing (Appendix table 4.4). Approximately half of them were satisfied with their apartments regardless of the quality of housing itself. Similarly, people who lived in good housing were generally satisfied with their apartments whether they made extensive or minimal use of the resources in the local area. On the other hand, among people who made moderate or minimal use of local resources, the quality of housing made a marked difference in their apartment satisfaction. Among people who lived in poor housing, satisfaction with the apartment was very strongly influenced by differences in their use of the local area. Thus, either good housing or extensive local participation were sufficient to induce apartment satisfaction for a great many people. Conversely, maximal use of local resources could partly counteract the negative effects of poor housing just as good housing could partly compensate for minimal local participation.

The compensatory effects of different features of residential experience in the West End operated for people at all social class levels. However, housing and neighborhood experiences had different significance for people in different social class positions. People of higher status have a wider range of housing options and alternative sources of satisfaction unavailable to people of lower status. Many poor people, on the other hand, have learned to accept the inadequacies of their situations. Thus, at each level of economic condition, approximately a third of the people who lived in poor housing were satisfied with their apartments. But among people who had good housing those who were poor were more likely to be satisfied than those in less strained financial status. Thus, of those who had good housing, the vast majority of the very poor (73 percent), a small majority of people in marginal economic conditions (59 percent), and less than half of those in modest or comfortable economic circumstances (43 percent) were satisfied with their apartments. The relevance of the availability of alternatives, of a wider range of options becomes even more evident when we consider the effect of housing conditions and satisfaction on people's plans to remain in the West End (before relocation) or to move elsewhere. Among those who lived in good housing, there were few differences in the proportions of people who planned to stay or to leave at different social class levels. People of higher status who lived in poor housing far less often planned to stay in the West End (39 percent) than those of low status who lived in poor housing (80 percent). Moreover, the objective quality of housing was more influential on plans to stay or to leave the West End than was the expressed satisfaction with the apartments people had.

Although people of lower status had few options but to remain in low-rent districts like the West End, they more often had alternative sources of local satisfaction. These sources of satisfaction, in turn, had greater consequence for housing satisfaction for working-class people than for people of higher status (Appendix table 4.5). Good housing led to somewhat higher levels of apartment satisfaction among low status residents than it did among those of higher status. But many forms of local involvement, participation, and relationships with local people also were more significant influences on apartment satisfaction among low than among higher status inhabitants of the West End. In fact, local participation or compelling social relationships like the local residence of parents were occasionally linked to dissatisfaction with their apartments among people of higher status although it is difficult to determine whether these involvements and commitments were actually sources of dissatisfaction or, rather, conditions that bound them to the West End in spite of their housing dissatisfaction. Certainly it was the case, however, that long-term residence led to greater housing satisfaction most consistently among those of lowest status. This supports an earlier hypothesis that people of lower status more regularly improved their housing over time if they continued to live in the West End than did people of moderate or higher status. Just as alternative forms of local involvement and participation more consistently led to apartment satisfaction among those of lower status, so did higher aspirations or potentialities more frequently lead to dissatisfaction among those of moderate and low status. Thus, low status people with relatively high family incomes or with aspirations for upward mobility or better housing were more likely to be dissatisfied with their current housing than were people of higher status with similar social aspirations or economic achievements.

It is quite evident from the analysis of housing and from the effort to locate the sources of housing satisfaction that uniform explanations across a wide range of social class levels may obscure important relationships. This would itself be a major aspect of housing behavior were it not a phenomenon that we shall find again and again in examining social class differences in behavior. Nonetheless, it is quite striking that the sources of satisfaction with the apartment varied so considerably from one social class to another. More specifically, few of the potential explanatory factors had much significance for apartment satisfaction among people of higher status while there were numerous influences on apartment satisfaction among those of lower status. When we take simultaneous account of a wide range of issues that might influence satisfaction with the apartment for people in different social class positions, we find that inevitably only a modest amount of the variation in such housing satisfaction can be explained.[22] The only influences that stand out as general and fairly substantial explanatory factors irrespective of social class are few in number: good housing led to satisfaction; older people were more frequently satisfied; people with mental or emotional difficulties were more readily satisfied; and people who were comfortable in their social relationships were more often satisfied with their apartments in the West End.

Apart from the quality of housing and general residential satisfaction, however, both of which were quite strongly associated with apartment satisfaction for people in all social classes, and the greater tolerance for poor housing among older people in all social class positions, the differences rather than the similarities among social classes stand out. For people in higher status positions, housing quality and residential satisfaction were mainly supplemented by transitory life situations that increased the importance of the convenience of the West End and its accessibility to the rest of the central city and to hospitals, universities, and other facilities nearby. For these people, predominantly young, often unmarried or without children, with considerable education and often of high occupational status but with relatively low incomes compared to their potential, the inexpensive, large apartments in the West End were particularly attractive. Frequently they obtained the best housing the area had to offer. Nonetheless, they were less often satisfied with their apartments than were people of lower status. Whether satisfied or not, they were less likely to be committed to the area with long-range plans to continue living there. For the low status residents of the West End, on the other hand, and those of moderate status who were quite similar in many cultural respects to their low status neighbors, the area had a very different meaning. Their apartments were, in a much more significant sense, their homes: their average duration of residence was longer, far more often did they plan to continue living there regardless of their level of satisfaction, they knew less of the world outside and more of the West End, and, particularly if they were long-term residents, they were more often satisfied with their apartments and with the area as a whole. Many of these considerations entered to influence their feelings about their apartments. In addition to the general significance of housing quality, of residential satisfaction, and of age, the entire range of physical and interpersonal resources, of local involvement and participation with people from the same ethnic origins, with relatives, and with neighbors all served to encourage a high degree of housing satisfaction. In fact, however, they had few options. For many people of low and moderate status, the West End was a personally meaningful environment, but dissatisfaction with their housing or even with the residential

area did not signify plans to leave. Only in the relatively rare instances of
real potentials for social mobility or of overt mobility aspirations did alternative residential situations seem feasible for people in lower social class
positions in the West End.

Residential Satisfaction: The Neighborhood

These findings provide considerable support for accumulated, but often
contested, impressions from numerous studies of working-class communities. Data from these communities in different parts of the United States,
in Puerto Rico, in England, and in France stress the vividness of working-
class neighborhood life, the extension and closeknit social interaction patterns in the local area, and a conception of the neighborhood as an extension of the home.[23] In the West End this kind of working-class neighborhood orientation dominated even so limited a sphere of experience as
apartment satisfaction and, in this respect, the differences between social
classes is quite marked.[24] It is difficult to document the full extent to
which there is a fundamental difference in conceptions of neighborhood
and community and of the ways in which the local area functions within
the life space of individuals from different social class positions. Working-
class people devote a much greater part of their time and focus more of
their activities within the local area. They know the area better, they are
familiar with a larger part of the area, they utilize the local resources to a
greater extent. But this is not entirely a matter of completely free choice.
Working-class people are more timid about moving out into the wider
metropolitan world, utilize the resources and facilities of the city less often
and less widely, and are generally less comfortable outside the neighborhood. These differences we can summarize as the emphasis on localism in
working-class life in contrast to a more metropolitan orientation and a
more selective use of territorial spaces among people of higher status. But
this distinction does not alone capture all of the difference. For, however
defined, there are marked differences in the use of space among people of
different social positions.

   People in higher status positions do not merely value housing quality
more than do people of lower status. They value neighborhood interaction
less. The apartment or the house in the middle class is a specialized retreat:
terribly private in one sense and the basic place of social interaction in
another. There is a relatively impermeable boundary between the walls of
the apartment or house and the street. Even in suburban life, in which the
conception of a wider community often has many similarities to working-

class neighborhood life, the extension of the home into the garden or yard is closely guarded and neighborly interaction is closely controlled.[25] In the working class, the apartment also has a private character and is certainly less likely to be the locus of social interaction than in the middle class. In a more casual sense, however, the apartment leads directly into the street, through sounds, through sights, through movement. Daily life is more often lived on the street and, particularly during mild weather, almost the entire population may congregate in front of the houses and on the street corners. It is here that we may best speak of community life in the working class. The social interaction occurring in the street is not only a basic feature of working-class life. It is also the core of a set of patterns of behavior and of social organization that invade almost all aspects of working-class life, from family relationships and shopping behavior to recreation and a sense of social participation.

We have already said that most people who lived in the West End liked it. Indeed, 37 percent were intensely positive about living in the West End and another 39 percent were more moderate but decidedly positive. Few people (10 percent) disliked the area or disliked it extremely. While the men were somewhat less deeply committed to the local area than the women, they too were predominantly positive about the West End. Less than a third of the women (28 percent) had no positive sense of the area, approximately the same number of people who had said they disliked the area or were ambivalent about it in describing their feelings. The most frequent positive reason was a global sense of basic satisfaction (31 percent) which often took a specific form of liking everything, a feeling that it was home, or the fact that they knew everyone there. Some people had difficulty expressing their positive feelings and said only that they had lived there all their lives. Many of the positive feelings about the area, colored by impending relocation, were deeply poignant. But a large proportion of people who were quite positive about the West End gave less intensely personal reasons: 22 percent spoke of the convenience of the area, 14 percent liked the West End because of their interpersonal relationships there, and 7 percent claimed they liked living in the area because it was inexpensive. Of the small number who had mainly negative feelings about the area, the most frequent explanations were global distaste and the physical deterioration of the West End.

Most people, including some of those who disliked the area, appreciated the fact that the West End was a true neighborhood. In fact, what is most striking about this is that relatively few people (14 percent) traced neighborhood quality to specific interpersonal affiliations and associations with kin, friends, or neighbors. Most people conceived of the neighborhood as something broader and more inclusive, because of a general sense of comfort and friendliness (24 percent), or because of widespread interpersonal relationships with other people living in the West End (29 percent). Many people interacted mainly with people who lived very close by but a more general sense of the integrity of the West End was widespread. Indeed, in contrast to the limited familiarity most people have of the urban areas in which they live, the majority of people in the West End (64 percent) knew most of the West End. So high a degree of localism and local involvement, of course, exacted its price. A remarkably large proportion of the women (32 percent) and only somewhat fewer of the men said they knew no other area of Boston beyond the West End. Many of those who said they knew no other area had, in fact, extensive contacts with other areas. But their responses revealed that for many people, leaving the West End was like entering a foreign territory and no matter how often they ventured forth to shop downtown or to go to work, they always felt like anxious strangers in other areas.

The full quality of attitude can only be appreciated by direct observation, but many comments capture the nuances of feeling. Asked what made the West End a neighborhood, some of the replies were:

I love it. My husband works in Cambridge and it's very convenient, my mother is here.
I've been here so long that I'm used to the place. You go someplace else and you feel strange.
The people. I have known the neighbors so long. We treat each other like sisters and brothers, even the colored people.
When you're brought up in a neighborhood, it's home to you. Your heart and roots are there.
The best people in the world are right here.
Everything, the shopping, the Esplanade, it's handy to a show, the friendly people.
I love it. It's home and handy to everything, to theaters, schools, parks, and town.
I know all the people casually and say hello.
I love it. All of it. I was born here, was married here forteen years ago.
I think 'cause we know one another, the same people you see everyday. We know everybody. You feel for one another. It's a community all by itself.
There was always someone to talk to. Visiting people, always different ages of people around. You know all the stores and who owns them. Sometimes when you need help, people would help out without making a fuss.

Certainly there was a wide range in these views of the West End, but even among those who had a more distant and impersonal view of the area, apart from the few who actively disliked living there, the quality of warmth and friendliness was almost omnipresent.

Most of the sources of differentiation in residential satisfaction are quite self-evident. The single most important independent source of such satisfaction was the degree to which the local resources in the area were utilized.[26] People who shopped in the area, who went to the various settlement houses and clubs in which the area abounded, who were widely familiar with the area and knew its informal facilities well were considerably more satisfied with the area than were those who made minimal use of the West End (Appendix table 4.6). The differences in residential satisfaction associated with differences in the use of local resources are large thoughout. While the extensive use of local resources and facilities and its function in supplementing, concretizing, and interweaving a host of other forms of interaction and common experiences captures the essence of working-class life in the West End and in other low status communities, other influences on residential satisfaction are also worthy of note.

We have already seen that social class differences in housing quality were relatively large but such differences in apartment satisfaction were relatively modest. Similarly, while people of higher status were less often highly satisfied with the West End than were those in lower social class positions, the differences were not very great. Moreover, the social class variations in the sources of residential satisfaction are less striking than the equivalent variations in the determinants of housing quality or of apartment satisfaction (Appendix table 4.7). However, social class differences are present and have a coherence that carry more general implications for explaining the reasons for local commitment among people in different statuses.

Among people of relatively high status, residential satisfaction in the West End was not only less frequent than for people in moderate or lower status positions but was rarely intense. However, at this status level, a high degree of residential satisfaction was linked to indications of parochialism. People of higher status who belonged to the dominant ethnic groups in the West End, who were quite limited in their knowledge of the metropolitan area, whose parents lived in the West End, who had few mobility aspirations, and who were low in personal efficacy or mastery were considerably more likely to feel a strong sense of satisfaction with the neighborhood.[27] The attitudes of West Enders who were of moderate status were generally more similar to those of lower status than to those of higher status residents. But they were distinguished from both higher and lower status people by the importance of traditional social affiliations as determinants of a high degree of local involvement. The availability of kin in the local area, ethnic involvement, the local residence of their parents, frequent interaction with family members, and closeknit network contacts were of prime importance as sources of residential satisfaction for them. The image of local community life as a source of intense satisfaction due to neighborliness and active participation in the informal networks of the neighborhood was particularly characteristic for people of lower status. For them, the use of local resources, extensive social interaction, and closeness to neighbors were investments of major significance and the dominant sources of residential satisfaction. While the sources of residential satisfaction varied in degree and, to some extent, in kind for people in different social class positions, these differences should not obscure many similarities. Regardless of social class position and despite variations in the strength of the correlations at different social class levels, extensive contact with neighbors, use of local resources, local friendships and a sense of neighborhood, long residence, good housing, and satisfaction with the apartment were universally important determinants of residential satisfaction in the West End.

Finally, it is essential to take account of a factor that is frequently mentioned but rarely sufficiently emphasized in discussions of residential satisfaction: length of residence. It is only reasonable that people who do not like an area are more likely to move out than those who do. The longer a person lives in an area, the more likely he is to establish ties and commitments that bind him ever more closely to that area.[28] As a consequence, we can anticipate that those people who have lived in an area for a very long time are far more likely to have profound involvements with the area than those who have lived there for a shorter period. In the West End, this is precisely what we find. The length of time a person lived in the area was one of the most potent influences on residential satisfaction for people in all social class positions (Appendix table 4.8). People of higher status, however, with a greater range of options and wider familiarity with other urban areas were less markedly influenced by sheer length of residence in the West End. But long residence in the area virtually insured a high degree of satisfaction, regardless of specific involvements or affiliations, just as quite recent residence usually meant only modest satisfaction for most people whether they had already established ties or not. It was mainly among those who lived in the West End for a moderately long time, who divided more sharply between those who were highly satisfied and those who were less deeply involved, that specific affiliations like the degree of closeness with neighbors made the greatest difference to residential satisfaction (Appendix table 4.9).

As we examine different aspects of West End residential experience and satisfaction, the impression grows that this, like other working-class communities, was a closeknit, warm, intensely interactive small community. This view of working-class community life has often been referred to as romantic. Whether the romanticism is that of the many observers of working-class communities who report similar findings or that of the residents themselves who have tried to make a meaningful way of life in an "urban village" under conditions of economic and social constraint within the larger society and in an impersonal industrial environment is not clear. No matter how we look at the results, the evidence persists that for the large majority of the people who lived there, the neighborhood had meaning far beyond that of a comfortable or even of a sociable residential area. For many, indeed, it meant home: a place in which they belonged, to which they belonged, and which belonged to them. Certainly it is clear that the warmth, the homelike quality, the friendliness of West End life were not the specific factors affecting everyone. Many people moved into the area for entirely different reasons, with different expectations, with different desires for meaningful residential experiences. The significance of these features of West End life, in fact, seems to have been of decreasing importance for people in successively higher status positions. At the same time, it was a way of life and an orientation to the local community that created a total and, in some respects, an inescapable atmosphere. Even for many people who did not seek this atmosphere, who could have lived comfortably without the neighborliness and friendliness, it often proved to have a captivating quality that made their experience of residence in the West End more significant and perduring.

In spite of this, slowly and gradually people moved out of the West End long before urban renewal forced a mass exodus. Some moved out because they had moved in only temporarily and tentatively and never became involved in the life of the area. Others moved out because they actively disliked the area. Many moved out, over time, as part of the long and painful transitional process from immigrant, lower-class life in an urban slum to lower-middle-class status in a slightly improved residential environment and with a slightly expanded world view. For some people, ambitions for their children led them to seek higher status areas before they themselves felt fully certain that they wanted to give up their neighborhood life. Indeed, the more highly concerned the household was with the children in the family and their needs, the lower was the level of residential satisfaction.

Concern with children as a factor influencing residential dissatisfaction and leading to movement out of the area appears to have been of significance over a long period of time. In trying to estimate the differences between the residual population of the West End living there just prior to relocation and former West Enders who had moved out of the area earlier, we interviewed ten people who left the West End voluntarily five to six years before there was any threat of urban renewal.[29] Strikingly enough, all ten early movers, without exception, indicated that a deep sense of commitment to the West End or involvement in the community life of the area had served as a restraint against moving. Many people had liked their apartments very much and were reluctant to give them up. But more important to them than housing were their general feelings about the area, about the friendliness of the atmosphere, or specific local social relationships which they experienced as irreplaceable even after the move. Ten years after moving, they still experienced a strong residue of these feelings about the West End. Although many found compensatory satisfactions in their new housing situations, they continued to regard the change in community orientations as a real and regrettable loss. The critical factor that overcame their initial resistance to leaving the West End was most often a striving for social mobility or, alternatively, desires for better housing after having achieved social mobility. Most consistently, however, the move represented a desire for residential improvement for the sake of the children.

These, indeed, are typical of the dilemmas of working-class status in modern, urban, industrial societies. Regardless of the satisfactions of working-class neighborhood life, the attractions of potential reward through upward mobility or through the realization of achievements in middle-class residential areas are too powerful to be neglected. Moreover, the widespread derogation of slums in our society and the history of their deprecation, often neglecting the important stabilizing functions of cohesive working-class communities, exacerbate these pressures. The dominant constraint against residential movement lies in working-class forms of communality within the local residential area which often overrides any specific considerations of housing improvement.

Housing Desires and Aspirations

The relatively poor quality of housing in the West End, the very modest conditions that produced housing satisfaction, and the effects of social class differences on levels of expectation and satisfaction have prepared us for highly temperate aspirations for future housing. That was precisely the case for people in the West End, as it is for a great many working-class people. Low status people become habituated to meager social rewards, whether these be educational opportunities, work situations, or housing and residence. As adaptive devices to minimize constant feelings of frustration and anger, their hopes and desires are often kept at a relatively low level. In some respects, this must inevitably become a feature of class culture and impede the full realization of opportunities that may become available sporadically. The most highly valued attributes in working-class cultures are restricted to those they can obtain for themselves despite constraints in the socioeconomic system. Close friendships, simple entertainments, family commitments, neighborhood involvements are among the most stable working-class values. Most notable are the relatively great significance of social relationships within the local area and a more global sense of community in the context of the impersonal, urban environment. These often become the determinants of housing decisions and satisfactions rather than more specific dwelling attributes that dominate the housing orientations of the middle class in our society.

Most working-class people, as a consequence of their experiences, are simply unwilling to allow themselves the dangerous luxury of high fantasies. Asked to describe their dream house, 28 percent of the people expressed only the most meager housing desires and the majority (64 percent) allowed themselves only simple wishes that hardly deserve to be called fantasies. Only 8 percent indulged themselves in fantasies like desires for a double-decker with four bedrooms, two baths, and a den or, at a rare extreme, a big house, with ten to twelve rooms, and land, along with fancy kitchens and baths. The specific features of housing toward which people aspired as ultimate fantasies confront us with the sad housing plight in which so many of the working class live. Many people expressed a yearning for simple, outdoor areas: a yard and a porch, land for lounging, a place to garden and plant flowers (27 percent). In view of the affluence and the luxury housing widely available in the mid-twentieth century, it is particularly startling to realize that 27 percent of the people in the West End dreamed about attributes that many American take for granted as minimal housing: a dining room, a separate living room, more rooms, a good refrigerator and a gas range, a nice tile bath with shower.

Certainly many people, if forced to move, wanted to own their own homes or to live in the metropolitan suburbs, desires that have become almost universal in industrialized countries. Indeed, 47 percent expressed a desire to move into suburban areas. As we know from subsequent events, these desires were doomed to failure for many while others acquired apartments outside the city of Boston in equally urbanized working-class regions of the metropolitan area. One may suspect that even in anticipation, the meaning of suburban life was more modest, in greater conformity with the housing they actually obtained, than the idea of a suburb itself implies to middle-class people.

Many said quite simply that it made no sense to them to talk about their dream houses or that they never thought about it because they knew they would never get them. Those who allowed themselves these simple fantasies, as we have indicated, desired mainly to live in housing that was only a trifle better than the housing they knew in the West End. Thus, 41 percent of the women said they wanted only basic, minimal rooms and another 29 percent desired additional space that was so modest that, for many Americans, these would also be considered basic minima. Even among those whose ambitions led them further, 22 percent allowed themselves the wish for one room that might be classified as a luxury (den, study, playroom, sunporch, television room) and only the few remaining people (7 percent) went beyond these small yearnings. While most people in the West End were extremely tentative about desires for housing, many more were conscious of the difficulties they were likely to meet in seeking the most modest dwellings. For the 42 percent who anticipated major difficulty in finding an apartment at rentals they could afford and for many of the others who expected difficulties which were indirect reflections of economic constraints, even these simple desires seemed like unrealistic flights of fancy.

In light of these modest desires and the focal importance of economic limitations, it is all the more impressive that so many people rejected public housing as a feasible alternative. Public housing remains the major form of income-supplemented housing specifically designed for occupancy by low-income working-class families despite several experimental programs providing different types of rental support for poor people. Nevertheless, almost three-quarters (74 percent) of the people in the West End completely rejected public housing and very few (11 percent) considered it a desirable objective. The major objection was particularly startling in view of the high areal density of the West End. Most people who were negative toward public housing felt that the density of population in housing projects was too high, that no privacy was possible in the projects. The comments people made captured the essence of their reactions: too many people; it's like being cooped up with people on a boat; too many families close together; each family would know what the others were doing and saying. A close second in frequency was a sense that the public housing projects contained many unacceptable people: lower class, prostitutes, people who used bad language. Finally, a widespread and typical reaction concerned the institutional, bureaucratic quality of public housing.[30] These views of public housing, in fact, make it quite clear that the low levels of housing aspirations of most West Enders hardly signified bland indifference to their dwellings but rather stressed the importance of a special set of values that informed people's housing decisions and choices. These values gave priority to the neighborhood, to the potentiality of maintaining close interaction with other, similar people, and while many West Enders might lavish enormous attention upon their dwelling units, realistic limitations of money and family size made them chary of striving for housing conditions they could not hope to realize. Indeed, the objective conditions that were likely to determine the possibility of moving into excellent housing were precisely the factors that actually influenced housing aspirations.[31] But no one factor is of overwhelming importance. Rather it is the summation of different potentialities or debilities, each contributing its share to the likelihood of achieving good housing, that results in different levels of housing aspiration.

The major factors that led to differences in housing aspirations were age and social class position. Older people had considerably reduced demands and considerably reduced hopes of obtaining excellent housing. Similarly, people with lower occupational levels, lower educational levels, lower per capita incomes all maintained lower levels of aspiration for housing. Thus, both age and social class position were important determinants of housing aspirations, but older people generally had reduced aspirations regardless of social class status (Appendix table 4.10). Nor was this merely a function of a general reluctance among older people or among people in lower class positions to indulge themselves even in modest fantasies. The same relationship appears in the specification of the kinds of rooms people desired in choosing a new place to live. Among the young, 39 percent of the higher status, 26 percent of the moderate status, and only 11 percent of the lowest status people signified a desire for modest "luxury" facilities in their new homes. At every status level, there was a sharp decline in expressed desires for modest additional rooms with increasing age. Thus, for people of high status, there was a decrease from 39 percent among the young to 16 percent among those aged thirty-five to forty-nine, and a further sharp decrease to 5 percent among higher status people aged fifty or over in such housing desires.

We have suggested, on several occasions, that derogatory images of lower class and of poor people are often based on quite superficial consideration of a few isolated and ill-understood facts. The housing behavior of low status populations is one issue that has lent itself to such abuse both of facts and of the human qualities of poor people. Indeed, slum clearance legislation was predicated, not on the grounds that low income populations needed better housing at low rentals, but on the basis of a view that if slum residents were dispersed, many of them would have to find better housing and, thus, their problems would vanish or diminish. As a consequence, well-financed developers rather than poor tenants were offered supplementary sources of support to accomplish the destruction of working-class slums. While manipulations that often led to redevelopment contracts in the past may have diminished and while the rationale for redevelopment has more recently emphasized urban tax gains rather than the dispersion of poor (and often black) residents out of desirable properties, the underlying conception of poor people has not altered much for example (Banfield, 1968). The data on housing aspirations confront these images with incontrovertible evidence that hard realities, rather than incompetence or lack of motivation, are responsible for the limited hopes, dreams, and strivings of most poor people.

Whatever factor we consider, the same evidence is revealed. Social class position may have some effect on housing aspirations but economic condition contributes a great deal in motivating higher or lower housing desires. Economic condition itself is influential mainly to the degree that it implies an expectation of continued poverty or a potentiality for economic improvement. Thus, when there was no husband in the household because a woman was single or widowed or divorced or separated or if the husband was unemployed or irregularly employed, women in poor economic circumstances had minimal housing aspirations, but if there was a husband in the household and he was employed, aspirations grew larger. For people in better economic conditions, it is quite understandable that the employment status of the husband was less relevant for housing aspirations. Similarly, for married people with both spouses in the household, poor economic circumstances currently left room for some modest hope of improvement and for modest housing aspirations. Women without a spouse almost invariably maintained extremely low aspirations for housing.

However, social class status often made a difference in the influence of other conditions and experiences on the level of housing aspirations. People of relatively high and even of modest status generally maintained moderate housing aspirations regardless of other circumstances in their lives. People of lower social class position, whose desires and ambitions were ordinarily quite depressed, felt freer to aspire to higher levels of housing when the family per capita income was more adequate or when the family was intact (Appendix table 4.11). Similarly, desires for social mobility or satisfaction with their housing and residential situations in the West End had no effect on the housing aspirations of people of higher status but led to somewhat higher levels of housing aspiration among those of moderate or low status. Thus, the uniformly low aspirations for housing among those of lower status were occasionally modified by special potentials or strivings while the higher housing aspirations among those of higher status followed from their generally wider range of potentials and opportunities. Conversely, several attributes only mildly improved the realistic chances of lower status people for obtaining better housing but had a much greater implication for improvement for those of higher status. Thus, younger people and the American born of native parents had the highest levels of housing aspiration. These characteristics potentiated such aspirations most fully among those of highest status. For people of lower status, youth and nativity could not counteract the realistic limitations of class position.

Another set of factors that differentially influenced housing aspirations for people in different social class positions were various social involvements and personal satisfactions: kinship and family experiences, closeknit network interaction, marital or more global role satisfaction. A high degree of involvement or of satisfaction often led to higher aspirations for housing among those of relatively high status but had a diminishing influence on the housing aspirations of people at lower status levels. The reasons for this are less clear, but one hypothesis stands out as a likely explanation. The irrelevance of social or interpersonal integration for housing aspirations among people of lower status can be traced to the fact that these experiences did not markedly affect their decisions to live in the West End in any event. Objective circumstances were more potent, but people of moderate or higher status sometimes restrained their aspirations for better housing and for residential areas of higher status because of commitments within the West End. Indeed, often they did not feel impelled to seek better housing because they found their total West End experience satisfactory. With the constraints diminished due to forced relocation and, in any case, due to the questions themselves that specifically asked for housing desires without consideration of any realistic limitations, they could more readily express their latent aspirations. Interestingly enough, differences in the purely local experiences of neighbor relationships or the use of West End resources had no effect on housing aspirations for people in any social class position. Rather, the more obligatory ties or the stable relationships that might persist regardless of place of residence were linked to high aspirations for housing among those in the higher social class positions.

On the basis of these findings, we can return to a question that arose earlier in the discussion of housing quality. To what extent were the differences in the effects of the quality of housing on apartment satisfaction a function of the strivings and demands of people at higher status levels or, conversely, of the indifference of people at lower status levels? It now becomes clear that there are many different parameters of housing orientations and these different parameters are affected by different factors. As the purest projection of future life chances seen by the person himself, it is of fundamental significance that housing aspirations are so thoroughly dominated by realistic conditions of age, marital status, social class, and financial or employment condition. But this is far from saying that people at lower status levels or in more restricted economic and social circumstances are indifferent to the housing environment in which they live. To some degree, they have learned both to set themselves lower goals and to be satisfied with more meager accomplishments. In this respect, they reflect a degree of tolerance, often for intolerable conditions, that is hardly evident to those who perceive every sign of anger and complaint from deprived people as an unjustified intrusion of conflict into a stable situation of peaceful complementarity.

However, the acceptance or relatively high degree of apartment and residential satisfaction in spite of poor housing betokens a difference in value systems as well. Whether due to the hopelessness of achieving the rewards defined by other values or generated through sources more basic to working-class cultural experience, they represent a widespread and distinctive orientation to the foundations of residential satisfaction. In contrast to the emphasis on a relatively impersonal, local social environment in the urban middle class (a conception that has given way, in recent years, with the development of higher status suburban communities), working-class people give primacy to the interpersonal commitments and more global, if informal, social organization of neighborhood life. That this is not merely due to a disregard for housing, however, is clear from the very high rates of apartment and even of residential satisfaction among those low status people who lived in good housing. Rather it is both the compensatory significance of local social relationships and of local participation and their intrinsic value for lower status people that is important. It is the successful accomplishment of this objective that leads to widespread residential satisfaction in most working-class communities and typifies the experience people had in the West End.

5 Working-class Community Life and Social Relationships

Community Commitment and the Sense of Community

A high degree of residential stability, deep commitment of people to their neighborhoods, and closeknit social organization within the local area are among the most striking features of working-class community life. These characteristics have been noted during more than a century of observations in urban slum areas. However, in the face of widely derogatory conceptions of these areas, those who commented on the community spirit also deplored this social cohesiveness as a source of resistance to other residential alternatives. Such complex issues require more adequate attention than has ordinarily been given to the psychology of low status people, to the social and economic contexts of their lives, and to some of the variations within and between working-class areas. There are undoubtedly working-class slums that are socially disorganized. The predominant pattern of highly effective forms of local social organization described by most studies of urban slums does not encompass all residents in these stable working-class areas. In trying to gain perspective on the structure of social relationships and affiliations in working-class slums, we have to recognize the intricacy of the patterns themselves and bear in mind that there are numerous instances of variations and deviations even from those patterns of functioning that appear most nearly universal.

The high degree of residential satisfaction in the West End and reports of similar levels of satisfaction in other working-class slums reveal the manifest devotion and personal investment that many working-class residents experience toward their neighborhoods. Many of the activities in which people engage, the breadth of local social relationships, and the use and sense of the community and its resources provide evidence of the sustaining quality

94

of working-class community life. Just as the home extends into the street, so is the boundary between family, kin, and community often virtually obliterated. Working-class residential areas reflect the sense of family life, of parents and their children, of close sibling ties in childhood and adulthood, of mature heads of household living close to their parents, and of neighbors who treat one another as many people treat family members. Indeed, the closeness of nuclear family relationships in adult social interaction and a kinship orientation extended to friends and neighbors give an exaggerated impression of the persistence of extended kinship arrangements. However, whether kin or kind, brother or sister or neighbor, friend or familiar, the working-class community is characterized by many overlapping, informal group affiliations.

Working-class social organization revolves around small, informal groups. Whyte (1943), in one of the earlier modern studies of working-class social organization, presses the importance of group relationships among working-class youth. These group relationships are so binding, Whyte points out, that an individual's role in the group tends to remain unaltered even after the individual has developed new styles of functioning outside the group. Gans (1962) refers to these patterns as the peer group society, in which close relationships between individuals are tightly embedded in the larger group of peers of the same age and sex. Teenagers in working-class communities typically hang together in highly localized, neighborhood or corner groups, usually boys and girls in separate groups. Close friendships develop within the group, but they are often sporadic and may reflect transitory patterns within the larger clique or group. It is the group itself, informal and undefined though it may be, that is the primary object of investment and loyalty. Hanging groups continue far into adulthood. Even married couples often interact in groups. Wives spend many afternoons and evenings with "the girls" and husbands devote their leisure to activities with "the boys." When husbands and wives visit or go out, they generally do so as a group of couples in which the men and the women tend to interact mainly with others of the same sex.

This group orientation is a distinctive feature of gregariousness within the local working-class community. High levels of local social interaction, however, and even larger localized networks of social affiliation are hardly limited to working-class communities. Specialized territories, like student housing projects, or suburban residential areas, or even exclusive areas of upper-class homes often reflect the broader significance of a high degree of social interaction and of common activities within a spatially bounded region.[1] But special characteristics like long-term residence within an area and the availability of a host of overlapping, daily relationships along with the sharp sense of discomfort beyond the local territory give the working-class form of community life a particular intensity that seems unique and more consistent than close community ties in other residential areas.

Like a number of other working-class areas, the West End included a rather wide range of people from different social classes, with different social origins and histories, with different current situations, and with different reasons for living in the area. Yet the vast reservoir of good will and sense of pleasure in the area largely transcended these differences. We have already said that most people were extremely positive about the area: a total of 76 percent, in fact, liked the area quite unambivalently. Nor is this an isolated instance. When asked "Do you consider the West End or some other place as your real home?" the largest proportion of the women by far (71 percent) specified the West End as their real home. Discussing what they disliked about the West End, many women (38 percent) could specify nothing and could only assert that they liked and would miss everything. Most of the others rejected physical attributes of the area, the run-down buildings or small apartments or narrow streets or garbage standing around, largely characteristics over which the residents had little control. But these features of the area were subordinate to the vividness of community life for most people. Most people planned to stay in the West End and, as we have indicated, mainly desires for social mobility for their children impelled the working-class inhabitants to seek neighborhoods of higher status.

Seen from this global vantage point, almost three-quarters of the adult women and men felt positive and committed to the local residential area. While precisely comparable quantitative information is unavailable from other working-class communities, the extent and intensity of involvement appears quite similar.[2] In a working-class residential area, it is not surprising that the higher the occupation of the head of household or the higher the education, the smaller were the proportions of people who were positive about the West End. But the consistency of strong positive feelings about the area for all social classes creates only modest relationships between status position and expressions of sentiment toward the neighborhood.

As we examine successive features of community life to determine the sources of these attitudes and involvements, an image begins to emerge. The consistency and interrelationships among these patterns seem to reflect almost a self-contained world in which each commitment leads to other commitments. Individuals who are implicated in the network of participation and affiliation become deeply and inextricably invested in them. We shall return to this issue as we press the question of causal sequences more closely. However, several individual attributes do stand out as influences on community commitment: age, length of residence in the West End, and ethnic embeddedness.[3] For the most part, young adults were less deeply committed to the local residential area than were people over thirty or thirty-five years of age. Certainly they had a wider range of options, of plans, and of expectations that had yet to be explored and fulfilled. The young adults were frequently people with relatively high educational attainments, highly assimilated with few foreign born among them, and frequently had low incomes relative to their educational levels and occupational potentials. Those young people who were more characteristically working class were often as deeply committed to the local area as were people past thirty-five years of age. The increase in commitment with increasing age, thus, tends to disappear when other factors like education, occupational status, or length of residence are simultaneously considered.

The length of time that people lived in the local area, however, was a pervasive force in accounting for many features of local behavior and attitudes. Most of the people who lived in the West End a very long time were deeply committed to the area while the moderately large number of recent residents were much more casual about local investments. A very large proportion of the people living in the West End (23 percent of the women, 13 percent of the men) had been born there and the majority (67 percent of the women, 60 percent of the men) had lived there for at least ten years. This degree of residential stability appears to be slightly higher than for other working-class areas and considerably higher than is true for the American population as a whole. Naturally, those who were less satisfied more readily moved out when other options were available, leaving behind the residents who became increasingly attached to their local community. The clear differences in localism associated with differences in length of residence are apparent in the expectations of losses due to relocation. Of those who lived in the West End a very long time, the majority (55 percent) expected to miss central neighborhood attributes while only a minority of those who lived there a relatively short time (27 percent) anticipated an equally severe loss.

Ethnic embeddedness was also an influence on local involvement. By embeddedness we refer to the fact that there were quite different proportions of different ethnic groups in the West End and people who belonged to the dominant ethnic groups were ethnically most readily integrated into the local community. Thus, they can be classified as ethnically embedded. At the other extreme were those people who belonged to ethnic groups with minimal representation in the local area. A wide array of correlations reveals the manifold but modest influence of ethnic embeddedness on localism: involvement with central West End activities, a sense of belonging, and a feeling about the West End as home were more frequent among the embedded ethnic groups. The reason that ethnic embeddedness was a less powerful influence than the emphasis on the ethnic orientation of working-class areas would suggest is evident in the irrelevance of ethnicity for most people in the West End. Asked how they would feel about living in a neighborhood in which there was practically nobody of the same ethnic origin and why they felt this way, some typical responses were:

No difference. People are the same regardless of race, color, or creed. We are all human beings.
Don't care. We have so many friends of so many different origins, it'd be a shame to limit yourself.
I no gonna like it very much. Because Italian people are better than American people. They understand me, and I understand them.
I don't care. As long as they good neighbors. I just don't care to live with the colored.
I wouldn't like it very much. We talk about the same things—food and things.
What's the difference? Makes no difference. Jews, non-Jews, they're all people, no difference.

Although differences in social orientation and psychological style were associated with differences in local investment and commitment, it is noteworthy that none of these contributed strongly to feelings about the local area. However, women who experienced a high degree of anxiety in social interaction more frequently limited themselves to local resources and facilities. Women who were more dependent on interpersonal ties to others were more frequently satisfied with the local community. Thus, for people who were fearful of extending themselves into unfamiliar situations and establishing relationships with unfamiliar people, the local area served an extremely important protective function. Different aspects of socioeconomic status, of social origins, and of social experience also contributed in a small way to the overall development of intense localism. But no one factor, nor even any combination of these, made a marked difference in localism or local satisfaction. It is mainly the relationships among different aspects of localism that are persistently powerful.

The Use of Community Resources

The integrity of a society or community implies that institutionalized patterns are interdependent with one another and understanding the community necessitates an appreciation of these interrelationships. But to clarify most aspects of functioning in a society, whether it be a nation-state or a residential community, discrete dimensions have to be examined as if they could exist apart from their interrelationships with a host of other features of life. The more closely woven the social fabric of a social unit, the greater is the degree of overlap between the same people in different role relationships. And when a wide range of activities is largely territorially bounded, the more fundamental are these interdependencies for the development and organization of social life within the community. Thus we must frequently anticipate interrelationships between different spheres of life and attributes of individuals even as we proceed to consider specific and isolated behaviors.

Like many of the old, ethnic communities in the United States, the West End contained a large number of local services. Settlement houses were abundant testimonials to the philanthropic efforts of Boston Brahmins eager to Americanize the immigrants or to the nostalgic yearnings of former residents who had made it in America. There were many clubs, playgrounds, and bars and restaurants. There were stoops and sidewalks and streetcorners where people might gather and establish a rudimentary sense of territorial identity. And there were stores and services to provide for local consumer needs. This wide array of local resources and neighborhood facilities is closely identified with European and Asiatic lower-class immigrants, as it is also linked to an era in which the melting pot was the model of effective incorporation of newcomers into society. Newer migrant populations have had to demand such locally-based opportunities anew in order to encourage social activity within the residential area.

People at low status levels generally engage in few formal organizational commitments and belong to few organizations.[4] Involvement in local, informal groups, however, and the use of local resources is a widespread and salient feature of daily life. In the West End the local settlement houses and other local organizations in which one could participate without a formal membership commitment were enormously popular. Technically these are formal organizations, but they were not seen as such by local residents. Thus, while most people claimed extensive participation in these local clubs and activities, few people said they belonged to organizations inside or outside the West End. Most people (60 percent) had some familial association with at least four or more of these local associations; few families living in the area were entirely without some contact with these organizations. The children engaged in many activities through the local settlement houses and clubs. The majority of the adult men and women also participated actively in these organizations, although the men generally preferred the most informal associational contacts.

Another activity that is even more typical in many working-class communities and little understood outside working-class areas is the use of local stores and services. Few women in the West End limited their shopping activities to local stores, particularly since there were major shopping areas within easy walking distance outside the West End. But most of the women did some of their shopping within the West End and even gave preference to local shopping. Only a small number (9 percent) had no preference at all for local shopping and a few more (7 percent) used local stores only as a matter of convenience. The great majority were more decided in their predilection for local stores and services. Some kinds of local shopping facilities were very meager. There were few clothing or furniture stores around. Yet most people (70 percent) shopped locally both for daily necessities and for other consumer needs. Even women who emphasized the more rational aspects of consumer behavior often revealed a subjective bias toward West End stores and services. Thus, despite considerable evidence that the local stores were more expensive than the nearby supermarkets, a number of women (11 percent) said they preferred shopping in the West End because it was cheaper.

Closer to the central meaning of local shopping behavior, the vast majority (77 percent) preferred a highly personal shopping arrangement in which they knew the owner and the owner knew them. Caplovitz (1963) has pointed out that the poor often pay more for several reasons. They cannot make the most economical purchases which require ready cash when bargains are available, and wide knowledge of consumer opportunities and flexibility in shopping behavior are essential to effective economizing. The low-income consumer is also often a target of unscrupulous merchandising practices. The search for low prices and, at the same time, the inescapable desire to acquire consumer goods beyond the means of low-income families often lead them either to impulsive purchases or to being easily convinced that they are getting a good buy. Within the local neighborhood, shopping in the same place day after day and buying from the owner whom one has known for many years, anxieties about being cheated can vanish. While the cost may be a bit higher, there is some assurance that one is paying a reasonably just price for items of reasonably adequate quality.

But local shopping is more than this. It is not merely extensive use and a sense of comfort that one will not be cheated. It is part of a set of local social relationships between merchant and consumer and between local neighbors. The embeddedness of shopping behavior in the culture and social structure of the local area makes it difficult for working-class community residents to shop with optimum rationality and efficiency. Shopping in the neighborhood is a basic form of participation in local, social activities with important economic origins. Regardless of income, weekly wage-earning working-class people who live in stable, working-class communities often shop on credit in the local area. This form of credit relationship is less widespread and effective in newer, disorganized, or more heterogeneous residential areas and is one of the problems created in public housing, in working-class suburbs, and in places where shopkeepers and consumers represent very different populations.[5] Credit purchases in the working class reflect a highly personalized relationship. Purchasing becomes an interpersonal exchange rather than a financial transaction. The extensive use of credit establishes an obligation for the consumer to continue buying at this store. The obligation established is reciprocal and unspoken; it requires the good faith of both. At times, even the working-class resident who is relatively secure financially may need this resource. If the main breadwinner is laid off or loses his job, if a costly illness occurs and exhausts their income temporarily, if some special event requires special purchases, the family can rely on the storekeeper to tide them over.

Beyond the reciprocity between consumer and storekeeper, many local shops also provide a rendezvous for social interaction among consumers. The stores of the West End were centers of the gossip mill through which information was passed along about who was doing what. Mainly in the stores, in the midst of casual shopping and chatting, residents found out about the tragedies or good fortunes that had occurred to their neighbors. These informal and almost incidental exchanges were so important to life in the area that many people seemed to make daily visits to the store primarily to participate in these relationships and events to the full. Complaints by social workers and public officials that working-class homes contain a meager supply of consumer resources can be better understood in this light. Since the store is an extension of the larder, readily accessible and socially significant, it is essential to have gaps in supplies in order to justify daily transactions in the store. Many people with moderate incomes and moderately high status as skilled workers had shifted to a familiar middle-class pattern of family shopping expeditions on Friday nights but deliberately omitted some items from their purchases in order to participate in these local social interactions at the neighborhood store.[6]

As with residential satisfaction and with other evidence of local commitment, the use of local resources was most strongly related to various forms of local participation. However, variations in the use of local resources were also mildly associated with differences in social role and position within the community. The use of formal facilities, participation in local organizations, and local shopping reflected the influence of length of residence, occupational status, and ethnic embeddedness. While it is hardly surprising to find that people who lived in the local area longest had the highest rates of participation in local organizations, the strength of this relationships leaves little room for doubt about its importance (Appendix table 5.1). For people who were generally resistant to formal organizations, participation in them had to take on the informality of other social ties. The longer a person lived in the West End, the more likely he was to become involved with organizations and clubs through friends and kin or through friends of friends and friends of kin. People of higher status were most often short-term residents but they were less likely to become fully integrated within these networks regardless of length of residence. Indeed, the people who most frequently utilized local formal facilities were those of moderate status, skilled workers and semiskilled white collar families. While 63 percent of these upper-working-class people used the local organizational facilities extensively, only 42 percent of the lowest status people did so, and even fewer (27 percent) of the higher status people became so actively involved in local clubs and settlement houses.[7] Consumer behavior, on the other hand, was equally often localized for people in the moderate and lowest social class positions although less frequent among people of higher status.[8]

We have already said that the different forms of localism were powerfully related to one another. Conversely, none of those attributes of more global status or role, except for length of West End residence, led to very large differences in diverse manifestations of localism. On these grounds localism may well be an endogenous and relatively self-contained pattern, historically influenced by ethnicity, length of residence, local kinship affiliations, and other forces that introduce a person into the community or ease his path, but with relatively little further consequence once these forms of local participation and use are themselves established.[9] Certainly other factors influenced the ease with which a person became involved in the community. We have already mentioned the effects of social anxiety or comfort with other people. While working-class people may be fearful of unfamiliar places and people, the high interaction level of working-class localism requires considerable relaxation in social relationships. This was most striking among long-term residents: those people who were most anxious in social relationships were least involved with widespread, local resource use. More recent residents generally made minimal use of local resources in any case and differences in social ease had little effect on the extensiveness of such usage.

It is particularly striking that diverse manifestations of purely local behavior as in close neighbor relationships were consistently and power-fully associated with local resource use regardless of social class. But the more traditional and obligatory relationships or identities, such as kinship ties or ethnicity or religious investment, led to very much greater use of local resources only among people of higher social class position. These class differences imply not merely different patterns of local behavior but the different forces that impelled people in different social class positions to live in the West End.

Another important and often neglected feature of localism is the wide-spread familiarity of many working-class people with their local communi-ties as physical entities. Most aspects of localism that we have considered were closely linked to the extensiveness of local social affiliations and, to some degree, so was the extent of local familiarity with the physical area. But knowledge of the physical community, like utilization of the larger metropolitan region, was partly independent of locally-based friendship and kinship contacts. The vast majority of both the women and the men knew a very large part of this area. Less than a third (27 percent) knew only a small part of the area and the men were even more frequently familiar with all or most of the area (77 percent). Widely familiar with the local area as they were, the boundaries of the free passage terminated at the borders of the West End for a great many people. We have already said that more than 30 percent of the women claim to have known only the West End within the larger metropolitan region and only 24 percent of them felt they knew any area beyond the immediately adjacent regions of the city. The men, naturally, had a broader range of familiarity with the metropolitan area but, nonetheless, revealed a high degree of physical parochialism. Almost a fifth of the men (19 percent) said they knew only the West End and less than half (47 percent) were familiar with areas beyond the West End and the immediately adjacent sections. It is this combination of a very high degree of local familiarity and a markedly bounded sense of the larger city that gave the West End, like so many other working-class neighborhoods, the quality of an urban village.

This is even more impressive when we consider that as a description of behavior, it was not entirely true. Many of the women shopped downtown or, at least, went window shopping in the downtown areas, and many of the men worked at some distance from the residential neighborhood. This, we have suggested, is one of the prices of working-class localism. As long as they were within the local area, peopled by familiar types, they felt *at home*. As soon as they moved into a different world, further removed socially than it was physically from their apartments, many people felt unknown, unknowing, and subject to myriad dangers. Their observations, thus, captured a basic, subjective reality: they did not feel they knew areas in which they felt utterly strange even if they had been there many times. Among those people who were more comfortable with areas beyond the West End, only 18 percent of the women and even fewer of the men (16 percent) went to these other areas frequently for volitional purposes like entertainment, leisure, and visiting. The boundaries of working-class life are thus narrowed, not merely by local commitments, but by the sense of estrangement from other areas and, especially, from other social classes.

Although the data are not sufficient to clarify the very different conception of space, territory, and property in different social classes, these findings lend support to more informal observations in the West End and in a number of other working-class communities. In discussing housing and residence we have already pointed out some of these differences, particularly the importance of the street, in contrast to the apartment or house, as the boundary of belonging and freedom of functioning in the working class. Quite apart from the fact that there is a visible difference in the number of people and their activities in middle-class neighborhoods, middle-class people more frequently know and use a wider range of resources and facilities in the larger metropolitan area. In practice, of course, people in all social classes are most likely to use resources that are nearby rather than those that are far away, but distance and even unfamiliarity are far less likely to deter people in higher status positions from using cars or public transportation to go considerable distances quite casually. While people in the working class are comfortable primarily in *places*, in areas in which they can function, middle-class people quite readily accept the impersonality of many areas of the city as passageways between places they know or want to go. It is a fundamental difference in the sense of spatial identity, in the conception of the physical environment as a personal region (Fried, 1963; Fried and Gleicher, 1961). The spatial identity that characterizes working-class people is a *territorial* one, based on and largely confined to a particular, bounded area. The spatial identity of higher status people is more generally a highly *selective* one, defined on the basis of desire or interest rather than propinquity or contiguity. Thus, the majority of people in the West End were, to characterize these differences in a typology, territorial locals who knew their own areas of residence extensively and did not venture far beyond them (57 percent). Only a minority (16 percent) were widely familiar with both the West End and with areas outside. Status, however, affected the degree of familiarity with areas outside the West End more markedly than it influenced the range of familiarity with locations within the West End.[10]

One other dimension of the sense and use of local and nonlocal space deserves attention, although we can only speculate about it. There is little doubt that those people who felt most comfortable within the local area and knew it best felt as if they belonged there. The ways in which people familiar with a large part of the West End spoke about it suggested, not only that they felt they belonged, but also that the West End belonged to them. To what degree this feeling about an area, a residential area that included many public places, reflected a difference in conceptions of property and proprietary rights one can only conjecture. People who own little property and do not expect to own property are more likely to conceive of proprietary rights in an entirely *functional* sense. If it is accessible to them, if it is used as part of their daily activities, if it is an area of quasi-familial relationships, it becomes a territory that belongs to the local inhabitants. And if it is further endowed with all the characteristics of home, it belongs to them and they belong to it, establishing a mutuality that is likely to treat the declaration of property rights as an invasion. Moreover, long-term familiarity and a feeling of control more readily absorb areas which, in a sense, belong to nobody. They are more readily seen as a semipublic realm in which one shares ownership with other users. This view of the neighborhood and its streets and public facilities seems to be the framework for much working-class behavior. It is this view, one may suspect, that not only defines localism of interaction and use but the feeling of strangeness and danger beyond the local world of the neighborhood.

Kin and Kin Contact

Although the use of local resources, facilities, and services are more important in stimulating a local orientation than is generally realized, local social interaction and the sense of sociability are also extremely important bases of localism among working-class people. The relevance of interpersonal relationships and of an atmosphere of local friendliness immediately becomes apparent in the reasons people gave for their positive feelings about the local area. If we include people who liked everything about the area, usually people who elaborated the highly interpersonal quality of their experience, more than 45 percent of the people felt that interpersonal relationships were among the most attractive features of the local community. Few people disliked the area because of the people: including those who disliked everything, only 7 percent specified or implied negative feelings about people living in the local community. Almost the same number (44 percent) anticipated that moving from the community would involve, among their most serious losses, the disruption of interpersonal ties. Many people also conceived the area as a neighborhood mainly because of friends and friendliness. In fact, it was the friendliness and community feeling and the long-term commitments far more often than specific relationships to kin, friends, or neighbors that made the West End a neighborhood for most people.[11]

Working-class neighborhoods have frequently been conceived as organized around relatively extensive kinship networks reflecting traditional kinship lines.[12] The evidence for this view is clear. The phenomenon known as chain migration leads to the gradual expansion of local kin from former cultural environments. For poor and often illiterate people, kinsmen served to bridge the new world and the old. Indeed, even in a population that was predominantly second generation, as in the West End, most people had relatives living nearby. Thus, 32 percent had small groups of relatives living in the West End within recent years and an additional 25 percent had four or more families of kinsmen in the West End.[13] Ordinarily we assume that kinship ties are both stronger and more essential for older people than for young adults, but kinship relations were often quite close even among younger people. Nearly half (45 percent) of the children numbered the children of kin among their friends, providing a childhood base for adult friendships among relatives. And 55 percent of the adults included some relatives among the five people to whom they felt closest. Most people gave some preference to kin over friends in highly personal issues: more people were likely to visit with relatives than with friends, the discussion of a family problem was more likely to occur among relatives than among friends, people more often expected emergency help from kin than from friends. There is little doubt from these and from qualitative materials that kinship was an important basis for social affiliations in the West End as it appears also to be in other working-class communities.

Kinship seems to be of great significance for social relationships in different societies mainly in certain conditions. (1) When there is economic interdependence among kin, regularized and close association is essential although it often leads to grave familial conflict as well. (2) Residence in the same locale or within the same tribal group over many generations results in extensive kin networks and ties. Kinship, in these circumstances, may be visible partly because it is indistinguishable from other bases for contiguity.[14] In urban, working-class communities, attenuated forms of these conditions often insure the perpetuation of social affiliations among kin. The entrepreneurial role of kin among new immigrants is undoubtedly supplemented by the forbidding social environment that greets the low status newcomer and gives particular emphasis to traditional forms of mutual obligation to insure some modicum of security.

But kinship may be a less potent force in the subjective experience of many working-class people and in their functional interactions. Despite the frequency of interpersonal reasons that led most people to consider the West End as a neighborhood, only a very small proportion (2 percent) mentioned relatives as the exclusive source of this attitude. More often neighborhood characteristics were attributed to the general community spirit or the friendliness of people. Considerably more people (53 percent) rejected the idea of moving near relatives than the number (38 percent) who found it a desirable objective. Friends were among the five closest persons far more often than relatives and those kin who were mentioned were mainly siblings and siblings-in-law. Thus, even for the large minority who saw their relations with kin as dominant, the kinsman was usually a member of the nuclear family or an in-law rather than a more distant relative.

Among people who lived close enough to parents, siblings, or married children to see them regularly, there was a great deal of interaction. Some parents (13 percent) lived with their children, almost exactly the same rate as in a similar working-class area in East London.[15] For those people whose parents were available, the majority (55 percent) saw them twice a week or more. An almost equally large proportion (49 percent) saw their married children this often. And most people (54 percent) saw their siblings at least once a week. Contact with extended kin was rarer: 69 percent saw many kin either once a year or less or several times a year. Among the five people who were seen as the closest persons (excluding parents and spouse), only 22 percent mentioned such relatives as aunts, uncles, cousins, nieces, or nephews even once. The importance of the parent-child relationship and, most particularly, the mother-daughter relationship, on the other hand, involved a very high frequency of interaction and was one of the most persistingly intimate ties known in the working class. Close relationships between mothers and sons and between siblings were only slightly less pervasive, although the relationship between fathers and children, for this generation, were more distant.[16] Whether these close ties are unique to the working class or far more characteristic in our society than is ordinarily realized remains uncertain, although a number of studies of relationships among kin in different social classes indicate that we have underestimated their importance more generally in the United States.[17]

To the degree that relationships with kin beyond the nuclear family were important to people, they were associated with other binding affiliations and conditions. People in the dominant ethnic groups much more frequently lived near kin in the West End than did people who were more ethnically isolated. Related to ethnic embeddedness, people from more rural origins were more likely to have kin living in the same community; the longer one lived in the West End, the greater the likelihood of having many kin nearby. The amount of contact people had with their parents also played a fairly crucial mediating role in closeness to nonnuclear relatives. If interaction with parents was infrequent, people were rarely close to their extended kin (11 percent), but among those people who saw their parents constantly, a moderate proportion were also close to more distant relatives (31 percent).

Frequent interaction with parents was even of considerable importance as an influence on the amount of contact people had with their own siblings. People who rarely saw their parents hardly ever had extensive contact with their siblings (6 percent). Those who saw their parents very often were quite likely (47 percent) to see their siblings often as well. On the other hand, frequency of contact with parents was a more highly personal matter, relatively unrelated to any other gross social forces. In general, propinquity had little effect on the frequency with which people saw their parents. But there was a difference by social class position. Among West Enders of high status, frequent interaction with parents was only to the slightest degree dependent on their living in the same neighborhood. However, among people of moderate and low status, parents were seen more often if they lived in the West End than if they lived at a greater distance, reinforcing the repeated observation of the greater importance of physical contiguity for social relationships among people of lower status.

If we shift attention from contact with parents to a composite measure of frequency of contact with close family members or an even more comprehensive index of kin involvement, we can see some of the factors that influenced these relationships more clearly.[18] People in the most embedded ethnic groups and those with long residence in the West End had the most frequent contact with their parents and with other close family members. Both ethnic embeddedness and length of residence were almost equally important. At the extremes, 58 percent of those people who lived in the West End a long time and were also ethnically embedded had frequent contact with their families while only 14 percent of recent West End residents who belonged to isolated ethnic groups had equally frequent family contact. On the other hand, social class differences in either family interaction or kin involvement were minor when the effect of differences in length of residence are taken into account. While there were evident differences in the significance of family and kin for people in different social class positions, these variations were less frequent and less striking than for many other social behaviors (Appendix table 5.2).

Interaction with family members or involvement with kin was quite markedly associated with both length of residence in the West End and with ethnic embeddedness at all social class levels. People who lived in the West End longer or were members of the more prominent ethnic groups in the community had more extensive relationships with their close relatives.[19] Interestingly enough, however, it is primarily among the people of moderately high status that a host of indications of conventionalism or constraint are linked to greater involvement with kin: a high degree of restriction to the local area, a markedly religious orientation, belonging to derogated ethnic groups, and, in personality characteristics, a low level of efficacy or mastery. For working-class people, involvement with kin is independent of these attributes, but those of higher status living in the West End were more likely to be close to their relatives if they were more generally committed to traditional orientations. For people of lower status, kinship involvement was part of a more widespread orientation to extensive sociability, although people at these status levels who had many ethnic commitments were also more likely to be close to their kin. These relationships, among others, suggest that continued residence in the West End for people of higher status is partly explicable on the grounds of a host of commitments that were most readily achieved within, although not entirely dependent upon, the local area. This view receives further documentation from the similarity between these class differences and those that influenced residential satisfaction.

In fundamental respects, relationships among relatives were quite distinct from other forms of working-class social or community involvements in the West End. As we have seen, a substantial minority engaged in close interaction with kin, particularly with parents, siblings, and married children, but such relationships were less widespread than were close interactions among neighbors and friends. Kin relationships, of course, were less confined by physical propinquity than were relationships among friends, but among lower status people interaction even among close kin was diminished if they lived at some distance from one another. The sense of different feelings about kin is captured by some of the responses people gave when asked if they would try to move near any of their relatives when they had to leave the West End:

No. Because we're very independent and they live too far out.
No. I wouldn't consciously make the effort to move near them but I wouldn't mind it either. Usually they don't live in places I'd like to live in.

They live in suburbia and I'm not fond of suburbia.
No. I have no relatives out here but you're better off away from your relatives. I am used to be by myself and I like to be alone.
No. I think they like you better when you're not too close to them.
Yes. I would like to. I want to be near them, they're my family. I have wonderful in-laws and such.
Yes. Well, I moved here because I found a flat that suited my fancy and so I could be near my son. I think it's nice to be near one of them so that I'd have someone in an emergency.
Yes. I thought it would be best to be near my mother to help her.
Yes. We help each other a lot. I have a built-in baby sitter.

Those people who did not plan to move near kin were less often strongly opposed than indifferent. Those people who wanted to live near their kin most often experienced this as a form of mutual aid or of a need to give or receive help. But while many people saw their kin moderately often and many felt quite close to them, affiliations among relatives rarely provided the major basis for the widespread localism and local involvement that characterized West End community life, especially for the working-class residents.

Neighbors and Neighborhood Friends

As a regular, daily basis for social interaction there were no relationships in the West End more important than neighboring and other affiliations based on physical contiguity. The significance of the neighbor relationship is often overlooked and our knowledge about neighboring remains inadequate. But there is enough evidence to indicate it is often of considerable importance in urban life. There are, however, variations in its importance for different people. In the very lowest status groups, the neighbor relationship may be less powerful and persistent than among stable, working-class people.[20] On the other hand, in the middle class there is a marked gradient of increasing localism in social relationships with increasingly suburban residence (Greer, 1956; Greer and Kube, 1959; Fava, 1958). This may be a more general form of the observation that special conditions that stimulate a sense of exclusiveness, due either to societal derogation or to a common identity, engender heightened group reciprocity. This, in turn, may be facilitated by the physical organization of housing.[21]

   The concrete forms of neighboring behavior, of course, may differ for different social classes. Thus, the relative infrequency of visiting in the home among working-class neighbors has occasionally misled observers to believe that these relationships were not close or intimate (Kerr, 1958). It indicates rather a different conception of, as well as different locales for, interaction among neighbors and a different view of the home and its functions. The evidence about neighboring behavior in different countries is far from adequate, but studies in many different places suggest that similar patterns of neighboring, at least in working-class communities, are fairly characteristic in all industrial societies. Close neighborhood ties, however, do not mean the abnegation of privacy. In virtually every modern community studied, regardless of social class status and certainly in the West End as well, respect for privacy is a highly valued characteristic of social relationships and such sensitivity often defines a good neighbor.

Local social affiliations can be separated into several overlapping types of relationships. We have already described the importance of regular relationships of daily interaction within the local area. Kinship, as we have seen, is of great importance for a large minority, especially relationships between parents and children and among siblings. For the majority of West Enders, neighbor relationships and close friendships with people more widely dispersed throughout the West End were of the utmost importance. We do not know exactly how a neighbor was defined. We assume that neighbors were people who lived in the same building or in an adjacent building or, at most, in nearby houses. Most people in the West End (74 percent) liked their neighbors, although only 38 percent had close contact with many neighbors. By contrast, the large majority (68 percent) reported that all or most of the five persons closest to them were current or recent West Enders, including siblings and other kin (apart from parents or spouse), as well as neighbors or friends (table 5.1). Within this predominantly local pattern of social organization there was room for individual preference for kin, neighbors, or people living elsewhere in the West End. For less than a third

TABLE 5.1   Residence of five closest persons

Residence of five closest persons	Percent	N[a]
All West End	48	203
Mostly West End	20	85
Equal West End or outside	3	13
Mostly outside West End	17	70
All outside West End	12	48
Totals	100	419

[a]There are 67 uncodeable cases.

(29 percent), however, were the five closest persons drawn mainly or exclusively from outside the local area.

As with many other aspects of community participation and social affiliations, the extent to which close social relationships were maintained primarily in the local area or were more widely dispersed was largely a function of ethnic embeddedness, length of residence in the local area, and social class position. Differences of status were of particularly great importance in the degree to which localism and local commitments dominated a person's closest social relationships. The greater importance of localism among people of lower status held for all ethnic groups and was evident, in varying degrees, despite differences in length of residence (Appendix table 5.3). Moreover, the importance of localism among people at lower status levels manifested itself in yet another way. For people in the higher status positions both friends and kin were distributed, with equal frequency, between the West End and areas outside the West End. However, among people of moderate and lower social class positions, local persons were relatively more often friends and nonlocal persons were relatively more often kin. In effect, for people in moderate or lower statuses, the pull of local relationships was so great that it was only mildly counteracted by the availability of close relatives outside the local area.

Separating these forms of social affiliation from one another provides a more differentiated sense of interpersonal relationships for the population of the West End, but there was a common thread running through all these relationships. In one sense, this common thread was its locally-based character. But it was more than that. Bott (1957) has given this pattern of social relationships a name that unifies the principle of social organization on which life in the West End and in other working-class communities rested: the closeknit network. Closeknit networks may involve kin, neighbors, other friends, or all of these. Indeed it is the overlap between relationships of different structural types and the somewhat ambiguous distinction between them that distinguishes the closeknit network pattern from other forms of the social organization of interpersonal affiliations. The existence of overlapping social relationships within a bounded region facilitates, if it does not generate, closeknit network patterns. A closeknit network pattern offers extensive opportunities to meet and to interact with friends or friends of friends, neighbors or friends of neighbors, kin or friends of kin in diverse circumstances and frequently quite informally. Moreover, when relationships have persisted over long periods of time, and are encouraged by meeting in the store or in the street or in the settlement house and involve not merely a contact between two people who know one another but also symbolize an entire set of additional relationships and links, we have the basis for closeknit network relationships. This is the form of social affiliation that characterized the social organization of interpersonal relationships within the West End.

One central aspect of the neighbor role was precisely its function of linking different relationships between people, of cementing the sense of friendliness, of neighborliness, of expanding and enveloping relationships among kin and friends. Virtually every form of local behavior and affiliation was associated with close neighbor relationships.[22] In turn, more than any other type of local affiliation or local resource use, close neighbor relationships depended upon that ease in interpersonal relationships that so often characterizes working-class behavior. Regardless of length of residence, people who were generally anxious in social relationships were least often close to their neighbors. Because of this, those people who were beset by anxiety and strain in social interaction were inevitably relatively isolated and could not participate fully in community life. To some degree, this may have been compensated by more active involvement with relatives since interaction with kin, who could more readily be taken for granted, was less dependent on social comfort and facility. But in the communal atmosphere of a working-class neighborhood, social anxiety was a serious debility. One had to learn to overcome it or suffer exclusion from the vitality of closeknit network ties.

The ways in which people talked about their neighbors captured, at one and the same time, the diversity of neighbor relationships and the widespread sense of closeness to people living nearby. Asked how they felt about their neighbors, most people were positive and many expressed their deeper attachment:

I liked them very much. Because of their being good neighbors, helping each other. I thought it was a terrific place for . . . well, they had more of an interest in you, a closeness, than you would find elsewhere.
You couldn't ask for anything better. I hope they're like that where I move.
Very nice. That warm feeling, that sisterly feeling. You feel as though you can call on them when you need them or have them call on you.
I like them very much.

On the other hand, the distance, impersonality, or anxiety that some people felt was also evident:

I couldn't tell you because I didn't mingle with anybody.
They're all right. They mind their business and I mind mine.
I felt I was a little out of my element down there. I didn't like it.
They're nice neighbors. I have no complaints about them.

The existence and prominence of a closeknit network form of social organization may be traced to yet another source in traditional kinship relationships, to which we are alerted by the occasional use of familistic terms like sisterly feeling, behaving like brothers, being at home. Social theory distinguishes two general types of statuses: ascribed and achieved. Ascribed patterns are those which are defined at birth: sex roles, kinship, ethnicity. Achieved patterns are those which an individual can reach through individual effort: occupation, marriage, friendship. But there is some interchange between these defining characteristics. Thus, sex roles in our society can be modified and occupation, particularly at higher status levels, is partly ascribed by the position of the parents. Kin relationships are, by definition, ascribed and generally include close forms of mutual obligation and reliability, although even kinship can be "achieved" as in pseudo-kin ties or in conferring kinship terms (uncle, cousin) on close friends of the family. In our society, attenuated kin relationships retain an obligatory character that is distinct from the norms for friendship. But the closeknit network pattern duplicates many features of kinship and of other traditional forms of local, social relationships.

The closeknit network encapsulates and institutionalizes orientations ordinarily characteristic among kin. For any individual, one or more relationships within the closeknit network may be its core. But far beyond this, an ascriptive orientation defines a degree of affiliation, even of obliga- tion, to any other person who can legitimately be included within that network by virtue of his close links to someone at the center of the net- work. Any resident of a working-class area is, in some sense, a potential participant in local closeknit networks and, thus, by virtue of his residence has a certain ascribed status in the neighborhood. In a more literal sense, one contact or one relationship or one form of participation readily leads to others. In this sense the closeknit network, locally based within an urban, working-class community, provides the framework of social organi- zation and the basis of interpersonal commitment and stability in the working-class world. This framework establishes the link between localism and close relationships whether they are sustained primarily with kin, neighbors, or friends.

Closely associated with closeknit network ties, a remarkably high degree of close mutual assistance persists in working-class communities despite the fractionated residential patterns of urban life. Almost a third (28 per- cent) of the people in the West End were closely involved in mutual help with neighbors and kin and another 30 percent were helped and helped others in more modest ways. Whether people were involved in relationships of mutual assistance or not was little influenced by the dominance of kin

or friends in their most intimate affiliations. But closely intimate relationships with kin, neighbors, or friends did not preclude more casual interaction with a much wider circle of people. Often more incidental relationships of sociability and friendliness included large numbers of people in the
local area. One situation of widespread interaction was the coffee klatch, a
popular phenomenon in the West End. As with other social relationships, it
tended to be group-oriented rather than a simple matter of chatting between two women. Only 22 percent of the women mentioned formal
activities like visiting, parties, dinner, or card games among their primary
activites with neighbors and friends. By comparison, for 75 percent of the
women the major activity with neighbors and friends was talking or having
coffee together. Some homes were centers of the coffee klatch to which
neighbors, friends, and kin wended their daily way. Other homes were
rarely seen by neighbors or friends.

Among the men, the corner hanging group was comparable, although
activites were not limited to staying on the corner. The men went out
together to the bar, to watch sports activities, to play games at the club or
settlement house, and occasionally to take a night on the town with wine,
women other than their wives, and song. Even among the men, however,
social affiliations were largely locally based. Although the men were less
locally oriented than the women, 36 percent of the men participated quite
regularly in corner hanging groups and an additional 20 percent associated
with corner groups once in a while. No matter how important interpersonal
relationships were on the job, these were quite transitory since they were
not part of the closeknit network pattern. The core of interpersonal
integrity was maintained, for the men as well as for the women, within the
local area. Approximately two years after moving from the West End, 55
percent of the men still preferred their West End neighbors to people who
were currently living nearby.

In emphasizing the localism of close relationships, the importance of
local kin, local friends, and local neighbors, we have neglected the fact that
for a substantial minority, social affiliations were nonlocal. Thus, 56 percent of the people had no kin within the West End, 22 percent had no
close contact with West End neighbors, and 20 percent of the people
indicated that most or all of their friends lived and had formerly lived outside the West End. Even if we assume that a small proportion of these
nonlocal ties represented kinship affiliations that crossed the boundaries of
residential contiguity, a moderately large number of people had no local
relationships. Another small proportion (at most 9 percent) were more
generally isolates and had few people or nobody close to them.

The main factors that stand out in accounting for these differences in local social affiliations were, as we have suggested, the degree of participation in other forms of local relationships and resource use. To a considerable degree, it was a semiclosed system and certainly a mutually reinforcing one. But, as with other aspects of localism, a number of influences made a difference in the degree of involvement a person developed: the longer a person lived in the area, the greater his reliance on local people; people who were members of the dominant ethnic groups were more likely to maintain close friendships within the local area; people who were more comfortable in the sociability of community relationships could more freely engage in local interpersonal affiliations. People of higher status were generally more selective and had a larger physical realm within which their social affiliations were maintained. However, as with kin involvement and residential satisfaction, religious commitments, restricted localism, and a low level of mastery or efficacy were particularly conducive to investment in local social affiliations among people of relatively high status. Among people of moderate status, youth, freedom from social problems, and ethnic involvement facilitated closeknit network interaction. Among those of lowest status, for whom such network ties were most frequent and more frequently taken for granted, little special stimulus was required for such local interpersonal investment beyond the more general influences of membership in the more prominent ethnic groups, long-term residence, and participation in other local activities.

There was probably no other single indicator of transitional status, of a readiness to move beyond the urban village and beyond the ascriptive orientation to social affiliations, than the establishment of close ties to people living outside the local area. Even among those who retained an integral association with closeknit networks, increasing status and economic freedom often led to the development of a few social relationships with people living at traveling distance. Indeed, among people of higher status, as we have indicated, a fairly exclusive commitment to local kin or friends was often an indication of more pervasive forms of traditionalism and parochialism. Among working-class people there can be little doubt that the neighborhood was more typically a closely woven world in which local intimacies formed the primary web. It is equally evident that as people were able to move out and to expand the range of their relationships and orientations, they did so voluntarily and effectively. But the process of disengagement was slow and involved the development of alternative patterns of functioning. Recent studies have raised a question about the possibility that local investments are dependent on the absence of affiliations outside the local area (Fellin and Litwak, 1963; Litwak, 1960).

To some extent, of course, and most particularly among people of higher status, the more exclusively local they were, the more thoroughly they were committed to the local area. More often, however, the expansion of social relationships beyond the local community did not impede intensive local commitments until other factors precipitated a decision to leave the local area. At that point, the availability of more widely dispersed contacts facilitated the transition to a new, more middle-class residential location.[23]

Community Participation and Local Satisfaction

In light of the enormous importance of localism in the daily lives of people living in working-class communities, it is all the more startling that patterns of affiliation and investment can be more easily described than explained. Usual forms of explanation, that affiliation and investment might be attributed to individual characteristics, statuses, or roles, account for few of the differences in community behavior, particularly among the working-class people in the West End. Length of residence, social class position, and ethnicity provide a context for explanation in their empirical correlations but do not really clarify the sources of diversity in social interaction. However, several clues suggest an explanation in the interweaving of different social affiliations.

Since the closeknit network pattern involves submergence within and conformity to the influence of group-oriented perceptions, conceptions, and behaviors, we can hardly expect that attributes of individuals will play as powerful a part as they do in accounting for highly individualized behaviors. Indeed, as we have already indicated, the different features of community participation and social affiliations seem to form a web of relationships and activities which become a self-contained, mutually reinforcing, endogenous system. Attributes or experiences or prior affiliations of individuals with kin or ethnic groups are likely to influence entrance into the community, the availability of community resources, and the degree and speed with which people become integrated within closeknit networks. But once neighbor role relationships and other local forms of participation are established, they supersede other, more obligatory relationships for many people or become integrated as part of a more general pattern of localism. Length of residence in the neighborhood is of great significance primarily because the longer people live in a community, the more opportunity they have to become engaged in diverse community activities and expanded relationships.

The historical significance of characteristics and identities that facilitated entry into community life and their reduced importance after people were established within the neighborhood was widely evident. Ethnic embeddedness was one such attribute that made initial contact easier. People who belonged to the dominant ethnic groups had close neighbor relationships more often than did those who were ethnic isolates. However, while ethnic embeddedness was an important determinant of neighbor relationships, continued residence in the area led even more consistently to expanded interaction with local people. Thus, ethnically isolated long-term residents more often had close neighbor relationships (43 percent) than did ethnically embedded short-term residents (25 percent). Along with ethnic embeddedness and length of residence, social class status was another interrelated source of expanded social interacton. Ethnicity made more of a difference to social relationships among people of higher status than for the average working-class person in the West End. And social class position more markedly modified the social interaction of short-term than of long-term residents. It is in this sense that such characteristics were a context for social relationships but cannot account for their existence, strength, or diversity.

On the other hand, the major forms of local participation and affiliation were all very highly interrelated with one another, further indicating the interweaving of many different forms of local relationships and activities (Appendix table 5.4). When we consider the simultaneous effects of many discrete attributes on each aspect of localism, it becomes apparent that the use of local resources and close neighbor relationships, particularly, had strong, independent influences on most of the other forms of local behavior. The great importance of the neighbor relationship has been shown in a number of studies of working-class communities, although these quantitative data document it more clearly. The use of local resources as a component of community life has been described or discussed less often but is only somewhat less critical than neighbor relationships for sustaining the full vividness of working-class neighborhood experience. Kinship involvement, on the other hand, while hardly negligible, is of less central importance for integration within the local community.[24] However, none of the objective indices of status, origins, or situation other than the length of time people lived in the area bears a strong and consistent relationship to any form of localism (Appendix table 5.5).

Beyond the interrelationships among different forms of local affiliations and participation, the central significance of neighbor relationships and of local resource use is most evident in their influence on satisfaction in the local area. No other form of local behavior and no other individual characteristic apart from length of residence contributed as highly to a total experience of gratification in the community (Appendix table 5.6). By contrast, the relatively weak associations between kinship involvement or family interaction and residential satisfaction indicate that such affiliations were less consistent determinants of gratification with neighborhood life, although they were certainly important for some people.

More substantial evidence of the relative importance of different factors in producing differences in community role satisfaction can be obtained from considering, simultaneously, the host of factors that are associated with such satisfaction (Appendix table 5.7). Apart from the overwhelming influence of local resource use, length of residence in the local area is followed immediately by closeness of neighbor relationships and by communal shopping preferences in the local area.[25] Clearly, people who lived in the West End longer were more satisfied with the neighborhood. Regardless of length of residence, people who had close neighbor relationships and people who enjoyed the communal atmosphere of shopping in familiar, local places were considerably more satisfied with their roles in the community than those who were distant from neighbors or did not participate in local shopping. At the same time, people who had a wider range of options because of greater objective or subjective resources, were also less likely to be readily satisfied with their community experience. Thus, younger people were less satisfied with the community than were older people; those with meager incomes were more satisfied with local community life than were those in moderate or comfortable economic circumstances; and people who had greater efficacy or mastery or were less dependent on interpersonal relationships were generally less satisfied with their total community experience than were those who relied more heavily on others for support and motivation.

For most people, the web of local social relationships was a source, thus, of considerable satisfaction. For those who had fewer options, more limited experiences, and less adequate external or internal resources, community roles were not only a major source of gratification, but their investment in the community and its activities was one of the few forms of meaningful participation in society available to them. On the other hand, some patterns of local involvement were more binding than satisfying. Interaction with family and kin and ethnic commitment followed these lines of tradition-based, obligatory patterns which led to other forms of local involvement but resulted in only modest levels of community satisfaction. Greater frequency of interaction with family members had little consequence for greater residential satisfaction except among quite recent residents. However, close neighbor relationships increased the level of residential satisfaction regardless of length of residence (Appendix table 5.5).

These interrelationships reveal with considerable clarity the nature of the internal system of community commitments that involved people in diverse behaviors and embedded them ever more deeply in the community. Integration within and participation in these networks proved highly gratifying. Despite the indirect influence of the length of time a person had lived in the community, people who were involved in these networks were most frequently highly satisfied with the community even if they had lived there only a relatively short time. Regardless of length of residence, the people of highest or lowest status were least likely to be fully integrated within local patterns of social affiliations and community participation. This was manifest in a wide variety of behaviors but perhaps most clearly and most importantly in the extent to which they developed close intimacies with their neighbors (Appendix table 5.8). Strikingly enough, the unskilled manual workers had among the lowest rates of closeness to neighbors and, by contrast, the semiskilled manual and clerical workers and the skilled manual workers, the prime representatives of the traditional and stable working class, along with the skilled clerical workers and small entrepreneurs, were the most deeply involved with their neighbors.[26]

The closeknit network pattern, with its manifold relationships and diverse expressions of localism is, indeed, the characteristic form of neighborhood life for the stable working class. While people of lower or of higher status may become involved in extensive and extended local affiliations and participation, these are not as typical or as central features of their lives or of their life styles. However, less central though it be, localism was often an extremely important source of satisfaction for some of the people of higher status just as it has been in many suburban communities of relatively high status. Localism may well have proved, not merely a source of satisfaction, but a major basis of stability and security for those people of the lowest status who had few other resources upon which they could rely. For the more typical person in the middle and upper ranges of working-class positions, it provided the core of an experience with other people, of a sense of belonging in an otherwise impersonal and scantly rewarding society, of opportunities for participation and activity that are rare in modern, urban societies.

6 Family Roles and Relationships

Marriage and the Family in the Working Class

Family and community life are central spheres of closely interdependent human relationships in most societies. Despite all the changes in modern forms of family life and despite many differences in family roles and relationships among people of different social statuses, the family is ultimately a most critical unit that determines more global experiences of satisfaction or dissatisfaction for the majority of people in all social classes. Culturally-derived expectations and values regarding marital and family relationships vary in important ways from one social class to another. Economic and social conditions markedly influence the structure of family roles and relationships and the affective atmosphere of the household. Yet, some of these differences become attenuated in the face of generic issues that confront all families in our society.

Marital ties and the relationship between husbands and wives in modern, working-class families are a far cry from the descriptions of working-class families during earlier centuries and even differ markedly from those of the early twentieth century, as Young and Willmott (1957) have observed. Working-class men may feel more strongly about maintaining traditional boundaries of masculinity than middle-class husbands, but they share a wide range of household tasks, participate actively in child-rearing, feel strongly about the importance of the family as a unit for which they bear fundamental responsibility.[1] Yet working-class people are less likely to maintain close relationships of companionship or sociability with their spouses or even to see these as desirable features of the husband-wife relationship. These are seen as relationships appropriate among kin, friends, or neighbors of the same sex. Women wheel their baby carriages in front of the house chatting all the while with their neighbors; or they stand around with groups of other women keeping half an eye on slightly older children

121

playing in the street. Men will often bring their little boys with them to the street corner or watch them sporadically while carrying on a conversation in the local drugstore or candystore. With so many people around and easily located, neither husband nor wife is quite as dependent on one another as in more isolated conditions of conjugal life. These differences may have diminished in the increased neighborliness of middle-class, suburban communities and the lower residential densities of many working-class areas. But the social class differences that exist in family relationships and interaction persist as a result of different cultural traditions, different expectations from life, and differences in current circumstances, resources, and opportunities.

The texture of family life is subtle and most easily grasped as a total experience, but some of the similarities and differences in the family life of different social classes obtrude themselves. Most working-class women marry when they are quite young. In the West End, a few were married by the age of sixteen, more than a quarter were married by the time they were nineteen years old, and the great majority (67 percent) who were ever married had married before the age of twenty-four. Among the younger people, aged twenty to thirty-four, 41 percent of the women in lower social class positions were married before the age of twenty, 38 percent of the women in the middle social class positions were married by this age, and only 22 percent of the women of higher status were married when they were so young. Among older people, the social class differences were smaller, although the general trend of marriage at an earlier age for people of lower social class positions was similar.[2] The vast majority (89 percent) of the women had been married at one time or another. A moderately large proportion were widowed (10 percent) or had been divorced or separated (11 percent).

The large class differences in family size of an earlier decade have virtually disappeared (U.S. Census Bureau, 1967). However, some differences were evident in the population of the West End. The median number of children in a family was 2.0. A moderately large number of families (20 percent) had four or more children and only 12 percent of the married people had no children. Among the youngest age group (twenty to thirty-four), only 12 percent of the people in higher social class positions had three or more children, while 51 percent of those in lower social class positions had families this large. Nor is this merely a function of a greater delay in bearing children among people of higher social class status since these differences in family size are even greater among people beyond the age of thirty-five. Moreover, children appear to be more crucial for family

life in the working class than in the middle class. The reasons for this are
not entirely clear. It may well be that only with the presence of children
can working-class husbands and wives depersonalize the unfamiliar intimacy between the sexes and mitigate the conflict potential inherent in
two-person interaction. Conversely, for many middle-class people, marriage
is predicated on a companionship ideal and the birth of children is readily
experienced as an intrusion, a disruption of the harmony between husband
and wife.[3] Under less happy circumstances, with the overt or covert
erosion of marital ties, children frequently serve to sustain a sense of family
integrity and to be a resource of affection and support for working-class
wives deprived of the closeness or the presence of their husbands.

It is not always easy to trace either class differences or class similarities
in family conceptions or behavior to cultural traditions, socioeconomic
circumstance, or the structural characteristics of class positions. Some
differences, of course, are clearly due to different social and economic
realities. Thus, for many working-class women, the most important characteristic of an ideal husband is his ability to support the family, an attribute that is generally taken for granted in the middle class. The source of
other attitudes is more ambiguous. Working-class women more often
assume that their husbands have a right to spend occasional evenings away
from home with their friends than do middle-class wives. In spite of this,
however, a great many register desires for the kinds of interpersonal
companionship which their husbands do not seem to need as strongly.[4]
Such desires for interpersonal responsiveness were expressed by 28 percent
of the women: "love, understanding, loyalty, and patience," "try to get
along with the wife," or "nice to wife and take her out places." On the
other hand, some women indicate that, despite a satisfactory adjustment to
marriage, they have despaired of such affective and closely interpersonal
exchanges:

When we first got married, we used to fight all the time. He would get
dressed every night to go out and I'd stay home. If I complained that he
didn't take me with him, he'd say "Why should I go out with you when I
can go out by myself and chew the fat with the boys?" They didn't go out
with other women or anything like that. He'd just meet the boys, have a
few beers, and come home. He'd go out every single night, just like he
wasn't married. But could I go out? No! And then he'd get mad when I did
go out. Most men when they first get married are not very grown up.
They're still little boys. It takes years for them to grow up and usually
there is their mother still around for them to be pampered by. I knew what
I was getting into, I didn't think it was going to be like it is in the movies.
I couldn't see any glamour in marriage. I knew all this but still you feel

inside that maybe yours might be different. But after marriage all that love and stuff flies out the window.

Some of the differences in conceptions of marriage among working-class men and women are inevitable sources of conflict. Few women conceived of the ideal husband primarily as a responsible head of household. On the other hand, among the men the most important characteristic of the ideal wife was precisely her management of family and household tasks.[5] The difference in conceptions of men and women is even sharper when we ask, not about ideals, but about responsibilities. Almost a third of the men (32 percent) saw their major and virtually exclusive role as overseeing the care of the household, while few of the women (14 percent) saw their husbands' major responsibilities in this light. However, both husbands (45 percent) and wives (35 percent) often saw the wife's familial responsibilities as primarily caretaking and managerial.

Superimposed on these sex differences in role conceptions, there are differences in expectations that are linked to social class position. Men and women in higher status positions gave greater emphasis to interpersonal relationships within the family while those in lower social class statuses more often gave primacy to household and caretaking roles. Similarly, people in higher status positions more often saw a successful marriage as one in which there was considerable love, reciprocity, and tenderness between husband and wife, while people in lower status positions, accepting the inevitability of conflict, more readily viewed a successful marriage as one in which the husband and wife were ready to compromise and recognize the needs of the other partner. However, with increasing age, social class differences in conceptions of marriage diminished.[6]

The romantic ideal that hypostasizes love as the core of a marital relationship has been more widely described than studied, but the importance of romantic love as an ideal or a treasured myth is evident far beyond the boundaries of Western civilization. Few of the women in the West End, however, even among those in higher status positions, believed that love was essential for marital success. In viewing their own marital relationships, love or affection was the most salient positive feature for only 5 percent of the women, although a somewhat greater number (8 percent) expressed their tender feelings in the adoration with which they described their husbands' qualities. Familial involvement was most often (24 percent) the positive feature that stood out for the women. Many of the men also relished their global involvement in familial life or the more specific forms of interaction with their wives and children (64 percent). Far fewer men (15 percent) than women (29 percent) were entirely disappointed with their marital relationships. Similarly, fewer men (19 percent) than women (28 percent) saw marriage as a restrictive experience with little compensatory gratification.

There are consistent social class differences in all of these respects, but these are not very strong and indicate mainly that the more global forms of positive relationship occur somewhat more often among people of higher status. Experiences of marital gratification are somewhat more frequent among people in higher status positions and marriage is seen as both less restrictive and more integrative. Men and women in lower status positions do have greater difficulty than those of higher status in accepting their own contributions to conflict and strain in marital or parent-child relationships. Most of the younger women and many of those past thirty-five in higher status positions sometimes felt that they were not as good wives as they wanted to be, a view that was rare among the women of lower status. A similar although weaker social class difference in feelings of inadequacy as a spouse occurred among the men. Exactly the same variation by social class position affects conceptions of self as a parent. Moreover, among people in higher status positions, poor economic circumstances intensified such feelings enormously so that 71 percent of the women and 100 percent of the men among those of higher social class status who were living in poverty often felt they were inadequate as parents. There was only a modest increase in the frequency of such self-doubts with very poor economic conditions among lower status mothers and fathers who took such deprivation more readily in stride.

These attitudes appear clear in their own right, but they are not entirely comprehensible apart from the differences in marital and familial roles and relationships. In order to clarify family roles and relationships we will distinguish separate components of family functioning: (1) the maintenance of a household and its variously defined activities, (2) the extension of the marital partnership to include children and their socialization, (3) the sexual and social interaction and gratification between marital partners, (4) the development of friendship intimacies and companionship between spouses, (5) the resolution of conflict that is inevitable in closely interrelated roles. Although all of these functions involve issues of general social and psychological importance, variations in conceptions about these roles and in the way they are handled reflect sociocultural regularities and situational differences among different social classes. But the realities of marital experience have a force of their own and often entail changes over the life cycle that contravene the initial patterns of people in different social class positions.

Family Roles and Relationships:
Household Functions and Child-Rearing

The affective quality of family relationships does not differ markedly from
that of other interpersonal relationships, but feelings about family members
are generally more intense and people attach special significance to them.
Much of the uniqueness of family relationships can be traced to structural
characteristics of family life, although these, in turn, are linked to their
psychological and social functions. At its core the family involves many
different role relationships between the same partners, interweaving one
function with another and one member with another in an intricate and
binding matrix. Interaction between people who work together may
occasionally expand to include friendship outside of work. Neighbors may
occasionally engage in many activities with one another. For most people,
however, different roles are usually carried out with different individuals.
In the nuclear family, many role relationships involving different functions
and different objectives are regularly carried out with the same family
members. While specialized family partnerships may develop for sustenance
activities, sexuality, recreation, companionship, child-rearing, and other
roles, most family members interact with one another in the performance
of at least several of these functions. The fact that some of these functions
like economic support, feeding and sharing of food, and sexuality are of
the most profound symbolic significance for the individuals involved
intensifies but does not entirely account for the sense of primordial
security the family can provide or the overt or covert violence that attends
major family disruptions. Another determinant lies in the increased separation of the conjugal unit from both kin and community brought about by
industrialization and urbanization. While this separation may facilitate
rational, economic organization, it places greater functional burdens on the
family and increases the mutual interdependence and affective significance
of relationships among family members.[7]

The family is also distinctive in the fact that its continuity hinges upon
the participation of a limited set of individuals. Business organizations,
community groups, extended kinship networks, even friendship cliques
may have long-term continuity but they are not dependent on the activities
of the same individuals. The persistence of families, however, is very much
at the mercy of the effectiveness and attitudes of a very small number of
persons. It is mainly as a household group that the family develops a
certain integrity and continuity that is not entirely dependent on individual
members, a fact that gives unique importance to the adequacy of house-

hold management. The household comes to represent the family both as the central domain in which the family meets as a unit and as a symbol designated by the idea of "home." Even with the loss of a nuclear family member by death or separation, the family may persist as a household unit. Roles and relationships that the departed member left unfilled may be redistributed to other family members or taken over by new family or household participants. The seriousness of the loss is, to a considerable degree, a function of the centrality and uniqueness of the role relationships of the lost member (Lindemann, 1944, 1960). The loss of the father through death, divorce, or desertion may be mitigated by the prominence of the role responsibilities of the female head of the household, so characteristic of young, low status families. Its consequences may also be modified by the availability of kin or friends who can provide a transition by taking over some of the role relationships of the father. The emotional loss or the real or fantasied deprivation are likely to be of great psychological importance even under these circumstances, but the acclimitization to crisis of working-class people provides mechanisms for coping with situations that might otherwise be disastrous. For families weakened by inadequate resources and excessive strain or conflict, such crises may prove to be the signal for maladaptive decline.

Because of interlocking role relationships and the fact that continuity hinges on interactions between very few people, the effective fulfillment of family role relationships is even more crucial for stability and satisfaction than is the case for other social units. There are many styles of maintaining effective role relationships in the family. All marital role relationships require some modicum of shared responsibility and exchange. This can vary from highly segregated forms of activity, in which the contributions of both partners are extremely imbalanced with minimal mutuality or reciprocity, to highly integrated forms with equal participation by both partners and a great deal of joint or reciprocal behavior. We shall refer to this as the segregated-shared dimension of marital role relationships.[8] Household activities, sexuality and sociability, and companionship exchanges can be carried out between marital partners with only the most minimal involvement of one of the partners or as highly interactive relationships. Even sexual behavior, so often considered as the embodiment of reciprocal love, can be a matter of mutual antagonism, sheer compliance, exchange of pleasure with little mutual involvement, or as an integrative interpersonal experience.

Working-class people more often appear to sustain segregated role relationships in marriage while higher status people more often demand and develop shared marital role relationships. These social class differences in marital role relationships, however, are easily exaggerated and readily misconstrued. The differences in ideology are greater than the differences in performance and social class differences in performance in many marital role relationships are not maintained through the life cycle.[9] While differences in the segregation or sharing of marital role relationships are functionally significant, they do not imply variations in specific affects like love or variations in such attributes like differential power. Both sharing and segregation have positive and negative potentials. Segregated role relationships are extremely useful in limiting conflict and averting its disruptive consequences, although sharing of role relationships has greater potential for experiences of marital gratification. But affection and love may attend either segregated or shared marital role relationships. Nor is there any simple relationship between sharing or segregation and dominance in marriage. The frequent interpretation of participation in marital decision-making as an aspect of power has little justification.[10] It is evident, for example, that a wife may make all the decisions in the household either because she is the dominant partner or because the husband is the dominant partner and has unilaterally decided that he would make none of these decisions.

In view of the fundamental importance of the integrity of the household for family functioning, we can expect household roles to reflect central features of family relationships. Similarly, we can anticipate that social class differences in family functioning will be manifested in the division of labor in the household. One feature of such variation is the greater involvement in household roles of men in higher than of those in lower social class positions.[11] However, in modern societies, most husbands in all social classes are quite actively involved in household decisions and tasks. Husbands in 65 percent of the West End households participated extensively in the household decision-making process and shared a great many of the household tasks in 69 percent of the households. Of even greater significance, however, is the fact that decision-making and task-participation are generally coordinated and those husbands who are active in household decision-making are usually active in task-participation as well. Thus, activity by husbands in decision-making does not signify their power in the household as much as it reflects the degree of total involvement of the husband in household activities. Conversely, the fact that women who take primacy in task-participation generally take primacy in decision-making as well means that dominance in household tasks is not necessarily a sign of subordination but may equally well represent involvement and definition of spheres of responsibility (table 6.1). Only a small number of households (18 percent) allocated almost exclusive responsibility for household activities to the wife alone, despite the prominent view among working-class people that the household ought to be the sphere of influence of the wife. In 26 percent of the households, husband and wife shared both decision-making and task-participation with full equality. The majority of the households reflected widespread involvement of the husbands in household activities.

While most husbands participated in the household to some degree, there are quite striking social class differences in the patterns of household role allocation. Husbands in higher social class positions were more often extensively involved in household functional roles than were husbands in lower social class positions. Only rarely (8 percent) did higher status husbands remain almost completely uninvolved in the household division of labor. At the other extreme, 34 percent of the lower status husbands had little to do with any of the household decisions or tasks (Appendix table 6.1). If we view these as differences in the segregation or sharing of the household role relationship, it is clear that husbands and wives in higher social class positions maintained a more integrated or shared household role relationship than did spouses at lower status levels.[12]

Any role relationship which is continuous over time is bound to undergo changes. This may be influenced by life-cycle events like the birth of children or the significance of status at different age levels. Age alone, implying long-term familiarity between marital partners and the gradual reorganization of their role relationships, is likely to produce changes in patterns of household functioning. These are not entirely predictable for individuals, as Zilbach (1968) points out, since each successive stage of family development may have a very different meaning for different individuals. Indeed, there is a general trend across different social classes for increased segregation in marital roles with increasing age.[13] Among young married people in the West End—those who were twenty to thirty-four years of age—segregated household role relationships were relatively infrequent (19 percent). In households of people who were fifty years old or older, greater responsibility for both household decisions and tasks on the part of the wife had become virtually typical (41 percent). One of the most striking features of changes in the household allocation of roles concerns the ways in which age differentially affects people in different social class positions. Among younger people, social class differences were sharp and clear: men in higher social class positions participated in the household considerably more than did men in lower social class positions. With in-

TABLE 6.1 Household decision-making by household task participation (in percentages of total sample)

Household decision-making	Household task participation				
	Husband directed	Both directed	Wife directed	N[a]	Percent
Husband directed	2	8	2	39	12
Both directed	8	26	14	171	53
Wife directed	2	11	18	116	36
N	67	157	102	326	
Percent	21	48	31		100

[a] In this and other tables dealing with the family, only those cases in which there is a spouse currently in the household are reported. The total N = 334, excluding women who are single, widowed, divorced, or separated. In subsequent tables on the family, the missing cases reported will be those missing from these 334. In this table there are 8 uncodeable cases.

creasing age, the clarity of this relationship vanished.[14] This gradual diminution in social class differences beyond the age of thirty-five was largely a
result of the fact that household activities were increasingly relegated to
the wife among the higher status households.

Like the organization of community affiliations, the family is an endogenous system, more responsive to current influences and to the particular
characteristics of the members, but self-sustaining in its adaptive or maladaptive organization to a very large degree (Appendix table 6.2).[15] Even
the increased allocation of household roles to the wife with increasing age
is only minimally explained by such life-cycle changes as the number or
ages of the children. However, the poorer the economic condition of the
household, the more often did wives take primary responsibility for
household decisions and tasks, a small but independent trend that increased with age. The employment status of the husband and wife had
little systematic effect on the household division of labor, although there
was a subgroup among the people of lower status in which the wife retained
primary responsibility for the household in spite of the fact that she was
employed while her husband was irregularly employed or unemployed.
Thus, although family role changes evidently occur in response to major
economic crises, endemic situational forces had surprisingly little impact
on the household division of labor.[16]

Close neighbor relationships and other indicators of community involvement bore no significant consequences for the household division of labor,
but those who had a great deal of contact with their kin more often maintained segregated household role relationships at all social class levels.[17] On
the other hand, personal characteristics like ego efficacy, which bears
directly on the ability to negotiate difficulties and to assume responsibility,
influenced the allocation of household roles in intricate but understandable ways. In high status households, women with high levels of ego
efficacy never took primary responsibility for the household and their
husbands played prominent household roles. In low status households, on
the other hand, women more often took primary household responsibility
but efficacy itself had no effect on household role distribution. If we
assume that efficacious women of higher status have alternative opportunities for manifesting mastery and control which are unavailable to women
of lower status, dominance in household roles by efficacious women in
lower social class position and rejection of such roles by efficacious, higher
status women may reflect situations of desire rather than of compulsion.

Child-rearing is one of the spheres of household responsibility in which
husbands participate most regularly in all social classes. But the socializa-

tion of children is so important and universal a family function and involves
so distinctive a set of role relationships that we can anticipate many differences in social class patterns compared to other areas of family life.
There have been numerous studies of social class differences in child-
rearing attitudes and behavior, but there is neither much consensus nor
even much useful information about parent-child relationships and the
experience of childhood.[18] The relatively limited data from the West End
allow us mainly to consider a number of child-rearing orientations. Informal observations and qualitative comments indicate both differences
and similarities in child care and in child behavior as well as in parental
attitudes among people in different social positions.

There has been considerable debate about the relative restriction or freedom of childhood in different social classes. Some of the conflict may be
traced to variations that occur at different ages. While very young, children
in working-class families are more freely indulged and given greater care
and attention than children at higher status levels. However, as Gans
(1962) points out, working-class children move in an adult world. Indulgence and attention are often somewhat routine and do not interfere with
household or social activities. Middle-class parents expect more independence at an early age but, in attending to the child, devote greater effort to
determining the needs or desires of the young child. Whether in feeding or
in play, working-class parents watch over their children with the utmost
care but within the limits they establish allow greater freedom than the
educative approach of middle-class parents permits. By school age, these
differences begin to reverse themselves. Among working-class youngsters
there is increasing freedom from parental visibility, while in the middle
class greater autonomy is only slowly granted. Moreover, at moderately
high status levels, the freedom of childhood is bounded by large demands
or encouragement to do household chores, homework, extracurricular
activities, and even formalized recreation. These are not merely matters of
constraint or freedom but of differential channeling since the developmental experiences of youngsters in different social classes prepare them
for adult life in those class positions.

Early in life, working-class children learn to live within restricted opportunities for material things, for play, and for learning. Once having gained
the freedom from immediate and constant parental control, they are very
much on their own among their peers. The peer group functions within
these limited opportunities, sometimes seeking out new sources of excitement but often biding its time in the security of a relatively inactive group.
The gulf between youngsters and adults tends only to widen. In the middle

class, reciprocal efforts at communication between children and parents frequently result in some modicum of mutual understanding and permit a generalization of such exchanges to teachers and other adults. Working-class youngsters are more likely to see the gulf as unbridgeable, especially when status differences are superimposed on the gap in age. The split between children and adults, supplemented by the early dominance of peers, may well be one source of preparation for the gregariousness and social conformity of working-class life.

Some of these differences have their parallels in the orientations of parents in different social classes. Strikingly enough, the attribution of punitive child-rearing practices to working-class parents finds little confirmation in the West End. Mothers at all status levels were equally affectionate to their children. Men of higher status were a little more openly expressive of affection to their children than men of moderate or lower status, but in describing their usual methods of dealing with child-rearing problems, physical punishment was as infrequent among lower status as it was among higher status parents. However, given a situation of ambiguity in which a child refuses to go to school, claiming that he is afraid of the teacher, social class differences were clear. Men and women of lower status were more likely to assume that the child was at fault and to punish him, while at higher status levels the parents more often tried to explore, to talk with the child and the teacher, and to mediate the difficulty.

While working-class parents are often extremely indulgent, particularly toward young children, and may go to great lengths to fulfill a child's needs, their general orientatons toward child-rearing are more autocratic and conventional than those of middle-class parents. This is manifested not merely in the stress on cleanliness, fears of spoiling, the importance of respect for parents, and occasional arbitrary rules or responses, but in the general concern with compliance and obedience. While working-class people are undoubtedly influenced by traditional conceptions of children and parent-child relationships to a greater extent than are people of higher status, their authoritarian child-rearing attitudes are undoubtedly exacerbated by their own sense of the gulf between themselves and their children. The difficulty of communicating and, thus, of clarifying complexities of relationship between parents and children in the working class may often lead to unnecessary and reinforcing conflicts. Many working-class parents never sat down to discuss a problem their child was having with a teacher and, for that matter, working-class children are not likely to reveal their private thoughts or feelings to their parents. At the same time, while they may be more punitive when they are compelled to deal with such complexities, working-class parents are most likely to overlook the matter entirely.

Although the difficulties of working-class life are rarely discussed by people in lower status positions, these feelings become quite evident in the frequency with which people hoped that their children's lives would be different from their own. Only rarely did parents want to see their children's lives completely different from their own, but working-class parents more often wanted to see such differences and wanted to see larger differences. Despite frequent denials of strivings for social mobility, the main changes they hoped to see were greater educational, economic, and occupational achievement. On the other hand, the relatively high degree of satisfaction with marital and family life was manifest in the frequency with which parents hoped their children's lives would be similar to their own in these respects (22 percent of the women, 18 percent of the men). The importance of social conformity is visible in the high proportions of mothers (19 percent) and of fathers (27 percent) who wanted to see their children follow their footsteps in maintaining a high level of moral and social responsibility. As we have suggested, class differences in family role relationships are adapted to differences in conception, in expectation, and in life circumstance. However there are few differences in the satisfaction that men or women in different social classes experience in their relationships to their children.

Although it is difficult to categorize child-rearing orientations along the dimension of sharing or segregation, it is apparent that the major social class variations in parental attitudes are precisely those that imply more segregated parent-child relationships at lower status levels and a greater emphasis on sharing and reciprocity among people of higher status. Indeed, as with the household division of labor and other family role relationships, the social class difference diminished sharply with increasing age. This was largely due to the much higher level of segregated child-rearing orientations among older people of high status than among younger, high status people.[19] At lower and moderate status levels, on the other hand, there were no variations in segregated or shared conceptions of child-rearing with age. As a consequence, the social class differences were sharpest among the younger parents. However, the similarity of the social class and age differences in child-rearing orientations and in the distribution of household roles suggests that these are not merely discrete but, rather, that there is a more general tendency for people of lower status to carry out family role relationships in more segregated fashion than do people of higher status, a tendency that diminished with age and the experience of family life.

Marital Roles and Functions:
Sociability and Companionship

Ultimately, the effectiveness of family role relationships is manifested in
the stability or instability of family structure and the extent to which these
relationships are enriching and satisfying for individual household members.
However in order to see more fully the significance of role functioning in
the family, we must go beyond the household division of labor and parent-
child relationships. Sexuality and sociability are hardly less fundamental
than household integrity to family relationships in our society. The continuity of the household as a unit may not rest as heavily on their successful performance, but they may be even more critical for the quality of
marital life. Partly as a result of strains in contemporary family life, there
have been drastic changes in the norms governing the exclusiveness with
which sexuality is viewed as inextricably tied to marital relationships along
with a greater sense of the importance of sexuality for effective marital
functioning. Sociability has also been seen increasingly as a central function
of marital and familial role behavior in urban, industrial societies, although
leisure, entertainment, and social interaction have rarely been conceived as
the exclusive province of joint marital or family life.

We know considerably more about the social than about the sexual behavior of people in the West End. Surprisingly few spontaneous comments
were made about sexual behavior except when a husband was evidently
spending a great deal of time with other women or a wife had betrayed her
husband's faith or confirmed his expectations by sleeping with another
man. Even when asked how they responded when their spouse did something that pleased them, few men or women made explicit reference to
sexual activity and such comments were often accompanied by a smile and
a passing reference.[20] Informal observation, conversations, comments by
people all suggest that the conclusions of other observers concerning
sexuality among working-class people are quite germane to the sexual behavior of West Enders.[21] The most important class distinctions in sexual
behavior appear to be the higher rate of extramarital sexual behavior
among young, working-class men; the contrastingly lower rates of extramarital sexuality among lower than among higher status women; and the
more widespread acknowledgment and appreciation of female sexuality
and pleasure in sexual behavior among people in higher status positions.
Although it is reasonable to assume that there is a close association between sexual and joint sociable behavior and, thus, that an understanding
of sociability in marriage may be extended to clarify sexual behavior, we

will discuss mainly the patterns of sociability among West Enders, for which information is available. However, sexual and sociable role relationships in marriage reflect a common social class difference. Shared sexual and social role relationships are the marital norms among people of higher status and are fulfilled in practice among those who are young. Separate social activites and occasional cheating on one's wife are more readily taken for granted among younger people in the working class.

To the extent that segregated role performance is reflected in nonmutual participation, lower status women more often fulfill their husbands' sexual desires without active sexual engagement than do higher status women although, at the extreme, shared love-making and sexuality appear to be as frequent among lower status as among higher status women. Similarly, and particularly among younger people, working-class men and women seek entertainment and recreation without their spouses more regularly and frequently than do people in higher status positions. Spending the evening with the boys at the corner or the bar and sitting around with the girls or going to a nearby club in the evening is characteristic for working-class people. In the middle and upper classes, numerous social commitments often separate the activities of husbands and wives, but joint recreation and entertainment, in the home and outside, also appear more frequent than in lower status families. While the striving for excitement, motoric activity, and immediate challenge described by Walter Miller (1958) were visible, these were most characteristic for teenagers and for very young, unmarried adults.

The simplest measure of marital sociability is the frequency with which husbands and wives go out together without their children. More than a third of the couples in the West End (37 percent) maintained extensive social activities together, although 25 percent of the spouses rarely or never went out together. The activities involved were quite varied but most often were locally-based visiting with friends or kin, going to the movies, sitting in restaurants or bars, and informal participation in local organizations or clubs. In the sociable or social role relationship in marriage, segregation ranges from rare participation in social activities together to more moderate forms of peripheral association in sociability. Integration implies frequent and interactive participation in leisure and recreation. But the significance of the concrete social activities in which couples engaged was partly modified by a more general atmosphere of segregation or sharing in other marital role relationships. Such patterns are evident in descriptions of joint sociability:

We may plan a picnic or go some particular place. If John [the husband] is not home, we go to Boston Common. In the summer we go to the beach, really right up the street. Two or three weeks of the summer we go to the mountains and rent a cottage. But John's never home. When he is home, we go out together. He goes out alone in the winter but in the summer he's too busy. He goes bowling or plays cards. We women get together too. Or we go out as couples to a night club. If we are at weddings, there are a large crew of us that know each other. John and I get along very well. We don't have too much time for arguments. If I feel like exploding, it's too late by the time he gets home. But we have an old standing agreement since we were married. We never go to bed angry. We always kiss and talk to each other by the time we go to bed.

We don't do anything really. We used to go out together but it's hard. He's up early. He's too tired to go out. And anything you do costs money. My husband will occasionally go off with the boys [their sons] to a hockey game but I don't go with them. I go off to visit my folks on Saturday night and they go their separate ways. I'd like social organizations but my husband isn't interested in that. Something like sports events, he likes but he doesn't go for social things like dances or where you just meet and talk. It's my fault. He's sort of in a rut and I haven't helped him get out of it. I think it's good to be among people, going different places.

Naturally, to the extent that sociability may be costly we can anticipate that its frequency will be lower among people in lower status positions. Most people in higher social class positions went out together at least moderately often (87 percent), while fewer prople of lower status (67 percent) went out together as often as once a month or more. A similar difference appears when we consider a composite index that includes a wider variety of forms of sociability that are also less dependent on adequate finances. Among people aged twenty to thirty-four, 9 percent of those of relatively high status and 35 percent of those in low status positions rarely participated together in social activities. Among older people, there was a slight decline in joint sociability and the differences associated with social class position diminished. It is of major significance that, as with other marital relationships, the gradual diminution of social class differences with age resulted mainly from diminished sociability among married couples of higher status, while the lower status people maintained their initially modest level of joint sociability when they were older.

Several studies show a decrease in joint leisure activities with increasing age (Komarovsky, 1962; Pineo, 1961). In the West End, there was also a general decrease in joint social activities with age, but the number and ages of children in the household were even more potent influences on the

social role relationship in marriage. Indeed, among childless couples the
social role relationship changed only slightly as people grew older. However, with the birth of children, people went out less often (Appendix table
6.3). For all social class levels, young children in the household meant a
marked reduction in the social activities of the parents. People in higher
status positions were able to maintain a fairly active social life despite the
initial impact of parenthood since the absolute level of their joint sociability was so high before they had children. People of moderate status also
experienced a marked decrease in joint sociability with the birth of children but began to go out quite readily once their children grew a little older.
The low initial level of joint sociability among those of lowest status,
however, meant that the decrease they suffered after children arrived in the
household left them with little social activity as married couples, and this
persisted until their children were considerably older. These low levels of
joint sociability were major sources of frequent complaints among working-
class women that their husbands were often absent from home and of
desires to go out together more often. When these restrictions were added
to other sources of strain, there was fertile opportunity for marital conflict. On the other hand, as we have implied, after the children had grown
older there was a striking increase in joint sociability among couples at all
social class levels.[22]

In some instances, social class differences in behavior are most meaning-
fully attributed to situational factors; in others, cultural or structural
aspects of social class position seem to be most prominent. It is already
evident that situational influences such as age and the presence or age of
children affected the extent to which people undertook social activities as
couples. Joint sociability in marriage among people in the West End was
also influenced by purely economic circumstances associated with social
class position as well as by other aspects of status. At all social class levels,
the poorer the economic circumstances of a family, the more segregated
were their sociable role relationships in marriage (Appendix table 6.4).
Moreover, when both the husband and the wife were working, husbands
and wives went out together most often. Differences in other resources
were also prominent influences on marital sociability. Not least among
these was the actual level of health. At all age levels, people in poor health
had more segregated social role relationships than those in good health.
Among the young, 39 percent of those in good health maintained active
social lives together while only 9 percent of those in poor health had similar levels of joint social involvement.[23] The greatest incursions on joint
sociability due to differences in physical health occurred among the people

in the lowest status positions. Thus, we are led to reaffirm the "them as has gits" hypothesis: the greatest impact on sociability in marriage occurs among those people with fewest alternative resources.

In other respects, joint social activities between married couples were affected by personal and social characteristics less clearly linked to cumulative deficits. Among people of relatively high status, marital sociability was encouraged by extensive interaction with family members (Appendix table 6.5).[24] The significance of such relationship with kin supplements the earlier impression of the dependence on traditional cultural and social commitments of those West Enders of higher status who truly resided there and were not passing through as a matter of convenience. On the other hand, personal difficulties manifested in extensive psychoneurotic symptoms or high levels of social anxiety seriously impeded joint marital sociability more uniformly, although people of moderate status, the upper working class, were relatively immune from such effects.

As with the household role relationship, the factors most significantly associated with marital sociability are other aspects of marital and family life. Indeed, joint sociability between husbands and wives is a core element of companionate marriages.[25] While the working-class housewife may enjoy many of the simple and readily available social resources of the local community, she is quite dependent on her spouse for social activities outside the home. The accessibility of friends, neighbors, and kin within the local community may diminish the felt necessity for marital sociability but does not decrease its occurrence. Occasionally, severely deprived women may seek out neighbors and friends to sustain them in the unavailability of their husbands. For the majority, however, there are few alternative resources to compensate for the lack of a meaningful social role relationship in marriage. Despite the fairly consistent desire for such sociability at all social class levels, shared social roles are less frequent for people in lower status positions and, thus, exacerbate other problems that occur with greater frequency for people with the fewest resources.[26]

The idea that the modern, middle-class family has developed a companionate form in which close interaction between spouses is the dominant stabilizing feature is familiar enough, but little is known about companionship in marriage.[27] Most married couples see communication, shared confidences, and a sense of mutual respect as important for successful marriage, but the salience of these companionate characteristics varies a great deal for people in different social class positions. In the middle and upper middle classes, these attributes are seen as integral to married life, but working-class people, especially men, rarely consider companionship to be a central feature of marriage. For many working-class people, premarital friendships, ties to parents and siblings, and group affiliations are maintained for a long time after marriage. Friends rather than spouses are ordinarily expected to be a person's main companions in the working class. This is occasionally a source of strain if the husband is jealous of his wife's intimacies with other women or if the wife is reluctant to accept the fact that her husband's friendships are quite separate from their married life (Komarovsky, 1962). More often than not, however, working-class men and women have very different interests from one another. The working-class wife may regret her husband's inability to listen to her conversation about daily doings and the lives of others more than he regrets her lack of interest in spectator sports or his work day or politics, but neither is willing to shift realms of involvement. Nor does the absence of companionship necessarily imply any diminished tenderness, affection, or regard, although in the absence of close communication these are frequently impeded by unresolved conflicts.[28]

The companionship role relationship in marriage can be conceived along a dimension of segregation and sharing as with other marital role relationships. But since the conception of companionship itself implies interpersonal transactions, the segregation of companionship roles is tantamount to their absence. There is, nonetheless, an intermediate form of companionship in marriage between the extremes of sharing and segregation. Mildly supportive interactions, occasional discussion of conflicts, subtle evidences of rapport in any marital role relationship all encourage a modest sense of companionship, but these fall short of the more global interpersonal relationship implicit in close companionship in marriage.

Class differences in companionship roles are quite marked. For people of moderately high status in the West End, the companionship role relationship was rarely segregated (11 percent), but more than a third (35 percent) of the people at the lowest status level had no companionship relationship with their spouse. Among young people aged twenty to thirty-four, the contrast by social class was even greater. Indeed the changes in marital companionship with increasing age, while similar to those that affected other role relationships in marriage, were sharper and more clearly demonstrated the life-cycle sequence among people in different social classes. As people passed the earliest years of marriage, those in higher status positions gradually developed more segregated companionship roles while those in lower status positions slowly became more companionate in their marriages.[29] It seems likely that many of the realities of intramarital and familial experiences which transcend social class differences weigh more heavily than ideals and class-based values in intensifying or reducing interpersonal closeness in marriage over the life cycle.[30]

Some of the reasons for these life-cycle changes are not difficult to unravel. We have said that the marital relationship among people in relatively high status positions is so often predicated on a model of ideal companionship and two-person intimacy that the birth of a child is experienced as a disruption of companionate bliss. This appears to have been part of the explanation for the decrease in companionship among those in positions of moderately high status. With the birth of a first child, high status couples experienced a very sharp drop in shared companionship, a phenomenon that occurred only with larger numbers of children (and less markedly) at successively lower status levels. Thus, for those in the highest status the decrease in companionship occurred with one child, for those at intermediate levels of status it occurred with two to three children, and for those at the lower status levels it did not occur until there were four or more children in the household.

For all the importance of the presence, age, and number of children as a constraint on companionship in marriage, a far more important influence on the companionate quality of the marital role relationship stems from economic forces (Appendix table 6.6). Economic circumstances and the employment status of husbands and wives affect the overall sharing of companionship in marriage and, thus, implicitly account for some of the class and age differences. At all social class levels, poverty markedly reduced the frequency of shared companionship in the marital relationship (Appendix table 6.7). But the greatest reduction in marital companionship due to economic circumstances occurred among the people of highest status and had less effect on those of moderately low and very low status. Moreover, although economic want affected marital companionship at all age levels, it had the most disastrous consequences for young married couples. The employment status of both husband and wife also clearly influenced the level of shared companionship in marriage.[31] If the economic circumstances of the family were poor, companionship rarely existed unless the husband worked. But among the poor, shared companionship was infrequent if the wife had to work even if the husband was regularly employed. Quite evidently, under these conditions employment was not an option the wife elected but a matter of sheer necessity that, in any event, did not remove them from poverty. For people in marginal, modest, or comfortable economic circumstances, however, the wife's employment never diminished the level of shared companionship in marriage and, at higher economic levels, led to the highest frequency of marital companionship.

Companionship in marriage, we have already suggested, is the most fulfilling aspect of a marital relationship and the most vulnerable to stress and conflict. The effect of these stresses on marital companionship, moreover, is greatest among those of higher status (Appendix table 6.6) and among the young for whom companionship in marriage is most frequent and appears to be most important. Indeed, in spite of the frequent observation of a disenchantment phenomenon in marriage over the life cycle, given a moderately high level of resources and stability, the diminution in marital companionship with increasing age is quite minor. When all of the economic, social, personal, and demographic factors are considered together, the importance of age alone disappears as an influence on marital companionship.[32] And the particular sensitivity of marital roles like sociability and companionship to incursion by economic situations and personal attributes becomes clear. Although we have stressed the importance of income and employment, characteristics that imply personal ease or difficulty in relating to other people are also of some significance as determinants of marital companionship (Appendix table 6.6). Thus, a high level of social anxiety or a low level of interaction with others markedly reduced the frequency of companionship roles in marriage.[33]

While numerous forces influenced marital companionship, no other factor had as potent an effect as the level of segregation or sharing in other marital role relationships. Marital sociability was the single most important influence on marital companionship. The degree of segregation or sharing of household roles was also of considerable importance for marital companionship. Certainly the overlap among all of these marital role relationships is considerable and they are difficult to tease apart. The issue is complicated by the fact that social class position, economic conditions of the family, the stability of employment of husband and wife, personality factors, and extramarital social relationships all have some effect on each marital role relationship. Nonetheless, the marital relationship seems to form an endogenous and somewhat self-contained system in which some external forces, like income and employment, enter quite directly but other social roles and relationships merely facilitate or impede increased marital closeness or, at the other extreme, provide support and compensation in instances of severe conflict and high levels of segregation short of disruption (Appendix table 6.6).

When we put many of these different role relationships together into a single composite index of segregated or shared role relationships in marriage, we find that many of the effects we have previously seen emerge more strongly than before. While there were sporadic indications that values or expectations regarding marriage had some effect on different marital role relationships, these value-laden conceptions of marriage had a moderately strong influence on the total marital relationship, although it was strongest among those people in relatively high or moderate social class positions. The effect of economic conditions becomes quite noticeable if we consider the consequences for the holistic pattern of segregation or sharing in marital functioning. But the impact of economic constraint diminished considerably for people in lower status positions who were more familiar with poverty. On the other hand the influence of intramarital role relationships upon one another was greatest for people in the lowest status positions. Thus, for people in lower social class statuses, shared household role relationships led to shared sociability quite regularly, and shared sociability led to a companionate marriage with great frequency. Among people of higher status, the same relationships held but were less consistent.

We have made little mention of marital conflict or its resolution. Certainly a great many people had many complaints about their marriages and described a great many sources of disagreement with one another. The largest single type of disagreement, oddly enough, concerned the children and child-rearing patterns. Only the great importance of children in working-class families and the great investment in the lives of children adequately accounts for this focus as an issue in marital conflict. But disagreements about material circumstances like lack of money, bills that could not be paid, jobs, and unemployment were only slightly less frequent. While many women were disturbed by their husbands' unemployment and it certainly interfered with shared marital role relationships, they did not ordinarily generalize this to a more global sense of their spouses' inadequacies. Some women did, however, perceive their husbands' failures to obtain or maintain jobs as reflections of more general incompetence, passivity, or lack of motivation. As one might expect, the most intense feelings of rage and the most bitter disagreements occurred when the husband neglected the household and family for the sake of gambling, drinking, other women, and occasionally for criminal activities.

The issues which were important for people in different social class positions varied considerably, but there was little difference in the overall level of conflict between husbands and wives of different statuses. On the other hand, the methods of conflict resolution were quite clearly differentiated by social class position. People in higher status positions communicated with one another more freely about differences and adopted shared patterns of conflict resolution as they did in marital role relationships. People in lower status positions more often preferred segregated forms of conflict resolution, retreating from the situation, ignoring it, suppressing their anger in the hope that the anger or the situation would disappear, or expressing their rage in volatile fashion with little further discussion or clarification.

Marital Satisfaction

In societies in which marriage is structurally integrated with larger kinship or community groups that retain coercive power, marital satisfaction often receives secondary attention.[34] Its importance in these societies is revealed by the frequent myths of overpowering romantic love, by the occasional efforts to diminish opportunities for close marital relationships when these are deemed to interfere with other solidarities, or by allowing some veto power to young couples whose marriages are to be arranged. The relatively high degree of independence of the conjugal unit in modern societies, however, places particular stress on marital satisfaction as one of the most effective bases for insuring family continuity. Paradoxically, those very factors that increase the potential for marital satisfaction in modern societies, the relatively high degree of freedom from overt coercion by kin or community and from the covert coercion of binding cultural perspectives, intensify, at one and the same time, the possibilities for gratification and continuity or for dissatisfaction and disruption.

The few available studies of marital satisfaction or marital adjustment and social class conclude that there is an inverse relationship between class position and marital satisfaction or adjustment.[35] Families in higher status positions more frequently show marital satisfaction or effective marital adjustment than do lower status families. But the differences are not very large. Similar and modest social class differences obtained for people in the West End.[36]

Many of the same issues that influenced the patterns of segregation or sharing in the household division of labor, child-rearing, marital sociability, and marital companionship also affected marital satisfaction. However, the social class variation in levels of marital satisfaction was less striking than the class differences in many of the concrete patterns of marital interaction. And the effects of diverse influences on marital satisfaction were often similar for people at different status levels (Appendix table 6.8).

Nonetheless, these class-differentiated patterns of marital role functioning and other conditions that directly affected the marital or family situation were the most potent determinants of marital satisfaction.

The critical dimension of marital role relationships that influenced marital satisfaction was the degree of sharing or segregation in marital role performance. Shared role performance in any marital role relationship led to heightened levels of marital satisfaction for people in all social class positions and at all ages.[37] Among these, the companionship role relationship was most consistently important as a determinant of marital satisfaction (Appendix table 6.8). At each social class level, approximately half the people with companionate relationships in marriage were highly satisfied with their marital experiences.[38] Indeed, the only striking social class variation in the effect of marital role relationships on marital satisfaction occurred for the household division of labor. Women in lower status positions were far more likely to be maritally satisfied if their husbands took a prominent role in household decisions and tasks while the distribution of household responsibilities held considerably less uniform significance for marital satisfaction among women at moderate or higher status levels. Although marital sociability and companionship led to marital satisfaction with equal regularity at all status levels, it seems likely that joint participation in the household provided a meaningful basis for marital interaction primarily for families of lower status. In this way, the lower frequency of shared social and companionship role relationships among people in lower social class positions could partly be compensated by interpersonal reciprocity in household decisions and tasks to produce marital satisfaction.

Despite the analytic importance of segregation or sharing in marital role relationships for marital satisfaction, these qualities of marital experience were rarely mentioned in specifying pleasant or unpleasant features of marriage. However, there were subtle differences in conceptions of marital satisfaction that betray different expectations and sources of meaningful relationships among people in different social class positions. These were evident in the responses people gave to questions about the nicest and worst features of their marriages. If we consider first only the women who were maritally satisfied from different social class levels, we find noteworthy differences. The following comments are each from one maritally satisfied woman at each status level, going from moderately high to very low status:

(Nicest) The fact that we've been able to accomplish so many things, and the children of course.

(Worst) Our financial situation. Just the financial situation.
(Nicest) Having your own family, to know that somebody loves you and enjoys staying with you.
(Worst) Nothing. Maybe living in three rooms [laughs].
(Nicest) We get along good. We very seldom or never argue. I've got a good man. He stays home nights and doesn't go out.
(Worst) I don't know. I am satisfied. I'd like to have a nicer place than this and I am going to have when we move to Boston. Everything has been satisfactory. But my husband is awfully cross at times. He hollers at me and sometimes if my friends come, he just goes into the other room and won't talk to them.

A similar range of variation existed among women with a moderate level of marital satisfaction. With the same social class sequence, from moderately high to very low status, some of the responses were:

(Nicest) Companionship. Talking things over.
(Worst) Sometimes we're short of money.
(Nicest) My three little girls. And my darling husband.
(Worst) Living with my mother-in-law. I don't think anyone should. But with my marriage there is no problem.
(Nicest) We have a nice home. My husband and I have a sense of humor.
(Worst) I'd like my husband to work more regularly. And the bills we have to pay. Money is always a problem.

Interestingly enough, the differences among women who were in different social class positions and were maritally dissatisfied are less evident. The successive examples of marital dissatisfaction from a woman of moderately high status, one of moderately low status, and one of very low status reveal mainly a uniform sense of discouragement:

(Nicest) I don't know even after 20 years.
(Worst) [Refused to answer.]
(Nicest) Getting married is the nicest part. There's nothing nice about my marriage now.
(Worst) My husband. I could use another husband. Everything is wrong, my husband and all his problems.
(Nicest) I no find anything nice about it. He been sick so long a time.
(Worst) He's been sick. That's the worst, where your husband don't bring the money.

In view of the consistent and powerful influence of segregated or shared marital role relationships on marital satisfaction, we can anticipate that an aggregate measure of sharing or segregation in several marital role relationships will more clearly reveal the effects of role functioning on satisfaction with marriage. Indeed, when we use such a composite measure of marital role integration, there is little residual effect of social class position on marital satisfaction (table 6.2). To the small extent that people in higher social class positions were more often maritally satisfied than people in lower social class positions, it was almost entirely due to the greater frequency of shared marital role relationships among people of higher status. Much of the difference in marital satisfaction among people of different ages similarly vanished, although there was a modest residual effect showing that even with relatively high levels of shared marital role relationships older people were somewhat less often satisfied with their marriages than were younger people.

We have previously suggested that the family is an endogenous system in which each pattern of interaction within the family influences other family relationships and, ultimately, defines a total family atmosphere. The interrelationships among different family role relationships and the fact that marital role relationships are the most powerful influences on marital satisfaction provide some documentation for this conception. Other factors do affect marital satisfaction, although the other effects are often indirect and influence marital satisfaction mainly through their significance for sharing or segregation in specific marital role relationships. To the extent that other issues affected marital satisfaction, they were predominantly situations and experiences that had quite an immediate impact on family life. Family income, the employment status of husband and wife, the standard of living of the family, and social problems were prominent factors influencing marital satisfaction (Appendix table 6.8). A fairly high family income increased the level of marital satisfaction among people in all social class positions. Regular employment on the part of the husband was essential for marital satisfaction regardless of the economic level of the family. However, as with marital companionship, if the husband was employed and the family had an adequate income so that the wife was not compelled to find a job, her participation in work led to even higher levels of marital satisfaction. Living conditions influenced by economic circumstances such as housing, the availability of a car, or the general standard of living were also important for marital satisfaction. For all levels of per capita income and at all social class levels, the higher the standard of living, the more often did people find marriage satisfying. On the other hand, the intrusion of social problems was a serious and potent impediment to marital satisfaction regardless of social class position.

While most of the economic and economically-derived influences on marital satisfaction were consistent in their effects on people of different status, other factors were occasionally more important for people of

TABLE 6.2   Marital role integration by marital satisfaction, with social class status held constant (in percentages)

Social class status	Marital role integration	Marital satisfaction				
		Highly satisfied	Moderately satisfied	Dissatisfied	N[a]	Percent
Moderately high						
	Shared	44	53	3	36	100
	Mixed	18	77	6	17	100
	Segregated	(11)	(33)	(56)	9	100
Moderately low						
	Shared	49	49	2	61	100
	Mixed	29	66	5	41	100
	Segregated	12	58	30	50	100
Very low						
	Shared	47	50	3	34	100
	Mixed	39	58	3	31	100
	Segregated	2	58	40	45	100

[a]There are 10 uncodeable cases. See footnote to Table 6.1.

higher status or, alternatively, for people of lower status. We have already
observed that there was a diminution in marital satisfaction with increasing
age, but this occurred primarily among people of higher status living in the
West End. Similarly, other forms of personal debility such as poor health
or a husband with neurotic symptoms led more often to marital dissatisfaction among people of higher status.[39] Conversely, women who themselves
had neurotic symptoms, a high degree of social anxiety, or a low level of
efficacy were more likely to be maritally dissatisfied if they were of low
status. Moreover, although an individual's own status did not have a great
influence on marital satisfaction, changes in status from parental origin
were associated with lower levels of marital satisfaction. Apart from general
observations of strain under conditions of social mobility, intergenerational
changes in status may engender pressures for new patterns of marital role
functioning for which the partners are unprepared by their prior, status-
connected experiences.

We have already indicated that children are more important for family
life in lower than in higher status families and that, in fact, the birth of
children may be perceived as an intrusion on companionate relationships
at higher social class levels. Confirmation for this view is evident in a
reversal in the effect of children on marital satisfaction for people in different social class positions. The presence of children diminished the level of
marital satisfaction among people of higher status and led to increased
marital satisfaction among people of moderate or lower status (Fitzgerald,
1967). In fact, at the lowest status level marital satisfaction increased
regardless of the number of children, while at moderate status levels satisfaction diminished when there were four or more children in the household.

In view of the significance of community life for a great many people in
the West End, we might have expected that a high degree of local social
interaction could counteract some of the deleterious effects of segregated
marital roles and, thus, lead to somewhat higher levels of marital satisfaction. We have already indicated that the prediction of a close association
between segregated marital roles and a high degree of closeknit network
involvement was only rarely visible among people in the West End. More
often those people who had extensive social affiliations in the local area
were also likely to sustain shared marital role relationships. However, in
the extreme, extensive interaction with local networks did compensate
for experienced inadequacies in the marriage and resulted in lower levels of
marital dissatisfaction. Quite consistently, we find that segregated marital
roles were less likely to lead to marital dissatisfaction among people who

engaged in other social relationships (Appendix table 6.9). The compensatory effect occurred only when the marital role relationships were extremely segregated and obtained for all social class statuses.

Although we have stressed the nature of family relationships as a self-contained system, it is clearly not a closed system. While most extra-familial forces are largely mediated through their effects on specific role relationships, there remain some independent influences on marital satisfaction. However, highly integrated family role relationships seem to be a bulwark against the incursion of problems until they become quite overwhelming and lead to a deterioration in the total atmosphere of family life. Certainly sustained crisis or long-term developmental changes may slowly erode the effective sharing of family role relationships. [40] But within the ordinary range of life stresses, shared role relationships within the family provide the basic conditions for a high degree of marital satisfaction. Indeed, when marital role relationships are shared, it is possible to sustain a high level of marital satisfaction in the face of considerable conflict between husbands and wives, although shared marital functioning inevitably reduces the amount of conflict as well (Appendix table 6.10). Conversely, other sources of satisfaction, of support, of economic or social advantage can bolster a flagging family environment but serve to integrate marital and family relationships only to a modest degree unless they alter the total pattern of family role functioning.

In the light of these findings, we can see some of the determinants of marital and family functioning and of marital satisfaction in broader perspective. Social class position defines a framework of expectations and conditions for the patterns of marital interaction. The realities of experience and of situational forces, however, affect the developmental process of family life and reduce the total impact of initial social class differences. Economic security, stable employment, children, close social relationships, and personal strengths increase the likelihood of effective family functioning and produce heightened levels of marital satisfaction. The role relationships internal to the marital and family systems, however, are the direct determinants of marital satisfaction; other forces that influence marital satisfaction do so indirectly through their effects on segregation or sharing in these role relationships. The unfortunate situation of people in lower status positions is that they have few of the resources that facilitate sharing in marital role relationships and, thus, frequently lack the patterns of family functioning that provide some insurance against the cyclical effects on both the individual and the family of economic and social deprivation.

Under these conditions it is hardly surprising that people in lower social class positions more often experience marital dissatisfaction, separation, and divorce. Higher rates of separation and divorce among people of lower status are quite widespread in many countries (Goode, 1962). That lower-class black families, suffering even more severe constraints than lower-class white families, should show even higher rates of marital disruption and alternative household arrangements is only to be expected.[41] But while marital disruptions may be necessary adjustments to reality, they invoke serious penalties. This is evident in the fact that, at all social class levels, regardless of the adaptations people may have made to the exigencies of economic and familial life, marital satisfaction is the most crucial component of more general satisfaction with life. In the West End and in other communities of different status, among whites and blacks, marital satisfaction is almost a necessary condition for a high degree of global contentment.[42] Other sources of gratification, like community satisfaction, may be extremely important in their own right, but neither these other satisfactions nor the availability of other resources can effectively counteract the effects of marital dissatisfaction (Appendix table 6.11). On the other hand, various resources and gratifications can facilitate the development of marital role relationships that are satisfying.

In the face of many debilities, endemic pressures, and even crises, and a host of unfulfilled desires and needs, it is all the more striking how large a proportion of people in the working class manage to sustain meaningful marital and family relationships that are enduring sources of satisfaction and make other difficulties more tolerable.

7 Work Experiences and Work Orientations

Occupations and Status in the West End

The conception of a working class, referred to by various terms, is ancient. All urban societies have known a class of persons who had to devote themselves primarily or exclusively to the most poorly rewarded manual, nonagricultural laboring jobs. Aristocratic societies, of course, have ordinarily considered the necessity of working for a living as demeaning. But the notion of working with one's hands and of working for others has generally carried with it an opprobrium that has extended, in both subtle and overt forms, into the era of industrialized democracy.

Although many people refer to the working class, there are different conceptions of its boundaries. The term working class does not refer to any precise concept, but it does capture an essential idea that is easily obscured by efforts to refine it except for specific and limited purposes. The essence of the concept of a working class lies in the existence of a large mass of the labor force, people who may differ in skills, in prestige, and in rewards within a narrow range but share many economic and occupational circumstances. Their livelihoods depend directly on daily labor since they own little property that can sustain them if they do not work. Economic recessions or personal difficulties like ill health that interfere with their functioning on the job are serious threats. Although workers with relatively high wages may begin to earn enough money to acquire some property on a small scale and to develop more expansive life styles, their life chances remain largely limited to the skills they can sell in a competitive labor market. But working-class occupational positions are precarious since, even at moderately high levels of skills, people are viewed as relatively interchangeable in jobs. Unionization has reduced the uncertainty of these positions, and established seniority systems offer some insurance to experienced workers. But the importance of unions is indicative of the concerted effort necessary for providing a modicum of security and of equitability in bargaining. Perhaps most of all, however, working-class positions are distinguished by their routinization and by the minimal control people are allowed over their own destinies. Even such rudimentary matters as adequate wages and work conditions require the coercive force of organized occupational groups, usually trade or industrial unions, to establish effective bargaining power based on mass representation.

People in the working class are often distinguished from others of lower status, sometimes called the lower class, who have no saleable skills or cannot use their skills because of external conditions or internal constraints. The distinction of an underclass, a *lumpenproletariat* as Marx and Engels designated it, or the undeserving poor, or a category of multiple problem families, has almost always implied a willing shiftlessness and rejection of self-support. While the assumption of irresponsibility has to be investigated rather than asserted, the separation of a lower class from the working class is occasionally useful. But the deficits they imply are, in large part, class-less. Divorce, child neglect, occupational instability, economic dependency, and delinquency occur at all status levels. However, the resources of people in higher status positions often enable them to conceal their difficulties and even permit them to retrieve their situations through available services ranging from bank loans to psychotherapy. We shall include these people of lowest status in the working class since we view their problems as super-imposed on and exacerbated by low status rather than as indications of a fundamentally different position in the social class hierarchy.

The boundary between the working class and the middle class is even more shadowy. If we use the distinction between blue and white collar workers, as is often done, the ill-paid clerk and salesperson would be categorized as middle class. Moreover, some blue-collar workers, particularly those who have inherited the mantle of the old skilled trades, often earn high wages and have considerable bargaining power. These affluent workers may even become suburban homeowners and develop life styles close to those of the middle class. But since their basic positions in society remain relatively uncertain and since the evidence suggests that they retain social and political orientations that reflect a working-class identity, we shall include them within the working class.

There remain a number of ambiguities according to these defining characteristics. In modern bureaucratic societies in which a large part of the professional activity of physicians, lawyers, teachers, engineers, and others is carried out within huge organizations, the structural position of profes-sionals is quite similar to that which has traditionally typified manual laborers. Despite high salaries and prestige and expertise associated with these positions, a sense of conflict of interest has often arisen with the administrative hierarchies of their organizations. However, the prestige, highly specialized education, and technical knowledge of professionals and of lower executives permit them extensive control over their daily occupational role activities and provide a sense of social esteem and a superior bargaining position that warrant their exclusion from the working class.

A more difficult problem is posed by the small entrepreneur, the small shopkeeper who runs his store as a family enterprise, or the small craftsman who services people himself and runs his business either out of his home or with only a small repair shop. Often people in these positions conceive of themselves as working class and their economic and social situations generally justify this self-concept. However, the fact of self-employment, despite the limited framework and stability of the enterprise, allows a degree of control over one's life situation that distinguishes them from the working class. In a purely occupational categorization, however, those whose activities are clearly manual are likely to fall within the upper working class as skilled laborers while shopkeepers, classified as skilled white-collar workers, will fall outside this class. Nonetheless, however defined, these are some of the more striking instances of ambiguity in so broadly conceived a social classification. Whether we include or exclude various categories of workers in this broadly-defined working class, we must ask repeatedly how differences in status and situation influence the behavior and attitudes of different individuals.

The vast majority of people in the West End fell quite properly and with little ambiguity into the working class conceived in this way. Both the poorly paid and least stable workers and the more affluent and secure manual laborers with high levels of skill were amply represented in the population. Although residential areas tend to be relatively homogeneous in the class positions of their inhabitants, most neighborhoods inevitably contain a moderate range of people from different educational and occupational levels (Duncan and Duncan, 1955; Tilly, 1965). In an area so convenient to the center of the city as the West End, we expect to find an even wider range, including some people of considerably higher status. The vast majority of the West End men, however, were manual laborers (79 percent). There were more semiskilled workers (37 percent) than either skilled laborers (17 percent) or unskilled workmen (25 percent). By an occupational definition, therefore, the West End was predominantly a residential area for low status blue-collar workers. It was extremely convenient both to the Massachusetts General Hospital and to the down-

town area and was known as an area in which many students and
professionals lived, but the proportions of people in higher status positions
were quite small. Thus, 15 percent of the population were white-collar
workers who bordered on, and often thought of themselves as, working
class (small business people and skilled and semiskilled clerical workers).
Only 6 percent fell into higher status categories of employment (professionals, semiprofessionals, and men in managerial positions). The women
who were employed were generally in lower occupational positions than
the men. The majority (64 percent) were unskilled or semiskilled manual
workers and very few women were skilled manual laborers. Many of the
women (25 percent) held low status or moderate status while-collar jobs
and a modest number (8 percent) were in semiprofessional positions. None
of the women from the West End were in managerial or professional
occupations.

The educational backgrounds of the men and the women were quite
similar to one another and extremely low. Naturally, many people in the
West End were of foreign, peasant origin, but this only partly accounts for
the large proportion (42 percent of the men; 43 percent of the women)
who had attained no more than an eighth grade education. Less than a
third of the men or women (29 percent in both cases) had finished high
school, although there was a linear increase in education among successively younger age groups and almost 50 percent of those between the ages
of twenty and thirty had completed high school. A small proportion (10
percent of the men; 11 percent of the women) had had some schooling
beyond high school and this rose to a peak of 28 percent of the men aged
twenty to thirty. Very few people, among the men or the women, had
completed college. Incomes were similarly low and a great many West
Enders were living on extremely meager wages.

The West End was by no means the lowest status residential area in
Boston but West Enders were predominantly members of the lower
working class. In fact, a great many people in the West End were severely
deprived. Since the economic condition of a family involves the number of
persons supported by a given income, per capita income estimates provide
a more accurate picture of the total economic situation of a family than
does the total income itself. Even by conservative standards, almost a
quarter (24 percent) of the people in the West End were living below
national standards of a minimum household income and, thereby, living
in poverty.[1] Another 32 percent were living in marginal economic conditions that forced a meager standard of living upon them and allowed for
no financial emergencies. Older people and women who had been divorced,

widowed, or separated and had children to support were in the worst
economic straits, though many of the families with husband and wife and
children in the household were also among those living below the minimum
or marginally. A major source of these severe economic strains is evident in
the fact that rates of unemployment and underemployment were high
compared to national figures. Fully 6.8 percent of the men were unemployed, a rate that rose to 9.9 percent during the recession of 1961.
Another 12 percent were underemployed and worked irregularly.[2]

Problems of poverty and unemployment were clearly quite frequent.
However, the large majority of the men (78 percent) were stably employed.
As is generally the case, men of lower occupational status and those who,
in other respects, were in the least competitive positions in the labor
market, had higher rates of unemployment. Even within the narrow range
of working-class positions, although more sharply evident in comparisons
between a wider range of occupations, status made a difference in many
aspects of the work situation and of work experiences. Thus, variations in
occupational position influenced, not merely objective differences like
income, supervisory responsibilities, and secondary jobs, but the kinds of
orientations men had toward work and the kinds of experiences they had
on the job.

To understand the status and situation of working-class people, it is also
necessary to recognize the high degree of stability in status from one
generation to another that influenced their total experience and orientation. Although the United States and other industrial countries are often
viewed as highly mobile societies, long-term upward mobility occurs least
frequently at the lowest levels of the working class (Blau and Duncan,
1967; Glass, 1954). There is widespread agreement that parental social
class position is the single most important determinant of educational
attainment and so it was among people in the West End. Despite the fact
that a fairly large number of people had moved up or down from their
parental statuses and despite the widespread sense among Americans in
general of status achievement relative to their parents, no other factor even
approximates parental status in its influence on the amount of education
a child received.[3] Indeed, apart from the higher levels of education among
younger people, only the early loss of the mother, lack of closeness to the
father, and rural origins amplify the markedly low levels of education of
people from low status origins.

In view of the many deleterious consequences of limited educational
background in our society, it becomes apparent that the large impact of
parental status on education also has wider ramifications. For example,

while a person's educational attainment is dominated by his social class
origins, the educational level he attains is the main influence, by far, on
his subsequent occupational career.[4] Thus, in the long run, through the
influence of parental status on educational attainment and the subsequent
effect of educational attainment on occupational achievement, social class
origins are powerful determinants of an individual's own social class
position. Nor are these findings easily explained away as a function of
foreign origins. While the effect of parental social class position on occupational achievement was certainly greatest among the foreign born, it was a
powerful influence regardless of assimilation status (Appendix table 7.1).
Those people who came from very low status origins were unlikely to rise
above the lower occupational levels whether they were themselves of
foreign birth, the second generation children of foreign parents, or
Americans of long ancestry. Although ethnicity was not a pervasive influence on occupation, the Italians manifested the signs of former disadvantage. Among the last of the white ethnic groups from past European
migrations to suffer considerable discrimination, the Italians of the West
End had achieved lower levels of occupational status even when they had
attained levels of education comparable to other ethnic groups. Thus,
among those who were high school graduates or had some college, 19
percent of the Italians were in moderately high occupational positions
compared to 44 percent of the moderately embedded ethnic groups (East
Europeans, Jews, and Americans of at least the third generation), and to
48 percent of those who had few other members of the same ethnic group
living in the West End (western and central Europeans, British, and
Canadians).[5] There were modest differences in status associated with
religion but the only generalization that can be made is that Protestants
in the West End had the highest status and Catholics were more
often in moderate to low status positions. Rural background was another
source of status deficits. People from rural origins had lower levels
of education, but, even given equivalent education, their occupational
achievements compared unfavorably with those of people from urban
origins.

Unlike many other issues we have discussed, social status measured as
education, as occupation, as income, or in other ways was strongly and
almost exclusively influenced by objective structural and situational forces.
Each aspect of status was itself influenced by other status accomplishments.
The most striking of these, as we have indicated, was the considerable
influence of parental status on an individual's own status. In view of this,
and its confirmation in other data, the forces producing intergenerational

continuity in status must be seen as reflections of the limitations to upward mobility of working-class people. Once given the effects of parental status on the education that people attain, other limitations to status achievements ensue because of educational requirements for obtaining skilled jobs and because of the influence of educational and occupational status on wages and other income. However, despite widely-held views about the effects of psychological assets in channeling people into different achievement paths, few personal or social factors influenced the educational or occupational careers or debilities of people in the West End. Indeed, even physical or mental health were minimally associated with education or with occupational status, although poor physical condition or psychological deficits limited job functioning. Only occupational aspirations, if seen as contributing causes rather than merely as consequences of status, had any substantial influence on occupational achievement.[6] Certainly, occupational aspirations increased with further education, but even given the same level of education, people with higher occupational aspirations achieved higher levels of occupational status.

Although the large majority of the men were unskilled or semiskilled manual laborers, a moderately large number (23 percent) carried modest supervisory responsibilities. About half of these men supervised one to three employees and the other half supervised more than three other men. However, supervisory status was almost entirely uninfluenced by differences in educational attainment and was less markedly affected by occupational status than one might have anticipated. Thus, although there is a very considerable degree of intergenerational continuity in occupational status levels, one realm of somewhat greater freedom, in which a man can experience modest achievements despite educational deficits, lies in supervisory statuses of modest dimensions.[7] However, the immediate advantages of supervisory positions were minimal. While there was some modest prestige associated with supervisory status, there was little increment in wages with increased supervisory responsibility except among white-collar workers and the highly skilled manual laborers. Differences in supervisory status had consequences mainly for job stability.

The range of incomes among West End men was remarkably narrow. Indeed, while men with more education or with higher occupational positions earned higher job incomes, the earnings of men with different backgrounds were more uniform than one would anticipate. Low income may be a factor of importance in accounting for the residential choice of a working-class slum area by people with higher levels of education and occupation and this may explain some of the homogeneity in earnings.

However, many of the men with the lowest incomes suffered some deficit, be it age, poor health, or foreign origins, that served to modify the linear impact of education and occupational status on earnings. Certainly rural background was a source of such disadvantage for incomes as well as for education and occupation. Men from rural backgrounds had less education and lower occupations than those from urban backgrounds. Moreover, at every occupational level, men from rural origins were quite disadvantaged in their earnings. At lower occupational levels, this decrement in the incomes of men from rural backgrounds was quite marked: 25 percent of the un-skilled or semiskilled laborers from urban origins earned less than $75.00 per week, while 65 percent of the men in the same occupational positions who came from rural backgrounds had such low earnings.

In general, however, neither job incomes nor family incomes nor per capita incomes are adequately accounted for by social origins, occupation, or education or by other social roles or psychological dispositions. The differences between people in poverty, in marginal economic conditions, and in more comfortable financial circumstances, in particular, were only modestly dependent on these stable social frameworks and positions that affected so many other aspects of life.[8] The reason, however, is fairly clear. Although both temporary and permanent poverty are major social problems in our society, a large proportion of the people in poverty suffer such economic deprivation periodically rather than for very long time spans. The majority (61 percent) of West End families living below a minimal economic level were no longer poverty-stricken three years later. Conversely, many of the families in poverty at a later date had been in better financial circumstances three years before. This shift from poverty to marginal economic status (or better) and the reverse shift from more adequate finances to poverty is quite general, although there is a substantial minority of poor families who cannot alter their situations at all.[9]

Thus, it is evident that situational forces determine a large proportion of the cases of poverty. As a consequence, we can expect individual or family situations, often superimposed on more stable, structural limitations, to be the critical determinants of economic deprivation. Marital disruption, aging, a large number of children, and poor health are among the most important factors that potentiate the significance of low education and low occupational status in producing income levels insufficient for a minimal standard of living. Naturally, poverty was most frequent among those who suffered a combination of these circumstances. Often one condition entailed a greater likelihood of other supplementary deficits. Poor health and aging independently increased the chances of poverty, but aging also led to more frequent and more serious health problems. Similarly, a relatively small proportion of families were in poverty if the wife was employed; but employment among low status women with young children was rare. In some instances, therefore, we have the basic conditions for long-term states of poverty while in others, as among families with many young children, poverty is likely to be more transitory. Aspects of status, like education and occupation, certainly define an overall probability of falling into poverty. However, the specific factors that led to poverty in the West End were predominantly situational and, in this sense at least, modifiable.

Short-term or long-term unemployment, which also influenced the economic status of the family, were themselves mainly accounted for by a host of situational forces. As with poverty, unemployment varied only moderately with differences in education or occupation while other, situational influences superimposed on these statuses were of considerable importance. Education was of greater significance for unemployment than it was for poverty, and serious psychological deficits also produced higher unemployment rates. However, the prominence of situational determinants of poverty, unemployment, and job instability imply that familiar views that attribute poverty and unemployment to lack of motivation or to other attitudes and personal traits are entirely insufficient. In recent years, these claims have most often been directed toward black, Puerto Rican, and Mexican-American populations. But the white, ethnic working class of European extraction is not entirely immune from such stereotyped attributions and accusations. The data from the West End reinforce other evidence that the immediate origins of serious economic and employment inequalities in our society can be traced to sources beyond the control of individuals.

Work Experiences and Satisfactions

Several features of working-class jobs provide a basis for understanding the occupational experiences and attitudes of workers. We have already pointed out that one distinguishing characteristic of working-class jobs is a lack of participation in decision-making. Indeed, a major achievement of American industry at the turn of the century was the subdivision, routinization, and mechanization of complex industrial processes, an achievement that facilitated the incorporation into the labor force of millions of immigrants without skill. One of the most widely known developments of this form of job reorganization, the assembly-line, became the prototype of modern factory production. In recent years, some industries have adapted the new potentialities of automation to allocate greater judgment and responsibility for complex operations to workers, but ordinarily automation has simply subserved more traditional conceptions of factory labor.[10] The concentration of authority and power and the centralization of decision-making are so fundamental to the usual conceptions of industrial organization that little attention is usually given to evidence of potentially greater productive efficiency with the decentralization and reorganization of work roles.[11] Thus, in most organizations, the major function of the worker remains one of fulfilling discrete tasks that have been designated by somebody else with little freedom to elect the best procedures for attaining work goals.

This feature of working-class jobs has several consequences. It creates distance between the worker and his job, diminishing the potential involvement he is likely to develop in work. This is reflected in conceptions of and satisfactions in work. It also reduces morale and motivation, an issue to which much attention has been devoted, although mainly around extrinsic mechanisms of stimulating job commitment.[12] Most immediately, of course, it accomplishes what it was designed to do in making workers quite interchangeable. Thus, it inevitably produces a sense of insecurity on the job. The growth of unions and of their influence in hiring and firing and the existence of seniority systems have done much to diminish these anxieties, but the sense of uncertainty that is tied to manifest dispensability has persisted.[13] It is not surprising, therefore, that so many workers prefer stability and security on the job to taking chances on their economic futures. Given a moderate range of choices, 49 percent of the men felt that steadiness and reliability were the most important aspects of a job and hardly any (4 percent) considered these entirely negligible considerations. Given a more limited set of choices between security and a chance to get ahead, 77 percent of the men chose security as the preferable feature of a job. These orientations toward the job, moreover, were clearly related to occupational position, although with increasing age most men opted for security regardless of their status (Appendix table 7.2).[14] While workingmen may often indulge themselves in the small risk-taking ventures of playing the numbers or of other forms of small-scale gambling for small stakes, they cannot afford to jeopardize their wages by ambitions that are likely to prove ill-fated, given the known odds.

Whatever forms of job advancement the workers from the West End might have dreamed about, active desires for upward mobility for themselves were relatively rare. Less than a third of the men said that, if they could have any job they wanted, they would choose a job at the semiprofessional level or higher and among these, 7 percent already held such jobs. Most blue-collar men conceive of self-employment as their major channel of mobility even though, given the insecurity of undertaking their own enterprise and the capital required, few of them do so (Chinoy, 1955; Goldthorpe et al., 1969; Lipset and Bendix, 1967). The vast majority of the men in the West End also would have liked self-employment mainly so that they could attain greater independence or freedom from control by others. The widespread interest in self-employment indicates that, while overt mobility desires among manual workers were constrained by many realistic considerations, there were latent and indirect mobility desires. Most of the men were quite cognizant of their limited marketability and of their restricted potential for finding meaningful jobs. A great many regretted this situation although they had learned to live with it and, under most conditions, to ignore it. The occupational opportunity structure dictates a very narrow range within which effective adaptation is possible in the world of working-class jobs.

If one presses beyond the realm of contemporary realities, dim ambitions and old yearnings often reveal themselves. Asked what changes they would most like to have made in their lives, 33 percent admitted to covert desires for higher educational or occupational attainment. Many of the men had wanted more schooling but had to leave for a variety of reasons. Many of them no longer felt sorry about this, but the great majority still regretted the interruption of their education. Even if we assume that some of the men who said they had wanted more schooling at the time they left have retrospectively refashioned their ambitions, their reasons for leaving school remind us that education is too costly a luxury for many people:

I was ill and had to drop out. Maybe it was bronchitis. If I had more schooling, I would be in a better position today. If I had been crooked, I wouldn't need the education.
My people needed money.
I had a fall fixing the porch and broke several vertebrae. I was hospitalized for three months.
My people couldn't afford it. Now I feel terrible about it.
I was the oldest of seven and had to work. I feel it has been my great loss.
I had to go to work. Now I'm too old. And I've done okay without it. But I have a lot of respect for education.
I had to support my mother. She was paralyzed.
I started to work with my father at the age of fifteen because my brothers were all too small. I'm sorry I didn't have more schooling.
We were very poor. I had to work. My father passed away when I was fourteen years old.
My father was not making much money and I had to support the home.

Quite a few of those who left school voluntarily were also unhappy that they had not gone further in their education.

It is difficult to estimate the significance of different objectives behind these latent ambitions. Higher incomes were certainly among them, although relatively few of the men and only a slightly larger proportion of the women visualized that having more money would bring about major changes in their lives or in their life styles. Overt status striving for themselves, involving more direct confrontation with current ambitions, was similarly rejected by a third of the men who preferred simple pleasures, including satisfaction at work, to successful achievement. While success strivings were vague for most of the men and women and generally were represented by wishes for more education or for wider occupational opportunities, both men and women in the West End were more ambitious for their children. Indeed, it was not simply a matter of trying to fulfill their own unrealized, and suppressed, desires for achievement through their children. The level of achievement that these working-class parents wanted for their children was fairly uniform and independent of their own strivings, blocked or fulfilled. Most of the parents felt that it would be ideal for their children to go to college, but relatively few insisted upon a college education for their children. Many parents who wanted their sons to go to college were adjusted to the fact that this was unlikely, and while the majority of fathers, given the choice, preferred that their daughter marry a successful professional man, a large proportion (37 percent) clearly felt that their own wishes should not enter into the daughter's decision. Thus, their ambitions for their children were frequently modified by an awareness of the many barriers to their realization and by a sense of tolerance for the career decisions their children might make for themselves.

Despite many latent desires for modest financial improvement, independence, opportunity, and esteem, most of the men lived within the realistic limitations of their positions. Few working-class people try to redefine reality or to transcend it following the idealized model of entrepreneurial or professional zeal (Fried, 1970). Thus, they often accepted their jobs with good grace if not with overwhelming satisfaction, although, given relatively routinized conceptions of job satisfaction and dissatisfaction, the level of satisfaction was surprisingly high. Most of the men maintained they would continue at their present jobs even if they won a lottery and no longer had to work. But if we consider a straightforward question, asking the men whether they liked their jobs as is, whether they would like it with changes, or whether they would like a different job, we find important differences with age. The very idea of anticipating changes in a job was predominantly a phenomenon of higher status positions at all ages (Appendix table 7.3). Men in lower status positions were inclined either to like their jobs as they knew them or, more often, to prefer different jobs. The preference for a different job, which we might expect to be very strongly associated with the occupational status of the position, was only moderately differentiated by status among the younger men (twenty to thirty-four) and, among the older men (fifty and over), those in the lowest status positions most often accepted their current jobs with no alternative desires. Only among those in the middle age group (thirty-five to forty-nine) did the men of lower status reject their current jobs much more often than did men of higher status.[15]

Job satisfaction is, to a considerable extent, influenced by individual expectations and the range of available options. More fundamental to an understanding of class differences in work experience, however, is the large variation in the sources of satisfaction on the job associated with occupational status. Certainly the tasks and challenges of jobs vary quite directly with the hierarchy of occupational positions. And, in turn, the sources of job satisfaction vary in parallel fashion with the availability of interesting tasks and opportunities at different occupational status levels. At all ages, West End men in lower status occupations more often liked their jobs because of good work conditions or because of the money they made, while men in higher occupations placed greater emphasis on the intrinsic features of their work roles (Appendix table 7.4).[16] Although independence and opportunity were important aspects of desires for self-employment among working-class men, the blue-collar worker does not ordinarily expect such intrinsically attractive jobs.[17] They rarely complained about the absence of such opportunities. Regardless of occupational status, the main sources of job dissatisfaction concerned work conditions, low wages, difficulty of the tasks, or long hours, although a number of men did complain about the monotony of their work.

When we shift our attention from the more limited conception of a job to inquire about more personal experiences of satisfaction in work, working-class men reveal a much wider array of work orientations and a clearer image of the sources and levels of gratification in work. By contrast with the sheer job satisfactions that people expressed, new elements of pride and pleasure were evinced. Relatively few of the men found work satisfaction merely in their earnings or in keeping busy, and total dissatisfaction was rare. In fact, many of the men expressed their feelings about earnings as a sense of fulfilling their responsibilities for support of the family or of pride in their work roles. Although fewer than half the men experienced more fundamental satisfaction with their mastery of difficult tasks or of pleasurable activities in the process of working, many of the men in lower status jobs found pleasure in tasks which seemed to offer little enough possibility of such self-fulfillment. Some of the workers, particularly those in skilled trades, occasionally described surprising potentialities within their limited opportunities for work satisfaction:

I feel like an important man there. (warehouse shipping clerk)
I have a sense of accomplishment in doing the best job I can, looking for better ways to do things. (ship handler)
To see work accomplished, something that will be there for years, leaving your mark. (pipe fitter)
When I get through, I know it's perfect. (auto body repairman)
Well, accomplishing something creative. (hair stylist)
Completing the best quality work and always striving to do better. And getting the approval of my supervisor. (electro-mechanical craftsman)
Creating, seeing things begin and be completed. (manager, printing office)

Although many men seemed able to get more out of their jobs than one might anticipate, the majority evidently had much more restricted experiences. For most of the men, therefore, work satisfactions were as narrow as an objective job description would suggest:

None. It's hard. (dishwasher)
Money in my pocket. (laborer)
Being active, doing things. (order assembler)
I meet different people and can learn a lot from them. (factory worker)
I meet the guys and meet other people. (laundry machine shop operator)
It is a friendly atmosphere. (mail handler)
I'm earning my keep. I'm able to provide for the family. That's about the biggest satisfaction I can get. (mail carrier)
I love to work. There's no one to bother me. (mortar man, construction)

However, the different sources of work satisfaction reveal a very marked differentiation according to occupational status. Largely independent of education, the men of higher occupational status enjoyed the more personal and self-fulfilling aspects of work far more often than did those men who were more clearly in working-class occupations and, thus, had only restricted tasks and work opportunities on the job (Appendix table 7.5).

From the wealth of data in various studies, the conclusion becomes inescapable that low status workers have few opportunities to experience work-oriented satisfactions on the job. Even given these limited opportunities, they often perceive a far wider range of satisfactions than we might expect. But these opportunities hardly fulfill their strivings or even, for that matter, their skills and potentialities. Working-class men and women often develop the internal resources for jobs that are more demanding of skill, investment, and imagination than those that ever become available to them. Work and job opportunities in industrial societies vary enormously with the occupational level of the job. Workers from rural areas, like most of the immigrants of the past and a great many of the minorities who currently occupy the lowest status occupations, move into urban areas with minimal preparation for complex industrial jobs. The most basic and immediate transition required of the newcomer is the development of those expectations, skills, and abilities associated with obtaining and maintaining a job in a competitive market. Even apart from problems of seniority and discrimination, the job situation for such migrants was and is precarious. Not only have they traditionally occupied the lowest positions in the job hierarchy but, given any increase in unemployment, the more recent migrants are generally the first to lose their jobs. Among West Enders, those who grew up in the West End experienced unemployment rates of 4.1 percent during the recession of 1961; 6.2 percent of those who came from other urban areas were unemployed. But 14.5 percent of those who came from rural backgrounds were unemployed in the same time period. Thus, the persisting sense of anxiety and insecurity, revealed by the extremely large number of West End men who felt that security was the most important feature of a job, had an entirely realistic basis in fact.

Indeed, many of the restricted orientations of workers toward their work stem quite directly from past disappointments, from limited opportunities for meaningful job satisfaction, and from overt constraints and internal insecurities about exploring wider work role opportunities on the job. Most people require a sense of certainty about the fulfillment of their essential needs and a high degree of confidence in future fulfillment before they can have the freedom to move on to forms of work expectation and work orientation that are both more demanding and more exciting. The process of learning to obtain and to hold a job and to feel secure that this will be possible in the future is the first level in a hierarchy of work orientations. We can refer to this primary orientation as *work as a job*. Although most West Enders were the children of immigrants rather than of rural, foreign birth themselves, the very precarious nature of low status manual occupations prolonged this most rudimentary conception of industrial work.

A great many of the men in the West End had essentially moved on to a second level of work orientation. This orientation is *work as a task* and implies an ability to shift from routinized performance of duties to a conception of discrete components of the work process as pleasurable and as an opportunity for manual or cognitive mastery. But to consider work tasks as exciting requires realistic opportunities for exciting tasks at work. Indeed, because so many West End men had already moved beyond the levels that their jobs readily allowed, they sought and occasionally found varieties of satisfaction and mastery where these were most difficult to perceive.

Beyond work as a job and work as a task, we move into a realm that requires identification with the work organization in return for few overt advantages. *Work as an occupation* involves a fairly large commitment without offering major economic rewards or even long-term job stability. Most workers have had little enough opportunity to enjoy the satisfactions of work as a task and, as a consequence, remain uncertain about their ability to assume even greater responsibilities. Moreover, work as an occupation depends upon an identification with those in authority who represent divergent interests and are likely to maintain an impersonal and relatively uncommited attitude toward the worker. At the same time, it often brings the worker into competition with his peers. In principle, work as an occupation differs from work as a task in two main respects: it includes a wider variety of tasks or a larger segment of the work process and it demands an obligation to fulfill, not merely job roles, but the larger work goals specified by management. In practice it includes jobs of a large supervisory nature or of moderately high status and technical skill. Pleasure in discrete tasks must be subordinated to an overall objective and to the responsibility of considering organizational goals. Compensation lies mainly in the possibility of developing a new sense of social participation through work. However, workers have learned to restrict their investments to visible and attainable ends. Such involvements, without additional rewards or greater security, are more often experienced as a threat than as an opportunity.

With a sense of security in an occupational role and a sense of meaning in contributing to a larger objective, there is the possibility of moving to a conception of *work as a career*. To speak of moving into work as a career gives a false impression of mobility. Few workers who enter the job market at the level of work as a job or work as a task are ever likely to have the opportunity to reach those executive or professional positions that involve a career orientation. While work as a career provides enormous intrinsic rewards, it often places a very large burden on the individual in its expectation that work goals take primacy in his life. While people in such career positions have opportunities to define their own goals or to participate actively in the decision-making process, it requires not merely great personal investment but the development of personal qualities which are often antithetical to effective functioning in other societal roles.[18] Frequently, however, such positions offer alternative rewards in the form of money, prestige, and wider opportunities.

Although few working-class people can ever hope to move beyond one major occupational level in their own lifetimes, social mobility almost inevitably requires a transition from one set of work orientations and satisfactions to another. For most people, the challenge never arises. Opportunities for upward mobility are limited. Many workers who have achieved a modicum of security and skill at their own occupational levels are ready to move on to new work orientations, but the range of options is very narrow. Indeed, 50 percent of the men in the West End were working at the same occupational status level as their fathers, while 29 percent had moved up in occupational positions and 21 percent were in lower positions than their fathers.[19] The largest proportions, by far, of both upward and downward occupational movement were single step moves rather than large changes in occupational status. In view of the hope that immigration seemed to offer, in principle at least, of great potentials for achievement, these rates of upward and downward mobility are sobering. Aspirations for occupational mobility, while modest, were higher than the actual rates of mobility. Few men wanted occupations lower than their current jobs (7 percent), 42 percent were satisfied to work at occupations in approximately the same status level as their actual jobs, and somewhat more than half, 51 percent of the men, aspired to occupations higher than those they held. That the aspirations of these men were, indeed, modest and readily fulfilled by modest achievements is evident when we compare actual achievements with aspirations. At each occupational status level, those people who had already experienced some upward mobility maintained *lower* levels of further aspiration than did men who had been nonmobile (Appendix table 7.6).

As we have already said, status strivings in the sense of desires for occupational prestige or for status-connected worldly goods and appearances were not of major importance to most West Enders. Latent ambitions and aspirations were mainly concerned with less financial strain, greater security, and more control over the experiences of daily life. As the comparison of occupational achievement and occupational aspirations further reveals, modest accomplishments seemed to satisfy their occupational ambitions and did not lead, as they might in the middle class, to further aspirational strivings. But if these occupational aspirations were only modest, were reasonably well adjusted to the reality of very small differences in wages among lower occupational levels, and gave some emphasis to independence, then we must still wonder if there were substantive gains they sought through their aspirations. We have maintained that many men had skills and abilities beyond those they could fully utilize in the narrow range of job and task opportunities available to them. In fact, at each occupational status level, those men who aspired to higher occupational status more frequently expressed the more highly developed forms of work role orientation or satisfaction than those whose aspirations were maintained at the same level as or lower than their achievements (Appendix table 7.7). Thus, it seems likely that the aspirations of these men were generated by desires for expanded opportunities for satisfaction at work. Different levels of work role orientation appear to reflect a readiness to perform at a given occupational level. For a number of working-class people, strivings for wider possibilities of meaning in work, rather than desires for status or higher incomes, are the major sources of aspirations for occupational mobility.

The problem of working-class men, in this view, is hardly one of insufficient motivation but, rather, of suppressing aspirations for satisfaction in work and of learning to find gratification where it is possible. Extremes of mental or emotional difficulty, of course, make incursions on work orientations and job functioning, although lack of gratification in work and the persistent frustration of occupational aspirations and desires may produce or exacerbate emotional problems. Thus, men with poor mental health were less occupationally mobile, had lower levels of occupational or social aspirations, and more rarely experienced highly developed forms of work satisfaction. These associations cannot be generalized to the average working man for whom differences in personality had minimal consequences for work behavior and orientations. However, some men maintain a struggle to find meaning in work through whatever task they do and despite limited potentialities for occupational mobility. Other men in the working class resign themselves more readily to the failure of working-class jobs that offer little challenge or opportunity for satisfaction. They work only so that they may live and support their families, hoping to find gratification and meaning through other channels and in other social roles which they can more readily define and control.

Working-class Women at Work

During the past few decades, accelerating a long-term trend, there has been a dramatic increase in the proportion of women in the labor force (Bancroft, 1958; Perella, 1968). For a number of reasons this has had far less effect on improving the economic situation of working-class people than of people in somewhat higher status positions. Most working-class wives have few credentials for decent jobs and, in the past, were often discouraged from getting an education. The difficulty of arranging for baby-sitters, the meager range of interesting jobs available at low status levels, and cultural orientations among many white ethnic working-class groups that have traditionally opposed employment for women also limit the number of working-class women in the labor market. As a consequence, the highest rates of employment among women in the United States occur for those of higher education and those whose family incomes are in the middle range. A large part of the change in the distribution of real incomes of middle-income families is a result, not of higher job incomes, but of the contribution of women wage-earners as secondary breadwinners in the household. Concomitant with the widening role of women in the work force, the causes and consequences of employment among women have attracted greater attention.[20] But relatively little of this concern has been directed to the employment, job opportunities, occupational experiences, or resistances to work among working-class wives.

Unlike women in middle and higher status positions, the major inducements to work among women in the West End were in the nature of compelling necessity rather than of voluntary preferences. The most powerful influences, thus, on the employment status of these women were their needs to support themselves because they were single, widowed, divorced, or separated or because their husbands' earnings were insufficient to support the household. Less than half (32 percent) of the married women worked at all, while 55 percent of the women who were widowed, separated, or divorced and the great majority of the single women (86 percent) were employed part time or full time. In fact, while most of the women without husbands in the household worked full time, those married women who worked were as often employed on a part-time basis as full time. Moreover, 37 percent of the wives of unemployed men worked full time, compared to only 20 percent of those whose husbands had very low incomes and 16 percent of the women whose husbands earned modest wages of $75.00 a week or more. When we consider simultaneously differences in marital status and the husbands' earnings among those women with husbands in the household, the full impact of these realistic pressures to work becomes quite evident (Appendix table 7.8).[21]

During the earlier years of marriage in working-class families young children in the household increase the drain on low incomes but, at the same time, the presence of children is one of the major deterrents to employment among women. Thus, there was a constant gradient with only 8 percent of the women who had a child six years old or younger being employed full time to 40 percent of the women with no child under eighteen in full-time employment. The number of children in the household was an almost equally potent factor. However, the biggest difference was between those women who had no children in the household and those who had only one child at home. Beyond that, larger numbers of children reduced the frequency of employment among women to only a modest degree.

Although a woman's marital status and her husband's employment status were among the most important pressures to work and, in turn, the number and ages of children in the household were among the most significant barriers to employment, several other considerations entered to determine the likelihood of employment among these predominantly working-class women. For those women who had a choice or for whom other factors militated against employment, health status made a significant difference. Among young women in particular and among women who had husbands in the household, those in poor health were far less often employed than were women in good health. On the other hand, with increasing age and for women who were without husbands in the household, even poor health did not markedly distinguish a woman's labor force status. With sufficient pressure from such realities as the need to support oneself or to help support the household and without the added restraint of young children who required maternal attention, most working-class women worked at least part time even if they were in the poorest health.

Among men, differences in education and occupational status affect their employment opportunities, but men have to work if they can possibly find a job. For women, however, better job opportunities linked to higher status are bound to influence the motivation to work. Most of the women in the West End, as we have already indicated, had attained only relatively modest educational levels and had few occupational skills. As with the West End men, the forces leading to intergenerational stability of status were considerable. Most of the women came from lower social class origins which led to low levels of education and further entailed the development of few occupational skills.[22] In view of the almost uniformly low levels of occupation among the women, it is not surprising that education was a more significant inducement to employment than were occupational skills. Most of the women who had gone to college were employed (80 percent), while only half of the women with grade school educations worked. More than that, however, the level of education a woman had attained strongly influenced the conditions that led to employment. Women who had some college education were most often employed regardless of their husbands' employment status or income, while women who had only been to high school were far more likely to be employed if they had to work because of financial necessity (table 7.1). Interestingly enough, at the very lowest level of education, differences in the employment or income of the husband also made little difference in the wife's working, although, more frequently than not, these women were not employed. This was largely due to the fact that, beyond the greater difficulty they had in obtaining jobs, the women with eight grades of schooling or less were mainly older women, often of foreign birth, who had little conception of or motivation toward work outside the home. However, just as financial necessity was generally a more powerful influence on the wife's decision to work at lower than at higher educational levels, so the presence of young children was a greater deterrent among women with less education. Whether education was itself an incentive to work or whether it simply provided greater freedom of choice in jobs, it was certainly one of the important influences on employment decisions among women. In fact, higher education often overrode other considerations in affecting the decision to work.

None of the personality factors that might suggest heightened motivation to work, even those involving determination and efficacy, had any differential consequences for the employment status of women in the West End. In a subtler way several personal factors did seem to lead to differences in employment. Thus, among women with children, those who were more child-oriented, who showed greater concern about their children and about the wishes and needs of their children, were less likely to be employed than were the women who viewed their children in a more perfunctory way. Certainly few women sought paid employment as an escape from housework. The majority of working-class women enjoyed their housework either because of the intrinsic satisfactions they found in the role or because they had what sometimes amounted to a passion for cleanliness. Most of the women with more education also enjoyed their housework. But women with less education were rarely ambivalent or unambivalently negative about household activities, while 30 percent of the women who had gone to college were quite willing to relinquish this role. However, the greater frequency of paid employment among women who did not like housework was largely accounted for by the fact that they had more often gone further in school and satisfaction or dissatisfaction with housework itself had relatively little independent consequence for the decision to work.

TABLE 7.1 Wife's education and husband's income or employment status by wife's employment status (in percentages)

Wife's education	Husband's earnings or employment status	Wife's employment status		N[a]	Percent
		In labor force	Not in labor force		
Some college or beyond	$75 per week or more	63	17	16	100
	$75 per week or less	(71)	(29)	7	100
	Unemployed	(67)	(33)	6	100
High school graduate	$75 per week or more	24	76	29	100
	$75 per week or less	62	38	24	100
	Unemployed	70	30	10	100
9–11 grades completed	$75 per week or more	22	78	50	100
	$75 per week or less	42	58	50	100
	Unemployed	57	43	14	100
0–8 grades completed	$75 per week or more	40	60	30	100
	$75 per week or less	46	54	66	100
	Unemployed	38	62	29	100

[a]There are 3 uncodeable cases

In evaluating the meaning of work for women, and for working-class women particularly, it is essential to distinguish between the reasons for working and the satisfactions that a woman may derive from being employed. The majority of the women (79 percent) claimed that financial need or, at least, the greater financial freedom that earning a living gave them was the major reason for their employment. Moreover, the very large proportion of women who worked mainly for economic support of the household is fairly typical for other populations (Hoffman, 1963; Sobol, 1963). But a subjective sense that one is working for financial reasons may have quite different meaning for different women. In fact, there was no relationship between the expression of financial motivations and objective differences in financial need. Women whose husbands earned fairly decent wages as often gave financial reasons as did those whose husbands earned less or were unemployed or those, for that matter, who had no husband in the household. On the other hand, women who had more education less frequently saw their employment as a function of financial pressure: only 67 percent of the women who had gone to college gave such reasons, while 84 percent of the women with grade school educations offered financial explanations for their employment.

Regardless of the initial impetus to work, some women may find greater satisfaction in their paid employment than they had anticipated. The variations in experience and orientation are evident from their responses when asked about the personal satisfactions they experienced in work:

I enjoy the feeling of helping others and seeing people grow. (social worker)
I enjoy working, training and watching the students get along, being able to help them. (clerical work instructor)
I like to do the things I do at work. (seamstress)
I like to do my work and to produce and to get money. (stitcher)
Accomplishing something and earning money besides, putting money away for the future. (billing clerk)
Makes you feel better to get out and work. You need another interest outside the home. You need a change. (domestic)
The satisfaction that you always have a dollar in your pocket. If you see anything and want it, you can buy it. I'm not rich but I'm never broke. (saleslady)
It keeps me busy and keeps my mind occupied. (counter girl)
I know I can buy more gifts. Also I'm away from all of them [the children] so I'm more relaxed. (factory worker)
To help the family finances. I know I'm sharing the load. (waitress)

A large proportion of the women found a variety of meaningful experiences in work beyond mere financial resources and beyond the opportunity to purchase luxuries. Often they felt that the sense of personal esteem, of well-being, or of task pleasure were important aspects of their work lives. Certainly women who were motivated to work primarily for financial reasons less often experienced these broader satisfactions, but many of them found that the work experience offered them some personal satisfaction. The most striking differentiating factors between those women who found only minimal or extrinsic forms of satisfaction in work and those who found more personal or intrinsic satisfactions in their experience of employment were, as for the men, their levels of education and occupation. Regardless of other factors, women who were in higher occupational positions or who had achieved higher levels of education more often found major sources of satisfaction in the work experience itself.

The work situation is quite evidently more complex for women than for men. While many of the same factors of social class position influence the work experiences of men and women, working women must more often weave their way through pressures and counterpressures from spouse, children, and expectations in other social roles. As a consequence, a great many women felt that it complicated their lives or caused difficulties for them. On the other hand, work roles often provide important compensations for women whose marital experiences do not include companionship or other forms of gratifying social interaction with their husbands or children. But whether employment serves to complicate a woman's life or not, whether she finds satisfaction in work only in the absence of such complications or in spite of them, and whether she takes pleasure in work in addition to gratifying relationships with her husband and children or only when she experiences frustration in other social roles is largely a product of differences in social class position and, at least implicitly, in the available opportunities for meaningful work. Women in the West End who had gone to college, thus, found major satisfactions in work whether they found that employment complicated their lives or not, while women with less education could experience such work satisfactions only if they were free of other burdens due to being employed.

The conditions for employment among women, and among working-class women particularly, vary considerably from those that obtain for men. The experiences women have on the job and as a consequence of their working are somewhat dissimilar from those of men in similar status positions. But many generalizations about the effect of social class on employment and on work experiences cut across sex differences. Working-class women more often seek employment under conditions of overt necessity than do women of higher status. Whether this reflects a difference in orientation or a difference in opportunity is not entirely clear, but it is

quite clear that those women with more education or with higher occupational skills find greater and more intrinsic satisfactions in work than do
women of lower status positions, and these differences in satisfaction, as
among men, fit quite reasonably with the freedom and challenge available
in jobs at different occupational levels. As part of the cumulative understanding of the pervasive effects of social class status on role opportunities
and role expectations in our society, the influence of social position on
the occupational situations and experiences of women add yet another
dimension. Clearly these differences in social class position invade almost
every sphere of human activity and influence the conditions, potentials,
and consequences of social functioning far removed from income differences alone and, in many fundamental respects, affect men and women
alike.

8 Sources of Working-class Attitudes and Values

Attitudes and Ethnic Communities

Attitudes have long been defined as evaluative predispositions to act (Allport, 1935; Rokeach, 1968; McGuire, 1968). Certainly the attitudes and values that people hold are singularly important in understanding their images of the society in which they live and of their own place within that society. In recent years, attitudes have gained renewed attention because they appear to be centrally aligned with vital social and political issues in industrial countries. Yet the behavioral consequences of attitudes are largely obscure, although the evidence indicates that attitudes and behaviors are often inconsistent with one another (Wicker, 1969).

The views of people in positions of economic or political power have never been systematically studied. More general investigations of different social classes have led to quite contradictory interpretations about the effects of social status on attitudes. Those in higher status positions have sometimes been seen as the bulwark of democracy because their voting behavior clearly reveals their ability to override self-interest, but, conversely, they have also been seen as the most cohesively self-interested parties in economic and political behavior.[1] Blue-collar workers have been described as fundamentally authoritarian, at least in their political propensities, and supportive evidence has been found in pockets of working-class votes for extreme right-wing political figures and in verbal or physical attacks by blue-collar workers on antiwar demonstrators, students, and ethnic minorities like blacks and Puerto Ricans. By contrast, the authoritarianism of blue-collar workers has been seen as a misinterpretation of the data and of workers.[2] The working class as a social and political entity has also been viewed as a dying force in the midst of the transformation of

177

workers into a new middle class, but this view has also been vehemently criticized and reinterpreted on the basis of additional findings.[3]

Ethnic attitudes have gained greater prominence in the last few decades in numerous highly industrialized and developing countries because of evidence of an expanding number of submerged minorities. The United States has been a major immigrant-receiving country since colonial days and has seen the influx of vast numbers of foreign ethnic groups who often formed distinctive minority populations. Advances in industrialization, as well as political transformations and the contrast between the wealth of the technological societies and the poverty of underdeveloped nations, has led, in more recent years, to migratory patterns into many European and Asiatic countries that have never before known or had only minimally perceived the existence of minority groups. Even in the United States, the existence, persistence, and disadvantages of ethnic minorities have reached a new level of visibility and concentrated interest. The economic potentialities of greater equality of opportunity have led to wider awareness of the political and social constraints that limit more egalitarian arrangements. Although Myrdal (1944) documented the underprivileged situation of the Negro in America almost three decades ago, these facts have been further revealed time and again in studies of discrimination and prejudice and similar investigations have extended the perception of ethnic inequalities to Puerto Ricans and Mexican-Americans as well.[4] Minority groups themselves have begun, increasingly, to clarify the underlying conflicts of interest by overt actions, often violent, that have produced a new wave of concern about widening the scope of opportunities. Partly out of discouragement with efforts at social absorption, the increased cohesiveness of the new urban minorities has shifted attention from assimilation and integration to involvement of people with their own ethnic groups. Indeed, many of the older ethnic groups that have remained targets of subtle prejudice despite educational and occupational achievements have shown renewed interest in establishing a degree of solidarity they have never been accorded by the majority group.

Issues of ethnic involvement and solidarity, on the one hand, and of prejudice and discrimination, on the other, have generally been closely linked in both evident and covert ways to social class discriminations. Americans, in their rejection of the facts of social class in our society, have displaced much of their underlying awareness and feelings about social differentiation onto ethnicity and minority group status. The ethnic groups themselves have generally fallen into compliance with this conception, even when it has produced or exacerbated divisions among working-class populations and has prevented their concerted efforts to achieve common goals. Discrimination and prejudice mean that people who belong to a given minority will be treated as members of that minority and stereotypically accorded the modal social status of that minority even when they have achieved far higher educational or occupational advantages. This must certainly be one of the important pressures behind the striving for cohesiveness among ethnic groups. Those minority group members who deviate from the modal statuses of the ethnic population are inevitably in an anomalous position. They have often had to develop personality characteristics, attitudes, and role conceptions that sharply demarcate them from dominant ethnic norms. Yet they must inevitably recognize their ethnic origins, commitments, and interests if only by virtue of the fact that our society has defined them in this way.

Ethnic involvement and ethnic intolerance are only two among many aspects of cohesiveness and exclusiveness in ethnic communities. Another frequent feature of cohesiveness in ethnic communities lies in a common religious orientation. A very large proportion of the ethnic minorities in the United States during previous decades were Roman Catholics. Subsequently, with the immigration of many Jews and, more recently, with the expansion of black communities that are predominantly Protestant, greater diversity developed in the religious composition of ethnic communities. Often, religious homogeneity was more apparent than real in view of conflicts between different strains of Catholicism, as among the Irish and Italians. However, because of the high correlation between religion and ethnic origin, it is difficult to distinguish the separate contribution of each factor to attitudes and behavior. In seeking some independence from this overlap, we shall consider the role of religious commitment as one expression of religious attitudes.

Beyond this, there are many attitudes concerning social class, politics, the economic system, work, and family life that may be influenced by social class position or ethnic or religious origins.[5] Most ethnic communities are residential areas for people at lower levels of the social class structure. Many class attitudes, including both self-concepts about social class and more general orientations about political and economic affairs associated with class position, are developed and confirmed within the residential community. In these particularly we may expect to find indications of common social influences, whether derived from class position or ethnic or religious orientation, that give greater homogeneity to beliefs of people living in ethnic slum areas.

Ethnic Involvement, Religious Commitment, and Ethnocentricity

The single most important force in maintaining a sense of continuing ethnic identity among American ethnic groups has been the existence of ethnic neighborhoods or communities. The significance of ethnic, residential communities as the core of ethnic awareness has a double focus: their existence has revealed the high degree of segregation by the majority population; and the propinquity induced by common residence has encouraged many opportunities for sustaining or even creating a vigorous sense of a common cultural heritage. Further support for the continuity in ethnic beliefs, practices, and commitments was provided by ethnic clubs and organizations that often cut across neighborhoods and by the large number of foreign language newspapers that once filled the local newsstands (Lopata, 1964; Park, 1922; Janowitz, 1967).

Historically, ethnic and kinship involvement were of major importance in introducing immigrants into a neighborhood and helping to overcome initial obstacles in a new land. Once elementary relationships were developed in the new area, as we have suggested, these relationships and informal networks became the core of a self-perpetuating system. Among people in the West End, cultural commitments to ethnic cooking, observance of ethnic holidays, and foreign language usage were considerably more widespread than interpresonal relationships based on common ethnic origin. Slightly more than a third of the women were of foreign birth, but most of them (72 percent) could speak the foreign language of their ancestry. The knowledge of the foreign language of origin was a major sign of identification with the ethnic group since it was more highly correlated with other manifestations of ethnic continuity than any of the other ethnic behaviors were among each other. However, many women often cooked their own ethnic foods and ethnic dishes and maintained some modicum of ethnic continuity in this fashion.

We have already observed the distribution of ethnic groups in the West End, dominated by Italians but with large proportions of Poles and Jews and a substantial number of many other ethnic groups. The relationship between an individual's own ethnic background and the size of the same ethnic population living in the neighborhood has been described as the level of ethnic embeddedness. Clearly enough the ethnic embeddedness of individuals was a significant determinant of the degree of their ethnic involvement. If we use a composite index of ethnic involvement, including diverse expressions of cultural commitments to their own ethnic groups, we find that a large number of the people in highly embedded ethnic groups (40 percent) had a very high level of ethnic involvement, while those who were ethnically isolated rarely (7 percent) manifested such ethnic involvement. However, even the highest rates among the embedded ethnic groups are low enough to challenge the view that ethnic involvement is the norm in different working-class, ethnic areas.

The idea of the United States as a melting pot was clearly a fantasy and, in any case, as Glazer and Moynihan (1963) have indicated, we have moved beyond the melting pot. However, there is little doubt that part-cultures, like ethnic communities in a larger society, are constantly eroded by residential and cultural assimilation. The acquisition of status characteristics like higher levels of education and of occupation particularly lead to a slow attrition of ethnic commitments. These and increasing distance from foreign origins, which we refer to as assimilation status, are bound to produce an increased desire to free oneself from the traditional modes of thought and belief that are ordinarily, although not necessarily, associated with various forms of ethnic commitment and practice. It is hardly surprising, therefore, that objective assimilation status had the most powerful effect on levels of ethnic involvement for people in the West End.[6] Of those women who were of native birth and had at least one native-born parent, very few (7 percent) were highly involved with ethnic traditions, while among the women with two foreign-born parents 24 percent showed a high degree of ethnic involvement. Even among the women of foreign birth, the frequency of high levels of ethnic involvement (42 percent) was considerably lower than one might have anticipated. The shift from the immigrant generation to their children was marked. As one young man put this change:

We were brought up to feel that we were Italian in the home . . . When I was young, the only people I knew were Italian, but when I started hanging together with other kids my age, they were from all groups. I learned to judge people according to who they are as a person. The older people divide people up according to their nationality. I don't believe nationality makes any difference. Years ago, I remember people would sit down and play cards. They would all be one nationality. Now we sit down and we're all mixed up. We're all Americans anyway.

Whether we conceive of ethnic involvement as cultural transmission, as an

aspect of reference group identifications, as the acceptance of traditionalism, or as an aspect of low status that entails clinging to a known and
supportive framework, the influence of assimilation status on the retention
of ethnic life styles is almost self-evident. It may be that all of these factors
play some part in ethnic involvement. More empirically, it is quite clear
that education, particularly for those who went as far as the completion
of high school, modifies the strength of involvement with ethnicity (Appendix table 8.1). Even among the foreign born, 46 percent of the women
who had not completed high school were committed to ethnic ways,
while only 18 percent of those who had completed high school continued
to adhere to ethnic patterns. This is a remarkably low proportion and, in
fact, exaggerates somewhat the picture of ethnic nonconformity. But even
if we distinguish the earlier immigrants and those who came after World
War II when many of these same countries had developed more widespread
educational systems and more pervasive urban influences, only 29 percent
of the earlier immigrants with at least a high school education and none of
the more recent immigrants showed high levels of ethnic involvement.[7]
Occupation, which has some of the same significance for introducing ideas
and options that can serve to modify traditional commitments, had similar
but weaker effects.

The West End was a multiethnic community in which ethnic characteristics were entirely accepted. The levels of ethnic involvement were almost
certainly higher than we are likely to find even among the foreign born and
their children in less homogeneous settings. Indeed, it is likely that the
ethnic character of the neighborhood attracted some people to the area
and held sway over the continued residence of others who retained many
ethnic commitments. Several factors indicate, not merely the influence of
general attributes of traditionalism on ethnic involvement, but the effects
of interpersonal ties that might help to sustain these orientations. We have
already observed the influence of assimilation status and of education on
ethnic involvement. Similarly, the people who belonged to the dominant
ethnic groups were most often involved with ethnic commitments. In
addition, people who came from higher status origins were less likely to
have extensive ethnic involvements than those whose parents were of lower
social class status. Other aspects of status or position were either irrelevant
to ethnic involvement or quite inconsistent in their relationships.

However, close neighbor relationships, the availability of local kin,
frequent interaction with family members, and more embracing closeknit
network ties were all quite strongly and quite consistently linked to a high
degree of ethnic involvement (Appendix table 8.2). Moreover, such involve-

ment with ethnic issues and traditions was primarily affected by interpersonal relationships in the local area rather than by more general forms of localism. Thus, the extensive use of local resources and narrowly localized familiarity with the urban area did not facilitate higher levels of ethnic involvement. Only the objective, cosmopolitan influences of education and assimilation status made a difference to ethnic involvement, and wider familiarity with the city, extensive use of a car, the availability of a telephone, or a higher standard of living did not lead to any marked reduction in the traditional orientation implicit in ethnic involvement. Some further clarification is offered by the fact that the personality attribute with the most consistent influence on ethnic involvement was ego efficacy. At all social class levels, women who were less efficacious were more likely to show a high degree of ethnic involvement. While less consistent, women who were more dependent or more conformist were also more likely to be ethnically involved. This constellation of personal influences on ethnic involvement implies that one function of such involvement was to provide a secure and familiar framework for those who were less capable of independent action and mastery.

There are many theories about the sources of cultural commitments. While these results do not permit any systematic test of alternative hypotheses, they do reveal some of the complex of issues involved and lend some weight to the importance of reference group influences in maintaining minority group cultural orientations.[8] Certainly the most potent dynamic influences on ethnic involvement in the West End were the concrete forms of reference group associations, the social affiliations people maintained with neighbors and kin in the local area. It is important to observe that availability or close interaction with kin were hardly more important in this regard than close neighbor relationships. In effect, while living in a community with people from the same ethnic background provided a basis for continuing commitments to ethnic ways of life, the main direct influences on ethnic involvement were relationships with close people in the local area who held similar ethnic orientations. At all levels of education and assimilation status, more extensive contact with kin and neighbors led to a higher degree of ethnic involvement. On the other hand, people with little education and those who were relatively unassimilated were more often ethnically involved regardless of social affiliations. Thus, the narrower horizons of people who had less education or were less assimilated established an ethnic framework regardless of the further encouragement of close persons from similar ethnic origins. Finally, the importance of personal qualities of dependency and conformity indicate that the potency of social relationships as determinants of ethnic involvement rested, in part, upon individual needs for security that can often be found in the stable and traditional orientations of ethnic minorities.

Without attempting to extricate all the different attitudinal concomitants and behavioral sequelae of ethnic involvement, a few important relationships are worthy of note. Although attitudes have been widely studied, the behavioral consequences of attitudes, as we commented earlier, are relatively little known. The evidence suggests that attitudes are more highly interrelated among themselves than they are with corresponding behaviors (Wicker, 1969). Often, however, the assumption is implicit in research that people will behave similarly if they hold similar attitudes, irrespective of differences in class, personality, or the conditions in which the behavior occurs. Even if we consider only class differences in the interrelationship among attitudes or in the effects of attitudes on behaviors, it is evident that the significance of attitudes varies for people according to their social class positions (Appendix table 8.2). Ethnic involvement was related to ethnocentricity and to the rejection of planning for the future, but far more so for people of lower than of higher status. Similarly, people who were more highly involved with ethnic traditions were more alienated from the society at large, more conformist, and more authoritarian in their conceptions of child-rearing, but these relationships were more powerful among people in higher than in lower social class positions. As we have already seen in numerous forms of social behavior, the different patterns associated with ethnic involvement for people in different social class positions are themselves among the most important phenomena concerning social attitudes.

Another indication of the acceptance of traditional orientations can be found in religious commitments.[9] Religious affiliation itself was only modestly related to social status and other social influences or to a wide range of possible consequences. A more dynamic manifestation of religious orientations, the religious commitments people maintained, was similar but stronger than religious affiliation in its associations. Social class position itself was quite clearly linked to differences in religious commitment. People of higher status less often held deep religious commitments. However, religious and ethnic commitments among people in the West End were so closely tied to one another that most of the same determinants and consequences were evident. Similar forms of local social affiliations with neighbors and kin facilitated religious commitments, although these were weaker and less consistent than with ethnic involvement. Thus, not only did a high degree of ethnic involvement and religious commitment coexist for the same people, but they served similar functions.[10]

Ethnic involvement among minority groups has only rarely been studied, despite its evident importance in understanding the adaptation of minorities to an alien society. Ethnic and racial prejudices, ethnocentricity, and various forms of discrimination and stereotypes, on the other hand, are classical problems in social psychology.[11] The degree of involvement people have with ethnic (or class or regional) collectivities influences the ease of developing negative stereotypes, prejudicial attitudes, and discriminatory behavior toward groups that are defined as out-groups. But common identities can expand or contract. The definition of a compatriot, a paesano, or a lanzman becomes more inclusive when we move from familiar surroundings to those in which people who are otherwise dissimilar share some common feature of origin, background, or interest. In the West End, as in many other ethnic communities, once the aftermath of immigration and initial adjustments were past, other "ethnics" frequently were seen as almost Italian or almost Polish or almost Jewish if they were residents of the same neighborhood.

Ethnocentricity is closely related empirically to ethnic involvement.[12] But the two are not, by any means, indistinguishable from one another in their subjective significance, their determinants, or their correlates and consequences. It is difficult to determine if the West End was very different from other ethnic working-class communities in the high degree of tolerance, even of determined inclusiveness, of people from diverse ethnic backgrounds.[13] Many people took great pride in its very heterogeneity. There were, moreover, clear historical roots for ethnic tolerance in the political organization of Martin Lomasny, a local political leader of the early twentieth century who fostered the absorption of Italians, Poles, and Jews into a neighborhood that had previously been predominantly Irish.

With the exception of moderately widespread but relatively subdued resistance to Negroes in the West End, most people rejected the idea that ethnic background might or should influence acceptance into the neighborhood. The vast majority (70 percent) insisted that they were entirely impartial toward differences in national origin or positively disposed toward ethnic heterogeneity. Even if we make estimates about prejudicial attitudes on the basis of statements about the people who were welcome in the West End and the attributes that would lead to acceptance or rejection, we find that almost half (49 percent) were either entirely inclusive or recognized only deviant familial or individual qualities as a basis for intolerance. Only a minority (20 percent) made statements that were quite clear in their explicit or implicit manifestations of ethnic, racial, or class prejudices.

These indications of an extremely low level of ethnic intolerance necessarily raise questions about the conditions in which working-class people do or do not show evidence of racial and ethnic prejudice. Anti-Negro prejudice appears to be quite high among blue-collar workers, but class comparisons in a variety of situations are not available. Stember (1961) points out that verbalized attitudes of low status people are often more discriminatory than those of people in higher status positions, while people of higher social class status are less accepting of any close involvement with minorities. There is also widespread, if mainly informal, evidence to indicate that ethnic prejudice among working-class people becomes prominent mainly in situations of stress or clear, economic threat.[14] But the results from the West End must also be seen in light of the long experience of living in an ethnically heterogeneous community for much of the population. In this sense, they imply a conclusion similar to the findings in the studies of racial prejudice during World War II (Stouffer et al., 1949). When joint experiences or common identities are superimposed on a prior sense of difference and discordance, there is a sharp diminution in ethnocentricity. The daily experience of living near people from different ethnic backgrounds, of meeting and interacting with them, of finding that anxieties diminish in the face of realistic opportunities for testing them, may have been a major factor in the ethnic tolerance or even the ethnospansive orientations of many West Enders.

As with ethnic involvement, education and assimilation status were the most powerful influences on ethnocentric or ethnospansive attitudes, although education was the more potent of the two (Appendix table 8.3). Other features of status and of socioeconomic position affected ethnocentricity even more strongly than they affected ethnic involvement. Low-status origins, rural background, low incomes, downward mobility, low occupational status, and unemployment were all conducive to ethnocentricity. However, their effects varied occasionally depending on other aspects of an individual's status. Thus, in high status families where the husband was unemployed, ethnocentricity was low; while in low or moderate status families where the husband was unemployed, ethnocentricity was high. While the evidence is not entirely clear, situations that made an individual's status or identity precarious or ambiguous seemed to evoke higher levels of ethnocentricity. In similar fashion, people with discrepancies in ethnic status, evidenced by those assimilated women who belonged to moderately embedded ethnic groups in the West End, had among the highest rates of ethnocentricity.

Unlike ethnic involvement or religious commitment, few other factors accounted for variations in ethnic prejudice. Neither associations with neighbors or kin nor a high degree of localism had any consistent influence on ethnocentricity. While this might suggest the importance of more highly personal qualities as determinants of ethnocentricity, there were no consistent differences in personality that were linked to different levels of ethnocentricity. There were, however, a few modest suggestions that support the view that differences in the feelings people had about their own status or identity influenced ethnocentric attitudes. Among women of moderately high status, localism, extensive relationships with kin or neighbors, even the restriction implied in failure to work outside the home were all associated with a high degree of ethnocentricity. Among those of low status, these indications of embeddedness in the community either made no difference or were linked to a high degree of ethnospansiveness. While we can only estimate the significance of these different patterns, it seems reasonable that for people in lower status positions, these forms of local integration represented a meaningful basis for identity and provided a source of stable status. Conversely, for women of higher status, these commitments were themselves reflections of a status discrepancy or of insecurity in accepting residential and social relationships that accorded more closely with the norms of their social positions. Indeed, people who were low on mastery, especially among those of relatively high status for whom a high degree of such mastery was more frequent, were also more ethnocentric in their attitudes. To this degree, the class variation in the factors that influenced ethnocentricity lends further support to the view that ethnic prejudice and exclusiveness are either produced or exacerbated by status insecurities or by a sense of uncertain identity.

There is a strong association between ethnocentric or ethnospansive attitudes of husbands and wives. Moreover the patterns of influence on ethnocentricity among the men of the West End are much the same as those for women. Neither among the women nor among the men were ethnocentric attitudes integral components of a larger orientation or value framework, but were dissociated from other attitudes that might appear similar (Appendix tables 8.4, 8.5). On the other hand, while the links between ethnocentricity and other attitudes were generally weak and only slightly stronger among high than among low status people, the significance of ethnocentricity for people in different status positions seemed to vary considerably. While these are only fragments of total attitudinal sets, it seems quite evident that ethnocentricity had different specific meanings for people in different status positions. There may, of course, be a deeper similarity in the underlying significance of these attitudes, as we have suggested in hypothesizing amibguous identity or status insecurity as determinants of ethnocentricity. The different discrete patterns of attitude among people in different social class statuses, however, are equally important manifestations of social class differentiation in our society.

The data on ethnic involvement, ethnocentricity, and religious commitment do not provide a comprehensive understanding of these important social attitudes but do present several important guides. Despite the fact that the West End was, in a most typical sense, a multiethnic, working-class community, neither the levels of ethnic involvement nor of ethnocentricity were strikingly high. Religious commitments were more frequent, particularly for Roman Catholics. Certainly it has been clear that educative and cosmopolitan influences reduced the levels of ethnic involvement, of religious commitment, and of ethnocentricity. Interacting with such educative influences on ethnic involvement, close interpersonal relationships in the local community, superimposed on personal qualities of dependency, sustained higher degrees of traditional ethnic attitudes and behavior. Nonetheless, the relatively rapid decline in importance of ethnic involvement with opportunities for a wider world view indicate that failures to absorb the immigrant must be seen largely as functions of societal rejection rather than of cultural inertia among the foreign born or their children. Similar forces affected ethnocentricity but to a smaller extent. Indeed, the few patterns revealed by ethnocentric attitudes in the West End provide support for hypotheses that have frequently been used in explaining prejudice and discrimination. Ambiguity of status and identity conflicts, stimulating anxiety in relation to people who are manifestly different, seem to be important motivating factors in ethnocentricity. These are not ideologically embedded issues but seem, rather, to be discrete and specific displacements of internal threat to external objects. As a consequence, extensive contacts with people from different ethnic origins that provide a basis for a more inclusive identity as neighbors or as working-class people with others from different ethnic backgrounds are likely to diminish the sense of ethnic exclusiveness.

Class, Class Consciousness, and Political Orientations

The attitudes of people in different social classes toward the class structure itself, to their own position within that structure, and to power and politics have been of recurrent interest. Ever since World War II, higher wages among working men and the victory of labor unions in obtaining bargaining rights for most blue-collar workers have led to a conviction that the working class, if it ever was a class in the United States, had disappeared. Added to this, the enormous increase in secondary workers and the rising standard of living that made available a wide array of consumer goods never before within the reach of workers seemed to spell the doom of an attenuated form of working-class solidarity.

The kind of working-class solidarity that Marx envisioned and which many observers have in mind in discussing the working class was largely a projection of revolutionary imagination. Marx and Engels spoke of working-class consciousness or self-consciousness as a necessary precondition of revolution. But they found such consciousness only in past conditions that did not lend themselves to careful, empirical analysis. More often than not, they located conditions that prevented the emergence of class consciousness in the contemporary situations they examined and never found it to exist as an effective force. Nor is it surprising that the extreme conditions Marx and Engels set for the definition of class consciousness are rarely met in reality. By the very nature of their life situations, limited education, traditional social affiliations, a sense of a compartmentalized world on the job and in society, blue-collar workers are bound to function within relatively limited horizons. Their work conditions within a specific organization are more likely to be in the center of their attention than the common situation of workers or of people in similar occupational statuses. Certainly the very ambiguity of the forces impinging on workers means that whether they conceive of themselves as members of the working class or middle class and whether increased affluence has altered self-conceptions or party loyalties, they are likely to hold a wide range of political and social views.

Using a different conception of class consciousness, these diversities may be merely variations superimposed on a basic identity with other people in similar social positions. In fact, despite the repetitive view that workers tend to think of themselves as middle class, the evidence is quite consistent that most people in lower social class positions conceive of themselves as working class.[15] Certainly most men and women in the West End considered themselves working class and conceived of the West End as a working-class neighborhood (table 8.1). The fact that working-class populations define themselves as working class does not, of course, mean that they see themselves as part of a mass working-class "group" or even of a more amorphous collectivity. It does mean that they hold few illusions often attributed to working-class people that they had now entered the middle classes. And it does mean that they conceive their positions in the class structure as relatively inferior although, like most people who have

TABLE 8.1   Self-estimate of social class of West End: males and females

Self-estimate of West End social class	Males		Females	
	Percent	N	Percent	N
Upper	2	6	1	5
Middle	22	73	28	137
Working	65	210	58	290
Lower	11	37	13	64
Totals	100	326[a]	100	496[a]

Self-estimate of own social class: males and females

Self-estimate of own social class	Males		Females	
	Percent	N	Percent	N
Upper	1	4	2	9
Middle	32	106	37	181
Working	64	211	57	282
Lower	3	9	4	22
Totals	100	330[a]	100	494[a]

[a] These data are based on postrelocation information for which the male N = 334 and the female N = 503. The discrepancies in the totals are due to uncodeable responses.

achieved stability in their positions and life situations, they often maintain pride in their working-class identity and in many of the life-style patterns they see as its concomitants. Very few women or men in the West End, however, thought of themselves as lower class since this has connotations for many people of something more derogatory than merely low occupation, low education, or low income. At the other extreme, a moderately large minority defined themselves as middle class, a self-concept that was more frequent among women than men in the West End.

A number of different attributes influence the social class self-conceptions that people hold but none of these approximates the power of objective social class position as a determinant of subjective conceptions. There are, however, some revealing discrepancies. Among women, education was of greater significance than the occupation of the head of household as an influence on self-conceptions of social class. Among men, on the other hand, their own occupational status was more potent an influence on their subjective views of their class position than was education. More highly educated men and women made more realistic appraisals of their own social class positions. This greater clarity among people who see the class structure from its higher reaches is even more sharply evident when we take account of social class origins. People whose parents were in higher social class positions clearly perceived the subjective implications of their objective statuses and defined themselves accordingly, while the self-estimates of people who came from moderate or low social class positions were hardly differentiated according to objective criteria and reflected mainly low occupational self-definitions. (Appendix table 8.6). Even more significantly, parental status retained its power as a determinant of the self-conceptions even of those people who had achieved relatively high social class positions themselves. However, the ways in which people defined their social class status were not simply compromises between their origins and achievements since low status on either of these dimensions had a similar effect in reducing the self-perception of objective differentiations.

It is quite striking how frequently people saw the neighborhood in which they lived in light of their estimates of their own social class position. Both men and women most often identified the social class position of West Enders in general with what they viewed as their own statuses. When we consider differences in education as they affect perceptions of the class position of people in the West End, however, we again find that higher education led to more accurate perception of the social class structure. Those who had completed high school or had gone on to college more regularly recognized the fact that the West End was a working-class area regardless of their perceptions of their own status.

One of the confounding factors of social class perceptions and their analysis stems from the fact that many people are influenced in their ideas about their own positions by status implications other than those carried by education, occupation, or income. Thus, women who were highly assimilated, and by virtue of this held relatively high "cultural" status, tended to upgrade their self-conceptions if they were actually of low or moderate status by the criteria of education and occupation (Appendix table 8.7). Even women who were native born of foreign parents often disregarded objective differences of status. Among the women of foreign birth, however, those who were of lower status most often considered themselves to be working class while those of moderately high status generally defined themselves as middle class. A similar although less marked phenomenon occurs among the men. The wider social acceptance of highly assimilated people that obliterates objective differences in their own statuses also functions at the community level. Those people who had status within the community by virtue of belonging to dominant ethnic groups in the neighborhood ignored their objective class placement in their self-definitions, while those who belonged to relatively isolated and locally marginal ethnic groups were keenly aware of the status implications of their positions. Complexities of this nature, that cut across objective class divisions but do have implications for the prestige and status people feel in the society in which they live, inevitably modify the subjective sense of social class belonging. Acceptance and esteem, whether in local or national terms, redefine the self-conceptions people have of their placement within the social class structure.

Although people generally conceive of their own social class positions in accordance with composite realities, there are a number of paradoxical features about class self-consciousness among working-class people and perhaps for those in other classes as well. Most West Enders might recognize their own class positions with some degree of objectivity, but they were quite reluctant to talk about class or to think in class terms. They realized that there were differences in education among people and that these had implications for occupation and income. They were quite cognizant of the fact that these differences, moreover, could be considered as differences in social class position. However, they frequently removed the issue at least one step by viewing education rather than occupation as the crucial determinant of social class position in spite of the objective fact that their own occupational positions influenced their status self-conceptions more than did their educational attainments. Among the men, 42 percent felt that education was the most important criterion of social class position and a modest minority considered the number of friends one had as the factor of greatest relevance. Interestingly enough, most of the men rejected nationality as an influence on social class position. The relative importance of different criteria was almost identical among the women. Many men and women, of course, realized that occupational position made a difference in our society, but they viewed it as quite secondary to education. Differences in income necessarily forced themselves upon the attention of most people in the West End but they were more conscious of the fact that there were people who were worse off than they and disregarded the fact that they were in the lower quadrant of incomes in the nation as a whole. When they did become more self-consciously aware of income differences that defined different styles of life, they readily rejected other styles as undesirable. Indeed, more often than not, they felt that when people had more money and began to live differently they lost some of the most highly valued attributes in life like simplicity, humility, and easy, informal friendliness.

Subjective self-estimates of social class position were not generally or consistently associated with any constellation of interrelated attitudes. Thus, while it is occasionally possible to make inferences about more general and underlying ideological implications of self-concepts, manifest clusters of attitudes were rarely associated with self-estimates of social class. And, as we have frequently found, such relationships occurred more frequently among people of higher than among those of lower status. Indeed, objective social class position was more often associated with different attitudes than were subjective self-estimates of social class. However, while people in the West End were reluctant to think about class differences, they were often sensitive to these differences in specific situations. Asked about accepting a dinner invitation from a neighbor of higher status whom they did not know too well, a very large proportion (46 percent of both women and men) said they would reject the invitation. The ease of moving across such class lines varied quite strongly with objective status but minimally with subjective social class. Women in lower-status positions were most frequently opposed to accepting the invitation and low status men were only slightly less often intimidated by this discrepancy in social class positions between themselves and the hypothetical neighbor.

Class membership, we have implied, is more often seen as a way of life than as an indication of large-scale economic and social forces. This inevitably influences social mobility orientations which, as we have indicated, are generally muted and displaced toward their children. Even expressed through their children, desires for mobility were clear but involved few expectations that they would be realized and little pressure toward fulfillment. Mobility aspirations, interestingly enough, were much more strongly linked to objective social class position than to subjective self-estimates of status. For the men, desires for occupational or social mobility were more clearly related to dissatisfaction and desires for more global change than they were for women. Among the women in the West End, social mobility wishes involved primarily desires for greater economic freedom and especially for freedom from financial anxieties. Among the men, ambition was more often associated with more general dissatisfaction with their lives and situations. Regardless of social class position, men who wanted to change their lives in many ways often had strong desires for upward mobility. But men who wanted no changes or few changes in their lives infrequently expressed desires for social achievement (Appendix table 8.8). Even in a more limited sphere, men who were dissatisfied with their jobs more frequently had higher occupational aspirations than their actual achievements, while those who were relatively content in their job situations preferred remaining at their current occupational level.

A relatively narrow definition of class position, of mobility aspirations, of the many specific issues we have discussed runs through diverse attitudes among working-class people. As a consequence, although many working-class men and women are quite sensitive to political and economic issues in concrete and immediately meaningful ways, when the problem is quite broad and general in scope, they are readily inclined to accept characteristic American norms and values. Despite their inferior status and the objective fact of a high degree of intergenerational stability in social class position, the majority of people in the West End believed that America is a land of opportunity. Concretely, they often recognized that opportunities were not readily available to them, but the majority felt that ability is more important for success than luck, opportunity, or personal connections. As we have already indicated, despite the fact that the amount of education they achieved was largely a function of the social class positions of their parents and of situational pressures that often forced them to drop out of school, they saw education as the major channel to social class position and as an opportunity they had failed to take.

When political issues have a direct and visible bearing on situations of immediate concern to working-class people and, particularly, when there is some hope that something can be done to change the situation, working-class people become more conscious of some of the economic and political forces that shape their lives.[16] Many people in the West End exhibited a clear perception of the origins of the redevelopment decisions that governed their immediate experience and frequently tried to take action to halt or delay the process in spite of an underlying sense of their own powerlessness to control the situation. While a large proportion of the women felt uncertain about the ultimate decision-making responsibility for the redevelopment of the West End, and, indeed, they had been subjected to diverse views about this matter, many of them allocated the responsibility either to urban political forces or to the financiers and real estate interests who were planning to build on the vacated land. While virtually everyone said that the local residents would suffer most from the redevelopment, 44 percent gave it a more general ideological turn by stressing the fact of loss for working people or poor people in general. The major beneficiaries of redevelopment were less clearly perceived, although many people recognized the economic benefits to be gained by the investors. Perceptions of redevelopment were, or course markedly influenced by education, and people with more education had a more realistic appreciation of the structure of the situation. Less educated West End residents were more dependent on local sources of information. Those women who lived in the West End longest, those who used local resources most widely, and those who had extensive networks in the neighborhood were more fully aware of the factors involved in the redevelopment of the West End than those who were more peripheral residents.

In light of these considerations it is evident that specific views of working-class people can readily be distorted in meaning and significance if seen only in the light of middle-class ideologies. Attitudes of working-class people are less clearly related to an entire framework of values and are, in a sense, more immediately practical, although this means that they must make ad hoc decisions on the basis of underlying images and feelings about social and political process (Rainwater, 1969; Rodman, 1963). Thus, we must wonder whether value-laden terms like liberalism, conservatism, or authoritarianism really carry the same meaning or whether the implied attitudes carry the same investment and stability for working-class people that they often do for middle-class people.

The actual economic and political positions of different social classes are influenced by the sense of power or powerlessness that people have or feel they have in influencing political decisions. If we take as our criterion of this sense the general trust or mistrust toward public officials, political processes, and a feeling of declining fortunes for low status people, most men and women in the West End showed high levels of alienation.[17] These are high, of course, only in view of the extent to which a democracy ultimately rests upon legitimate and responsible political and social organization. On almost every specific issue, a little more than a third of the people adopted an anomic or alienated view of the political or world situation rising to a peak in the large number, almost half, who said that one couldn't be sure of whom one could count on these days. When we put these together into a composite alienation scale, we find that, as in many other instances of both attitudes and behavior, social class stands out as one of the most critical determinants of differences. Among the women differences in education were more potent than differences in occupation, while among the men the largest variations were associated with occupational status. Apart from status as such, experiences of disappointment, frustration, and lack of opportunity which encourage alienation and occur more often among low status people were, in fact, also associated with a more pervasive sense of alienation.

It is this sense of impotence, of defeat, and of the futility of efforts to change unsatisfying situations that is more distinctively characteristic of working-class people than any specific attitudes toward political and social events. Not only is this important in indicating the degree of involvement people are likely to have in making efforts to change their own immediate circumstances or more general social conditions, but it almost certainly influences the content of their attitudes as well. People who feel that they have little control over their own life situations, particularly when such views are reinforced by daily experience and daily observation, are likely to see issues in starkly realistic ways and to treat them on the basis of their most evident consequences rather than to appreciate the intricacies and interconnectedness between events. It is also likely that much of the evidence suggesting political authoritarianism among working-class people is based on the fact that, under conditions of stress, working-class support has often gone to demagogues who promise easy, rather than authoritarian, solutions. The attractiveness of ready-made solutions is intimately dependent on this general sense of low esteem and its expression in feelings of powerlessness.

Although the more specific data on authoritarian attitudes among people in the West End are limited in scope and refer only to child-rearing orientations, the different types of authoritarian attitudes are at least moderately highly correlated with one another.[18] Authoritarian attitudes toward child-rearing or rigidities of discipline among parents in different social classes have been widely studied with quite ambiguous results.[19] As we have already indicated, the views of West End men and women about children and child-rearing do not easily lend themselves to simple categorization as authoritarian or nonauthoritarian, as disciplinary or indulgent. Somewhat more than half of the West End men and women felt that it was more important for a child to learn to keep himself clean when he was young than to enjoy himself. Even more (55 percent of the women; 62 percent of the men) felt that it was critical for a child to be taught explicitly to respect its parents rather than to allow this to develop spontaneously. At the same time, most of the parents were indulgent and more than half of the women and men felt that a child should be picked up when it cries without concerning oneself about spoiling the child. In discussing more complex issues of parenthood, moreover, many of the women and men were quite sensitive about psychological needs of children.

Status differences in the expression of authoritarian child-rearing attitudes are themselves less clear-cut than we might expect. The only marked variations were between the people of highest status and everyone else. Moreover, authoritarianism manifested in child-rearing orientations was integrally related to an entire set of attitudes among people of higher status and minimally related to a more integrated set of values among those of lower status (Appendix table 8.9). Among higher status people, both men and women alike, a high level of indulgence toward children was closely associated with independence of judgement, a relatively moderate and independent view of political issues, and an ethnospansive attitude toward ethnic differences. For the men it was also linked to a high degree of work satisfaction and to a more cosmopolitan urban orientation.

Many of the attitudes and values that have often been described as characteristic for working-class people do not reveal sharp class differences among men and women in the West End. However, there is one striking social class difference among both the women and the men that seems of far more general significance for a wide range of attitudes. This difference emerges for social conformity, a characteristic of great importance for working-class life.[20] Men and women of higher status were decidedly more independent, while people of lower status were more socially conformist (Appendix table 8.10). We have already described the conditions of community life in which working-class people live and the importance of maintaining close social relationships with a relatively wide network of friends, neighbors, and kin. While this undoubtedly is a factor of significance in encouraging compliance with the views and expectations of others, the issue seems to lie deeper than that. Certainly it is the case that working-class men and women, caught in a dilemma between their own personal views and those of a group of peers, are likely to go along with the group. This became manifest when people were asked about joining in a strike decision. Those in lower status positions most often went along with the strike despite their disagreement with its objectives, while higher status people who disagreed generally refused to go along with the decision. Moreover, while the relationships between social conformity and other attitudes are not huge, they are considerably more strongly integrated with other attitudes and behaviors among both working-class men and women than are most of the other attitudes we have considered. Thus, conformity is not perceived merely as an aspect of life that one must take for granted; it is also tied to a host of other attitudes and values.

The importance of social conformity among working-class people has been dealt with extensively in the literature.[21] What is of particular importance is the fact that conformity is so much a way of life among people of lower status. For people in higher status positions, conformity depends very much on personal characteristics. Those who were more dependent on others were more conformist. But among working-class people, no such relationship obtained. Regardless of their own personal dispositions, most working-class people generally accept group orientations or opinions. But if this is the case, it also means that many of the attitudes and values we have considered, which we often consider to be generated by a more comprehensive view of the world, function in this way only minimally for working-class people. In order to understand working-class attitudes, we must know the context in which the question has meaning for them and the reference group pressures, explicit or implicit, that are likely to operate. Not only do working-class attitudes reflect the ways in which other working-class people look upon the world, but they are also bound to be more readily affected by situational forces that may modify the significance of a given attitude at different times. Since these attitudes and values are not generated by a confirmed ideological position, they can be altered more easily by transitory conditions or group attitudes. It is this orientation of social conformity that also makes working-class people so vulnerable to provocation by group atmospheres and, under certain conditions, such easy prey to attitudes and actions that are antithetical to their own best interests.

We have said that many of the attitudes we have discussed—ethnocentrism, authoritarianism, alienation, and social conformity—have often been conceived as different manifestations of a single syndrome. In the influential study of authoritarianism by Adorno and his colleagues (Adorno et al., 1950), it was considered to be a generic personality disposition.[22] Within the West End, as we have indicated, there was no evidence of powerful interrelationships among the different attitudes that would justify a unitary conception. Those interrelationships that were of moderate strength appeared mainly among people in higher status positions and were rarely so strongly associated that they could be regarded, on empirical grounds, as components of a multidimensional attitudinal set.

We have stressed one major distinction in the attitudes of people in different social class positions. Many attitudes appear to have an ideological base for people in higher status positions but seem more specific, more often determined by both reference group influences and by situational variations among working-class people. Moreover, in view of the different patterns of relationship of many attitudes for people in different social class positions, the same apparent expression of attitude may have quite different meanings. Through different routes, however, attitudes may serve similar functions for people in different social classes. For people of higher status, they provide a sense of integrity by fulfilling distinctive ideological commitments which they may or may not realize in action. Indeed, the attitudes of people in higher status positions often imply an effort to modify or control the world. It is, of course, not at all clear that people of higher status, excluding those in evident positions of power, actually succeed in influencing social policy any more than do working-class people. But the sense of social efficacy, so often frustrated in reality, can be asserted (if not confirmed) by the expression of attitudes that imply more general conceptions of process and policy.

For people of lower status, attitudes may also provide a sense of integrity by affirming the group identity of individuals through common beliefs. Indeed, to the extent that working-class people experience a sense of social efficacy, it most often occurs in a group context or in the knowledge of widely shared working-class attitudes. Sometimes, however, the attitudes expressed may involve sharing a sense of futility that is more palatable by virtue of being shared. Sometimes they may imply general negativism to people in authority. These may even coalesce with a very different set of economic or political objectives of high-status interest groups and produce support for conservative or even truly antidemocratic forces and movements (Horton and Thompson, 1962).[23] But since a high degree of social conformity is built into the very conditions of life for working-class people, it cannot itself be modified except by providing real changes in the opportunities that people have, individually or as groups, to influence and affect their own lives and to modify some of the conditions that define the world of working-class people.

9 Personality and Social Behavior in Working-class Life

Personality and the Social Context of Class Differences

The examination of human differences in personality and in personal styles of functioning has a long history. There are numerous theories to account for individual differences in personal dispositions. The most prominent of these theories is psychoanalysis which has influenced ideas about personality far beyond Freudian and post-Freudian dynamic psychologies. Large-scale differences of personality have also been studied in that field known as national character, the study of modal personality characteristics of a nation or group that distinguish one population from another. And there are a few, very important analyses of fundamental forces that link the personalities of individuals with the social structures or cultures in which they live.[1] But there have been only a few studies of personality differences associated with social class position or of the processes by which these are developed (for example, Aronfreed, 1968; Hess, 1970). As one result of the paucity of work in this entire area, personality characteristics of people in different social classes are generally ill understood and discussed mainly on the basis of impressions, unsystematic studies, or extrapolations from pathological models.

Another consequence of the neglect of sophisticated studies of social class differences in personality and their behavioral ramifications is that one of the most readily available fields for investigating social influences on personality formation and for studying the interaction between social processes and personality as determinants of behavior has been neglected. There appear to be a few striking differences in behavior and role performance and in personality between people in different social class positions. But we have few grounds for tracing these differences in behavior and role to modal personality characteristics in different social classes. Certainly it is impossible to formulate serious propositions on the basis of available empirical evidence to show how personal dispositions related to social class can influence behavior differently depending on the social conditions or the social context in which they occur. In fact, the problem goes deeper than this. In some respects people in different social class positions are so evidently different from one another that conclusions are easily drawn about the stability or the meaning or the results of these class-related attributes. However, we do not know if the differences we find between people in different social class positions involve those relatively enduring traits that we call personality. Assuming such personality dispositions are implicated, we have no adequate basis for designating these personality characteristics as causes, consequences, mediating factors, or incidental concomitants of class-related behaviors.

We cannot hope to deal effectively with this range of issues in examining characteristic personal styles among working-class people or even in comparing the personal dispositions of people in different social class positions within a single community. Within limits, we can investigate the extent to which there are patterned differences in personality by social class position across the moderately wide spectrum of West End residents. However, by virtue of their willingness to live in a working-class community, those people in the lower and upper middle class who made their residence in the West End are likely to differ less sharply from working-class people than are middle and higher status persons living in areas consistent with their own class positions.

We can also consider the effects of these personality differences on behaviors, roles, and attitudes and, in this way, estimate whether social class or personality traits independent of social class or personality differences derived from social class position are most influential as determinants of behavior. But a fuller evaluation of basic propositions will require systematic studies deliberately planned to examine alternative hypotheses.

One of the more evident differences in personal style among people in different social class positions concerns differences in patterns of social relationship. We have already discussed the great importance of the local community for working-class people and the less closely involved and more widely dispersed forms of social affiliation among people in higher status positions. Working-class people reveal a marked concern about social relationships, sociability, social facility, and the approval of others, a concern that goes to the very core of their personalities. The working-class social orientation involves a sense of being a part of the group, of being taken for granted and assuming that one can take others for granted, of being among the same kind of people.[2] Friendships were certainly a very central part of the daily lives of people in the West End. Most people felt that friendships "were worth more than money" and that "a person is very happy to have friends." Among men and women alike, the great majority saw friends as extremely important or even as the main thing in life.[3]

The qualities people sought in friends, both the diversities and the repeated theme of similarity, acceptance, and the absence of status threats, are evident in their actual statements about what made them like a person and want to be friends:

Sincere, honest people who are friendly and are like you.
Kindness. If he has heart, I like them. If you have no heart, I don't bother. In my heart is always for the person that cannot afford it. My heart is open to the poor person.
If they're truthful and sincere. That's about all.
Well, if they didn't think they are high-toned. I like a regular Joe.
If they're sociable and my type and don't try to put their airs on . . . like I'm poor and you're rich type.
Their friendliness, their warmth, their intelligence. That's all.
I like people in general. Appearance and whether they have money or not makes no difference to me.
If they're friendly and don't ask personal questions.

The desire for warmth, camaraderie, and a sense of commonality are as evident in these characteristics as is the precarious sense of self-esteem that is easily threatened by a feeling of status differences.

It is not merely the importance or qualities of friends and close associations that varies by social class; the meaning of friendship differs as well. Few West End men thought of friendship primarily as a sharing of confidences or of joint sociability. While loyalty, trust, and mutual respect were extremely important, the dominant feature involved the expectation of reciprocity and of assistance in need. Thus, 44 percent of the women and 57 percent of the men regarded such assistance as the main thing they would expect of a friend. A large number of women who felt affection for someone were likely to demonstrate this by helping them in some way, by showing affection directly or inviting social participation, or by some other attempt to sustain contact (47 percent). On the other hand, quite a few women were content simply to feel the warmth of the friendship or to indulge themselves in a feeling of contentment (47 percent). The statements by both men and women about the main things they would expect of a friend reveal these conceptions. Some of the men said:

If you need assistance, they'd help.
Respectability. And to help one another if need be. Not just a good time
friend.
Companionship. Do things together and for each other in emergencies.
That's about it.
Companionship. To agree on a lot of things, to enjoy the same things. Talk.
Personal warmth. They should be interested in you as a person, not what
he can get out of you.

The emphases among the women were quite similar:

If I need help, they should help me. If I were sick, they might take care of
my child.
To be true, loyal, helpful if needed. Can expect this in the West End but
nowhere else.
I'd expect them to ask for help, advice, financial or otherwise. And I would
expect the same from them. But if I needed it, I'd hesitate.
Talk nice, not gossip, mind their own business.
A friend is a person who knows all about you and likes you just the same.
A person who will do helpful things for you.

The differences between social classes in underlying personality characteristics related to social relationships are often subtle since sociability is a
trait that cuts across class lines. But there are fine differences. Women of
higher status were somewhat more sensitive about feelings of loneliness or
mild frustrations in social engagements; lower status women were more
likely to be saddened by overt rebuffs and interpersonal difficulties. On
the other hand, while working-class people are more familiar with the
exigencies of life that often interfere with expectations, they are far less
capable of being alone. Thus, 54 percent of the lower status women
envisaged depressive reactions (sadness, crying, dejection) when they
thought of being left alone, while only 31 percent of the higher status
women reacted in this way. These differences reflect a fundamental variation in the need for other people. But there are other variations in the
constellation of interpersonal reactions. There were only minor class
differences among both the men and the women in the degree to which
they felt confident of the good will of other people or in general suspiciousness about others. However, the embeddedness of working-class people
in familiar groups led to greater discomfort with strangers and in other
situations of social uncertainty. Women of higher status were more comfortable than lower status women in relatively impersonal or unfamiliar
situations, while those in lower social class positions were more relaxed
than women of higher status in close or familiar groupings.

Several separate but interacting trends seem to account for the subjective importance of social affiliations among working-class people and to distinguish the quality of personal needs for sociability of people in different class positions. Feelings of security are particularly important for working-class people whose lives are generally beset by many uncertainties and who do not have the basic security of ample resources. We have already pointed up work conditions that foster an emphasis on security and diminish the freedom for self-expression or risk-taking.[4] Indeed, satisfaction is often translated into security. While women in higher status positions often sought social engagements or thought that the purchase of luxuries would be gratifying, lower status women sought mainly simple comforts, the safety and presence of family and friends, and freedom from severe strains and anxieties. The same needs for security and warmth and peace of mind recurred whether in conjunction with satisfaction, happiness, or even excitement. Closely related to this, although it stems from issues of negative sanctions rather than positive goals, is the consciousness of the social esteem of others. Few working-class women were terribly concerned about their personal atrributes, while a great many women of higher status gave primacy to their personal appearance. On the other hand, women of higher status were considerably less bothered by attributes of social position and moral transgression (17 percent), while a relatively large number of lower status women (41 percent) considered their homes, neighborhoods, poverty, or sexual and aggressive behavior to be major sources of shame. These differences in the importance of social relationships as sources of security and of social conformity as some insurance of social esteem appear to lie behind the emphasis on obedience and compliance in parental values and behavior.

In this light, it is not surprising that to be misunderstood is extremely disturbing to working-class people. More than half the women responded to the thought of such a situation by sadness, tears, feelings of hurt, nervousness, or withdrawal. A relatively small number of women became angry or struggled with the problem, but most of the women felt helpless in the face of such social rejection. Social class differences were clear. Among the high status women, 34 percent tried to cope with misunderstanding by explaining themselves, trying again, working at the problem, while only 14 percent of the low status women could visualize engaging in such efforts. Conversely, 30 percent of the higher status women and 49 percent of the lower status women reacted to this situation with a sense of passive helplessness.

As we have already indicated, class differences in punitiveness toward children are ambiguous, but in a number of situations working-class parents are more likely to feel that punitive action is required instead of seeking clarification with their children. Whatever the reasons, moreover, working-class children seem to experience their parents as more restrictive, somewhat more severe in their punishment, and more demanding of obedience.[5] An understanding of working-class parental orientations can be found in the insecurity of working-class experience itself, in their fears of transgression, in the threat of social rejection. Their conceptions of punishment, whether translated into action or merely verbalized, engender similar conceptions of the world among their children. Thus, it would not appear to be the slight differences in punitiveness as much as the stress on social conformity in child-rearing and the influence of situational forces on parental behaviors that distinguishes the child-rearing techniques of different social classes. The child rapidly learns the importance of compliance with peers and adults and develops a high degree of sensitivity to the immediate feelings of other people. Working-class people, operating with fewer reliable resources and fewer sources of long-term stability other than their relationships with close people, are more affectively responsive to situations and events that can markedly influence their lives. This is readily communicated to children. A rapid assessment of the affective tone of parents and peers becomes one of the great assets of effective social interaction in the working class.

Partly because of the importance of social relationships, partly because of the importance of situational determinants of affective behavior, working-class people feel easily threatened by their own or other people's anger and hostility. In a wide variety of situations, working-class women were more fearful of threats from people in authority positions, including men in general, than were women of higher status. In fact, the major sources of fear among women in lower social class positions were interpersonal threats or hostility (46 percent), while women of higher status were relatively unconcerned about such aggression and were more often (42 percent) phobic about many impersonal and often unrealistic dangers. In some respects, anger and hostility lead to active and cathartic expression quite frequently in the working class. Nonetheless, while such volatile expressiveness does occur, characteristic responses to feelings of anger and hostility are various forms of withdrawal from the situation, suppression, and denial. As a consequence, women of lower status were more likely to control their anger (42 percent) than were the women of higher status (29 percent). The same social class gradient was evident among the men. Men of higher status were more likely to deal with threats by open confrontation. Men of lower status more often withdrew from the field. The price that working-class men and women thus pay is a sense of frustration, of anger and hostility turned in upon themselves. At the same time they are able to maintain smooth interpersonal relationships and retain a sense of being accepted members of a group.

We have considered the importance of social relationships, approval, and conformity up to this point. Another realm of personality characteristics that are also significant in distinguishing people in different social class positions are those involving mastery or efficacy or, more technically, the executive functions of the ego. These refer to attributes that are the most highly prized and most highly rewarded traits in our society: persistence, competitiveness, confrontation, achievement, self-esteem. Moreover, despite their great value for success and achievement, all the forces in our society militate against the development of these characteristics in working-class people. Child-rearing practices may contribute to the readiness to accept defeat among working-class children, but these developmental experiences are fully confirmed by daily situations outside the home, at school, beyond the community, and eventually at work. The frequent failure to develop such characteristics of mastery, efficacy, and an overriding strain for achievement, however, diminish the rewards that working-class people can hope to obtain in a society that so highly values these attributes.

These characteristics are a set of interrelated traits; they are manifested in diverse ways. If we consider difficult and stressful situations, less than a quarter of the women were able to cope with these problems with the personal fortitude necessary to sustain efforts at mastery. Certainly, in the face of many realistic, daily struggles, working-class people develop many routine skills for dealing with impediments. Working out budgets within narrow constraints, maintaining privacy in minimal space with many people around, dealing with a host of anxieties and realistic pressures all require a considerable level of mastery. But when problems are conceived as barriers, frustrations, or difficulties, working-class people are more likely to retreat than to confront them.

A frequent reaction to frustration among women in the West End was anger (50 percent); criticism of their work evoked anger almost as often. As we have pointed out, however, feelings of anger were often suppressed or withheld. Withdrawal was a more common response to anger than was either cathartic or calm communication of these affects. Many women responded to frustration or criticism by feeling sad, crying, or becoming more passive. Only a quarter of them tried to marshall their personal resources to overcome the problem or even to seek assistance in dealing directly with frustration or criticism. Women in higher status positions more often manifested such attempts at mastery. The same distinction appeared in the kinds of people they admired. Working-class women generally admired people who were friendly, responsive, or had estimable character traits. Only 15 percent admired competence in people, while 41 percent of the women of higher status deemed such competence to be the most admirable quality.

Closely related to mastery, achievement motivation has been widely studied and some striking social class differences have appeared (Douvan, 1956; McClelland et al., 1953; Rosen, 1956). Achievement motivation involves a persistent struggle to maintain control and to overcome threats and challenges. For people in the West End as a whole, confrontation with a situation in which someone else was better than they at a task they were both doing led most often to either of two opposite reactions: competitiveness or indifference. Among the women, indifference took priority, while the men more often reacted with competitiveness. But the social class differences were striking. Those men who were of relatively high social class status most often became openly competitive and tried to outdo the other person (46 percent) and considerably fewer remained indifferent (29 percent). The patterns for men of lower status were reversed: many more (44 percent) ignored the fact that the other man was better than they, while relatively few (24 percent) responded with competitiveness. The social class trends among women were similar but the class differences were weaker.

Personality characteristics are laden with social meaning and may have quite different significance for people in different social contexts. This is quite evident and yet is often overlooked. Competitiveness, outdoing others in the same position, maintaining equanimity in the face of disapproval all place a strain on the sociability, social conformity, and group orientations of working-class people. Other characteristics associated with efficacy, self-determination, a sense of internal strength, and a high level of self-esteem are also influenced by and often limited because of these pervasive social orientations and needs as well as by other aspects of working-class experience. The reliance upon groups fosters needs for external support. The experience of insecurity, derogation and low regard in the society, minimal opportunity, and the lack of freedom to determine one's own destiny produce a low sense of self-esteem. Child-rearing practices may facilitate the development of these working-class orientations. But societal forces further reinforce these characteristics in the working class.

There is considerable evidence to indicate that a low sense of self-esteem is quite widespread among people of lower status.[6] One manifestation of low self-esteem among the West End women was the frequency of angry responses to the lack of support from others, to feelings of being neglected, or to feelings of one's own inadequacy. In these situations, women of higher status more often responded with less concern and expressed anger mainly in the face of open hostility from others. The existence of generalized depressive potentials is also linked to low self-esteem, although the psychological mechanism involved is more complex.[7] We have already pointed to depressive phenomena among women of lower status. In fact, women in lower social class positions are depressed quite frequently, a wide variety of circumstances evoke depression, sadness, or withdrawal, and they accept these depressive feelings with few attempts to overcome them. Less than half of the women in lower social class positions (41 percent) tried actively to master their depressive affects, while many more of the women in higher social class positions (69 percent) made efforts to do so.

Indirectly related both to depressive reactions and to a low sense of self-esteem is the severity and rigidity of guilt feelings. People who maintain irrevocable (and often traditionally-based) moral standards are more likely to castigate themselves for a variety of transgressions than those who define a more flexible and personal variant of moral norms for themselves. In a variety of shame or guilt-evoking situations, such differences in response were clearly related to social class position. Among the lower status women, the most frequent source of guilt was moral transgression, often ambiguously phrased as "she did wrong," "she sinned," "she was to blame," and occasionally stated in explicit sexual terms as "she went out with other men" (44 percent). This form of guilt feeling occurred among only 28 percent of the women of higher status. On the other hand, supplementing the other evidence of the differential importance of efficacy and control, failures of personal mastery were the most frequent sources of guilt for women in higher status positions (38 percent) but occurred less frequently (20 percent) for women of lower status.

Through many channels, internal and external forces encourage low self-esteem among women in lower social class positions. Women of higher status are, if not entirely free from these influences, more likely to experience both pressures and encouragement to think more highly of themselves, to rely more heavily on themselves, and to engage in active efforts that provide greater security in one's own effectiveness and thus heighten the sense of self-esteem. These differences in self-esteem also link up with differences in anxiety about competitiveness, with readiness to accept defeat or to try to master it, with uncompromising moral codes that invoke self-punitive feelings or more general moral principles that allow for learning and development, and with differences in orientations to achievement. In the long run, these produce social class differences, not only in the subjective sense of self-esteem, but also in the capacity for efficacy and for the mastery of challenge and difficulty.

In a comprehensive sense, the characteristics we have discussed as differentially distributed among people in different social class positions fall within two broad spheres of personality traits. One of these involves orientations to other people: the need for approval, support, social responsiveness and its consequences for interpersonal dependency, social conformity, and social anxiety. The other major set of personality attributes, most generically referred to as ego efficacy, ego mastery, or ego control involves competitiveness, confrontation and effective coping with difficulty, achievement motivation, self-esteem, and depressive or optimistic expectations. Many other individual characteristics have been considered in studies of social class differences in personality. Some of them, like differences in the reliance on internal or external sources of control and influence are closely related to ego efficacy. People who are highly efficacious or strongly motivated toward achievement must inevitably rely on internal controls and internal approval rather than on external determination and support. Other characteristics, like class differences in language behavior, we have not considered although the data are substantial and, at the least, observations in the West End are congruent with their results (for example, Bernstein, 1961). Yet other attributes that have been described as differentiated by social class, like the capacity to defer gratification, are ambiguous (Straus, 1962). The available findings are weak and inconsistent and receive little support from the distribution of characteristics among the people of the West End.

In considering the consequences of personal characteristics for social behavior related to status differences, we shall focus mainly on the two major constellations of attributes we have discusses: those related to social interaction and those related to personal mastery.

Social Class, Interpersonal Dispositions, and Social Behavior

People in lower status positions learn, quite early in life, that they can anticipate an indulgent and tolerant if not always consistent response of friendliness and support from a close and available network of parents, neighbors, relatives, and peers. Middle-class children find out during child-hood that they must earn both affection and autonomy, that they are expected to present age-graded accomplishments in order to maximize their social advantage even within the close circle of home. However, there are enough conflicting and contradictory social experiences for children and adults in all social classes to urge caution in any simple formulation of differences in interpersonal dispositions. Most Americans expect at least casual sociability from others, learn to feel at ease in group situations, and develop social skills that often seem surprising and superficial to foreigners who assume that overt friendliness must necessarily be tied to friendship. Thus, even though it is possible to discern a number of differences in sociability and social relationships among people in different social class positions, these variations can easily be overstated. They generally reflect different frequencies in the occurrence of social patterns rather than any more extreme and irreconcilable distinction in the social behavior of people in different social classes.

It is hardly surprising, in this light, that while we have shown some striking social class differences in interpersonal orientations and affective relationships, when we put these diverse personality characteristics associated with social interaction into composite indices, we find relatively small social class differences in basic interpersonal or social dispositions (table 9.1). Although people in lower status positions and, particularly, people with less education are more often passive and feel helpless in situations of interpersonal stress, only a relatively small proportion of people in any social class position are extremely passive or helpless in such situations. Many of these social class differences, clarifying though they may be about the meaning of social class, are variations on some basic, common patterns among people in our society. Nor are there major differences among people in different social class positions in the degree to which fear of rejection is a general personality attribute, and such fears are not characteristic for Americans or for West Enders in any event. People who have evidently experienced the extreme buffeting of circumstance reflected in marked downward mobility, however, have more often internalized such fears. Similarly, people whose lives are centered around close, familiar, and reliable friends, neighbors, and kin conform more readily to others, feel that compliance is the best route to friendship, and are somewhat less trusting of unfamiliar people. But levels of conformity and compliance are not extremely high, just as distrust of others is rarely marked. The broader experiences that men generally have, particularly in the working class,

TABLE 9.1   Mean scores within social class subgroups for
selected personality variables: female and male

Personality variable	Social class status		
	Moderately high	Moderately low	Very low
Female			
Interpersonal responsiveness	4.03	4.11	3.90
Social anxiety	4.76	4.66	4.74
Interpersonal dependency	2.46	3.10	3.10
Social conformity	2.17	3.11	3.63
Interpersonal trust	3.30	3.45	3.00
Ego efficacy	4.02	4.05	3.47
Male			
Interpersonal responsiveness	3.03	2.70	3.19
Social conformity	2.48	2.69	3.38
Interpersonal trust	2.16	1.99	1.79
Ego control	4.69	4.25	4.02

reduces these class variations even further for them. Among the traits that
are often discussed clinically, there is some social class differentiation in
interpersonal dependency, but it is not so sharp or clear or linear as many
conceptions of working-class people would suggest.

   In the discussion of attitudes, we have already pointed out the importance of social conformity for working-class people and the very extensive
consequences of social conformity at lower status levels. Although there
are many factors stimulating social conformity among working-class people,
one influence upon the development of compliance and conformity is the
dependence upon other people for acceptance, approval, or support.
Although interpersonal dependency is not as strongly or consistently
associated with social class position as is social conformity, people of
lower status tend to be more dependent on others than people of higher
status. However, in view of the fact that it is often difficult to determine
whether a personality characteristic is primarily a consequence of social
class position or its cause, it is worth noting that the social class status of a
person's parents is a more potent influence on interpersonal dependency
than is the person's own class position. However, those women from
relatively high status origins who attained little education and those from
very low status origins who went on to college, the two most dramatic
instances of downward and upward mobility, were particularly dependent

on others.[8] But while social class origins influenced interpersonal dependency and these were supplemented by aspects of an individual's own status, there were few consequences of this personal characteristic and these are mainly self-evident. Thus, among women of low and moderate social class position, those who were more dependent maintained closer relationships with neighbors and family members than did women who were freer of reliance on others for their sense of esteem. Interpersonal dependency among working-class women even influenced their relationships to their husbands. Low status women who were interpersonally dependent had relatively high levels of marital companionship, although this personality attribute had little effect on companionship between husbands and wives at moderate or higher status levels. Women at all social class levels who were interpersonally dependent more often conceived of the West End as their real home. Among high status women particularly, interpersonal dependency led to a high degree of ethnic involvement. Thus, while interpersonal dependency influenced the immediate social relationships of women at lower status levels, it led to more general embeddedness in the local area for women of higher status and helps to account for their decision to live in the West End.

One of the most crucial features of living in a closeknit, working-class community, more generally important than sheer interpersonal dependency, is the ease and relaxation people feel in social interaction. The social skills required in working-class life do not hinge so much on dependency as on comfort and pleasure in interpersonal relationships with close people. A composite measure of social anxiety distinguishes between the sense of fear and feelings of relaxation and ease in social interaction.[9] Although there were only minor social class variations in social anxiety among women in the West End, it seems clear that social ease is a particular asset to working-class women in a working-class community. Social anxiety must create a double indemnity for women who are, in the first place, of low status and, in the second, cannot utilize the social resources a working-class community can provide to help in coping with daily experience and periodic stress.

The special limitation of low status women who were socially anxious appears when we compare different kinds of social relationships, both those involving local neighbors or kin which were most prominent for people in lower social class positions and those of a more widely dispersed nature more characteristic for the people of higher status. At all social class levels, women who were socially relaxed more frequently maintained close neighbor relationships, while those who were socially anxious were more often distant from neighbors (Appendix table 9.1). A similar con-nection held for relationships with kin, although social anxiety did not interfere as markedly with the routines of kinship interaction as it did fo[r] more optional contact with neighbors. Thus, for neighbor and kinship relationships, social anxiety was an impediment but interfered with or otherwise diminished social interaction to an equivalent degree at all so[cial] class levels. When we consider a broader range of social relationships, including those that cut across traditional or local ties, we discover that women who were socially relaxed and of moderate or low status had m[ore] extensive interpersonal relationships than did women of higher status w[ith] were equally at ease in social situations (Appendix table 9.2).[10] The debility created by social anxiety among working-class women, howeve[r] was evident at the other extreme. Women of low status who were anxie[ty] ridden in social interaction maintained much lower levels of interperson[al] relationship than did anxious women in higher social positions. Indeed, effects of social anxiety and status invaded even the sphere of marital relationships. Lower status women who were at ease in social interactio[n] less often maintained shared companionship role relationships with the[ir] husbands than did women of moderately high status who were relaxed [in] social interaction. In view of their more extensive social relationships w[ith] other people, this was infrequently a source of major strain. But the anxious women of lower status had the worst of all fates since, not only were they deprived of interpersonal ties outside the home, they also suffered lower levels of marital companionship than relaxed, low status women or than anxious, high status women.

One other sphere in which social anxiety itself had important conse-quences that were particularly serious for women of lower status was in both physical and emotional types of symptom formation and in the development of social problems. Relatively little is known about the precise constellation of internal and external forces that produce physical, mental, or social symptom formation beyond general notions like maladap-tation or poor fit between personality and social context. In this situation, we have clear evidence of the importance of both personality and social context and of their somewhat divergent manifestations in different types of symptom formation. For this purpose, we can use an index for each major symptomatic sphere: health status, psychoneurotic symptoms, and social problems.[11] Social anxiety had a consistent effect on health status in all social class positions (Appendix table 9.3). Women high on anxiety more often had poorer health. The difference by social class position was marked, and anxious, low status women had the highest rates of poor th. The interrelationships between social anxiety, psychoneurotic ptoms, and social class were almost identical. But the relationship veen personality difficulties and psychoneurotic symptoms is more ct than that between personality and health and the effects were spondingly sharper. Socially anxious women had considerably more verer psychoneurotic symptoms than socially relaxed women at all al class levels, and the most extreme levels of psychoneurotic symptom- ogy were to be found among the socially anxious women of lower us.

ne most powerful consequences of the interaction between personality social class occurred in the sphere most directly related to social iety: social problems. Lower status and higher levels of social anxiety h led to marked increases in social problems. By far the most severe ial problems, however, existed for the lower status women who were ially anxious. The disadvantage of social position was, moreover, ent. Despite low levels of health problems and psychoneurotic ptoms, the socially relaxed women of low status had higher rates of al problems than the women of higher status who were equally com- able in social relationships.

we return to our original general questions about the relationships ween personality and social behavior, several factors emerge quite irly. Although differences in personality characteristics associated with iability, interpersonal dependency, and social anxiety or relaxation are markedly influenced by social class position, they do have conse- ences for social behavior. Moreover, these consequences are not identical r people in different social classes. The social context of working-class ople living in a working-class community requires extensive social inter- ction, and, largely as a result of this, women in the working class who vere socially anxious suffered marked deficits. They could not utilize the resources readily available to them and could not conform to the norma- tive expectations of the community. Women of higher status, who ordi- narily have an entirely different set of social expectations and, in any event, did not generally participate in the life of the community fully, were less affected by differences in social anxiety. They were freer to behave as they pleased, regardless of these personality characteristics. Whether these differences in turn account for the very marked effects of anxiety on symptom formation is not certain, but it seems quite likely that, at the very least, socially anxious, lower status women are among the people most vulnerable to pathological reaction in the face of stress and difficulty.

Social Class, Ego Efficacy, and Social Behavior

Personality characteristics that reflect needs for and ease with other people blur the outlines of distinctive class differences because our society so widely encourages social interaction for people at all social class levels. But those attributes that represent the executive functions of the ego show the manifold ramifications of different class experiences in our society. Whether we consider the mastery of difficulties, achievement orientations, conceptions of self-blame, optimism, or other traits that contribute to the modern, competitive, entrepreneurial personality, we find that people in higher social class positions approximate this model more closely than those in lower status positions.[12] Similarly, when we put a number of these attributes together into a composite index of ego efficacy or ego control we find this to be strikingly true and to reveal a number of other aspects of ego strengths, and social position as well.[13] Indeed, an important generalization that is manifested in the data for the West End is that those people with a high degree of ego efficacy or control approximated the ideal personal qualities of modern man mainly when they were of moderately high status. Among working-class people, these same internal strengths resulted in a very different pattern of personal and social characteristics adapted to the realities of working-class life.

With variables reflecting interpersonal and social dispositions, there seemed little doubt that these were primarily determinants rather than consequences of social experience. Questions of causal position, however, must be raised more sharply about ego efficacy since heightened status achievement could so easily provide an increased sense of self-esteem and increased confidence in competitiveness as well as greater motivation for further achievement. The social class relationship among the women was very strong: 58 percent of the women in higher social class positions were highly efficacious and only 27 percent of those in lower social class positions were equally efficacious. When we examine the separate components of social class, we find that education was a greater influence on ego efficacy than occupation. The occupational status of the head of household, generally viewed as the major defining characteristic of family social position, added little further differentiation in ego efficacy to the variation explained by education. Moreover, differences in ego efficacy appear to have antedated educational attainment since parental social class position also influenced the level of ego efficacy (Appendix table 9.4).

Personality differences in efficaciousness had numerous consequences for social behavior, but the consequences varied for women in different social class positions. Among women in higher and moderate status positions, those who were high on efficacy were often residentially mobile. Women in higher social class positions who were highly efficacious quite frequently used the West End as a temporary home and rarely were long-term residents. At the other social class extreme, on the other hand, high efficacy was more likely to be linked to stable residence, and women who were low on efficacy more often followed a transient pattern of residence. A similar pattern of relationships and social class variation influenced many forms of local involvement. Efficacious women of relatively high status were generally less satisfied with the West End than women of low efficacy and of equally high status. But among working-class people, for whom the neighborhood was more generally significant and meaningful, differences in ego efficacy were unrelated to residential satisfaction. Social relationships and the use of local resources were similarly influenced by differences in ego efficacy among women of higher status and minimally or not at all among the more typical working-class women of the West End. At all social status levels, efficacious women had more widely dispersed, less localized friendships than those who were less efficacious; but efficacy influenced friendship patterns most strongly among the women of moderately high status. Women who were of relatively high status and low efficacy had closer relationships to kin and neighbors than did women of the same status who were efficacious but, as before, these differences associated with ego efficacy disappeared among the women of low status. Along the same lines, women who were more effective in coping behavior were more cosmopolitan in orientation regardless of social class position: they knew less of the West End and more of the larger, metropolitan region. But the most marked variations in cosmopolitanism associated with differences in ego efficacy occurred among the women of highest status.

Differences in ego efficacy also had consequences for social attitudes, although this was clearest among people of relatively high status. Ethnic involvement, which often implies a fear of moving beyond the known and traditional, was higher among women of low ego efficacy than among those of high efficacy. But this was particularly true at moderately high status levels. Among women of low or moderately low status, for whom ethnic involvement was more characteristic in general, the same relationship obtained but was weaker. Religious commitment was also more frequent among women of low efficacy although this relationship obtained at both high and low status levels. An even more clear-cut manifestation of the limits that powerful, class-linked behaviors place on the influence of individual personality differences is evident in attitudes toward participation in a strike despite objections to its goals. Among women of relatively high status, ego efficacy most frequently led to resistance toward joining the strikers, while among women of low status, for whom compliance with the strike was most typical, differences in ego efficacy had no consequence for participation or resistance (Appendix table 9.5). Indeed, social conformity itself was quite strongly related to low ego efficacy among women of relatively high or moderate status while among women of low status, those who were more efficacious were also more socially conformist. Among high status women, furthermore, those who were efficacious were less alienated, less authoritarian in child-rearing, more socially ambitious, and more accepting of change. But the total pattern of strong relationships between personality and attitudes among women of high status and weak associations or no effect of ego efficacy on attitudes among those of low status was quite pervasive and held for these orientations as well.

We have already observed the very strong influence of differences in social anxiety on physical health, mental health, and social problems. Differences in ego efficacy were also associated with a number of personal deficits, but low levels of efficacy were not as strong and consistent in their effects on problems. By contrast with the frequent pattern in which differences in ego efficacy were most visible among the women of higher status, low efficacy affected personal problems mainly for the women of moderate or low status. Although physical health was unrelated to ego efficacy, the severity of social problems, extensive psychoneurotic symptoms, and more general mental health problems were exacerbated among women who were low on efficacy and of lower social class positions. Although low efficacy was not as potent an influence on personal difficulties as social anxiety, the greater vulnerability of lower status women is inevitably increased by the summation of both independent effects. If we add to this the greater frequency of low ego efficacy among women of low status, we obtain some clarification about the mediating factors that, in the face of greater provocation and stress, produce heightened levels of symptomatic behavior among people in lower social class statuses.

The personality data for the men are less adequate. But a related characteristic, which we have called ego control, reveals both similarities and differences in the significance of personality for social behavior and attitudes among men in different social class positions (Appendix table 9.6). As among the women, men of higher status had higher levels of ego control than men of lower status, although the differences were less marked than among the women. Education had an effect on ego control but this relationship was not as strong as the association between higher levels of occupational status and a high degree of ego control. While the causal position of personality variables is inevitably difficult to estimate, several factors suggest that, whatever the initial impetus to the development of ego control among men, a high degree of ego control facilitates achievement and, in turn, successful experiences further expand the level of ego control. Thus, parental status had little effect on differences in ego control, but men with higher levels of ego control were more often upwardly mobile compared to the occupations of their fathers. That higher levels of ego control were of motivational significance for achievement, moreover, is suggested by the fact that one of the strongest associations is that between ego control and occupational aspirations among the men. Interestingly enough, while a high degree of ego control was strongly linked to high aspirations among men of high status and moderately associated with high aspirations among men of moderate status, it led to low aspirations for men of low status. Since ego control implies desires to master situations, when occupational ambitions are likely to be frustrated by realistic limitations of opportunity, diminished aspirations are a means of resolving potential internal conflict. That such conflicts continued to manifest themselves indirectly, however, is suggested by the frequency with which major life changes were desired by men of low status and high ego control. By contrast, the efficacious men of high and moderate status more often wanted relatively minor changes of a social situational nature.

A number of patterns of social behavior and social attitudes were associated with differences in ego control. Rarely were these consistent for people in all social class positions. However, unlike these relationships among the women in which the strong associations between personal ego strength and behavior almost invariably occurred among those of highest status, for the men this varied depending on the behavior or attitude involved. As with the women, a greater degree of localism and traditionalism was linked to low levels of ego control primarily among men of relatively high status. Thus, at this status level, weak ego control led to greater dependence on the local area, embeddedness within familiar West End social interaction patterns, close neighbor relationships, and involvement with kin. Among men of lower status, personality differences had little effect on these diverse forms of localism. The significance of these social class differences is brought into sharper focus by the effects of personality variations in ego control on several social orientations that are fairly characteristic for working-class people. We have already observed that social conformity is considerably more frequent among men of lower status. Among men of higher status the acceptance of group norms implied by social conformity was associated with weak ego control. But among men of lower social class position, social conformity was one expression of a high degree of ego control. A similar pattern occurred in the expression of compliance with the demands of co-workers planning a strike in spite of personal reservations about the strike. Among the men of high status, those with lower levels of ego control were more likely to join the strikers as a matter of compliance. Among the men of low status, on the other hand, this relationship is reversed: participation in the strike occurred most frequently as a manifestation of a high degree of ego control. It is evident, thus, that social relationships and orientations that are typical of working-class people occur less frequently among those of higher status despite common residence in a working-class area. When such working-class behaviors or orientations do appear at higher status levels, they are often expressions of low ego control. But the occurrence of these same behaviors or orientations among men of lower status is either independent of differences in personality or, occasionally, in class-relevant instances like those discussed, it is a manifestation of ego strengths.

In these reversals of the association between personality and behavior for men in different status positions, the same behavior seems to have a different significance depending on the social class of the person. But even in instances of less apparent reversals of relationship, a similar behavior or orientation may have a different meaning for people of different status. Such a difference in meaning is implicit in the fact that a high level of ego control led to marital satisfaction among men of high status, but among men of low status such ego strength engendered marital dissatisfaction. In light of the analysis of marital and family relationships, a reasonable hypothesis to account for this contrast is that a high degree of ego control, more frequently taken for granted among people of higher status, is essential for maintaining the complex interaction in integrated, marital role relationships. At lower status levels, the difficulty of establishing highly integrative marital role relationships in view of normative expectations for segregation in marital roles leads to frustration and dissatisfaction. This hypothesis is given further support by the fact that at high status levels, ego control led to specific forms of integrated marital roles like companionship, while, at lower levels of status, ego control had no effect on marital companionship. That there was a conflict between personal desires and realities, particularly among the men of lower status, is evident from information about the features that men believed would lead to successful marriage. Among men of lower status, a high degree of ego control led to fairly atypical conceptions of marriage based on mutuality and integration and it was the failure to achieve this that most frequently led to marital dissatisfaction.

We might assume that because work and the job are such central areas of achievement, the implications of ego strength would cut across social class differences in work orientations. To a small degree, this is the case. But as we have seen with occupational aspirations, differences in realistic opportunities for men in different social positions can result in very different outcomes for similar strivings. Thus, among men of high status, a high level of ego control led to more complex forms of work orientation involving the mastery of problems, pleasure in challenge, satisfaction with achievement. Since these are less frequently available as opportunities in lower status jobs, the effect of ego control on these work orientations was considerably reduced among men of lower status. The lack of opportunity also invaded the sphere of generalized forms of job satisfaction. Despite many indications of desires for more demanding jobs and for achievement, ego control made little difference to job satisfaction among men of low status. Among men of high status, on the other hand, a high level of ego control led to overt desires for job changes.

By contrast with most of the behaviors and attitudes we have observed so far, when there are no clear-cut class norms or typical working-class reactions, ego capacities seem to make more of a difference to men of low than of high status. This was not the case for women and one can only conjecture that the wider social range of working-class men allows for a wider range of ideas than most working-class women have opportunities to meet. Although there was a class difference in the readiness people felt about accepting a dinner invitation from a new neighbor of relatively high status, the situation was sufficiently hypothetical and unusual to be free of consistent, working-class expectations. It is hardly surprising, of course, that acceptance or rejection of the invitation by men of high status was independent of differences in ego control. Among the men of lower status, however, those who were high on ego control more readily considered accepting the invitation than did men with low ego control. A number of social attitudes reflected this same pattern of social class differences. At lower status levels, ego strength led to low levels of alienation, an indulgent rather than authoritarian attitude toward child-rearing, preferences for planning ahead, and social mobility strivings. None of these attitudes were influenced by differences in ego control among men of higher status.

We have already discussed the effects of variations in ego efficacy on symptomatic behaviors among women in the West End. A similar conclusion can be drawn from the evidence of problems and difficulties among the men. In general, men with lower levels of ego strength were more likely to manifest diverse symptomatic patterns regardless of social class position, but the effect of differences in ego control was most telling among men of low status. Men with low levels of ego control were in poorer physical health, had more psychoneurotic symptoms, and had more severe social problems than men with strong ego controls. But the association between low ego control and problems or difficulties, especially in the sphere of physical health and psychoneurotic symptoms, was very marked among men in the lowest social class positions.

Although we have found marked differences in the interrelationships between aspects of housing and residence, community experience, family relationships, work orientations, and attitudes among people at different social class levels, these class variations are even more striking with respect to the determinants and consequences of personality characteristics. In this light, it is noteworthy that significant relationships between personality and social behavior so often fail to materialize in many studies. After the fact, however, it is reasonable to observe that the influence of personality on social behavior is regularly conditioned by the social context in which it occurs and by the various meanings of any behavior depending on an individual's social position. Even granted this, the influence of personality differences on behaviors and attitudes are rarely as powerful as the influence of social class or of other discrete statuses and roles. To some degree, this is due to the fact that many personality differences are already embedded in social class differences and even in different statuses and roles. Beyond this, however, the significance of personality characteristics for social behavior appears to be extraordinarily pervasive despite the limited potency of any individual personality trait.

Of the two major personality dispositions that proved of value in accounting for social behavior and attitudes of people in the West End, variations in social anxiety seemed most consequential for people of low status and variations in ego efficacy or control were most significant for people in moderately high social class positions. In view of the great importance of sociability for working-class people, social anxiety creates limitations to the possibility of realizing those behaviors that are the major functional adaptations to working-class life. The rejection of immigrants and people of different ethnic origins, the segregation of residential opportunities, obstacles to a range of options in work have all contributed to the heightened importance of the community and local social relationships in working-class experience.

Among people of high status, high levels of social anxiety are easily compensated by other resources available to them. But for people in lower status positions, it is a particularly grave deficit since it limits the adequate utilization of typical working-class resources in the form of neighbors, kin, and local facilities within the residential community. Ego efficacy or control presents a different set of issues. Since opportunities for advancement and for the successful realization of ambitions and strivings are so limited for working-class people, high levels of ego efficacy are only minor assets for them. But a high degree of ego efficacy or control is essential for effective functioning at higher status levels. And, in fact, we have found that, by and large, differences in these ego strengths are generally inconsequential for people in lower status positions, while they make a substantial difference to social behavior and attitudes among people of higher status.

From a more theoretical vantage point, it is evident that a number of personality differences characterize the personal styles of people in different social class positions. These differences are most apparent in the response to discrete situations representing specific conditions. Differences in broader personality constellations, reflecting general dispositions without regard for the specific conditions that may evoke them, are less striking. It may be that these differences are more substantial among people who are more typical representatives of these different statuses. However, the small number of studies of social class differences in personality reveal a similar trend of relatively modest differences. The major personality distinction that varied for people of different status positions in the West End appeared for those characteristics we have referred to as ego efficacy or control. For these and other attributes, the origins of differences are difficult to determine without longitudinal studies. But the patterns of relationship suggest that parental status provided some of the initial impetus to personality differentiation, although later experiences and, particularly, the different conditions, achievements, and resources associated with social class positions sharpened (or counteracted) these earlier influences on personality formation.

Although personality differences are influenced by social class origins and by class-linked adult experiences and, thus, encapsulate class differences, class-related personality characteristics do not account for most of the variation in behavior of people in different social class positions. The independent significance of social class position, as a summary measure of differences in personal history, current status, and the availability of resources and opportunities, persists. One reason this must inevitably be the case is that the behavioral or attitudinal consequences of a given personality characteristic are not uniform but vary depending on social class position. We can only conclude that personality mediates the impact of any situation on the individual by defining the meaning of an event or situation for that person given the realities of social class and of other status and role positions. Thus, extensive, local social interaction, so typical in a working-class community, was seriously impeded by social anxiety among people of lower status. But social anxiety did not affect such relationships for those of higher status for whom, in any event, such local involvement was less frequent and less crucial. Another instance can be found in the varying effects of ego efficacy or control on the behavior and attitudes of people in different social positions. At moderately high status levels, people who were efficacious manifested all the strivings and individualism associated with these ego capacities. But at lower status levels, efficacious people behaved quite differently, often in opposite ways. Since their desires for mastery and control could not be fulfilled through the channels of work and achievement in our society, such unrealistic strivings had to be suppressed or channelized into other areas in which they might be realized.

What is this? What's all
this questions anyhow?
All I know is I'm living.
The rest is details.
    —A West Ender

10 Working-class Life and the Structure of Social Class

The Working-class Experience: A Summary

Patterns of working-class behavior and the ways in which the lives of
workers differ from those of people in other social class positions reveal
some of the consequences of stratification in our society. Yet several
important questions remain unclarified. Although we have considered the
specific determinants of social class differences in many different areas of
behavior, attitude, and personality, we have not dealt with the larger
implications of these findings for understanding the dominant social forces
that account for global social class differences in functioning. Moreover,
we have yet to examine the nature of the social class system of our society
as a source of influences and experiences that affect the daily lives of
working-class people. After reviewing some of the data, observations, and
conclusions about working-class roles and role functioning, we can turn to
these fundamental questions about causal relationships and sequences.

    Broadly considered, the history of low status populations is a repetitive
experience of deprivation and minor crises interrupted by periodic gains
and major catastrophes. In the long run of social change, progress in
economic and occupational life, in expanding social opportunities, and in
wider political participation have inevitably filtered through to the working
class. Some of these have been fundamental changes in the structure of
society that have affected the organization of social classes and the
meaning of social position. Even when such progress has been quite profound, its potentials have been only slowly realized by the great mass of
the population. Certainly the Marx-Engels prediction that society would
become increasingly polarized around an increasingly wealthy and powerful
upper class and an increasingly impoverished and powerless lower class has
not been verified by social events. At the same time, during successive

periods of progress, the lowest status populations have been the beneficiaries of the smallest gains in both an absolute and a relative sense. Moreover, from a human point of view, even these gains have been too little
and too late since the earlier phases of change have so often left a wreckage
of lives and hopes among the poorest people. In the perspective of history,
we can see how each crisis that affected low status populations was
eventually mitigated by later social developments. But the inequity in the
distribution of benefits has often persisted through the later experience
of different social classes.

In many respects, the immigrant experience in the urban slums of the
United States was a recapitulation of this situation. Most immigrants were
destined to fill the lowest occupational ranks, particularly as the tide of
immigration increased. They were in a poor competitive position to
demand decent wages, adequate housing, a modicum of social recognition.
But many of the immigrants or, at least, their children established levels of
living and experienced opportunities that were superior to those in their
native lands. The underlying hostility they may have felt because of
deprivation and ostracization were readily displaced toward other ethnic
groups, often in competition with one another for jobs, housing, and
esteem. Rarely did they develop a basic sense of a common working-class
identity generated around a feeling of common interests. But the ethnic
communities in which they lived provided some compensation for feelings
of worthlessness and powerlessness and bridged the gap between the human
needs of low status immigrants and the impersonal, labor force functions
they served in the larger society.

Many aspects of housing behavior among low status populations reflect
this central importance of the local community. The condition of buildings,
of crowding, of neighborhood maintenance may often be deplorable. These
conditions have generally improved with declining rates of immigration,
but even in old, working-class slums like the West End the basic housing
stock is often poor. Even within so narrow a range of housing conditions,
higher social class positions tend to be associated with better housing.
Many working-class people make the best of these limitations and create
a decent living environment by extensive efforts to paint, decorate, and
clean their apartments. And the neighborhood often has a personal
meaning beyond the quality of housing. Indeed, variations in housing
quality did not adequately account for apartment satisfaction in the West
End. People of lower status frequently adjust their housing expectations
to the limited opportunities they find. However, when poor people in the
West End lived in good housing, they were more likely to be satisfied than

were people in more adequate financial circumstances. Satisfied or not, they accepted the situation and rarely planned to move. But for many people, local commitments and satisfactions provide recompense for inadequacies of housing and life situations. More than that, many working-class people become so deeply involved with their residential communities that we can only describe it as a sense of territorial identity. The price of such investment is frequently a narrow conception of the world and restricted boundaries within which people feel free to carry out their daily lives.

The residential orientations of people in the West End who were of moderate or relatively high status were also influenced by the general working-class atmosphere of friendliness, warmth, and participation. While some people of high status lived there only as a temporary convenience, others maintained ethnic, kinship, and friendship ties that deterred them from moving to housing commensurate with their social and economic positions. But the overall embeddedness in closeknit network relationships, the dominant pattern of the organization of social interaction in working-class residential areas, was more crucial for working-class people than for those of higher status. For people of higher status, locally-based, community commitments may become quite meaningful but higher status implies a wider of range of options. For people in lower status positions, such commitments are often the only investments they can make and such investments are an essential basis for stability and a sense of meaningful social participation. Even given this, there is a residual class difference that is difficult to capture except metaphorically. The image of home, of a feeling of kinship among unrelated individuals, and a sense of belonging and of proprietary rights establish the quality of working-class conceptions of neighborhood. The significance of kinship in working-class life has often been noted; undoubtedly close ties among parents and their adult children and between siblings are widespread. But it is the expansion of a kinship orientation to a wider realm of local friends and neighbors, rather than actual kinship relationships, that so uniquely typifies community life in the working class.

By contrast with community behavior, marital and family life are less strikingly different for people in different social positions. Certainly social position affects conceptions and expectations of marriage. The marital behavior of young couples fits these culturally-based orientations. But the experience of living together can drastically modify traditional conceptions and expectations. With increasing age, many of the social class differences in marriage become attenuated. Marital role performance among people of higher status becomes increasingly segregated with age, while among working-class people it either becomes more highly shared or remains relatively unchanged. Nonetheless, at all ages the total family pattern among people of lower status is more often segregated than among people of higher status. And because shared marital role relationships are such powerful determinants of marital satisfaction, these small but persisting differences lead to modest differences in levels of marital satisfaction. Moreover, since shared marital role relationships diminish the impact of crises and stresses, the greater vulnerability of people in lower social class positions, combined with the more frequent occurrence of situational pressures and threats, leads to more severe difficulties in personal adaptation.

Social class differences in work and jobs are almost self-evident. Working-class jobs are more routinized, more dependent on supervision and external control, more limited in scope. Although many manual workers develop orientations that would enable them to perform more demanding and challenging jobs, such occupational opportunities are extremely limited at lower status levels. Desires for achievement occasionally reveal themselves in covert job aspirations, in the kinds of tasks people would like to do on the job, and in hopes for the education, occupational careers, and incomes of their children. However, while working-class men are rarely enthusiastic about their jobs, a surprisingly large proportion describe themselves as satisfied. The sources of their satisfactions are most often the external rewards they obtain or pride in the sense of supporting the family, a contrast with men of higher status for whom intrinsic features of work roles are more often the reasons for job satisfaction. Although the range of job opportunities for working-class women are even narrower and there are greater impediments and more limited motivations to work, the total work situation is similar. Many working-class women, initially impelled to seek jobs for financial reasons, find work quite pleasurable. But status as clearly defines the kinds of jobs that are available and the possibilities of intrinsic work satisfactions as for men.

As with attitudes toward work, other social attitudes of working-class people are readily misunderstood without an understanding of the context and meaning of these views. The working class has been described as conservative, self-interested, authoritarian, and ethnocentric, and these attributions have as often been rejected by other observers. However, the attitudes of working-class people are not as ideologically committed as these terms imply. Their attitudes are more pragmatic and reflect the pressures of social conformity and the impact of situational forces and immediate experiences. Most working-class people have little access to and familiarity with the complex interplay of ideological or social forces. Intricate political structures and governmental or industrial bureaucracies are given a personalized meaning in the assumed attitudes of politicians or bureaucrats. Thus, working-class support of political candidates from the radical right may be due to the attractive public relations of candidates with easy solutions to complex problems (better law enforcement, no support for people who won't work) rather than reflections of ethno-centricity or other ideological commitments. Working-class attitudes often indicate an underlying conflict between a deep, if inchoate, sense of class differences and common interests and the blandishments of potential success. But the contrast between working-class realities of limited oppor-tunity and, simultaneously, widespread beliefs in the importance of ability for achievement and the freedom for enterprise in industrial democracies inevitably intensifies self-derogation. The importance of social conformity stems, in part, from this sense of individual inadequacy and the necessity of group support to achieve a sense of personal value or a rudimentary feeling of concerted strength.

Although social class differences in personality are only of moderate strength, people in different social class positions respond differently to many evocative situations in many subtle ways. The precarious sense of self-esteem among many working-class people is evident in sensitivity to rebuff, to being misunderstood, to feelings of social isolation, to status differences. Effective skills in developing and maintaining close social rela-tionships are of central importance to people at lower status levels. Conversely, feelings of internal control and mastery are dominant sources of security for people in higher status positions. These make less difference to people of lower status whose lives are influenced by forces over which they have little control. Thus, ego efficacy or control at higher status levels produces the characteristics associated with an achieving society: success-striving, individualism, freedom from traditional ties. For the working class, efficacy and control do not lead to the same behaviors but are exercised in the few spheres in which fullfillment can be anticipated. Personality characteristics, thus, function primarily to invest experiences with a special meaning that is influenced by the different opportunities and expectations associated with differences in social class position.

Determinants of Working-class Behavior

The conditions of life, life styles, attitudes, and behavior of working-class people are manifestly different from those of people in other social class positions. While there are numerous ambiguities and conflicting findings, diverse studies from many different populations in different places and of different ethnic, religious, and social composition, reveal a number of consistent and important features of social class differentiation. The implications of these differences and similarities, however, lend themselves to varied interpretations. These have been variously formulated as the products of working-class or lower-class culture, as the psychological functioning of low status populations, as matters of economic and other situational limitations that confront working-class people, and as the results of the structural positions of working-class people in the larger society. The two most familiar are the extreme views that conceive working-class behaviors as the derivatives of relatively autonomous, self-perpetuating cultures, unresponsive to changes in class conditions; or, almost at the opposite pole, these behaviors are seen as fairly direct functions of economic realities and deprivations, of poverty, poor housing, low levels of employment, and lack of opportunity.[1] Both views are founded on a core of relevant observation but do an injustice to some of the complexities of human and societal functioning.

Cultural patterns are themselves the result of economic, political, and social realities in the past and present. Although references to cultural forces often imply a very high degree of stability, cultures can be drastically modified by changes in the environment while maintaining the symbols and appearances of continuity. It is difficult, however, to estimate the cultural significance of working-class community life and to disentangle it from immediate functional influences. That working-class communities serve fundamental functions in a highly stratified society seems unambiguous. Such communities offer some of the internal security and support that are otherwise unavailable in the larger society, facilitating a sense of belonging and participation that counteracts experiences of exclusion and exploitation. When insecurity is too profound or exclusion too pervasive, the sense of a common identity necessary for effective community life in the working class may be undermined. This can be seen in populations suffering severe poverty coupled with ostracization and hoplessness. But working-class populations in industrial societies generally develop those minimal standards of living that make such communities possible although they rarely achieve the resources and acceptance that make them superfluous.

The integrity and utility of working-class communities are maintained for most people only to the extent that the structure of inequality in rewards and opportunities persists. That stability of subcultural commit-

ments occasionally occurs in working-class communities regardless of
greater opportunities and rewards is evidenced by those high status people
in the West End whose continued residence in the area hinged upon the
intensity of these commitments. However, the high degree of investment in
traditional beliefs and in a limited set of relationships was partly fostered
by personal constraints and anxieties. Indeed, the process of social mobility
regularly draws off cohorts of people from working-class communities
precisely because the subjective and objective rewards of higher status override subcultural commitments and identities and local social relationships.
Common values, beliefs, and life styles seem to have little retentive power
in their own right, dissociated from the patterns of working-class social
organization which they supplement. The dominant influences of the
immediate, working-class environment stem, rather, from concrete patterns
of local, social interaction and community involvement. But important
though these are, their direct effects, at least in the West End, were central
mainly for defining the geographical boundaries of social relationships and
resource use and for providing a sense of personal security.

It is reasonable to speak of working-class subcultures (or cultures of
poverty) as these are concretely embodied within working-class residential
areas or within other environments in which working-class people regularly
meet and interact. Such environments are inevitably part-cultures or part-
societies, organized around relatively homogeneous communities of
interest in complex, differentiated societies (Foster, 1953). They are themselves products of and adaptations to institutionalized stratifications in
society. Although ethnic or regional attributes have frequently been the
ostensible bases for the rejection of working-class people and especially of
newcomers to the urban, industrial environment, cultural assimilation
within the larger society seems to be a minor difficulty for most people.
It is the denial of acceptance and esteem by the larger society, rather than
any resistance to assimilation among working-class people, that makes
working-class communities viable and even essential. And it is their
relatively high degree of isolation from the larger society that results in
that amalgam from diverse origins and diverse current forces that we can,
descriptively, refer to as working-class cultures. Under these conditions,
social facilitation among neighbors, friends, and kin, or among teenage
peers, as distinguished from cultural commitment, may encourage some
behaviors and discourage others. But such modest influences are far from
indicating the coercive power of the culture itself. Indeed, there are few
evidences of monolithic, class-related behaviors or attitudes that would
imply the power of cultural norms or other purely cultural influences.

The historical and contemporary significance of working-class communities also implies that any model that conceives of purely situational forces, incomes, employment, or housing, as exclusive or even primary determinants of the behavior of working-class people must necessarily be oversimplified. Working-class communities and community life are themselves, in part, adaptations to marked inequalities in income, employment, and housing. The community as a system serves both to soften the impact of poverty, of job insecurity, and of poor housing conditions and to mitigate optimism stemming from improvements in the economic, employment, or housing situation. At the extremes, of course, changes in these conditions may doom the existence of working-class communities. Unrelenting, long-term poverty, continued unemployment, degraded housing conditions may lead to so severe a deterioration of morale that little semblance of social organization can persist. Even within a stable, working-class community, those people who suffer these conditions in the extreme are least capable of sustaining a high level of social and community participation. At the other end of the scale as well, long periods of affluence, of full employment, of superior low- and moderate-income housing opportunities are likely to reduce the population of working-class communities and gradually to draw off the residents who have or can achieve these goods. However, despite more than two decades of prosperity and industrial advance that have affected the character of the labor force and of working-class movements in Western countries, working-class communities have continued to exist and to serve important, integrative functions. More affluent workers and those whose jobs provide new sources of security and esteem may have moved out of these communities in larger numbers, but they have been replaced by new incumbents to low status positions in almost every Western European country as well as in the United States. Many of the workers who have achieved new status or higher incomes have retained a traditional suspiciousness about the future or have remained invested in the closeknit networks within working-class communities. Naturally, extensive programs of urban renewal and the widespread development of new forms of low- and moderate-income housing have further diminished the availability of old-style working-class communities, although new, even suburban, communities have frequently taken over their functions.

Many of the discussions of deprivation which stress situational forces and overlook the social class context in which poverty or unemployment or poor housing exist are focused primarily on the most severely underpriviliged populations. In such instances, there can be little doubt that improvements in income, employment, or housing are likely to have fairly dramatic consequences in stemming the tide of demoralization and deterioration. In light of the fact that the origins of these conditions can be traced quite regularly to societal forces, programs to ameliorate extreme underprivilege are matters of social responsibility and need no justification on the basis of their consequences for the society as a whole.[2] Even under these circumstances, one must recognize that from a psychological viewpoint, it would be far more meaningful and consequential to experience an increased range of opportunities or a better competitive position in the society. Such opportunities and competitive positions, however, derive from the position of different social classes within the total structure rather than from an immediate sense of marginal instead of submarginal existence.

In less severe conditions of poverty, unemployment, or poor housing, the issues are more complex but are even more integrally linked to the total social class context. Even within a working-class community like the West End, with a narrow range of differences in housing quality and a narrow range of rents, higher status led to better housing. This was not merely a function of income differentials but involved many other aspects of social class origins, social class position, age, and future expectations. Indeed, many other factors such as marital adjustment and personal difficulties were implicated in assessing the determinants of housing, factors that were indirectly related to the total position of low status individuals in our society rather than to low income alone. Except for truly degraded housing, however, the consequences of poor physical housing seem to be fairly limited and are, to some degree, compensated by other residential experiences. Poverty and unemployment have wider ramifications. They lead readily to deteriorating personal and family situations and create a context in which only rudimentary and readily accessible satisfactions are possible. But poor economic circumstances and unemployment also have complex consequences which vary for people in different social class positions, with different past experiences and different future potentialities. Although immediate improvements in income or jobs for the unemployed are clearly consequential, the larger and longer-range issues concern marked improvements in earning power, opportunities for job security, more meaningful work, and conditions that allow the development of initiative and self-esteem. Deprivations of this nature, rather than the more severe forms of underprivilege that are less frequent and more transient, influence the total experience of working-class people. These are inherent in their social class situation rather than in the concrete consequences denoted by a list of deprivations.

Another approach to the determinants of working-class behavior finds its source in the psychology of working-class people. Many aspects of working-class life, including poverty, unemployment, and low occupational status themselves, have been attributed to low levels of motivation or aspiration. Sometimes they are traced to such personal characteristics as dependency or incompetence. The findings on personality in the West End provide no more support than other studies for tracing social class differences in behavior to personality alone. The issue of personal dependency, in particular, has clearly been misunderstood and overstated. Working-class people are somewhat more dependent on close ties to familiar people than are those of higher status. But the majority of West Enders were moderately or markedly independent regardless of social class position. Moreover, few differences in behavior could be traced to social class differences in dependency. Among people in the West End, the important distinction in behavior grew out of differences in the effectiveness of establishing meaningful interpersonal relationships. This was largely a function of the level of anxiety. At all social class levels, anxious people were less capable of maintaining extensive interpersonal contacts than those who were relaxed in social intercourse. The toll was greatest for people of low status but this was due to the absence of alternative sources of security and satisfaction, not because of higher levels of anxiety. People of higher status were more often efficacious or showed a capacity for ego control and these differences did have behavioral consequences. But even these behavioral consequences were, at best, of modest proportion and were simultaneously influenced by social class position itself. Indeed, the very different consequences of attitudes and personality for people in different social class positions can only be understood in the context of the very great variations in social class realities, a difference, fundamentally, in the likelihood of fulfilling or being frustrated in the effort to realize personal potentials.

Behind the importance of working-class culture, supplementing the impact of situational forces, defining the meaning of attitudes and personality among working-class people, lies the structure of social class in society. Cultural patterns, economic influences, or psychological forces alone account for relatively small segments of working-class experience and are themselves explicable mainly as products of a particular system of social stratification. The effects of working-class culture, of low incomes and unemployment, of personality and attitudes, in fact, of working-class social organization, can be appreciated only within the framework of a relatively enduring, institutionalized social class system. The comparisons among people living in a single neighborhood, who occupy different social class positions, and vary along all these other dimensions as well, provides a very useful basis for assessing these interrelationships.

The conclusion that stands out with the starkest clarity is that while each explanatory dimension—cultural commitment, community involvement, economic and employment status, or personality and attitudes—is occasionally of considerable value in accounting for class differences in behavior, the only pervasive and frequently powerful determinant of role functioning in many different areas is the position an individual holds in the social class structure. Not only did social class itself explain some of the behavioral differences in many spheres, but the influence of other specific factors generally differed for people in different social class positions. In effect, the meaning and consequence of any given experience are markedly affected by the different life chances, the different competitive positions of people in different social class statuses.

In fact, such findings are eminently reasonable if one takes account of the ramifications of social class position in our society. Social class, as we have used this concept operationally, reflects differences in educational attainment and in occupational status. In a most direct and immediate sense, the realistic expectations of people with different levels of education and with different levels of occupational achievement vary enormously. Whatever the current family income, people with more education and with greater technical skills can anticipate higher future incomes. The likelihood of employment, except under unusual conditions of recessions that differentially affect those sectors of the economy that rely on higher levels of skill, is directly affected by education. Even other influences, like the effects of age on future expectations, are modified by differences in social class position. Beyond the more evident material benefits of social position, differences in social class status signify differences in prestige. Although the foundations of self-esteem may lie in childhood experience, differences in prestige, reflected in objective circumstances and in a host of subtler relationships, are bound to influence such self-estimates. Indeed, as we have shown, slight variations in the prestige of attributes more distantly linked to status, like degree of assimilation or ethnicity, produce different perceptions of one's own social class position. All of these factors, in turn, influence the range of options available to individuals and, thus, the kinds of expectations one may reasonably maintain. Even in the midst of difficulties, financial or personal, people of higher status are more likely to know about the resources for getting help, to find readier access to these resources, to be treated with greater consideration, and, ultimately, to receive more assistance.

One can only conclude that the realistic consequences of these differences in social class position are themselves primary factors in any explanation of differences in behavior. Their further influence on expectations of resources, opportunities, power, and control inevitably affect the meaning of any situation and the interpretation of any role or function. Other factors may occasionally be of great significance and certainly contribute to a total explanation. But their very significance itself varies for people who see the issue from different social class vantage points. Even at the extremes of deprivation, where situational forces may have quite potent consequences, ameliorative efforts that do nothing to alter the short-range or long-range social class position of individuals or to modify that structure itself can only be palliative in consequence.

In this light, the fundamental feature of inequality in our society lies in the nature of the social class system itself rather than in any of its symptomatic manifestations. It is the positional relationship of individuals to a population spread over a wide hierarchically-ordered range that accounts for major differences in behavior and perspective. These positional relationships encapsulate a host of invidious distinctions and inequalities of opportunity, access, and potentiality as well as differences in resources and competitive status. But they are integral to a highly differentiated system of social stratification. In order to understand the significance of social class position more fully, we must turn from its behavioral consequences to an examination of the system itself. In this way, we can determine its dominant characteristics and its implications for a population that must inevitably be distributed through the range of positions that the system defines.

Dimensions of Stratification in Modern Societies

Many of the economic, social, and political inequalities of our society are well documented and widely accepted.[3] That these inequalities can reasonably and usefully be conceived as manifestations of a social class structure, however, is more frequently challenged by theoretical analyses. One alternative conception views inequalities as largely functional: differential rewards are necessary for the recruitment of individuals into socially valued and difficult or demanding roles.[4] This is compatible with a social class model but implies a more rational process of assigning rewards and of allocating positions than is justified. Another view regards widespread social mobility as a force that disrupts the organization of social positions in a class structure; from this vantage point, social class formulations should be limited to societies with relatively fixed and extreme status distinctions.[5] Finally, questions frequently arise concerning the applicability of social class conceptions to a society in which there are several discrete hierarchies of status, in which there is little consciousness of class interests, and in which no single elite functions as a unilateral ruling class.[6] While these factors are important in describing the characteristics of different class systems, the utility of the social class model is independent of these considerations. Neither the functional allocation of statuses, the extent of social mobility, nor the characteristics of social strata warrant the conclusion that the rigidities of social class divisions have virtually disappeared from our society.

There are two major sources of confusion in placing modern, industrial systems of stratification in perspective. One of these is the heritage of Marxist analyses of social class which has influenced both adherents and critics disproportionately in conceptualizing social class.[7] For Marx and Engels a differentiated conception of social class was essential for historical and economic analysis, but a gross dichotomy, encapsulated in the opposition of ruler and ruled or of oppressor and oppressed, served as their basis for formulating a revolutionary program.[8] Their revolutionary goals led them to stress class consciousness, the awareness of common interests, as a defining characteristic of social classes. But such vivid consciousness of common interests occurred only in relatively transitory situations of imminent change and could hardly serve to assert or deny the existence of social classes. Their concern with revolutionary potentials in society led them to misinterpret the development of capitalism as an increasing polarization of two extreme classes in direct conflict with one another.[9] Although fundamental changes in capitalism were taking place during their lifetimes, Marx and even Engels refused to recognize the full extent to which the structure of capitalism itself had altered. Even their fundamental criterion for distinguishing social classes, access to and control over the means of production, became insufficient for characterizing the complex distributions of industrial and managerial power in modern societies.

Another source of confusion about social class lies in misconceptions concerning stratification in other social systems. The status hierarchies of former European societies and of other nonindustrial countries are often conceived as far more rigid and ascriptively defined than the evidence warrants. When these images are contrasted with an exaggerated view of the fluidity and equality in modern societies, there seems to be little basis for conceptualizing the patterns of industrial social structures in terms of social class.[10] Even in the modern world, distinctions are often made between the United States and other industrial societies with the assumption, on this side of the Atlantic, that social class differences are less patent here and, on the other side, that the United States represents some of the most marked class inequalities in the Western world. On the basis of the few studies that permit comparison, however, differences in the degree of social class inequality among industrialized nations seem to be relatively minor compared to the fundamental similarities in the structure of social class, in the consequences of class position, and in the patterns of social mobility or stability. These similarities, moreover, cut across political distinctions between capitalist, socialist, and communist societies, although there are undoubtedly major differences in the determinants of class position and in the sources of power and influence.[11]

In a general sense, we can assume that the stratification systems of modern, industrial societies are less extreme, more flexible, and reveal higher rates of social mobility than those of preindustrial societies. But the stratification systems of different, industrialized countries are distinctive from one another, not by virtue of flexibility and mobility patterns, but because of differences in the criteria and interrelationships of social positions. There are three main criteria or dimensions by which social position may be accorded: legal-political, economic-occupational, and social-psychological.[12] All stratification systems involve all three dimensions of classification and one major distinction among societies is the primacy of one or another dimension in providing the prerogatives and resources the society can offer. The term social class can be used quite generally to include all the forms of stratification based on these dimensions or, in a narrower and more specific sense, to designate the economic and occupational criteria of stratification.

The *legal-political* dimension is represented by inequalities in prerogatives, resources, and responsibilities (power, prestige, access, authority, influence) in the systems of social control, decision-making, and the adjudication of conflict. The extreme forms of political and legal monopoly are represented by the classical caste system of India, the oriental despotisms, and the feudal domains of the early Middle Ages. But there are numerous systems like the estate systems of renaissance Europe in which legal and political dimensions of stratification predominate although the prerogatives, resources, and responsibilities are not monopolized by any single elite. In modern societies, the legal-political dimension of stratification is primary mainly in fascist and communist dictatorships. Even in a highly industrialized country like the Soviet Union, party affiliation confers many legal and political prerogatives, resources, and responsibilities and provides access to other forms of status.

It is in the spheres of legal and political control that the industrial democracies have come closest to a potentially egalitarian distribution of prerogatives. However, political power, the essential medium of exchange in this sphere, can and does remain unequally distributed despite the ultimate sanction implied in universal suffrage.[13] The development of organizations and other collectivities that can assert some degree of "countervailing" power gives greater reality to the widespread exercise of citizenship. At the lowest levels of the stratification system, however, there remain people who are essentially disenfranchised by virtue of a sense of powerlessness, of alienation, of inability to relate personal needs to political objectives, of difficulty in reaching or dealing with bureaucracies, and, sometimes, because of overt impairment of voting rights.

The *economic-occupational* dimension of stratification is the dominant criterion of social position in the industrial democracies but is influential in all industrial and industrializing countries. Economic-occupational status is defined by access to and competitive priority in the commodity, service, investment, and labor markets which determine the life chances of individuals. Economic and occupational prerogatives include purchasing power for goods and services, opportunities for jobs, the availability of resources for financing a desired standard of living or capital investments, and considerable autonomy in economic and occupational activities. Responsibilities in this sphere involve obligations for administrative decision-making or rendering of services and opportunities to exercise control beyond personal economic position. This dimension of stratification became uniquely significant with the emergence of medieval cities as centers of exchange and manufactures. With the development of industrial society economic and occupational criteria gained precedence at a national level.[14] In particular, the prerogatives, resources, and potential responsibilities provided by wealth or a highly marketable skill or occupation were slowly liberated from the influence of legal-political or other prior status distinctions.[15] However, like political-legal status, economic and occupational resources and opportunities are transmitted from parent to child. This resuts in elite groups with many aristocratic pretensions and a very high standard of living and, at the other extreme, an underclass of poor, occupationally disabled, virtually powerless people largely deprived of responsibility, autonomy, and social esteem. While upward mobility is possible for the working class, just as downward mobility is possible for the economic and occupational aristocracy, major interchange within a generation or even between two generations is rare.

The third dimension of stratification is represented by prerogatives, resources, and responsibilities in the *social-psychological* sphere and is often referred to as social status. It depends upon judgments and acceptance by peers and may be based on birth, wealth, skills in social interaction, or on ethnicity, residence, or cultural orientation. This dimension includes those psychological attributes related to social prestige or social inferiority: a sense of power or powerlessness, of self-esteem or self-derogation, of autonomy or dependency, and of responsibility or futility.[16] Status differences in child-rearing and in other developmental experiences, as well as the realities of economic and occupational opportunity, perpetuate class-based personality characteristics, self-conceptions, and social expectations. Personality or intellectual achievements may occasionally overcome social status deficits and facilitate inclusion in groups which might otherwise be impervious to the newcomer. But these highly selective processes affect only a small proportion of individuals. On a massive scale, ethnicity, residence, and cultural orientations readily lead to social exclusion despite status achievements in other spheres. Being Negro or Jewish or Japanese often suffice to insure status inequality despite high income, occupational skills, or political positions.

The potency of social selection and cohesiveness among social strata in the United States was one of the striking findings in the early investigations of American communities. Social status was clearly a major basis for social interaction in this country and a source of influence on other dimensions of achievement in the social class system.[17] Moreover, it proved to be a characteristic feature of social organization among all strata in small communities as well as in local neighborhoods of large urban areas. However, social and psychological factors are rarely, if ever, the predominant dimensions in a social class system. They serve primarily as a basis for stabilizing or amalgamating power and privileges or for generalizing the prestige of positions achieved in other spheres. In the working class, the social-psychological dimension may be of considerable importance in creating impediments to economic or occupational mobility. Efforts to amalgamate community resources may also occur among low status people, but the lack of power and privilege implies that there are few prerogatives and opportunities that can be aggregated or distributed.[18] But working-class ethnic groups have utilized collective action: when voting in bloc, strengthening the demand for new or improved representation or local facilities, and even to press for wider political or economic opportunities.

The powerful tendency for the amalgamation of status and privilege is a characteristic of all societies and one of the major factors behind the stability of social class positions over many generations. At both the individual and the class level, there is a propensity for the privileges of status to extend beyond the sphere of achievement. People who achieve political power or influence are likely to use these as a basis for attaining greater wealth and prestige; those who gain economic or occupational status strive for political influence and social esteem; and prestige, which almost invariably implies former if not current status on other dimensions, proves extraordinarily useful in gaining economic-occupational or political advantages. The prerogatives and resources of higher social class positions function as circulating social currency which are useful in facilitating the acquisition of additional opportunities and privileges. As a consequence, even in a system that emphasizes functional criteria for status achievement, the influence of people who have inherited (or acquired) other attributes of status must be weighed against a standard of pure ability in selecting people for positions that carry status prerogatives. As the British conservatives more readily acknowledge than do Americans, the mere fact of inherited position provides some insurance that an incumbent is socially and ideologically, if not intellectually, the right kind of person for roles of high occupational or political status (McKenzie and Silver, 1968). In its most concrete form, strivings for the amalgamation of power and privilege may be viewed as efforts to attain status consistency (Benoit-Smullyan, 1944; Lenski, 1966). Many individuals in our society have several discrepant statuses (for example, between education, occupation, and income), and those who find themselves in this position generally seek consistency at the level of their highest achievement. Beyond this, however, the nature of opportunities in our society is such that, even apart from deliberately seeking advantage, the acquisition of status in any sphere opens up new options and vistas that facilitate any further search for greater wealth, security, or power.

The amalgamation of privilege in industrial societies, however, is not merely a consequence of individual strivings. The availability of power, control, and influence in political, economic, and social life is largely structurally determined and often fulfilled through organizations, associations, and group affiliations. Such combined endeavors, whether in the form of corporations, political parties or interest groups, or social organizations, may provide enormous funds and massive concentrations of effort to obtain legislation, preferential contracts, judicial decisions, or influence in local, regional, and national political structures. However, the constant competition for scarce rewards among business, professional, consumer, union, and special-interest groups occasionally encourages new combinations of power.[19] Underprivileged populations, groups, and the organizations that represent them are effectively ruled out of the opportunity to compete since it is a costly and demanding battle and, even at the level of local communities, involves relatively powerful and prestigeful antagonists. As a consequence, the inequalities of opportunity experienced by working-class people, particularly by its most visibly underprivileged members, are relegated to a position of one among many needs for public intervention or policy change and remain largely unmodified, except for token programs, in an economy of abundance.

Although all systems of according social position by hierarchical rank are based on the relative importance of each of these three dimensions of stratification, inevitably those who can be highly ranked on more than one are in that much more advantageous a position. Nonetheless, except at the very top of the status hierarchies in the industrial democracies, the total position of an individual in our society is generally dominated by his economic or occupational position. Thus, social mobility occurs most frequently and results in alterations of social class position most effectively through economic and occupational achievements. Whatever the forces encouraging status stability in a society, other attributes of an industrial society (and of most other societies as well) necessitate some degree of social mobility. Major limitations to mobility are inevitable sources of strain and deprive the society of the optimum use of human abilities. The accessibility and striving for mobility create a dynamic in the social class structure even of the most rigidly stratified system. Certainly in modern societies the patterns of social mobility are essential components of the functioning of social classes. In view of this, we shall consider the distributions and changes in distribution of incomes and occupations to provide a wider perspective about our system of social stratification and then turn to a fuller analysis of the processes of social mobility in our society.

Structure of Social Class in the United States

During the past century, technological change has led to a major decrease in the population devoted to agricultural labor and to a marked diminution in the unskilled labor force in industry. Economic expansion and structural development have increased the numbers of white-collar workers, administrators, supervisors, and executives. There has been an impressive growth of the gross national product which has filtered through as long-term gains in the standard of living of most industrial workers. Among the rewards of productive efficiency and affluence, the highly-paid service occupations and professions have grown in proportion. But in spite of many changes in the occupational structure and the diffusion of improved standards of living, the huge gap in income between the higher and lower socioeconomic segments of the population has changed but little. The very rich lost some ground during the Great Depression to the advantage of adjacent strata. But the poor received no substantially greater share of the national income in 1965 than in 1929 and remained relatively as poor as before. A similar pattern of stasis is characteristic for many industrialized nations.[20]

The relationships between different income or occupational levels is best revealed by examining the total distribution of incomes and occupations within a society. Within broad limits of precision, both income and occupation can be ranked hierarchically and compared for different periods and for different regions or countries. The shape of this distribution of the population at different income or occupational levels defines the most important features of the economic-occupational class structure. The graphic expression of these distributions in the United States during recent decades immediately reveals the wide gap between top and bottom positions (figures 2 and 3). The major changes that have taken place are also manifest. Changes in the occupational structure since the mid-nineteenth century have sometimes been conceived as a shift from a pyramid with a broad base to a hexagon and, more recently, to a diamond-like shape (Cole, 1955). The estimates of occupational change during recent decades lend some support to this image, the most dramatic change being a gradual diminution of the lowest working-class positions. The effects of technological advance during the last half century are remarkably depicted by changes at each occupational status level. The most striking shift in the occupational structure has been the reduction in size of the lowest status category consisting of unskilled workers and the commensurate increase in size of the adjacent categories of higher manual and lower clerical occupations. Even the highest occupational categories, however, show consistent expansion, but until very recently they have represented only a small proportion of the total labor force.

Changes in the structure of incomes (figure 3) are less dramatic but are roughly consonant with the occupational changes. Indeed, given a time-lag of about two decades, the income distribution follows a course quite parallel to that of the occupational distribution. The income figures

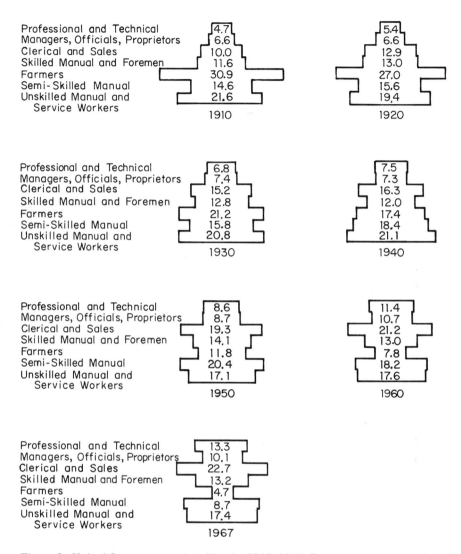

	1910	1920
Professional and Technical	4.7	5.4
Managers, Officials, Proprietors	6.6	6.6
Clerical and Sales	10.0	12.9
Skilled Manual and Foremen	11.6	13.0
Farmers	30.9	27.0
Semi-Skilled Manual	14.6	15.6
Unskilled Manual and Service Workers	21.6	19.4

	1930	1940
Professional and Technical	6.8	7.5
Managers, Officials, Proprietors	7.4	7.3
Clerical and Sales	15.2	16.3
Skilled Manual and Foremen	12.8	12.0
Farmers	21.2	17.4
Semi-Skilled Manual	15.8	18.4
Unskilled Manual and Service Workers	20.8	21.1

	1950	1960
Professional and Technical	8.6	11.4
Managers, Officials, Proprietors	8.7	10.7
Clerical and Sales	19.3	21.2
Skilled Manual and Foremen	14.1	13.0
Farmers	11.8	7.8
Semi-Skilled Manual	20.4	18.2
Unskilled Manual and Service Workers	17.1	17.6

	1967
Professional and Technical	13.3
Managers, Officials, Proprietors	10.1
Clerical and Sales	22.7
Skilled Manual and Foremen	13.2
Farmers	4.7
Semi-Skilled Manual	8.7
Unskilled Manual and Service Workers	17.4

Figure 2. United States occupational levels, 1910–1967. Percent distribution of labor force for selected years.

Sources: U.S. Department of Labor, *Manpower Report of the President* (1963, 1968).

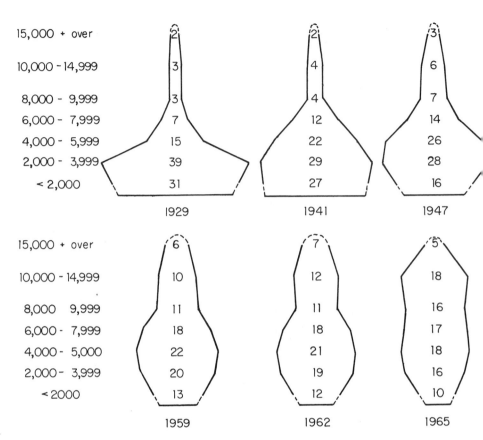

	1929	1941	1947
15,000 + over	2	2	3
10,000 - 14,999	3	4	6
8,000 - 9,999	3	4	7
6,000 - 7,999	7	12	14
4,000 - 5,999	15	22	26
2,000 - 3,999	39	29	28
< 2,000	31	27	16

	1959	1962	1965
15,000 + over	6	7	5
10,000 - 14,999	10	12	18
8,000 9,999	11	11	16
6,000 - 7,999	18	18	17
4,000 - 5,000	22	21	18
2,000 - 3,999	20	19	16
< 2000	13	12	10

Figure 3. United States family personal incomes, 1929–1967. Percent distribution of families and unrelated individuals for selected years.
Sources: Herman P. Miller, *Income Distribution in the United States* (U.S. Bureau of the Census, 1966); *Current Population Reports,* series P–60, no. 51 (U.S. Bureau of the Census, 1967).

graphically represent the huge bulge at the bottom of the income distribution and the long, narrow peak of high incomes in 1929 (figure 3).[21] By 1965 the proportions at the bottom of the income scale had diminished quite sharply while the proportions at the top had increased. The large proportion in the center of the distribution had gradually become more evenly spread over a wider range of middle income categories. If the purchasing power of each income category is viewed as identical in 1929 and in 1965 (with incomes adjusted to 1962 dollars), we can see that only a small proportion of the population (10 percent) were in the very lowest income categories in 1965 compared with almost one-third of the population (31 percent) at this level in 1929. In absolute terms, therefore, the decades between 1929 and 1965 have witnessed a marked expansion of incomes and of purchasing power for the American population. But further consideration of these changes and their implications modifies the initial impression of a significant equalization of incomes.

The increases in real income over the last few decades at every income level are mainly due to the expansion of the economy itself, resulting in an increase in the total national income. Because of this, the standard of living of the population as a whole rose considerably. In addition to a gross increase in the incomes of individuals, moreover, the expansion of the economy has encompassed an enormous increase in the number of secondary breadwinners, especially working wives.[22] Some of the appearance of equalization of incomes, particularly the decreased proportion of the population at the lowest income levels and the increased proportion in the middle of the income distribution results, thus, from the fact that two salaries per family are frequently being counted in more recent years in place of the salary of a sole breadwinner that obtained more widely in earlier decades. While this is a form of redistribution it must be recognized as the product of many secondary breadwinners since this also entails many additional but invisible costs (child care, transportation, food, clothing, and so forth). Finally, we must note that there has been an enormous increase in transfer payments in the form of social security, welfare, and necessary services and any evaluation of the meaning of income distributions must take account of these supplements to income.

In spite of all these factors, and despite the expansion of purchasing power throughout the entire range of incomes due to increases in the national income, the *relative economic position* of different segments of the population remained almost unchanged. Indeed, in view of these several considerations, it is likely that the additions to the national income between 1929 and 1965 were distributed *more* unequally than the earlier distribution of incomes itself. If we consider only the gross pattern of relative income shares of the population, the original inequalities in the income distribution of 1929 were largely sustained during the economic expansion of the intervening years (table 10.1)[23]

Closer analysis reveals even more clearly what occurred during almost four decades. Calculated as the share of the national income received by successive fifths (or quintiles) of the total population, the major change between 1929 and 1965 was a drop from 54 to 43 percent in the share received by the upper 20 percent of the population. Indeed, even this loss was in reality sustained only by the top 5 percent since the remaining 15 percent at the top experienced a major gain in its share of the national income. The loss among the top 5 percent filtered down as a gain to adjacent fifths of the population. The lowest 20 percent of the population received least benefit from this loss. Its share rose only 1 percent from 4 percent of the national income in 1929 to 5 percent in 1965. In effect, those who already had substantial incomes benefited most from the proportional loss by a small number of very rich just as they benefited most from the expansion of the national income.[24] Thus, while there has been a rise in income levels for the population as a whole, each income group gained in almost exact proportion to the grossly unequal shares of the national income that existed in 1929. Far from an equalization of incomes, even the gains of the economy have served to maintain the relative position of each income group by perpetuating former inequalities.

TABLE 10.1   Proportion of total national income received by each fifth and by top 5 percent of population, United States, 1929–1965

Population (families and unrelated individuals) divided into income ranks	Percentage of total national income received					
	1965	1962	1960	1944	1941	1929
Lowest fifth	5	5	5	5	5	(4)]
Second fifth	11	11	11	11	10	(9)] 13
Third fifth	17	16	16	16	15	14
Fourth fifth	24	23	23	22	22	19
Highest fifth	43	46	45	46	49	54
Total	100	100	100	100	100	100
Top 5 percent	16	20	20	21	24	30

Source: Data for the period 1929–1962 from Miller, 1966, table 1–1. Data for 1965 from U.S. Bureau of the Census, 1967.

The graduated federal income tax did not alter this pattern since it is more than counteracted by the regressive taxes of state and local governments like sales and real estate taxes which are disproportionately burdensome on the lowest income groups (Miller, 1966).

From an objective point of view, it is the relative distribution of rewards which is fundamental for the social class structure. Since changes in income during the past few decades have not substantially altered the relative distribution of incomes or of purchasing power, they have not contributed to any marked change in the social class structure of the United States. In fact, this is a very conservative interpretation of the data since there are many suggestive indications that inequality has actually increased. At the very least, we would assume that a dramatic change in the occupational distribution would lead to a commensurate change in the income distribution. The lack of such equivalence suggests either that the change in occupational structure is somewhat illusory or that, despite greater skill and status, incomes have not kept pace and reflect the persistence of old inequalities in a new pattern of occupational distribution.

On the other hand, the sense of affluence and of improved standards of living appears too widespread to be dismissed. Certainly there are diminished proportions of people with very low economic and occupational positions, and a small but important expansion of population into upper levels of income and of occupation. By criteria of income, occupation, or standard of living, a large proportion of the population has experienced improvement compared to their parents, although people at higher levels of the social class system experienced equal or greater improvement. Of equal importance for the subjective sense of change is the fact that individuals may be economically or occupationally mobile and effectively experience objective changes in status. The process of social mobility is an integral feature of the analysis of a social class system. While the structure of social classes, as an abstract system of positions, may persist unchanged and be little affected by individual changes in position, the rates of upward and downward social mobility in a society have many consequences for the sense of deprivation or opportunity in a population. We shall turn to an examination of social mobility to determine its effects on the system of social class positions.

Social Mobility and Social Class Dynamics

Social mobility, the upward or downward shift in social class positions, occurs in all societies but the rates and patterns of movement vary considerably from one nation to another. Several major forces determine the opportunities for social mobility and may act in concert in producing relatively high rates of social mobility.[25] In the United States, the long-term growth of the economy has been of fundamental significance in providing larger opportunities for upward social mobility. Technological change has produced an increase in higher occupational statuses and a decrease in the lowest occupational positions. But social mobility is a movement of individuals within an existing structure and may occur even in a static society. Thus, if people in high status positions have a lower birth rate than do those in low status positions, increased opportunities for upward movement arise. Other changes in social structure—in the openness of the educational system, or an increase in interclass marriage, or more rational job recruitment practices—alter the opportunities for social mobility.[26]

Despite many variations, the rates and patterns of occupational mobility are moderately consistent among the industrialized nations.[27] Certainly the rates do not vary in any evident way with differences in egalitarian ideology. While rates of social mobility have not deteriorated during the past half century in this country, neither have they risen remarkably.[28] However, in comparison with other industrialized nations, the United States has relatively high rates of upward mobility and relatively low rates of downward mobility. But the rates of downward mobility are quite substantial. A rough approximation is given by the ratio of those moving up or down across the barrier between blue-collar and white-collar workers. In the United States this ratio is calculated as 33 percent who move up to 26 percent who move down within a generation.[29] Thus, the *net* rate of upward mobility is exceedingly small. Moreover, those who have been upwardly mobile represent only a small fraction of the people in higher status positions (S. M. Miller, 1960). A great many more nonmanual workers come from nonmanual families than from manual families. Intergenerational movements are widespread but small in scale, leading mainly to shifts into adjacent occupational categories. Movements across many occupational levels are infrequent. The mythical image of the highly motivated and able young man whose self-discipline and ambition soar to the highest achievements is rarely manifest in reality. As studies of top executives suggest, when it takes place it is more likely to be a desperate escape from unhappiness and a frustrating environment than a triumphant flight toward a luminous goal.[30]

Since there is no objective basis for determining what is a high or a low rate of social mobility, it is possible mainly to note that a large minority of the population in our society achieves modest intergenerational changes of occupational position. The extent of deviation from an ideal egalitarian model, however, is revealed by applying a concept of "perfect mobility" in empirical analysis.[31] The criterion of perfect mobility requires a completely random redistribution of occupational positions from one generation to the next as the extreme degree of interchange. The degree of deviation from this criterion is, therefore, a measure of intergenerational occupational stability or inheritance. By this standard there is a great deal of stability in the transmission of occupational statuses from parents to children both in the United States and in other industrialized nations. Intergenerational occupational stability is most frequent among professional, executive, and proprietor statuses and among unskilled workers, while occupational achievement most often occurs among mid-level skilled manual and white-collar workers (Blau and Duncan, 1967; Glass, 1954; Rogoff, 1953). Thus, the highest occupational statuses show the least downward mobility and the lowest occupational statuses have the least upward movement. The division between blue-collar and white-collar workers appears more difficult to cross than are subdivisions within these social class groupings suggesting that this is, indeed, a point of structural division among occupations.[32] Intermarriage between people of similar occupational origins and positions predominates and further supplements tendencies toward stability of social class placement (Blau and Duncan, 1967; Glass, 1954).

Social mobility is not a simple and continuous upward progression. With each stage in the life cycle, the chances of change become progressively narrowed. Intergenerational mobility is more frequent than changes from first to subsequent jobs. And a very large proportion of the upward moves among blue-collar workers and of the downward moves among white-collar workers are quite temporary (Lipset and Bendix, 1959; S. M. Miller, 1960). Most strikingly, there is some indication that those families which show upward mobility in one generation tend to be downwardly mobile in the subsequent generation and, conversely, downward mobility in one generation is often followed by upward mobility in the next generation. This phenomenon of "intergenerational regression toward the mean" is a further limitation to the conception of occupational mobility as a source of major changes in the structure of occupational statuses (Allingham, 1967; Glass, 1954). At the lower levels of the occupational scale, occupational gains and losses are often reflected in (but not calculated as) rates of employment or unemployment and are closely linked to relatively small changes in economic and occupational conditions. During periods of continuous economic expansion, the most seriously underprivileged workers achieve some of the greatest gains, but even minor economic contractions take the greatest toll among the lowest status and lowest income occupations.[33]

The lower economic and occupational strata are distinguished from more advantaged people by many social and psychological deprivations and by numerous differences in opportunity and preparation for mobility during development. These produce an overwhelming disadvantage in occupational achievement. Since education is the major route to occupational mobility in our society, the most serious limitation to occupational achievement among low status people is their educational disadvantage. Parental status is of great importance in determining overt educational opportunities and attainments.[34] There are also marked differences by social class in the quality of schooling available, in the level of preparation children receive for formal education, in the personality characteristics that are likely to foster empathy among teachers, in aspirations and expectations for school achievement, and in available sources of assistance to remedy deficits and difficulties.[35] These forces tend to perpetuate social class differences in education despite the ostensible freedom and equality of opportunities and resources and the vast increase of educational attainment for the entire population. Nor does educational attainment guarantee equivalent achievements of occupational status or income for all people. Education is almost essential for achieving economic or occupational prerogatives, resources, and responsibilities among all social classes, but the consequences of education are less rewarding for the children of working-class parents than for those of higher status, for Negroes or Japanese than for whites, for Americans of southern or eastern European birth and ancestry than for those of western European origin or native Americans of native parentage.[36]

To what degree the transmission of educational and occupational positions is due to the inheritance of status and opportunity or to social class differences in ability or motivation remains a matter of debate. There is little basis, however, for believing that either inherited limitations of ability or class-related deficiencies in ambition explain much of the intergenerational inheritance of status. The conviction that immutable genetic factors account for human intelligence and ability has persisted throughout the history of psychology, but the cumulative evidence makes it increasingly untenable as a general proposition.[37] Experimental data reveal that even fundamental biological functions like vision, hearing, and motor skills develop effectively only if they are actively deployed and if there is sufficient feedback to allow neuromuscular learning.[38] More complex organismic functions and abilities are necessarily more completely dependent upon opportunities to use these biological potentialities and to learn from their success or failure. Despite contradictory evidence, many statistical and experimental studies reveal a marked increment in cognitive functioning among underprivileged children in improved and enriched learning environments. While genetic determinants of ability cannot be ruled out, their relative importance in complex functions can, at best, be quite limited (Farber, 1965; Gottesman, 1968). Nor is there adequate justification for the view that low status people are less highly motivated to achieve educational and occupational rewards than are higher status people. There are notable class differences: the higher the social class, the higher are absolute aspirations for education, occupation, or income. But lower status boys want positions of higher status than those of their fathers and the major limitation to their aspirations is due to a realistic appraisal of limited opportunities.[39] Given tangible and meaningful opportunities for reward, young people from lower status backgrounds show marked increases in motivation to achieve and in actual achievement (Douvan, 1956; Zigler and deLabry, 1962). Social class differences in encouragement and support for achievement and independence appear to be homeostatic mechanisms which lead to lower expectations and, thus, limit frustration and disappointment. But increased opportunities are ready spurs to heightened aspirations and performance.

Whatever the initial impetus to the development of abilities stemming from biological inheritance, the enormous significance of social inheritance at every stage of development and the mechanisms of social structure that further limit the opportunities in spite of manifest abilities among lower status people reduce the eventual consequence of genetic factors to a minimum. Indeed, much of the empirical work in this field has been devoted to the extremes of unusual ability and unusual disability and however genetic factors may influence the transmission of such traits, the results cannot be generalized across a broader spectrum of human qualities or qualifications. Within the broad range between rare intellectual or other gifts and serious deficits, there can be little doubt that mobility achievements are possible. But they are limited by the lack of adequate stimulus to the development of these skills and determined ambitions during childhood. They are futher constrained by the realistic limits of the opportunity structure which also produce adaptations among working-class people that restrict ideas of achieving status and its rewards to those that have a reasonable chance of being fulfilled.

From a theoretical point of view, even unambiguously high rates of social mobility do not affect the conception of a social class structure. Social class is essentially an abstract idea, a system of positions to which individuals are allocated. The character of the social structure is, to a large degree, independent of changes in the positions of individuals. From an empirical point of view, however, it is evident that the rates of upward social mobility in our society are not sufficiently high or sufficiently marked and are not equitably enough distributed to challenge seriously the hierarchical and differentiated organization implied by the notion of a social class system.

Social Class: Structural and Cultural Significance

It is now possible to return to several major questions about social class in our society in order to answer them more systematically. To what extent can we properly refer to inequalities in a modern industrial democracy as features of a social class system? What are the major dimensions of hierarchical placement and functioning? And how does the structure of social inequality affect behavioral differences among people in different positions?

Social class is a useful concept if and only if it helps to explain human behavior and social processes in our society. Most of the data and analyses presented have dealt with the consequences of social class position for role functioning in many different areas. Several social class variables—occupational position particularly, but a combined measure of education and occupation even more clearly—show extraordinarily pervasive although only moderately strong associations with many different behaviors. The reasons for the absence of stronger empirical relationships, however, is quite clear. On the one hand, social class functions in two rather different ways. Social class position provides a context in which other factors take on a specific meaning and influence that differs for people in different social class positions. Inevitably, this must reduce the apparent empirical effect of social class. The persistence of this form of social class influence, simultaneous with other determinants, has repeatedly emerged. Social class position also functions as a specific input, as a variable reflecting actual experience and the direct consequences of low status, low incomes, and low esteem. In this respect, it is a less pervasive but very potent determinant of behavior. Another reason that powerful empirical relationships between social class position and behavior do not appear lies in the fact that often the relationships are not completely linear or monotonic. Thus, social isolation or sporadic social relationships may be quite frequent at the very lowest levels of the social class structure while stable, working-class people may have among the most active patterns of social interaction and involvement. But these quite different levels of social interaction may not be visible and may even counteract each other unless they are deliberately separated and the discrete relationships sought in empirical data.

More generally, however, the ramifications of social class positions are so broad that many characteristics that influence role functioning themselves reflect the current or prior impact of differences in social class position. This necessarily mitigates any direct, empirical manifestation of social class effects. At the same time, the varied repositories of social class influence reinforce the evidence of global consequences of social position for the environments in which people live, for the roles they fulfill, and for their behaviors within these roles.

Another question concerns the degree of inequality that exists in our society and whether the trajectory of change during recent decades points toward the equalization or redistribution of prerogatives, resources, and responsibilities. Analyses of income distributions in absolute and relative terms and of changes in the distribution of occupations are among the most crucial sources for understanding the structure of inequalities. Two findings stand out. Because of the growth of the national income, technological development, increased educational attainment of the population, and a long-term rise in secondary breadwinners contributing to family incomes, there are more families in middle income brackets, more people in higher occupational positions, and a general increase in standards of living. Despite these changes the basic structural characteristics of economic inequalities have remained relatively unchanged. The most striking changes since 1929 have been the loss of the fabulous incomes among the very richest 5 percent of the population and, with the aid of a vast increase in social security, a diminution in the proportions of people in direst poverty.[40] For everyone else, however, incomes have become even *more* unequally distributed over the last four decades. The lowest income group has had only the barest increase in its share of the national income and each successively higher income group has gained successively larger increases.

The effect of occupational changes on the redistribution of occupational prerogatives is more difficult to estimate since it is not quantitatively measured. A larger proportion of the labor force occupies positions of higher prestige than in the recent past. However, the occupational upgrading of the labor force has not resulted in commensurate or uniform improvements in economic compensation or occupational conditions. Among blue-collar workers, occupational demand provides a moderately high level of job opportunities for a highly skilled labor force, but the less skilled members of the working class continue to have high rates of involuntary unemployment and suffer major reverses during minor recessions.[41] More generally, it is unclear whether the changes in the occupational structure of the last few decades have produced as marked a change in the occupational experience and status of the labor force as the distributions of occupational titles would imply. The largest increases in higher status occupations have been in the lowest levels of these categories. Indeed, the persistence of economic inequalities in spite of the increase in educational attainments, occupational skills, and higher occupational positions suggests that the structure of rewards has failed to keep pace with increased occupational skills and competence and has produced greater relative inequality.

Although widespread, small-scale social mobility creates subjective experiences of improvement for those who move up, neither the rates nor the patterns of mobility vitiate the utility of conceptualizing objective inequalities as functions of the social class structure. Rates of upward mobility in the United States are high compared to other countries but deviate markedly from a model of an open system of opportunities. Occupational inheritance, particularly among the highest and lowest occupations, is dominant among some occupations and frequent at all occupational levels. Freedom of opportunity for education is limited by obvious and subtle restrictions to equality and, thus, this major route to occupational mobility itself contributes to intergenerational occupational stability. While the view that we may be developing a hereditary underclass is unwarranted by available data, the debilities of underprivileged populations in competition for higher positions results in an inordinately stable pattern of low occupation, frequent unemployment, and poverty or deprivation. Most important of all, however, is the fact that current rates of social mobility and the existence of occupational opportunities among low status working-class people have been due to high levels of economic and technological growth and, thus, are independent of the intrinsic structural inflexibility of the social class system.

The concept of social class implies a hierarchical system of positions and a structure that differentiates these positions by unequal prerogatives, resources, responsibilities, and more evident rewards. Functional theories of stratification suggest that a moderately high degree of inequality is essential for maintaining adequate recruitment into difficult, demanding, and scarce positions.[42] However, in the absence of stable criteria for distinguishing the most useful occupational skills, individual potentials, or the "true" reward-value of performances, personal and class predilections influence decisions in the name of universalistic judiciousness. Functional theories are useful only for clarifying the fact of inequality, not its degree or exact form. Some degree of differentiation in reward seems inextricably tied to a highly elaborated division of labor and to manifest differences in skills and abilities whatever their origin. Certainly efforts to maintain classless societies or communities appear quite unsuccessful in the modern world.[43] Indeed, the fact of inequality does not itself seem to pose as serious a problem for society as its inordinate range, its intergenerational stability, its nonfunctional aspects, and its perversion through the amalgamation of powers and privileges.

While the level of economic inequality seems considerable in the United States, this is neither necessary nor sufficient for defining it as a structure of social classes. The critical factors that warrent the conceptualization of these inequalities as aspects of a social class system are that: (a) economic inequalities have been remarkably stable over time in spite of large additions to the national income; (b) changes in the distribution of occupations have not resulted in commensurate improvements in the structure of rewards and opportunities; (c) changes that have occurred are direct products of economic development and industrial productivity and do not derive from (although they might eventually produce) changes in socioeconomic structure; (d) these inequalities appear to be structured in broad groupings or classes with similarities of reward, opportunity, and behavior that are greater within than between the groupings or classes; (e) the inheritance of resources and opportunities encompasses more than economic, social, or psychological assets and results in inequalities of opportunity for achievement; (f) social status and social relationships sustain economic and occupational differentiation and particularly exclude low status people from equal participation; and (g) despite universal suffrage and a diversity of elites, political power, influence, and access are moderately concentrated and low status working-class populations remain alienated and powerless in achieving balance in political control.

Thus, in spite of the widespread sense of classlessness in our society, the objective evidence indicates the existence of a social class system that is continuous with the preindustrial systems of stratification in Western societies. Inequality has almost certainly diminished, but the most striking feature of modernization in the West has been a gradual shift from the primacy of legal and political dimensions of stratification to the primacy of economic and occupational dimensions. Social status as a manifestation of social acceptance has been secondary in importance to the economic dimension in determining access to prerogatives, resources, and responsibilities. However, social and psychological features of stratification assumed a unique pattern in the United States. In the form of ethnic discrimination, social and psychological status became the major bases for excluding working-class people from social acceptance as well as from economic, occupational, legal, and political equality. It is this interplay between membership in derogated minorities and lower social class positions that characterizes working-class experience in the United States and has helped to obscure the importance of social class positions.

The absence of a feudal tradition in the United States is often regarded as the major reason for our personalized view of social positions in which success and failure determine status rather than an inexorable transmission of social heritage (for example, Hartz, 1955). Other factors also modified the conception of social class and its apparent importance in the United States (Main, 1965; Warner, 1968). The movement of new ethnic groups into the lowest economic and occupational positions fostered the illusion that in-migration, minority status, and cultural inadequacy, rather than social class differences in opportunity, accounted for differences in achievement. Social rejection took the form of nativist sentiment and ethnic hostility. The newcomers also saw themselves, not as members of a class, but as members of a foreign ethnic group. The fact that they were competitive threats to the established working class helped to delay any alignment between the old and the new laborers. The discrimination, derogation, and deprivation experienced by newer urban groups, Negro Americans, Puerto Ricans, and Mexican Americans, has also focused attention on racist attitudes and has perpetuated the tendency to minimize the importance of the objective position of these minorities at the bottom of the class structure. Distinctive cultural characteristics of different minorities and distinctive forms of derogation experienced by them have accentuated ethnic rather than class status. But the situations and experiences of ethnic minorities are variants of stable class patterns. Enforced dependency and submission, powerlessness and alienation from the larger society are common to most low status populations in this country.

The importance of these patterns of the organization of social classes in industrial societies is great. It may be that with the development of a corporation-dominated economy in the United States and in numerous of the highly developed European countries, the power and influence of individual members of various elites has diminished. In this respect, the power of corporate economic groups in capitalist societies may begin to approximate the dominance of corporate political groups in communist countries. But if this gradual change in the monopoly of power diminishes the potency of individual members of the elites, participation in such corporate groups remains far more accessible to people in the upper class. In modern societies, with highly differentiated social class structures, it is not merely the existence of an elite or of elites, nor the forms of its power and influence, that is important. Concentrations of wealth, power, and prestige are, of course, critical since by definition concentration is antithetical to widespread distribution. An examination of such concentrations are beyond the scope of this analysis although they have been given only minimal attention in systematic investigations during recent decades.[44] Theoretical considerations of the social class structure have too often relied heavily or even exclusively on an anslysis of the view from above, from the situation of elites and those in other high status positions. But if we consider the effects of inequalities at levels of the social class structure below those occupied by top elites, we find all the evidences of maldistribution.

It is this social class structure within which the behaviors, attitudes, and personalities of working-class people must be understood. The working class of the late twentieth century may not be as desperately impoverished as the working class of the early twentieth century. Even those in poverty may not be quite as poverty-stricken as the much larger number of poor in underdeveloped societies. And prejudice, discrimination, and segregation may not be as severe, unremitting, and restrictive as the most extreme forms experienced by the lowest castes in India. But these are hardly adequate comparisons since the wealth and affluence, the spread of educational institutions, the geographical mobility, and the actual and potential resources of industrialized societies are incomparably greater than can be found in any undeveloped society. Whether inequality is inevitable or not and whether or not one form of status acquisition must inevitably place individuals in a better competitive position to achieve other forms of status prerogatives, the level of inequality in industrial societies can not be justified on rational or functional grounds. One of the functions of our social class system, alongside the allocation of positions to people with the ability and preparation to handle them effectively, is to maintain the integrity of the class system itself. While the structure may have developed out of functional necessity, it has become somewhat autonomous. Although the organization of social classes is not impervious to change, and individuals persistently change their rank positions, it has remained remarkably stable and resistant to the forces that periodically seem on the verge of effecting major egalitarian modifications.

The invidious distinctions of a class system affect everyone in the system.

If we take account of social and psychological as well as economic and political factors, it is not clear that the results are a net benefit for those at the top. But clearly they lead to tragic experiences for those at the very bottom and, even for the stable and effective working class, the character of our social class system produces an insecure and conflictful existence. That it may be possible to attribute some of these difficulties to the cultural commitments, community involvements, or personal dispositions of working-class people themselves—an attribution that is popular but vastly overstated—should not obscure the fact that the ultimate causal source is to be found in the social class systems of industrial societies. Institutionalized social class systems define most of the characteristics of the environment in which working-class people live and determine the behaviors and orientations of people whose lives are dominated by these systems. The conditions of social class structure that invade almost every sphere of life provide the ultimate foundation for the world of the urban working class.

Methodological Note

General Problems in Studying Complex Processes

The major objective of this study is to develop a number of empirically-based generalizations about the nature and causes of working-class behavior and patterns of social organization. This involves many small-scale models concerning discrete spheres of functioning, but we have tried to keep the larger objective and the need for more comprehensive models in view throughout.

These objectives are integrally related to the current situation of this field of inquiry. Disciplinary boundaries diminish the potential inter-penetration of models, concepts, and orientations between different fields of study dealing with similar substantive issues. Each separate field has generally produced sparse and narrowly-conceived results of short-range value. There is a dearth of effort to develop systematic theoretical (as opposed to conceptual) analyses and a paucity of models or data concerning social issues of contemporary relevance. As a consequence, the foundations are inadequate for formulating propositions or generating models that begin to approximate complex human and social realities. We believe there is an insistent need (a) for models and propositions that begin to integrate the diverse forces—economic, social, psychological, political, cultural—that seem to influence human behavior and social processes, (b) for formulations that attempt to bridge the gap between basic scientific questions and trenchant issues that affect the lives of many people, and (c) for empirical analyses that link themselves both to modest general propositions and to problems of broader scope. Whether the outcomes are confirmed by subsequent studies or not may be less important at the present time than their consequences for the conclusions of other studies.

In the study of working-class behavior and social organization, the need for this orientation has been particularly great. Generalizations about the working class abound but are infrequently associated *either* with theoretical propositions or with systematic data and analysis. Because of this, we have given particular attention to pulling together diverse bits and frag-

ments of extant information in trying to understand and generalize from
the data immediately at hand. However, the general methodological
position we have taken is also influenced by the current state of our
knowledge. A number of methodological problems arise in studies of
complex behaviors within natural environments. Most of these issues have
been discussed in the literature, but they remain as dilemmas in which the
advantages and disadvantages of each position are apparent but the precise
trade-off remains ambiguous. Thus, it becomes essential to adopt a methodological position that may vary with both the nature of the problem
and the stage of scientific development in a particular area of investigation.

It is widely recognized that there are many sources of error in obtaining,
recording, and processing data about individuals, groups, institutions, and
populations. These errors intrude themselves into all studies of human and
social processes but their consequences become magnified as we move from
highly controlled studies to those that attempt more nearly to approximate
the natural flow of behaviors or events. In the more complex and "natural-
istic" study, particularly, the problems of error are predominantly those
of extensive, indeterminate, and inconstant *random* error. We believe the
compounded, random error in such studies is greater than is generally
realized or affirmed. If the size of random error is so great, it raises important matters of decision in each study concerning the trade-off between
Type I and Type II errors, those that involve a false statement in rejecting
the null hypothesis and those that involve a false statement by virtue of
accepting the null hypothesis of no difference or no effect.

If the amount of error in the measurement of individual variables is
large and both the size and direction of the error are unknown, the interpretation of relationships between variables will inevitably be problematic.
Moreover, a large amount of random error in a data set is more likely to
diminish or obscure the strength of true relationships than to increase the
strength of false relationships. But if the error is differentially distributed,
it will differentially affect different observations. Thus, any criterion for
distinguishing strong from weak relationships or for asserting the degree of
confidence we have in a finding must be used with considerable caution.
Similarly, exact quantitative statements about the distribution of attributes
or about the size of relationships cannot be made solely on the grounds of
a high statistical probability of being confirmed. The major advantage of
statistical tests of significance under these circumstances is that, given the
need for some criterion for initial evaluations of results, statistical tests
provide a consistent, observable, and communicable criterion. But the
criterion is often less consistent than appears in view of the degree to
which different tests of significance are influenced by different characteristics of the data. Such attributes as marginal distributions, interactions,
and linear or nonlinear form may raise or lower the strength of a relation-

ship and its probability value without having corresponding substantive significance. Naturally, the examination of the form of a distribution or relationship may itself become a major target of inquiry if the stage of development of knowledge about systems of variables warrants such clarification.

A major solution to the problem of evaluating data and specifying relationships lies in replication. Replication in laboratory studies has, as a major objective, the control of bias, although random error may be a consequential issue. In the study of complex functions with large samples, in which data collection and processing are beyond the immediate control of the major investigators, systematic bias is generally a less serious (although everpresent) danger than is large, random error. However, repeated studies by different investigators using different instruments and different techniques of inquiry are not likely to replicate the same kinds of error even though the amount of error may be similar. Thus, the repetition of observations provides a primary basis for narrowing the "confidence limits" within which data may be differentially evaluated on the basis of the strength of relationships or even given a quantitative formulation. To a considerably smaller extent, the same holds true for quasi-independent observations made within a single study. The repetition of the same or similar findings with different indicators and with a variety of statistical controls provides some modest confidence that the result is less likely to be a product of random events (or of measurement bias).

One might argue, as has frequently been done, that when a considerable amount of random error is present in a data set, it necessitates an even more rigorous use and perhaps heightened criteria of tests of significance. Such a procedure, of course, implies a willingness to commit a larger number of Type II errors because of caution about committing Type I errors. From a long-range viewpoint, this may more seriously limit the development of knowledge than a lower criterion that allows a greater probability of committing Type I errors in order to be more sensitive to the danger of Type II errors. But this too must be gauged by the state of knowledge and the level of development of a given substantive issue. If we concern ourselves, however, not with the conclusions of a single study, but with the repetition of findings in different studies, then there is the practical matter that there can be no replication of results that have been excluded from a report because they have been, perhaps prematurely, rejected as too weak. Since it is impossible, and would be meaningless, to report all findings of "no relationship," this problem inevitably arises at some point or other. Conventional use of statistical tests of significance and of a single standard of "significance" imply that there is a single solution to this problem. Indeed, several considerations are relevant in dealing with the report of findings, particularly those findings that indicate the absence of a relationship. Internal replications of the type described provide some insurance that the absence of a relationship is a stable finding at least within a given data set. The consistency of this finding with other related findings, either supporting a more general conclusion or reflecting a hypothesis test, may also determine whether or not the absence of a relationship warrants interpretation and reporting. Finally, the relevance of the issue either for confirming or disconfirming other findings in the literature and its relevance for theoretical or social issues is an important basis for interpreting and communicating the result.

In this study, we have tried to deal with this problem in a number of different ways. We have decided, by and large, not to report the results of tests of significance on the grounds that they provide inadequate validation or invalidation of conclusions while offering a false sense of confidence. Some of the more popular tests of significance, like the X^2 test with nominal data, moreover, are so responsive to marginal distributions that, given great unevenness in such distributions, they prove inadequate even as the crudest sorting procedure. The rejection of tests of significance, however, is hardly adequate to the problem. Confronting the fact that there is an intrinsic dilemma that cannot be resolved with complete satisfaction, we have placed the greatest weight on several forms of replication. Despite the rejection of tests of significance, we have used "estimates" of significance levels for tabular and correlational analysis as a rough sorting device. These estimates were based on the differences in percentage required or the level of correlation necessary to achieve a probability level of .05, given "model" sample sizes and "model" distributions of marginals. This provided a basis for initial judgments about relationships.

On the assumption that the use of indices, based on several similar individual items, reduces the ratio of noise to signal, we have relied heavily on such composite variables. However, we have steered clear of indices built from a great many different items (and many dimensions) which tend to increase the frequency and decrease the substantive meaning of relationships. We have also tried, wherever possible and within obvious limits, to develop these indices as ordinal scales. The greatest weight has been placed, throughout, on the replication of results from different studies, from different variables that had common dimensions, from the consistency or inconsistency of results with different controls, from testing hypotheses on the basis of observations within the data with variables or relationships that had not been included in the prior observations. Most of the time, several of these procedures have been employed in dealing with any one issue. In addition we have quite generally tested propositions with several different statistical procedures.

Naturally, we cannot regard any of these formulations as conclusive.

However, there are differences in the confidence one may have about different types of conclusions. Although we have frequently presented quantitative results, these are presented only to document and exemplify our general statements and to provide a basis for future confirmation or disconfirmation, not as evidence of exact quantitative distributions or relationships. There are instances, moreover, in which we draw conclusions about variations (for example, by age or by class) in which, on the basis of the criteria of replication we have asserted, we might have simply regarded the variation as a form of *dis*confirmation. We have preferred to take the chance of overstating such conclusions rather than to chance understating them in the absence of clear-cut bases for decision. Even under these circumstances, however, we have never drawn such conclusions on the basis of a single finding of such patterns but only when such findings have repeated themselves. In effect, we have tried to develop small-scale models based on repeated observations in which a single negative finding might be a basis for rejecting, but never for confirming, the applicability of the model. It is such models, whether explicitly formulated as models or implicit in the general theoretical argument, in which we place the greatest confidence since they have been subjected to numerous tests both within this set of data and in comparisons with the findings from other studies. The present stage of inquiry in most of the social sciences seems to demand great attention to the development of such models and the examination of data for adequacy of fit, and particularly, to the designation of the status of different variables within systems and subsystems. Conclusions about their quantitative relationships or effects seem, in many instances, premature and, in the absence of adequate information about models and larger sets of variables, potentially misleading.

Sample Design

The ultimate objective of the study of a sample of West End residents was to evaluate the effects of residential relocation on the lives and experiences of a normal population representing a range of statuses, a spectrum of personal characteristics, and a diversity of role relationships within the community and outside. As a consequence, the framework for the study was a before-after design in which the same sample of respondents was seen before they moved and again after they had moved. For numerous reasons, it was impossible to include a control sample in the design, although we have used internal controls throughout to estimate the differential relationships among different subsamples and have tried to take account of sample biases.

The sampling procedure itself used the results of a population survey required of redevelopment agencies by federal law. The Boston Redevelopment Authority carried out such a survey with a 99 percent return rate. We used their records to sample one out of every fifth case. The records were filed geographically and, thus, provided a systematic probability sample of the West End relocation area. In practice, several problems arose that limited the subsequent sample of respondents. (1) Once the redevelopment survey was completed and the process moved rapidly to land-taking by the city of Boston, people began to move out of the area quite rapidly. In many instances, they left before we were able to interview them. We followed our initial sample to their new homes and interviewed them there. While this provided us with a less biased sample in general, it meant that interviewer reports about housing in the West End were unavailable for approximately one third of the sample. (2) During the prerelocation period, there was considerable resistance to being interviewed by some of the sample since we were occasionally identified with the relocation office. The total sample drawn was N = 583. Of these, a total of 97 persons either could not be found or refused to be interviewed initially. This left a prerelocation sample of 486 cases or a return rate of 83 percent. In the postrelocation situation, we returned to all individuals or families within the original set of 583 cases. Because of assiduous efforts to trace and to interview these families, the female postrelocation return rate was higher with a final response rate of 86 percent. Since some of the women were interviewed only before *or* after relocation, the sample for pre-post analysis was smaller, with an N = 434 or 74 percent of the total. At some point 552 of the women were interviewed, providing some information about 95 percent of the original sample. The men were not included in prerelocation interviews but were interviewed after relocation. Considering those households in which there was no male available for interview, the total possible sample size was N = 393 of whom 334 or 85 percent were interviewed. Analysis of the refusals, with the meager information available for them, revealed no systematic differences from the sample of respondents.

Interviewing and Coding

The interview was lengthy, with an average duration of two and a half to three hours. It covered a very large number of topics and included both open-ended and closed questions. For the analysis of experiences with health and welfare agencies, record data was obtained concerning mental health and social service contacts and court appearances. While there is bound to be error in such record data and it only includes contacts in Massachusetts, several methodological checks suggest that our subsequent indices provide reasonably accurate ratings and are probably more precise than it is possible to achieve by alternative procedures. The interviewers were primarily advanced graduate students in the social sciences (particularly psychology) or people who were already established in their careers as social workers, psychologists, or psychiatrists. The research staff members themselves also conducted a number of interviews throughout the field work phases. Some of the interviews were carried out by foreign-language interviewers. Participant observers who were widely familiar with a large number of residents read many of the cases in order to assess the accuracy of reporting. We have every reason to believe that, despite a great many errors that are introduced at this stage, the accuracy of interviewing was somewhat higher than one ordinarily finds in field studies. None of the tell-tale indications or grape-vine reports of fudging data or distortion, overt or covert, appeared.

The coding itself was a large-scale operation since approximately one-third of the questions were open-ended. This required a lengthy period of code construction, careful training of coders, and supervision of the coding staff. Reliability checks were carried out throughout the coding operation. A criterion of 80 percent agreement was considered essential for the coding of any individual item to be acceptable. Any code that did not reach this level was returned for a revision of the code itself and resubmitted for coding after preliminary reliability checks indicated that it showed a higher level of agreement. For the majority of codes, a higher level of agreement (90 percent or better) obtained. In a very few instances in which it was impossible to achieve this level of agreement because of the complex evaluative judgments required and when the item was of central importance, a double-coding system was used. In these instances, two coders coded every case and all discrepancies went to a third coder for independent coding, with the final code to be determined by the agreement between two coders.

Index and Scale Construction

Partly as a method of compensating for some of the error in individual items and partly to attain operational measures of more complex conceptual variables, indices were constructed for most of the major variables in the West End study. They reflect a history of increasing use of empirical procedures for index construction. It is not entirely clear that the indices based on factor analytic or regression procedures are, in any sense, better than those based on a priori judgments, but they do carry some conviction that the faultless computer was responsible for the index rather than error-prone humans. In some instances it is clear that the use of multivariate statistics alerted the investigator to index patterns that he might otherwise have overlooked or pointed up prior errors of judgment. In the last revision of the data, every effort was made to transform virtually all of the variables into scalar form. Thus, most of the variables are minimally ordinal scales and a few approximate interval scales.

Data Analysis

In the social sciences we are confronted with the problem of empirical relationships which, even if occasionally confirmed, might be affected by an almost infinite number of variables. As we move from two-variable problems to the simultaneous analysis of three or four variables, we do far more than provide controls in the literal sense of that term. Controlled analysis is primarily intended to determine whether or not a relationship between two variables is spurious, that is, whether that relationship is (indirectly) produced because of the relationship between either or both those variables and some third factor. Empirically, when this is the case we find that the former relationship vanishes (or approaches the vanishing point) if we hold the third factor constant. To the extent that we can control for a large number of such factors and find that the original relationship persists relatively unmodified, we can more confidently assert general conclusions based on that relationship. However, many other possible patterns can emerge other than the disappearance or persistence of an original two-variable relationship. We may find that the relationship becomes stronger, that under one condition it becomes stronger and under the other it becomes weaker, or that whole categories of "control" variables produce one type of effect while others produce another effect. Thus an increase in information results in addition to the discovery that an empirical relationship is or is not spurious. Indeed, whether we decide to call such a result "spurious" or regard it as evidence of an "intervening" variable is itself the product of the three-variable models we can propose and test. By the use of multivariate techniques such as multiple regression analysis, we can extend the analysis of this set of issues particularly to consideration, simultaneously, of an entire array of independent and control variables and their effects on a single dependent variable.

In the analysis of the West End data, it has been possible to utilize the most sophisticated analytic procedures only in part, although the reasoning behind them has influenced the entire conception of the data. The study was not designed with these procedures in mind, although extensive revision of the data format expanded the range of possible data analytic techniques. We have, however, moved back and forth between correlational techniques (particularly controlled correlations), tabular analysis, and relatively simple multiple regression analysis (single equation, stepwise multiple regressions). Unfortunately, tables of means based on three or four variables and analyses of variance derived from these were not readily possible for the analysis of interaction effects because of the difficulties with computer programs that would facilitate large numbers of such analyses. We have relied, instead, on tabular techniques for determining interactions and nonlinear relationships. For all the crudeness of tabular distributions of proportions, these do provide the sharpest view of the pattern of interrelationships among small numbers of variables.

The major justification for the many causal interpretations presented in the text rests upon the theoretical or logical sense they make, implemented by the fact that they are not empirically invalidated by evidence within the wide range of analyses employed or by observations in other studies. However, the use of many different data analytic techniques, the formulation of hypotheses in the light of prior analyses that were then tested with a "new" set of variables, and the clarification of complex interrelationships afforded even by simple forms of multiple regression analysis provides greater confidence in presenting these interpretations.

Multiple regression analysis has only recently come into vogue in sociology and psychology and, since there are many alternative views about their interpretation, the criteria we have used in interpreting the results warrant a word of explication. Since we have used the multiple regression technique mainly to evaluate those variables, among a large set, that had major effects on a dependent variable, questions arise regarding (a) the exact measures to be used as a basis for estimating the differential strength of different variables in relation to the dependent variable, and (b) the criteria for "terminating" the interpretation of results. In each of these instances, we have employed the following as the basis for judgments:

(a) The amount of variance explained and the measure of the strength of effect by beta-weights, have both been used. Using the beta-weight at the point of termination of the interpretation provides a more accurate estimate of the relative strength of different variables as they affect the dependent variable, while the variance explained provides a clearer picture of the variability accounted for by a set of measures.

(b) The main criteria employed for "terminating" the analysis of a stepwise multiple regression equation were (1) any reversal of sign between the beta-weight and the original correlation coefficient at the point of entrance of a new variable into the equation, and (2) any marked increase in the covariance ratios at the point of entrance of a new variable into the equation. Although we also set another criterion, the diminution of the additional variance explained to less than .5 percent, in practice we were primarily concerned with those variables that accounted for larger proportions of the variance or had larger, independent effects. However, statements that indicate the total variance explained by a set of variables utilize this criterion as well, provided neither of the other considerations had already become operative.

Ultimately, the validity or invalidity, the generality or limitation, and the utility of these observations, interpretations, and models must rest upon further comparisons of these data and analyses with other empirical studies. We have tried to keep in perspective the long-run contribution of any one study to the cumulation of evidence and to give it priority over other considerations of caution or precision in making statements that conform more closely to the empirical observations. While the loose interpretation of results or the free exercise of imagination in formulating hypotheses as if they were conclusions may be as disastrous as excessive caution is unproductive, the synthesis of findings by an investigator is an essential part of the scientific endeavor. Too often, social scientists withhold this synthesizing activity and, thus, deny the reader the supplementary knowledge, familiarity, and observations that immersion in a subject and in a data set must inevitably provide. Within the limits of the crude criteria one can employ, within the limits of currently irresolvable dilemmas of empirical interpretation, we have tried to analyze and to synthesize these data, along with all the supplementary and often implicit information that has accrued, to formulate as coherent an understanding of the working-class world as we felt it was possible to document.

Appendix Tables, Bibliography, Notes, Index

Appendix

APPENDIX TABLE 4.1   Family per capita income by housing quality, with social class status held constant (in percentages)

Social class status	Family per capita income	Housing quality				N^a	Percent
		Good	Fair	Poor			
Moderately high							
	Moderate	50	29	21		34	100
	Marginal	44	23	23		18	100
	Minimal	(0)[b]	(0)	(100)		4	100
Moderately low							
	Moderate	38	38	24		63	100
	Marginal	28	32	40		43	100
	Minimal	15	36	39		33	100
Very low							
	Moderate	30	30	40		30	100
	Marginal	21	35	44		34	100
	Minimal	26	24	50		38	100

[a]There are 31 uncodeable cases on the two independent variables, in addition to the 158 cases for which the housing quality index is unavailable.
[b]In this and subsequent tables, all percentages based on an N of less than 10 cases are presented in parentheses.

APPENDIX TABLE 4.2   Respondent's social class status by housing quality, with parental social class status held constant (in percentages)

Parental social class status	Respondent's social class status	Housing quality				N[a]	Percent
		Good	Fair	Poor			
Moderately high							
	Moderately high	56	36	8		25	100
	Moderately low	44	41	15		34	100
	Very low	29	35	36		14	100
Moderately low							
	Moderately high	47	32	21		19	100
	Moderately low	28	50	22		46	100
	Very low	23	42	35		26	100
Very low							
	Moderately high	27	26	47		15	100
	Moderately low	17	59	24		58	100
	Very low	24	44	32		50	100

[a]There are 199 uncodeable cases. See footnote to table 4.1.

APPENDIX TABLE 4.3   Housing quality by apartment satisfaction, with residential satisfaction held constant (in percentages)

Residential satisfaction	Housing quality	Apartment satisfaction			N^a	Percent
		Highly satisfied	Moderately satisfied	Dissatisfied		
Highly satisfied						
	Good housing	68	28	4	25	100
	Fair housing	49	49	2	45	100
	Poor housing	33	54	13	15	100
Moderately satisfied						
	Good housing	60	36	4	46	100
	Fair housing	53	42	5	44	100
	Poor housing	46	31	23	40	100
Dissatisfied						
	Good housing	28	60	12	25	100
	Fair housing	34	44	22	51	100
	Poor housing	8	48	24	25	100

[a]There are 170 uncodeable cases. See footnote to table 4.1.

APPENDIX TABLE 4.4 Housing quality by apartment satisfaction, with local resource use held constant (in percentages)

Local resource use	Housing quality	Apartment satisfaction			N^a	Percent
		Highly satisfied	Moderately satisfied	Dissatisfied		
Maximal use						
	Good	48	48	4	23	100
	Fair	45	48	7	29	100
	Poor	53	34	13	15	100
Moderate use						
	Good	55	37	8	51	100
	Fair	46	45	9	72	100
	Poor	23	54	23	39	100
Minimal use						
	Good	57	38	5	22	100
	Fair	43	38	19	38	100
	Poor	33	25	42	25	100

[a]There are 172 uncodeable cases. See footnote to table 4.1.

APPENDIX TABLE 4.5 Apartment satisfaction: correlations with selected measures, with social class status held constant

	Social Class status[a]			All social class statuses combined
	Moderately high	Moderately low	Very low	
Family per capita income	-.04	-.06	-.01	-.05
Social problems	.07	.01	-.01	.05
Assimilation status	-.02	.10	-.08	-.03
Parental social class status	.05	-.04	.07	-.01
Ethnic embeddedness	-.03	.07	.17	.10
Global social interaction	-.02	-.11	.15	.00
Closeness of neighbor relations	-.07	.05	.25	.11
Local resource use	.02	.00	.26	.11
Ethnic involvement	-.08	-.07	.19	.05
Intergenerational mobility	.10	-.12	-.19	-.11
Housing quality	.21	.29	.32	.27
Household orientation to children	-.13	-.14	-.30	-.21
Length of residence	-.15	-.10	.21	-.00
Total family income	.01	-.14	-.10	-.11
Social mobility orientation	-.06	-.10	-.21	-.15
Housing aspirations	-.07	-.14	-.13	-.15
Health self-estimate	-.18	-.08	.02	-.08
West End residence of parents	-.25	-.12	.14	-.04
Marital satisfaction	-.12	.06	.04	.01
Parental satisfaction	-.23	.03	-.17	-.10

[a]In this and similar tables, the correlations are not partial correlations but are the correlations within the designated subgroups.

APPENDIX TABLE 4.6   Local resource use by residential satisfaction, with social class status held constant (in percentages)

Social class status	Local resource use	Residential satisfaction				
		Highly satisfied	Moderately satisfied	Dissatisfied	N[a]	Percent
Moderately high						
	Maximal	53	41	6	17	100
	Moderate	35	46	19	43	100
	Minimal	20	40	40	35	100
Moderately low						
	Maximal	66	30	4	44	100
	Moderate	44	40	16	111	100
	Minimal	14	41	45	51	100
Very low						
	Maximal	67	33	0	42	100
	Moderate	53	41	6	80	100
	Minimal	31	43	26	58	100

[a]There are 5 uncodeable cases.

APPENDIX TABLE 4.7   Residential satisfaction: correlations with selected measures, with social class status held constant

	Social class status			All social class statuses combined
	Moderately high	Moderately low	Very low	
Ethnic embeddedness	.21	.18	.16	.19
Local vs. metropolitan orientation	.23	.17	-.02	.15
West End residence of parents	.17	.19	.02	.12
Conceptions of neighborhood	.34	.26	.20	.27
Respondent's age	.23	.14	.17	.20
Social mobility orientation	-.31	-.19	-.17	-.25
Ego efficacy	-.19	-.09	-.02	-.13
Closeness of neighbor relations	.25	.27	.37	.31
Local kin in West End	.01	.20	.13	.13
Ethnic involvement	.08	.16	.06	.14
Frequency of family interaction	.03	.15	.12	.12
Closeknit networks	.19	.35	.29	.29
Housing quality	-.04	.21	.10	.11
Global social interaction	.16	.27	.27	.23
Local resource use	.42	.47	.45	.44
Home ownership	.09	.12	.16	.12

APPENDIX TABLE 4.8   Length of residence by residential satisfaction, with social class status held constant (in percentages)

Social class status	Length of residence	Residential satisfaction			N[a]	Percent
		Highly satisfied	Moderately satisfied	Dissatisfied		
Moderately high						
	Very long	46	42	12	43	100
	Moderately long	21	58	21	19	100
	Short	21	36	43	33	100
Moderately low						
	Very long	55	30	15	116	100
	Moderately long	33	41	26	51	100
	Short	13	56	31	39	100
Very low						
	Very long	61	35	4	112	100
	Moderately long	37	46	17	35	100
	Short	20	47	33	30	100

[a]There are 8 uncodeable cases.

APPENDIX TABLE 4.9   Closeness of neighbor relations by residential satisfaction, with length of residence held constant (in percentages)

| Length of residence | Closeness of neighbor relations | Residential satisfaction | | | | |
		Highly satisfied	Moderately satisfied	Dissatisfied	N[a]	Percent
Very long						
	Very close	64	31	5	140	100
	Moderately close	51	39	10	85	100
	Distant	46	32	22	46	100
Moderately long						
	Very close	58	36	6	31	100
	Moderately close	28	46	26	46	100
	Distant	11	47	32	28	100
Short						
	Very close	22	39	39	18	100
	Moderately close	24	42	34	38	100
	Distant	11	54	35	46	100

[a]There are 8 uncodeable cases.

APPENDIX TABLE 4.10 Social class status by housing aspirations, with respondent's age held constant (in percentages)

Respondent's age	Social class status	Housing aspirations			N^a	Percent
		High	Moderate	Low		
20–34 years						
	Moderately high	60	33	7	45	100
	Moderately low	43	46	11	65	100
	Very low	26	61	13	31	100
35–49 years						
	Moderately high	32	53	15	34	100
	Moderately low	19	68	13	99	100
	Very low	12	64	24	67	100
50 years or older						
	Moderately high	18	35	47	17	100
	Moderately low	9	50	41	44	100
	Very low	6	46	48	84	100

[a]There are no uncodeable cases.

APPENDIX TABLE 4.11 Housing aspirations: correlations with selected measures, with social class status held constant

	Social class status			All social class statuses combined
	Moderately high	Moderately low	Very low	
Family per capita income	.08	.04	.26	.18
Marital status	.16	.33	.34	.26
Housing quality	.01	-.14	-.10	-.05
Apartment satisfaction	-.07	-.14	-.13	-.15
Residential satisfaction	.00	-.17	-.17	-.16
Social mobility orientation	.04	.16	.24	.22
Respondent's age	-.44	-.36	-.37	-.43
Assimilation status	.30	.15	.02	.20
Frequency of family interaction	.31	.02	.01	.07
Kin involvement	.27	.13	.03	.11
Marital companionship	.32	.10	.04	.16
Marital satisfaction	.17	.14	.09	.16
Closeknit networks	.33	.12	.03	.13
Closeness of neighbor relations	.16	.12	.09	.10
Local resource use	.14	.03	-.04	.02
Ethnic embeddedness	.13	.11	.04	.03
Household orientation to children	.20	.37	.27	.33
Social problems	-.29	-.18	-.23	-.28
Household size	.41	.33	.41	.36

APPENDIX TABLE 5.1   Length of residence by participation in local organizations (in percentages)

Length of residence	Participation in local organizations			N^a	Percent
	Extensive	Moderate	Minimal		
Very long	59	32	10	272	100
Moderately long	38	42	20	104	100
Short	11	47	42	102	100

[a]There are 8 uncodeable cases.

APPENDIX TABLE 5.2 Kinship involvement: correlations with selected measures, with social class status held constant

	Social class status			All social class statuses combined
	Moderately high	Moderately low	Very low	
Respondent's age	-.01	-.16	-.12	-.10
Length of residence	.40	.31	.31	.34
Assimilation status	-.14	.00	.05	-.02
Family per capita income	-.08	-.01	.02	-.02
Ethnic embeddedness	.33	.25	.34	.31
Ethnic derogation status	.23	.10	.04	.11
Religious affiliation: male	.23	.14	.17	.18
Local vs. metropolitan orientation	.33	.15	-.02	.14
Ego efficacy	-.27	-.04	.01	-.08
Global social interaction	.48	.45	.42	.44
Closeness of neighbor relations	.27	.15	.23	.21
Ethnic involvement	.22	.31	.19	.24

APPENDIX TABLE 5.3   Social class status by localism of five closest people, with length of West End residence held constant (in percentages)

Length of residence	Social class status	Localism of five closest people				
		Mostly West End	Mixed: West End and outside	Mostly outside West End	N[a]	Percent
Very long						
	Moderately high	51	22	27	41	100
	Moderately low	61	24	15	102	100
	Very low	59	24	17	96	100
Moderately long						
	Moderately high	13	24	63	16	100
	Moderately low	33	23	44	46	100
	Very low	59	31	10	29	100
Short						
	Moderately high	26	15	59	27	100
	Moderately low	28	22	50	32	100
	Very low	43	18	39	28	100

[a] There are 69 uncodeable cases.

APPENDIX TABLE 5.4 Community activities and social affiliations: correlations with local satisfaction indices

	Closeness of neighbor relations	Plans to move near relatives	Communal shopping orientation	Local resource use	Ethnic involvement	Closeness to kin	Frequency of family interaction	Area of West End known	Urban familiarity
Plans to move near relatives	.21								
Communal shopping orientation	.09	-.05							
Local resource use	.48	-.18	.11						
Ethnic involvement	.15	.19	.03	.05					
Closeness to kin	.28	-.41	.01	.24	.23				
Frequency of family interaction	.23	-.36	-.01	.15	.25	.46			
Area of West End known	.30	-.06	.05	.56	.03	.16	.18		
Urban familiarity	-.10	.07	-.11	-.09	-.10	.00	-.02	.01	
Community role satisfaction	-.50	.23	-.11	-.62	-.16	-.23	-.19	-.56	.09
Residential satisfaction	-.31	.13	-.09	-.44	-.14	-.17	-.12	-.28	.09
Number of places expected to miss	-.26	.17	.02	-.61	-.08	-.13	-.13	-.19	.06

APPENDIX TABLE 5.5 Closeness of neighbor relations by residential satisfaction, with length of residence held constant (in percentages)

Length of residence / Closeness of neighbor relations	Residential satisfaction			N^a	Percent
	Highly satisfied	Moderately satisfied	Dissatisfied		
Very long					
Very close	64	31	5	140	100
Moderately close	51	38	11	85	100
Distant	46	32	22	46	100
Moderately long					
Very close	58	35	7	31	100
Moderately close	28	46	26	46	100
Distant	10	58	32	28	100
Short					
Very close	22	39	39	18	100
Moderately close	24	42	34	38	100
Distant	11	54	35	46	100

[a] There are 8 uncodeable cases.

APPENDIX TABLE 5.6   Community activities and social affiliations: correlations with demographic, status, and personality measures

	Family per capita income	Ethnic embeddedness	Social class status	Standard of living	Respondent's age	Head of household occupational status	Total family income	Respondent's education	Parental social class status	Social anxiety
Closeness of neighbor relations	.08	-.26	.08	.18	-.06	.12	.11	.08	.16	.22
Plans to move near relatives	.01	.21	-.13	-.11	.01	-.12	.00	-.17	-.12	.01
Shopping orientations	.02	-.07	.06	-.01	-.07	.04	.06	.02	-.05	.13
Local resource use	-.01	-.14	.05	.19	.13	.09	.01	.05	.12	.17
Ethnic involvement	-.07	-.50	.27	.01	.17	.16	.03	.39	.31	.02
Closeness to kin	-.03	-.31	.09	.18	-.14	.09	.01	.14	.19	.07
Frequency of family interaction	.07	-.32	.10	.19	-.10	.09	.11	.14	.17	.07
Area of West End known	-.13	-.15	.06	.02	.05	.08	.10	.06	.19	.09
Urban familiarity	.05	-.02	-.19	.02	-.13	-.15	.09	-.18	-.16	.06
Community role satisfaction	.09	.25	-.16	-.12	-.19	-.13	.10	-.19	-.20	-.16
Residential satisfaction	.02	.19	-.14	.09	-.20	-.10	.05	-.13	-.13	-.10

APPENDIX TABLE 5.7 Determinants of community role satisfaction[a]
(variance explained and beta weights from stepwise multiple regression)

Variable name	Cumulative variance explained	Beta weights
Length of residence	25.0	.287
Closeness of neighbor relations	35.7	.351
Communal shopping preferences	38.8	.186
Respondent's age	40.5	.096
Ego efficacy	41.6	.098
Family per capita income	42.3	.086
West End home ownership	42.9	.082
Interpersonal dependence	43.5	.077

[a]The beta weights given are those that occur at the cut-off point based on the criteria used for terminating the multiple regression results described in the Methodological Note.

APPENDIX TABLE 5.8   Head of household occupational status by closeness of neighbor relations, with length of residence held constant (in percentages)

Length of residence	Occupational status of head of household	Closeness of neighbor relations			N^a	Percent
		Very close	Moderately close	Distant		
Very long	Highly skilled	(43)	(43)	(14)	7	100
	Skilled	43	37	20	74	100
	Semiskilled	61	21	18	118	100
	Unskilled	47	39	14	66	100
Moderately long	Highly skilled	(0)	(67)	(33)	6	100
	Skilled	33	45	22	27	100
	Semiskilled	37	39	24	46	100
	Unskilled	20	44	36	25	100
Short	Highly skilled	5	35	60	20	100
	Skilled	31	50	19	16	100
	Semiskilled	17	32	51	47	100
	Unskilled	22	45	33	18	100

[a]There are 16 uncodeable cases.

APPENDIX TABLE 6.1   Social class status by household role relationship (in percentages)

| Social class status | Household role relationship | | | | |
	Husband directed	Both directed	Wife directed	N[a]	Percent
High	57	36	8	62	100
Moderate	30	37	33	156	100
Low	33	34	34	116	100

[a]There are no uncodeable cases. See footnote to table 6.1 in text.

APPENDIX TABLE 6.2   Household functional patterns: correlations with selected measures, with social class status held constant

	Social class status			
	Moderately high	Moderately low	Very low	All social class statuses combined
Family per capita income	-.17	-.14	-.05	-.14
Ethnic embeddedness	-.01	-.04	.06	-.02
Health self-estimate	.17	.08	.03	.11
Standard of living	.05	-.01	-.01	-.04
Employment status: male	.18	.03	-.01	.05
Employment status: female	.07	.06	-.09	.02
Respondent's age	.41	.07	.25	.24
Assimilation status	.07	-.02	-.16	.00
Number of children in household	.01	.07	-.05	.02
Religious commitment	.12	-.03	-.02	.05
Closeness of neighbor relations	-.04	.03	.10	.06
Local resource use	.18	.00	.13	.10
Frequency of family interaction	-.19	.16	.07	.09
Marital sociability	-.16	-.11	-.27	-.21
Marital companionship	-.27	-.16	-.30	-.26
Level of marital conflict	-.24	.07	.13	.06
Social problems	.26	.18	.17	.23
Psychoneurotic index	.10	.08	.15	.14
Ego efficacy	-.23	-.21	.13	-.14

APPENDIX TABLE 6.3   Age range of living children by marital sociability, with social class status held constant (in percentages)

Social class status	Age range of living children	Marital sociability			N^a	Percent
		Extensive	Moderate	Minimal		
Moderately high	No children	(89)	(0)	(11)	9	100
	Oldest child 0–11 years	43	47	10	29	100
	Oldest child 12 years or over	18	59	23	17	100
	All children 18 years or over	(67)	(33)	(0)	6	100
Moderately low	No children	50	43	7	14	100
	Oldest child 0–11 years	22	54	24	67	100
	Oldest child 12 years or over	33	48	19	41	100
	All children 18 years or over	47	40	13	29	100
Very low	No children	42	33	25	12	100
	Oldest child 0–11 years	17	44	39	18	100
	Oldest child 12 years or over	22	45	33	43	100
	All children 18 years or over	42	32	26	37	100

[a] There are 12 uncodeable cases. See footnote to table 6.1

APPENDIX TABLE 6.4   Family per capita income by marital sociability, with social class status held constant (in percentages)

Social class status	Family per capita income	Marital sociability			N^a	Percent
		Extensive	Moderate	Minimal		
Moderately high						
	Maximum	53	38	9	34	100
	Moderate	47	32	21	19	100
	Minimum	(0)	(80)	(20)	5	100
Moderately low						
	Maximum	35	49	15	79	100
	Moderate	32	45	24	38	100
	Minimum	23	52	26	31	100
Very low						
	Maximum	33	47	21	43	100
	Moderate	38	24	38	37	100
	Minimum	18	46	36	33	100

[a] There are 15 uncodeable cases. See footnote to table 6.1.

APPENDIX TABLE 6.5   Marital sociability: correlations with selected measures, with social class status held constant

| | Social class status | | | All social class statuses combined |
	Moderately high	Moderately low	Very low	
Respondent's age	-.19	.03	.06	-.04
Number of children in household	-.26	-.13	-.09	-.14
Family per capita income	.27	.20	.16	.22
Total family income	.22	.28	.10	.23
Husband-wife employment scale	.16	.20	.17	.20
Employment status: male	.10	.17	-.19	.19
Employment status: female	.27	.04	-.02	.08
Health status	.14	.18	.21	.20
Psychoneurotic index	-.31	-.11	-.23	-.21
Closeness of neighbor relations	-.10	.09	.01	.01
Frequency of family interaction	.22	.11	.06	.09
Ego efficacy	-.05	.08	.02	.08
Social anxiety	-.13	-.05	-.24	-.14

APPENDIX TABLE 6.6 Marital companionship: correlations with selected measures, with social class status held constant

	Social class status			
	Moderately high	Moderately low	Very low	All social class statuses combined
Respondent's age	-.28	.08	.03	-.05
Number of children in household	.07	.09	-.04	-.04
Family per capita income	.37	.19	.23	.27
Total family income	.38	.27	.28	.33
Employment status: male and female	.41	.24	.15	.26
Employment status: male	.32	.22	-.12	.22
Employment status: female	.10	.09	-.07	.01
Health status	.02	.15	.16	.14
Psychoneurotic index	-.06	-.17	-.09	-.14
Closeness of neighbor relations	.17	.04	.10	.08
Frequency of family interaction	.17	-.02	.16	.07
Ego efficacy	-.18	.18	-.19	.03
Social anxiety	-.18	-.15	-.17	-.16

APPENDIX TABLE 6.7   Family per capita income by marital companionship, with social class status held constant (in percentages)

Social class status	Family per capita income	Marital companionship			N^a	Percent
		Intense	Moderate	Minimal		
Moderately high						
	Maximum	63	29	9	35	100
	Moderate	44	44	11	18	100
	Minimum	(0)	(80)	(20)	5	100
Moderately low						
	Maximum	51	32	18	79	100
	Moderate	41	30	30	37	100
	Minimum	26	45	29	31	100
Very low						
	Maximum	42	29	29	45	100
	Moderate	31	31	37	35	100
	Minimum	24	36	39	33	100

[a]There are 16 uncodeable cases. See footnote to table 6.1.

APPENDIX TABLE 6.8   Marital satisfaction: correlations with selected measures, with social class status held constant

	Social class status			All social class statuses combined
	Moderately high	Moderately low	Very low	
Household role relationship	.14	.17	.38	.26
Marital sociability	.54	.49	.52	.52
Marital companionship	.63	.68	.68	.68
Level of marital conflict	-.29	-.33	-.39	-.35
Marital role integration	.60	.61	.68	.65
Family per capita income	.34	.17	.15	.21
Total family income	.28	.26	.22	.27
Husband-wife employment scale	.31	.17	.14	.20
Standard of living	.25	.09	.10	.26
Social problems	-.74	-.65	-.62	-.66
Health status	.03	.18	.25	.20
Psychoneurotic index: husband	-.17	-.23	-.23	-.23
Psychoneurotic index: wife	-.24	-.13	.10	-.08
Respondent's age	-.33	.04	-.03	-.09
Closeness of neighbor relations	.07	.08	.06	.06
Frequency of family interaction	.26	.08	.25	.16
Closeknit networks	.12	.15	.16	.15
Ego efficacy	-.15	.16	-.32	-.02
Social anxiety	-.19	-.17	-.24	-.20

APPENDIX TABLE 6.9 Marital role integration by marital satisfaction, with closeknit networks and social class status held constant

		Closeknit networks										
		Extensive					Minimal					
		Marital satisfaction					Marital satisfaction					
Social class status	Marital role integration	Highly satisfied	Moderately satisfied	Dissat- isfied	N[a]	Percent	Highly satisfied	Moderately satisfied	Dissat- isfied	N[a]	Percent	
Moderately high	Integrated	43	54	3	37	100	43	55	3	40	100	
	Mixed	33	62	5	21	100	26	74	0	19	100	
	Segregated	23	59	18	17	100	10	40	50	20	100	
Moderately low	Integrated	55	45	0	31	100	52	44	4	23	100	
	Mixed	30	63	7	27	100	32	64	5	22	100	
	Segregated	3	74	23	31	100	3	47	50	36	100	

[a]There are 10 uncodeable cases. See footnote to table 6.1.

APPENDIX TABLE 6.10 Level of marital conflict by marital satisfaction, with marital role integration held constant (in percentages)

Marital role integration	Level of marital conflict	Marital satisfaction			N^a	Percent
		Highly satisfied	Moderately satisfied	Dissatisfied		
Shared						
	Low	59	39	2	61	100
	Moderate	36	60	4	45	100
	High	43	57	0	21	100
Mixed						
	Low	39	58	3	36	100
	Moderate	29	71	0	38	100
	High	13	67	20	15	100
Segregated						
	Low	17	50	33	18	100
	Moderate	8	66	27	61	100
	High	0	38	63	24	100

[a]There are 15 uncodeable cases. See footnote to table 6.1.

APPENDIX TABLE 6.11   Marital satisfaction by desires to change life, with community role satisfaction held constant (in percentages)

Community role satisfaction	Marital satisfaction	Desires to change life				
		Not at all	In some ways	In every way	N[a]	Percent
Highly satisfied	Highly satisfied	75	21	4	24	100
	Moderately satisfied	64	32	5	44	100
	Dissatisfied	40	30	30	10	100
Moderately satisfied	Highly satisfied	71	24	4	45	100
	Moderately satisfied	50	38	12	102	100
	Dissatisfied	17	54	30	24	100
Dissatisfied	Highly satisfied	55	35	11	29	100
	Moderately satisfied	33	53	14	36	100
	Dissatisfied	27	46	27	11	100

[a]There are 9 uncodeable cases. See footnote to table 6.1.

APPENDIX TABLE 7.1   Parental social class status by respondent's occupational status, with assimilation status held constant: males (in percentages)

Assimilation status	Parental social class status	Respondent's occupational status					
		Highly skilled & high white collar	Skilled	Semiskilled	Unskilled	N[a]	Percent
U.S. born: one or both parents U.S. born	High	30	15	33	22	27	100
	Moderate	5	38	19	38	21	100
	Low	16	25	24	33	12	100
	Very low	(0)	(0)	(50)	(50)	2	100
U.S. born: both parents foreign born	High	29	29	42	0	14	100
	Moderate	14	50	30	6	36	100
	Low	9	38	36	17	47	100
	Very low	3	18	49	30	33	100
Foreign born	High	63	11	15	11	19	100
	Moderate	14	23	45	18	22	100
	Low	5	14	52	29	21	100
	Very low	3	13	32	52	31	100

[a] These data are for male respondents with a total possible N = 334. There are 49 uncodeable cases.

APPENDIX TABLE 7.2   Respondent's occupational status by preference for job security vs. advancement, with respondent's age held constant: males (in percentages)

Respondent's age	Respondent's occupational status	Job security vs. advancement		N^a	Percent
		Job security	Advancement		
20–34 years					
	Highly skilled	18	82	22	100
	Skilled	68	32	19	100
	Semiskilled	70	30	30	100
	Unskilled	82	18	11	100
35–49 years					
	Highly skilled	67	33	12	100
	Skilled	81	19	43	100
	Semiskilled	80	20	50	100
	Unskilled	94	6	32	100
50 years or over					
	Highly skilled	(89)	(11)	9	100
	Skilled	83	17	24	100
	Semiskilled	88	12	34	100
	Unskilled	97	3	31	100

[a] These data are based on male, postrelocation information for which N = 334. There are 17 uncodeable cases.

APPENDIX TABLE 7.3   Respondent's occupational status by attitude toward job, with respondent's age held constant: males (in percentages)

Respondent's age	Respondent's occupational status	Attitude toward job			N^a	Percent
		Like job as is	Like job with changes	Like different job		
20–34 years						
	Highly skilled	32	50	18	22	100
	Moderately skilled	40	35	25	20	100
	Unskilled	41	28	31	39	100
35–49 years						
	Highly skilled	42	50	8	12	100
	Moderately skilled	55	31	14	42	100
	Unskilled	53	17	30	79	100
50 years and over						
	Highly skilled	40	30	30	10	100
	Moderately skilled	68	11	21	19	100
	Unskilled	74	13	13	55	100

[a]There are 36 uncodeable cases (male postrelocation data).

APPENDIX TABLE 7.4   Respondent's occupational status by reasons for job satisfaction, with respondent's age held constant: males (in percentages)

Respondent's age	Respondent's occupational status	Reasons for job satisfaction				N[a]	Percent
		Minimal satisfaction	Job conditions	Independence	Work pleasures		
20–34 years	Highly skilled	9	18	36	37	22	100
	Moderately skilled	25	25	5	45	20	100
	Unskilled	24	32	32	12	41	100
35–49 years	Highly skilled	0	17	25	58	12	100
	Moderately skilled	17	19	26	38	42	100
	Unskilled	26	33	24	17	81	100
50 years and over	Highly skilled	10	20	40	30	10	100
	Moderately skilled	27	18	27	28	22	100
	Unskilled	36	27	29	8	63	100

[a]There are 21 uncodeable cases (male postrelocation data).

APPENDIX TABLE 7.5 Respondent's occupational status by work satisfaction, with respondent's education held constant: males (in percentages)

Respondent's education	Respondent's occupational status	Work satisfaction				N^a	Percent
		Work as necessity	Source of pride	Mastery pleasure	Role fulfillment		
Some college or beyond							
	Highly skilled	5	9	18	68	22	100
	Skilled	(13)	(25)	(13)	(49)	8	100
	Semiskilled	(20)	(40)	(20)	(20)	5	100
	Unskilled	(0)	(100)	(0)	(0)	1	100
High school graduate							
	Highly skilled	(0)	(11)	(67)	(22)	9	100
	Skilled	17	9	48	26	23	100
	Semiskilled	32	47	16	5	19	100
	Unskilled	(22)	(67)	(11)	(0)	9	100

APPENDIX TABLE 7.5 (*continued*)

Respondent's education	Respondent's occupational status	Work satisfaction				N^a	Percent
		Work as necessity	Source of pride	Mastery pleasure	Role fulfillment		
9–11 grades completed							
	Highly skilled	(17)	(17)	(0)	(66)	6	100
	Skilled	33	0	38	29	24	100
	Semiskilled	28	29	20	23	40	100
	Unskilled	33	59	8	0	13	100
0–8 grades completed							
	Highly skilled	(33)	(0)	(50)	(17)	6	100
	Skilled	19	27	23	31	26	100
	Semiskilled	49	26	23	2	47	100
	Unskilled	61	24	13	2	45	100

[a]There are 31 uncodeable cases (male postrelocation data).

APPENDIX TABLE 7.6 Achieved occupational mobility by occupational aspirations, with respondent's occupational status held constant: males (in percentages)

Respondent's occupational status	Intra-generational mobility	Occupational aspirations				N^a	Percent
		High	Moderate	Low	Downward		
High							
	Achieved upward mobility	(78)	(0)	(0)	(22)	9	100
	Nonmobile	85	0	0	15	13	100
Moderate							
	Achieved upward mobility	22	63	0	15	27	100
	Nonmobile	44	44	0	12	43	100
Low							
	Achieved upward mobility	19	19	56	6	16	100
	Nonmobile	30	45	22	3	103	100
Downwardly mobile		33	44	23	0	48	100

[a]There are 75 uncodeable cases (male postrelocation data).

APPENDIX TABLE 7.7   Work role satisfaction by occupational aspiration-achievement discrepancy

Respondent's occupational status	Occupational aspirations	Work role satisfaction				N[a]	Percent
		Work as career	Work as occupation	Work as task	Work as job		
High							
	High	53	47	0	0	19	100
Moderate							
	High	17	67	8	8	36	100
	Moderate	23	38	30	9	56	100
Low							
	High	0	42	41	17	46	100
	Moderate	2	25	50	23	57	100
	Low	2	26	51	21	43	100
Achievement higher than aspirations		6	44	33	17	18	100

[a]There are 59 uncodeable cases (male postrelocation data).

APPENDIX TABLE 7.8   Marital status and husband's earnings, by employment status of wife (in percentages)

| | Employment status of wife | | | | |
Marital status	Works regularly	Works irregularly	Not in labor force	N^a	Percent
Married, with husband in household earning:					
Over $100 a week	14	20	66	50	100
$75–$99 a week	15	17	68	94	100
$50–$74 a week	16	37	47	117	100
Under $50 a week	18	29	53	56	100
Separated, widowed, and divorced	45	22	33	91	100
Never married	76	18	6	50	100

[a] There are 38 uncodeable cases

APPENDIX TABLE 8.1   Assimilation status by ethnic involvement, with respondent's education held constant (in percentages)

Respondent's education	Assimilation status	Ethnic involvement			N^a	Percent
		Highly involved	Moderately involved	Minimally involved		
Some college or beyond	U.S. born: parents U.S. born	0	4	96	22	100
	U.S. born: one parent foreign born	(0)	(20)	(80)	5	100
	U.S. born: both parents foreign born	9	45	46	11	100
	Foreign born: migrated 1947 or before	(17)	(50)	(33)	6	100
	Foreign born: migrated after 1947	(20)	(60)	(20)	5	100
High school	U.S. born: parents U.S. born	7	14	79	14	100
	U.S. born: one parent foreign born	20	50	30	10	100
	U.S. born: both parents foreign born	13	44	43	54	100
	Foreign born: migrated 1947 or before	(29)	(14)	(57)	7	100
	Foreign born: migrated after 1947	(0)	(100)	(0)	4	100

9–11 years

U.S. born: parents U.S. born	9	18	73	33	100
U.S. born: one parent foreign born	7	26	67	15	100
U.S. born: both parents foreign born	26	46	28	76	100
Foreign born: migrated 1947 or before	7	57	36	14	100
Foreign born: migrated after 1947	(25)	(25)	(50)	4	100

0–8 years

U.S. born: parents U.S. born	9	9	82	11	100
U.S. born: one parent foreign born	(0)	(33)	(67)	9	100
U.S. born: both parents foreign born	33	49	18	51	100
Foreign born: migrated 1947 or before	42	37	21	67	100
Foreign born: migrated after 1947	66	30	4	40	100

[a]There are 28 uncodeable cases.

APPENDIX TABLE 8.2   Ethnic involvement: correlations with selected measures, with social class status held constant

	Social class status			All social class statuses combined
	Moderately high	Moderately low	Very low	
Ethnic embeddedness	.41	.47	.55	.50
Parental social class status	-.34	-.19	-.30	-.31
Family per capita income	-.06	-.04	.06	-.07
Husband-wife employment scale	-.02	-.02	-.03	-.06
Respondent's age	.31	.05	.07	.17
Frequency of family interaction	.13	.30	.24	.25
Closeness to kin	.30	.32	.09	.23
Localism of five closest people	.09	.11	.19	.17
Closeness of neighbor relations	.21	.13	.11	.15
Closeknit networks	.18	.30	.11	.20
Local resource use	.26	.08	-.08	.05
Local vs. metropolitan orientation	-.11	-.11	-.04	-.14
Standard of living	-.01	.16	.00	.01
Ego efficacy	-.21	-.16	-.14	-.21
Social conformity	.19	.05	.15	.16
Residential ethnocentricity	.28	.34	.43	.41

APPENDIX TABLE 8.3 Assimilation status by residential ethnocentricity, with respondent's education held constant (in percentages)

Respondent's education	Assimilation status	Residential ethnocentricity			N^a	Percent
		Highly ethnospansive	Moderately ethnospansive	Ethnocentric		
Some college or beyond						
	U.S. born: one or both parents U.S. born	65	31	4	23	100
	U.S. born: both parents foreign born	64	27	9	11	100
	Foreign born	64	27	9	11	100
High school						
	U.S. born: one or both parents U.S. born	54	29	17	24	100
	U.S. born: both parents foreign born	41	36	23	53	100
	Foreign born	36	36	28	11	100
0–11 years						
	U.S. born: one or both parents U.S. born	55	25	20	60	100
	U.S. born: both parents foreign born	35	35	30	127	100
	Foreign born	26	30	44	128	100

aThere are 38 uncodeable cases.

APPENDIX TABLE 8.4   Residential ethnocentricity: correlations with selected measures, with social class status held constant (females)

| | Social class status | | | |
	Moderately high	Moderately low	Very low	All social class statuses combined
Parental social class status	-.27	-.09	-.16	-.20
Rural-urban background	.01	-.08	-.31	-.21
Family per capita income	.02	-.13	.01	-.11
Intergenerational mobility	-.18	.05	.02	-.14
Husband-wife employment scale	.03	-.09	-.06	-.09
Employment status: male	-.13	.10	.13	.11
Employment status: female	.22	.15	-.09	.07
Frequency of family interaction	.16	.06	-.02	.06
Closeness of neighbor relations	.22	.12	.02	.10
Local resource use	.36	.11	-.19	.02
Urban familiarity	.03	-.08	.01	-.07
Ego efficacy	-.18	-.14	-.05	-.16

APPENDIX TABLE 8.5 Residential ethnocentricity: correlations with selected measures, with social class status held constant (males)

	Social class status			
	Moderately high	Moderately low	Very low	All social class statuses combined
Parental social class status	-.14	-.39	-.01	-.23
Rural-urban background	-.15	-.12	-.15	-.21
Family per capita income	.05	-.45	-.16	-.26
Intergenerational mobility	.08	.10	.13	-.07
Employment status: male	.16	-.45	-.09	-.17
Employment status: female	-.10	.05	.07	.01
Frequency of family interaction	-.12	-.07	-.43	-.17
Closeness of neighbor relations	.03	-.21	.13	.04
Local resource use	.06	.01	.26	.12
Urban familiarity	.16	.03	-.12	-.03
Ego control	.14	.08	.31	.13

APPENDIX TABLE 8.6   Parental social class status by self-estimate of own social class, with social class status held constant: females (in percentages)

Social class status	Parental social class status	Self-estimate of own social class			N^a	Percent
		Middle class	Working class	Lower class		
Moderately high						
	Moderately high	68	32	0	44	100
	Moderately low	38	59	3	29	100
	Very low	37	63	0	24	100
Moderately low						
	Moderately high	46	54	0	46	100
	Moderately low	42	57	1	74	100
	Very low	40	53	7	89	100
Very low						
	Moderately high	29	57	14	21	100
	Moderately low	34	57	9	56	100
	Very low	23	72	5	108	100

[a]There are 12 uncodeable cases (female postrelocation data).

APPENDIX TABLE 8.7 Social class status by self-estimate of own social class, with assimilation status held constant: females (in percentages)

Assimilation status	Social class status	Self-estimate of own social class			N^a	Percent
		Middle class	Working class	Lower class		
U.S. born: one or both parents U.S. born						
	Moderately high	54	46	0	39	100
	Moderately low	48	50	2	62	100
	Very low	43	47	10	30	100
U.S. born: both parents foreign born						
	Moderately high	46	51	3	41	100
	Moderately low	43	53	4	100	100
	Very low	27	60	13	55	100
Foreign born						
	Moderately high	59	41	0	17	100
	Moderately low	34	62	4	47	100
	Very low	22	76	2	97	100

[a]There are 15 uncodeable cases (female postrelocation data).

APPENDIX TABLE 8.8   Desire to change life by social mobility orientation, with head of household occupational status held constant (in percentages)

Head of household occupational status	Desire to change life	Social mobility orientation			N[a]	Percent
		Highly mobile	Moderately mobile	Minimally mobile		
Highly skilled						
	In all or many ways	(67)	(33)	(0)	3	100
	In a few ways	27	33	40	15	100
	Not at all	(0)	(43)	(57)	7	100
Skilled						
	In all or many ways	(60)	(20)	(20)	5	100
	In a few ways	31	46	23	13	100
	Not at all	(25)	(25)	(50)	8	100
Semiskilled						
	In all or many ways	45	33	22	18	100
	In a few ways	24	43	33	46	100
	Not at all	29	38	33	21	100
Unskilled						
	In all or many ways	46	27	27	37	100
	In a few ways	33	33	34	76	100
	Not at all	27	18	55	75	100

[a]There are 162 uncodeable cases

APPENDIX TABLE 8.9   Child-rearing authoritarianism: correlations with selected measures, with social class status held constant

	Social class status			
	Moderately high	Moderately low	Very low	All social class statuses combined
Females				
Social conformity	.15	.08	-.10	.05
Economic liberalism-conservatism	-.16	-.12	-.08	-.14
Residential ethnocentricity	.20	-.07	.03	.04
Work satisfaction	-.22	-.01	-.11	-.13
Urban familiarity	-.15	.16	.24	.09
Self-estimate of social class	-.35	.00	-.07	-.12
Husband's child-rearing authoritarianism	.43	.20	-.06	.22
Males				
Social conformity	.18	.01	-.08	.08
Work satisfaction	-.21	-.06	-.20	-.19
Urban familiarity	.02	-.08	.01	-.04
Self-estimate of social class	-.04	.07	-.15	-.08

APPENDIX TABLE 8.10   Social class status by social conformity (in percentages)

Social class status	Social conformity				
	Independent	Moderately conforming	Highly conforming	N	Percent
Males[a]					
Moderately high	67	25	8	63	100
Moderately low	46	39	15	150	100
Very low	30	49	21	108	100
Females[b]					
Moderately high	51	38	11	99	100
Moderately low	37	43	20	210	100
Very low	31	35	34	181	100

[a]There are 13 uncodeable cases (male postrelocation data)
[b]There are 13 uncodeable cases (female postrelocation data).

APPENDIX TABLE 9.1 Social anxiety by closeness of neighbor relations, with social class status held constant: females (in percentages)

Social class status	Social anxiety	Closeness of neighbor relations			N[a]	Percent
		Very close	Moderately close	Distant		
Moderately high						
	Very anxious	32	24	44	34	100
	Moderately anxious	26	42	32	19	100
	Relaxed	33	44	23	43	100
Moderately low						
	Very anxious	31	43	26	86	100
	Moderately anxious	42	44	14	50	100
	Relaxed	55	27	18	67	100
Very low						
	Very anxious	31	35	34	77	100
	Moderately anxious	43	34	23	40	100
	Relaxed	57	29	14	58	100

[a] There are 12 uncodeable cases.

APPENDIX TABLE 9.2   Social anxiety by interpersonal isolation-integration, with social class status held constant: females (in percentages)

Social class status	Social anxiety	Interpersonal isolation-integration			N^a	Percent
		Highly integrated	Moderately integrated	Isolated		
Moderately high						
	Very anxious	32	42	26	19	100
	Moderately anxious	18	61	21	34	100
	Relaxed	23	51	26	43	100
Moderately low						
	Very anxious	27	53	20	41	100
	Moderately anxious	35	42	23	94	100
	Relaxed	39	49	12	67	100
Very low						
	Very anxious	13	25	62	32	100
	Moderately anxious	27	46	27	82	100
	Relaxed	45	38	17	58	100

[a]There are 16 uncodeable cases.

APPENDIX TABLE 9.3   Social anxiety by health status, with social class status held constant: females (in percentages)

Social class status	Social anxiety	Health status			N^a	Percent
		Good health	Fair health	Poor health		
Moderately high						
	Very anxious	53	32	16	19	100
	Moderately anxious	56	29	15	34	100
	Relaxed	61	33	7	43	100
Moderately low						
	Very anxious	33	38	29	42	100
	Moderately anxious	44	40	16	94	100
	Relaxed	55	37	8	67	100
Very low						
	Very anxious	24	38	38	34	100
	Moderately anxious	41	31	28	83	100
	Relaxed	45	41	14	58	100

[a]There are 12 uncodeable cases.

APPENDIX TABLE 9.4 Ego efficacy: correlations with selected measures, with social class status held constant: females

	Social class status			All social class statuses combined
	Moderately high	Moderately low	Very low	
Family per capita income	-.05	.04	-.10	.05
Ethnic embeddedness	-.30	-.13	-.24	-.23
Standard of living	-.11	.00	.09	.07
Parental social class status	.23	.14	.05	.22
Length of residence	-.26	-.15	.10	-.13
Residential satisfaction	-.19	-.09	-.02	-.13
Local resource use	-.33	-.03	-.07	-.13
Local v. metropolitan orientation	.21	.19	-.06	.18
Closeness of neighbor relations	-.27	-.05	-.11	-.13
Frequency of family interaction	-.38	-.09	.02	-.15
Closeknit networks	-.28	-.10	-.03	-.12
Closeness to kin	-.22	-.04	-.01	-.09
Religious commitment	-.18	-.02	-.22	-.18
Change proneness	.15	.14	-.03	.10
Anomie scale	-.25	-.34	-.10	-.28
Ethnic involvement	-.21	-.16	-.14	-.21
Child-rearing authoritarianism	-.20	-.13	-.04	-.16
Social conformity	-.11	-.26	.08	-.17
Strike participation	.20	.10	.03	.15
Social mobility orientation	.21	.08	.00	.17
Marital satisfaction	-.15	.16	-.32	-.02
Marital role integration	.02	.17	.20	.08
Work role satisfaction	.15	.00	.04	.08
Mental health rating	.12	.25	.34	.22
Social problems	.11	-.12	.27	-.02

APPENDIX TABLE 9.5 Ego efficacy by participation in strike decision, with social class status held constant (in percentages)

Social class status	Ego efficacy	Participation in strike decision			N[a]	Percent
		Vote for	Undecided	Vote against		
Moderately high						
	High	27	9	64	45	100
	Moderate	56	11	33	18	100
	Low	53	12	35	17	100
Moderately low						
	High	39	22	39	65	100
	Moderate	46	22	32	46	100
	Low	53	14	33	60	100
Very low						
	High	57	10	33	30	100
	Moderate	63	17	20	30	100
	Low	58	16	26	62	100

[a]There are 61 uncodeable cases.

APPENDIX TABLE 9.6   Ego control: correlations with selected measures, with social class status held constant: males

	Social class status			All social class statuses combined
	Moderately high	Moderately low	Very low	
Parental social class status	-.21	-.07	.02	-.01
Intergenerational mobility	.14	.02	.10	.19
Occupational aspirations	-.23	-.14	.12	.05
Desire to change life	.12	-.31	-.01	-.06
Family per capita income	-.01	-.02	-.04	.05
Length of residence	.05	.05	-.14	.00
Local resource use	-.05	.06	.05	.03
Frequency of family interaction	.07	.06	.00	.02
Closeness of neighbor relations	-.15	.18	.21	.10
Closeness to kin	.18	-.16	.01	-.04
Urban familiarity	.33	-.10	-.09	-.02
Social conformity	-.15	-.13	.21	-.08
Strike participation	-.07	-.04	.21	.01
Child-rearing authoritarianism	.20	-.05	-.14	-.03
Desire to plan ahead	-.04	.02	.24	.11
Response to neighbor invitation	-.04	-.10	.13	.02
Anomie scale	.15	.09	-.14	.00
Marital companionship	-.19	-.01	-.06	-.07
Marital satisfaction	.19	.13	-.21	.00
Work role satisfaction	.23	.04	.08	.17
Job satisfaction	.33	.06	.05	.11
Social problems	.12	-.06	.07	-.02
Psychoneurotic index	.00	-.23	-.23	-.18
Health status	.08	.13	.32	.19
Mental health rating	-.05	.04	.14	.08

Bibliography

HISTORICAL BACKGROUND OF MODERN SOCIAL
CLASS STRUCTURE

Abrahams, Israel. *Jewish Life in the Middle Ages.* New York and Philadelphia: Meridian Books and Jewish Publication Society of America, 1958 (first published 1896).

Ashley, Maurice. *England in the Seventeenth Century.* Baltimore: Penguin Books, 1961.

Ashton, T. S. *The Industrial Revolution 1760-1830.* New York: Oxford University Press (Galaxy Books), 1964 (first published 1948).

Barber, Elinor G. *The Bourgeoisie in 18th Century France.* Princeton: Princeton University Press, 1955.

Beech, George T. *A Rural Society in Medieval France: The Gatine of Poitou in the Eleventh and Twelfth Centuries.* Baltimore: Johns Hopkins Press, 1964.

Behrens, C. B. A. *The Ancien Regime.* London: Harcourt, Brace and World, 1967.

Bennett, H. S. *Life on the English Manor: A Study of Peasant Conditions, 1150-1400.* Cambridge: Cambridge University Press (paperback edition), 1960 (first published 1937).

Bloch, Marc. *Feudal Society,* trans. L. A. Manyon. 2 vols. Chicago: University of Chicago (Phoenix Edition), 1964 (first published as La Société féodale, 1940).

——*French Rural History*, trans. Janet Sondheimer. London: Routledge and Kegan Paul, 1966 (first published as *Les caracteres originaux de l'histoire rurale française*, 1931).

Blum, Jerome. *Lord and Peasant in Russia: From the Ninth to the Nineteenth Century.* Princeton: Princeton University Press, 1961.

Burkhardt, Jacob. *The Civilization of the Renaissance in Italy.* New York: Phaidon Publishers, 1950 (first published 1860).

Checkland, S. G. *The Rise of Industrial Society in England 1815-1885.* New York: St. Martin's Press, 1964.

Chevalier, Louis. *La Formation de la population Parisienne au XIXe siecle.* Paris: Presses Universitaires de France, 1950.

Cipolla, Carlo M. "Four Centuries of Italian Demographic Development," in D. V. Glass and D. E. C. Eversley, eds., *Population in History: Essays in Historical Demography*. London: Edward Arnold, 1965 (first published 1958).

——*Money, Prices, and Civilization in the Mediterranean World*. Princeton: Princeton University Press, 1956.

Coulton, G. G. *The Medieval Village*. Cambridge: Cambridge University Press, 1931.

Davis, James Cushman. *The Decline of the Venetian Mobility as a Ruling Class*. Baltimore: Johns Hopkins Press, 1962.

Dawson, Christopher. *The Making of Europe: An Introduction to the History of European Unity*. New York: Median Books, 1956 (first published 1932).

Deane, Phyllis, and Cole, W. A. *British Economic Growth 1688-1959: Trends and Structure*. Cambridge: Cambridge University Press, 1967.

Denman, D. R. *Origins of Ownership*. London: George Allen and Unwin, 1958.

De Schweinitz, Karl. *England's Road to Social Security*. Philadelphia: University of Pennsylvania Press, 1943.

Dovring, Folke. "The Transformation of European Agriculture," in H. J. Habakkuk and M. Postan, eds., *Cambridge Economic History of Europe Vol. VI (Part II)*. Cambridge: Cambridge University Press, 1965.

Eden, Sir Frederick Morton. *The State of the Poor: A History of the Labouring Classes in England, with Parochial Reports*, abridged and edited by A. G. L. Rogers. New York: E. P. Dutton, 1929 (first published 1797).

Elton, G. F. *Reformation Europe: 1517-1559*. Cleveland: World Publishing Co. (Meridian Books), 1963.

Engels, Frederick. "Prefatory Note to the Peasant War in Germany" (1874), in Karl Marx and Frederick Engels, *Selected Works, Vol. 1*. Moscow: Foreign Languages Publishing House, 1962.

Feldmesser, Robert A. "Social Classes and Political Structure," in Cyril E. Black, ed., *The Transformation of Russian Society: Aspects of Social Change Since 1861*. Cambridge, Mass.: Harvard University Press, 1960.

Ganshof, F. L. *Feudalism*, trans. Philip Grierson. New York: Harper and Bros. (Harper Torchbacks), 1961 (first published in French, *Qu'est-ce que la féodalité?* 1944).

George, M. Dorothy. *English Social Life in the Eighteenth Century*. London: The Sheldon Press, 1923.

——*London Life in the XVIIIth Century*. London: Kegan Paul, Trench, Trubner and Co., 1930.

Gerschenkron, Alexander. "Agrarian Policies and Industrialization: Russia 1861-1917," in H. J. Habakkuk and M. Postan, eds., *Cambridge Economic History of Europe, Vol. VI (Part II)*. Cambridge: Cambridge University Press, 1965.

——*Bread and Democracy in Germany*. New York: Howard Fertig, 1966.

——*Economic Backwardness in Historical Perspective*. Cambridge, Mass.: Harvard University Press, 1962.

Graus, F. "The Late Medieval Poor in Town and Countryside," in Sylvia
L. Thrupp, ed., *Change in Medieval Society: Europe North of the Alps,
1050-1500.* New York: Appleton-Century-Crofts, 1964.

Habbakkuk, H. J. "The Economic History of Modern Britain," in D. V.
Glass and D. E. C. Everesley, eds., *Population in History: Essays in
Historical Demography.* London: Edward Arnold, 1965.

Hamerow, Theodore S. *Restoration, Revolution, Reaction: Economics
and Politics in Germany, 1815-1871.* Princeton: Princeton University
Press, 1958.

Hammond, J. L., and Hammond, Barbara. *The Town Labourer 1760-1832:
The New Civilisation.* London: Longmans, Green, 1966 (first published
1917).

——*The Village Labourer 1760-1832: A Study in the Government of
England Before the Reform Bill.* London: Longmans, Green, 1927
(first published 1911).

Hartz, Louis. *The Liberal Tradition in America.* New York: Harcourt,
Brace, 1955.

Hayek, F. A., ed. *Capitalism and the Historians.* Chicago: University of
Chicago Press, 1954.

Heaton, Herbert. *Economic History of Europe.* New York: Harper, 1936.

Heckscher, Eli F. *Mercantilism,* trans. Mendel Shapiro. 2 vols. London:
George Allen and Unwin, 1934 (first published in Swedish, 1931).

Heitland, William E. *Agricola: A Study of Agriculture and Rustic Life in
the Greco-Roman World From the Point of View of Labour.* Cambridge: Cambridge University Press, 1921.

Hexter, J. H. "The Myth of the Middle Class in Tudor England," in
Bernard Barber and Elinor Barber, eds., *European Social Class: Stability and Change.* New York: Macmillan, 1965.

Hilton, R. M. "Peasant Movements in England Before 1381," in Eleanor M.
Carus-Wilson, ed., *Essays in Economic History, II.* London: Edward
Arnold, 1962 (first published 1949).

Homans, George C. *English Villagers of the Thirteenth Century.* Cambridge,
Mass. Harvard University Press, 1941.

Hoskins, W. G. *The Midland Peasant: The Economic and Social History of
a Leicestershire Village.* New York: St. Martin's Press, 1965.

Landes, David S., ed. *The Rise of Capitalism.* New York: Macmillan, 1966.

Lefebvre, Georges. *The French Revolution From Its Origins to 1793,* trans.
Elizabeth Moss Evanson. London: Routledge and Kegan Paul, 1962
(first published in French, 1930; rev. ed., 1957).

Lestocquoy, J. *Les Villes de Flandre et d'Italie sous le gouvernement des
patriciens (XIe - XVe siecles).* Paris: Presses Universitaires de France,
1952.

Link, Edith Murr. *The Emancipation of the Austrian Peasant 1740-1798.*
New York: Columbia University Press, 1949.

Lopez, Robert S. *The Birth of Europe.* New York: M. Evans and Co.,
1967 (first published in French, 1962).

Lucas, Henry S. "The Great European Famine of 1315, 1316, and 1317," in Eleanor M. Carus-Wilson, ed., *Essays in Economic History, Volume II.* London: Edward Arnold, 1962 (first published 1930).

Luzzatto, Gino. *An Economic History of Italy: From the Fall of the Roman Empire to the Beginning of the Sixteenth Century,* trans. Philip Jones. London: Routledge and Kegan Paul, 1961.

Mack Smith, Denis. *Italy: A Modern History.* Ann Arbor: University of Michigan Press, 1959.

Main, Jackson Turner. *The Social Structure of Revolutionary America.* Princeton: Princeton University Press, 1965.

Maitland, Frederick William. *The Constitutional History of England.* Cambridge: Cambridge University Press, 1908.

——*Domesday Book and Beyond. Three Essays in the Early History of England.* Cambridge: Cambridge University Press, 1921 (first published 1897).

——*Township and Borough.* Cambridge: Cambridge University Press, 1898.

Mantoux, Paul. *The Industrial Revolution in the Eighteenth Century.* New York: Harper (Harper Torchbacks), 1961 (first published in French, 1906).

Maynard, Sir John. *Russia in Flux.* New York: Macmillan, 1949. Abridged and edited by S. Haden Guest from *Russia in Flux,* 1941, and *The Russian Peasant and Other Studies,* 1942.

McConnel, John W. *The Evolution of Social Classes.* Washington, D.C.: American Council on Public Affairs, 1942.

Moore, Barrington, Jr. *Social Origins of Dictatorship and Democracy.* Boston: Beacon Press, 1966.

More, Sir Thomas. *Utopia.* New York: D. Van Nostrand Company, Inc., 1947 (first published 1516).

Mumford, Lewis. *The Culture of Cities.* New York: Harcourt, Brace, 1938.

Nef, John U. *The Conquest of the Material World.* Chicago: University of Chicago Press, 1964.

——*Industry and Government in France and England, 1540–1640.* Philadelphia: American Philosophical Society, 1940.

Ogg, David. *Europe in the Seventeenth Century.* London: Adam and Charles Black, 1961 (first published 1925).

Pirenne, Henri. *Economic and Social History of Medieval Europe.* New York: Harcourt, Brace, 1937 (first published in French, 1933).

——*Medieval Cities: Their Origins and the Revival of Trade,* trans. Frank D. Halsey. Garden City: Doubleday and Co., 1956 (first published in English, 1925).

Plumb, J. H. *England in the Eighteenth Century.* Baltimore: Penguin Books, 1950.

Polanyi, Karl. *The Great Transformation.* New York: Farrar and Rinehart, 1944.

Poole, Austin Lane. *Obligations of Society in the XII and XIII Centuries.* London: Oxford University Press, 1946.

Prest, John. *The Industrial Revolution in Coventry.* London: Oxford University Press, 1960.

Raftis, J. Ambrose. *Tenure and Mobility: Studies in the Social History of the Medieval English Village.* Toronto: Pontifical Institute of Medieval Studies, 1964.

Rorig, Fritz. *The Medieval Town,* rev. ed. London: B. T. Batsford, 1964 (first published 1932).

Rosenberg, Hans. *Bureaucracy, Aristocracy and Autocracy: The Prussian Experience, 1660-1815.* Cambridge, Mass.: Harvard University Press, 1958.

Rudé, George. *The Crowd in History: A Study of Popular Disturbances in France and England, 1730-1848.* New York: Wiley, 1964.

Sachar, Abram Leon. *A History of the Jews,* 4th ed. New York: Knopf, 1955 (first published 1930).

Sée, Henri. *Economic and Social Conditions in France During the Eighteenth Century,* trans. Edwin M. Zeydel. New York: Knopf, 1927 (first published in French, 1925).

——*Les Classes rurales et le regime domanial en France au moyen age.* Paris: Librairie Felix Alcan, 1901.

Simpson, Alan. *The Wealth of the Gentry, 1540-1660*: East Anglian Studies. Chicago: University of Chicago Press, 1961.

Slicher van Bath, B. H. *The Agrarian History of Western Europe, A.D. 500-1850.* London: Edward Arnold, 1963.

Smelser, Neil J. *Social Change in the Industrial Revolution: An Application of Theory to the British Cotton Industry.* Chicago: University of Chicago Press, 1959.

Stone, Lawrence. *The Crisis of the Aristocracy, 1558-1641.* Oxford: Clarendon Press, 1965.

Tawney, R. H. *The Agrarian Problem of the Sixteenth Century.* New York: Burt Franklin, undated (first published 1912).

Thompson, Edward P. *The Making of the English Working Class.* New York: Pantheon Books, 1963.

Thrupp, Sylvia L. *The Merchant Class of Medieval London, 1300-1350.* Chicago: University of Chicago Press, 1948.

Trevor-Roper, Hugh Redwald. *The Gentry, 1540-1640.* Cambridge: Cambridge University Press, 1953.

Ullman, Walter. *The Individual and Society in the Middle Ages.* Baltimore: Johns Hopkins Press, 1966.

Unwin, George. *Industrial Organization in the Sixteenth and Seventeenth Centuries.* London: Frank Cass, 1963 (first published 1904).

Vinogradoff, Paul. *The Growth of the Manor.* London: Swan Sonnenschein, 1905.

——*Villainage in England: Essays in Medieval History.* Oxford: Oxford University Press, 1892.

Vucinich, Wayne S., ed. *The Peasant in the Nineteenth Century.* Stanford: Stanford University Press, 1968.

Webb, Robert K. *The British Working Class Reader, 1790-1848.* London: George Allen and Unwin, 1955.

Weber, Max. *The City,* trans. and ed. Don Martindale and Gertrude Neuwirth. New York: Free Press, 1958.

Williams, Raymond. *Culture and Society*. Garden City: Doubleday (Anchor Books), 1960.

Wilson, Charles. *England's Apprenticeship, 1603-1763*. New York: St. Martin's Press, 1965.

Winston, Richard. *Charlemagne: From the Hammer to the Cross*. New York: Random House (Vintage Paperback), 1960.

PEASANTRIES AND THE CONDITIONS OF MIGRATION

Antin, Mary. *The Promised Land*. Boston and New York: Houghton Mifflin, 1912.

Arensberg, Conrad M. *The Irish Countryman*. New York: Macmillan, 1937.

——and Kimball, Solon T. *Family and Community in Ireland*. Cambridge, Mass.: Harvard University Press, 1948.

Balch, Emily Greene. *Our Slavic Fellow Citizens*. New York: Charities Publication Committee, 1910.

Banfield, Edward C. "Reply to J. Davis," *Comparative Studies in Society and History,* 12 (1970), 340-353.

——with assistance of Laura Fasano Banfield. *The Moral Basis of a Backward Society*. Glencoe, Ill.: Free Press, 1958.

Beckett, J. C. *A Short History of Ireland*. London: Hutchinson University Library, 1958 (first published 1952).

Bernot, Lucien, and Blanchard, René. *Nouville: un village français*. Paris: Institut d'Ethnologie, 1953.

Berthoff, Rowland Tappan. *British Immigrants in Industrial America, 1790-1950*. Cambridge, Mass.: Harvard University Press, 1953.

Beshers, James M., Laumann, Edward O., and Bradshaw, Benjamin S. "Ethnic Congregation-Segregation, Assimilation, and Stratification," *Social Forces,* 42 (1963), 482-489.

Bienenstok, Theodore. "Social Life and Authority in the East European Jewish Shtetel Community," *Southwest Journal of Anthropology,* 6 (1950), 238-254.

Bogardus, Emory S. *Immigration and Race Attitudes*. Boston: D. C. Heath, 1928.

Boody, Bertha M. *A Psychological Study of Immigrant Children at Ellis Island*. Baltimore: Williams and Wilkins, 1926.

Bourne, George (pseudonym for George Sturt). *Change in the Village*. New York: George H. Doran Co., 1912.

Brown, James S., Schwarzweller, Harry K., and Mangalam, Joseph J. "Kentucky Mountain Migration and the Stem-Family: An American Variation on a Theme of Le Play," *Rural Sociology,* 28 (1963), 48-69.

Browning, Harley L., and Feindt, Waltraut. "Selectivity of Migrants in a Developing Country: A Mexican Case Study," *Demography,* 6 (1969), 347-357.

Brunner, Edmund de S. *Immigrant Farmers and Their Children*. Garden City: Doubleday, Doran, 1929.

Carlyle, Margaret. *The Awakening of Southern Italy*. London: Oxford University Press, 1962.

Carpenter, Niles. *Immigrants and Their Children, 1920.* Washington, D.C.: Government Printing Office, 1927.

——and Katz, Daniel. "A Study of Acculturization in the Polish Group in Buffalo, 1926-1928," *University of Buffalo Studies,* 7 (1929), no. 4, 103-131.

Child, Irvin L. *Italian or American? The Second Generation in Conflict.* New Haven: Yale University Press, 1943.

Commons, John R. *Races and Immigrants in America.* New York: Macmillan, 1920.

Connell, K. H. *The Population of Ireland.* Oxford: Oxford University Press, 1950.

Cornelisen, Ann. *Torregreca: Life, Death, Miracles.* Boston: Little, Brown, 1969.

Covello, Leonard. *The Social Background of the Italo-American School Child,* ed. Francesco Cordasco. Leiden: E. J. Brill, 1967.

Davie, Maurice, R. *World Immigration.* New York: Macmillan, 1936.

Davis, J. "Morals and Backwardness," *Comparative Studies in Society and History,* 12 (1970), 340-353.

Dickinson, Robert E. *The Population Problem of Southern Italy: An Essay in Social Geography.* Syracuse: Syracuse University Press, 1955.

Dovring, Folke. *Land and Labor in Europe in the Twentieth Century: A Comparative Survey of Recent Agrarian History.* The Hague: Martinus Nijhoff, 1965.

Eisenstadt, Samuel N. *The Absorption of Immigrants.* London: Routledge and Kegan Paul, 1954.

Erickson, Charlotte. *American Industry and the European Immigrant 1860-1885.* Cambridge, Mass.: Harvard University Press, 1957.

Ernst, Robert. *Immigrant Life in New York City, 1826-1863.* New York: King's Crown Press, 1949.

Ex, J. *Adjustment After Migration: A Longitudinal Study of the Process of Adjustment by Refugees to a New Environment.* The Hague: Martinus Nijhoff, 1966.

Fein, Rashi. "Educational Patterns in Southern Migration," *Southern Economics Journal,* 32 (1965), 106-124.

Foerster, Robert F. *The Italian Emigration of Our Times.* Cambridge, Mass.: Harvard University Press, 1919.

Foster, George M. "What is Folk Culture?" *American Anthropologist,* 55 (1953), 159-173.

Fried, Marc. "Deprivation and Migration: Dilemmas of Causal Interpretation," in Daniel P. Moynihan, ed., *On Understanding Poverty: Perspectives from the Social Sciences.* New York: Basic Books, 1969.

Friedmann, Frederick G. "The World of 'La Miseria,' " *Community Development Review,* 10 (September 1958), 16-28.

Galitzi, Christine. *A Study of Assimilation Among the Roumanians in the U.S.* New York: Columbia University Press, 1929.

Garavel, J. *Les paysans de Morette: Un siècle de vie rurale dans une commune du Dauphine.* Paris: Librairie Armond Colin, 1948.

Glazer, Nathan, and Moynihan, Daniel Patrick. *Beyond the Melting Pot:*

The Negroes, Puerto Ricans, Jews, Italians, and Irish of New York City. Cambridge, Mass.: Harvard and MIT Press, 1963.

Goodhart, Arthur L. *Poland and the Minority Races.* New York: Brentano's, 1920.

Goodrich, C. A., Bushrod, W., and Hayes, M. *Migration and Planes of Living, 1920–1934.* Philadelphia: University of Pennsylvania Press, 1935.

Gordon, Milton M. *Assimilation in American Life: The Role of Race, Religion, and National Origins.* New York: Oxford University Press, 1964.

Halpern, Joel Martin. *The Changing Village Community.* Englewood Cliffs, N.J.: Prentice-Hall, 1967.

——*A Serbian Village.* New York: Columbia University Press, 1958.

Hamilton, C. Horace. "Educational Selectivity of Migration from Farm to Urban and to Other Nonfarm Communities," in Mildred Kantor, ed., *Mobility and Mental Health.* Springfield, Ill.: C. C. Thomas, 1965.

Handlin, Oscar. *Boston's Immigrants: A Study in Acculturation,* rev. ed. Cambridge, Mass.: Harvard University Press, 1959 (first published 1941).

——*Immigration as a Factor in American History.* Englewood Cliffs, N.J.: Prentice-Hall, 1959.

——*The Uprooted.* Boston: Little, Brown, 1951.

Hansen, Marcus Lee. *The Atlantic Migration 1607–1860,* ed. Arthur M. Schlesinger. New York: Harper (Torchback Edition), 1961 (first published, 1940).

Heiss, Jerold. "Sources of Satisfaction and Assimilation Among Italian Immigrants," *Human Relations,* 19 (1966), 165–177.

Hobbs, A. H. "Specificity and Selective Migration," *American Sociological Review,* 7 (1942), 772–781.

Hobsbawm, E. J. *Primitive Rebels: Studies in Archaic Forms of Social Movement in the 19th and 20th Centuries.* New York: Frederick A. Praeger, 1959.

Hutchinson, E. P. *Immigrants and Their Children, 1850–1950.* New York: John Wiley and Sons, 1956.

Illseley, Raymond, Finlayson, Angela, and Thompson, Barbara. "The Motivation and Characteristics of Internal Migrants: A Socio-Medical Study of Young Migrants in Scotland, I," *Milbank Memorial Fund Quarterly,* 41 (1963), 115–144.

——"The Motivation and Characteristics of Internal Migrants: A Socio-Medical Study of Young Migrants in Scotland, II," *Milbank Memorial Fund Quarterly,* 41 (1963), 217–248.

Jerome, Harry. *Migration and Business Cycles.* New York: National Bureau of Economic Research, 1926.

Jones, Maldwyn Allen. *American Immigration.* Chicago: University of Chicago Press, 1960.

Joseph, Samuel. *Jewish Immigration to the United States: From 1881 to 1910.* New York: Columbia University Press, 1914.

Kirkpatrick, Clifford. *Intelligence and Immigration.* Baltimore: Williams and Wilkins, 1926.

Kosa, John. "Hungarian Immigrants in North America: Their Residential Mobility and Ecology," *Canadian Journal of Economics and Political Science,* 22 (1956), 358–370.

——*Land of Choice: The Hungarians in Canada.* Toronto: University of Toronto Press, 1957.

Kuznets, Simon, and Rubin, Ernest. *Immigration and the Foreign Born.* Occasional Paper 46. New York: National Bureau of Economic Research, 1954.

——Thomas, Dorothy Swaine, et al. *Population Redistribution and Economic Growth: United States, 1870–1950.* Philadelphia: American Philosophical Society, 1964.

Laing, Samuel. *Notes of a Traveller: On the Social and Political State of France, Prussia, Switzerland, Italy and Other Parts of Europe During the Present Century.* London: Longman, Brown, Green, and Longmans, 1854.

Land, Kenneth C. "Duration of Residence and Prospective Migration: Further Evidence," *Demography,* 6 (1969), 133–140.

Levine, Edward M. *The Irish and Irish Politicians.* Notre Dame, Ind.: University of Notre Dame Press, 1966.

Lewis, Oscar. *The Children of Sanchez: Autobiography of a Mexican Family.* New York: Random House, 1961.

——*Five Families: Mexican Case Studies in the Culture of Poverty.* New York: Basic Books, 1959.

——*La Vida: A Puerto Rican Family in the Culture of Poverty–San Juan and New York.* New York: Random House, 1966.

——*Life in a Mexican Village: Tepoztlan Restudied.* Urbana, Ill.: University of Illinois Press, 1951.

Littlejohn, James. *Westrigg: The Sociology of a Cheviot Parish.* London: Routledge and Kegan Paul, 1963.

Lodge, Olive. *Peasant Life in Yugoslavia.* London: Seeley, Service and Co., 1941.

Lopreato, Joseph. *Peasants No More: Social Class and Social Change in an Underdeveloped Society.* San Francisco: Chandler Publishing Co., 1967.

Maraspini, A. L. *The Study of an Italian Village.* Paris: Mouton and Co., 1968.

Marris, P. *Family and Social Change in an African City.* London: Routledge and Kegan Paul, 1961.

Martin, E. W. *The Shearers and the Shorn: A Study of Life in a Devon Community.* London: Routledge and Kegan Paul, 1965.

Mendras, Henri. *Etudes de sociologie rurale: Novis et Virgin.* Paris: Librairie Armand Colin, 1953.

Miller, Anna. *Peasant Life in Germany.* New York: Scribner, 1858 (published under name Anna C. Johnson).

Miner, Horace. "The Folk-Urban Continuum," *American Sociological Review,* 17 (1952), 529–537.

Mintz, Sidney. "The Folk-Urban Continuum and the Rural Proleterian Community," *American Journal of Sociology,* 59 (1953), 136–143.

Murphy, H. B. M. "Culture and Mental Disorder in Singapore," in Marvin

K. Opler, *Culture and Mental Health: Cross-Cultural Studies.* New York: Macmillan, 1959.

——"Migration and the Major Mental Disorders: A Reappraisal," in Mildred Kantor, ed., *Mobility and Mental Health.* Chicago: C. C. Thomas, 1965.

——"Social Change and Mental Health," in *Causes of Mental Disorders: A Review of Epidemiological Knowledge, 1959.* New York: Milbank Memorial Fund, 1961.

Museum of English Rural Life, with contributions by D. S. Thornton and P. D. Wood. *Estate Villages: A Study of the Berkshire Villages of Arlington and Lockinge.* London: Lund, Humphries and Co., 1966.

Myers, Jerome K., Jr. "The Differential Time Factor in Assimilation: A Study of Aspects and Processes of Assimilation Among the Italians of New Haven." Ph.D. dissertation, Yale University, 1949.

Odegaard, Ornulv. "Emigration and Insanity: A Study of Mental Disease Among the Norwegian Born Population of Minnesota," *Acta Psychiatrica et Neurologica* (1932), supplement 4.

Park, Robert E., and Miller, Herbert A. *Old World Traits Transplanted.* New York: Harper, 1921.

Petersen, Gene B., and Sharp, Laure M. *Southern Migrants to Cleveland: Work and Social Adjustment of Recent In-Migrants Living in Low-Income Neighborhoods.* Washington, D.C.: Bureau of Social Science Research, Inc., 1969.

Pitt-Rivers, Julian A. *The People of the Sierra.* Chicago: University of Chicago Press (Phoenix Books), 1961.

Porak, René. *Un village de France: psycho-physiologie du paysan.* Paris: Doin et Cie, 1943.

Potter, George. *To The Golden Door: The Story of the Irish in Ireland and America.* Boston: Little, Brown, 1960.

Price, Daniel O. *A Study of Economic Consequences of Rural to Urban Migration.* Washington, D.C.: Procurement Division, Office of Economic Opportunity, Contract No. 889–4594, 1969 (mimeograph).

Redfield, Robert. *The Folk Culture of Yucatan.* Chicago: University of Chicago Press, 1941.

——*The Primitive World and Its Transformations.* Ithaca: Cornell University Press, 1958.

Redford, Arthur. *Labour Migration in England, 1800–1850.* Manchester, Eng.: Manchester University Press, 1964 (first edition 1926).

Richardson, Alan. "Some Psycho-social Characteristics of Satisfied and Dissatisfied British Immigrant Skilled Manual Workers in Western Australia," *Human Relations,* 10 (1957), 235–248.

Rubin, Ernest. "United States," in Brinley Thomas, ed., *Economics of International Migration.* London: Macmillan, 1958.

Schwarzweller, Harry K. "Sociocultural Origins and Migration Patterns of Young Men from Eastern Kentucky," *Bulletin 685* (December 1963). University of Kentucky Agricultural Experiment Station, Lexington, Ky.

——and Brown, James S. "Social Class Origins and the Economic, Social and Psychological Adjustment of Kentucky Mountain Migrants: A Case Study," in Eugene B. Brody, ed., *Behavior in New Environments: Adaptation of Migrant Populations.* Beverly Hills: Sage Publications, 1969.

Shannon, Lyle W., and Shannon, Magdaline. "The Assimilation of Migrants to Cities: Anthropological and Sociological Contributions," in Leo F. Schnore and Henry Fagin, eds., *Urban Research and Policy Planning.* Urban Affairs Annual Reviews, vol. I. Beverly Hills: Sage Publications, 1967.

Shuval, Judith T. *Immigrants on the Threshold.* New York: Prentice-Hall, 1963.

Sjoberg, Gideon. "Folk and Feudal Societies," *American Journal of Sociology,* 58 (1952), 231–239.

Smith, William Carlson, *Americans in the Making: The Natural History of the Assimilation of Immigrants.* New York: Appleton-Century, 1939.

Solomon, Barbara Miller. *Ancestors and Immigrants: A Changing New England Tradition.* Cambridge, Mass.: Harvard University Press, 1956.

Speare, Alden, J. "Home Ownership, Life Cycle Stage and Residential Mobility," *Demography,* 7 (1970), 449–458.

Spengler, J. J. "Effects Produced in Receiving Countries by Pre-1939 Immigration," in Brinley Thomas, ed., *Economics of International Migration.* London: Macmillan, 1958.

Stephenson, George M. *A History of American Immigration, 1820–1924.* Boston: Ginn, 1926.

Stinchcombe, Arthur L. "Agricultural Enterprise and Rural Class Relations,' *American Journal of Sociology,* 67 (1962), 165–176.

Taeuber, Karl E. "Duration-of-Residence Analysis of Internal Migration in the United States," *Milbank Memorial Fund Quarterly,* 39 (1961), 116–131.

Taft, Ronald. *From Stranger to Citizen: A Survey of Studies of Immigrant Assimilation in Western Australia.* London: Tavistock Publications, 1966.

Thomas, Brinley. *Migration and Economic Growth: A Study of Great Britain and the Atlantic Economy.* Cambridge: Cambridge University Press, 1954.

Thomas, William, and Znaniecki, Florian. *The Polish Peasant in Europe and America.* Chicago: Chicago University Press, 1918 (New York, Knopf, 1928).

Tolles, Newman Arnold. "Survey of Labor Migration Between States," *Monthly Labor Review,* 45 (1937), 3–16.

Tracy, Michael. *Agriculture in Western Europe.* New York: Praeger, 1964.

U.S. Immigration Commission. *Reports of the Immigration Commission.* 42 vol. Washington, D.C.: Government Printing Office, 1911.

Vance, Rupert. *Research Memorandum on Population Redistribution Within the United States.* New York: Social Science Research Council, 1938.

Walker, Mack. *Germany and the Emigration 1816-1885.* Cambridge, Mass.: Harvard University Press, 1964.

Warriner, Doreen. *Economics of Peasant Farming.* New York: Barnes and Noble, 1964 (first published 1939).

——ed. *Contrasts in Emerging Societies: Readings in the Social and Economic History of Southeastern Europe in the Nineteenth Century.* Bloomington, Ind.: Indiana University Press, 1965.

Weinberg, Abraham. *Migration and Belonging: A Study of Mental Health and Personal Adjustment in Israel.* The Hague: Martinus Nijhoff, 1961.

Willcox, Walter F., ed. *International Migrations, Volume II, Interpretations.* New York: National Bureau of Economic Research, 1931.

Williams, W. M. *Gosforth: The Sociology of an English Village.* Glencoe, Ill.: Free Press, 1956.

——*A West Country Village: Ashworthy: Family, Kinship and Land.* London: Routledge and Kegan Paul, 1963.

Wittke, Carl. *We Who Built America: The Saga of the Immigrant,* rev. ed. Cleveland: Western Reserve University Press, 1964 (first edition 1939).

Wolf, Eric R. *Peasants.* Englewood Cliffs, N.J.: Prentice-Hall, 1966.

——"Types of Latin American Peasantry," *American Anthropologist,* 57 (1955), 452–471.

Wood, Arthur Evans. *Hamtramck Then and Now: A Sociological Study of a Polish-American Community.* New York: Bookman Associates, 1955.

Woodham-Smith, Cecil. *The Great Hunger: Ireland, 1845-1849.* New York: Harper and Row, 1962.

Wright, Gordon. *Rural Revolution in France.* Stanford: Stanford University Press, 1964.

Wylie. Laurence. *Village in the Vaucluse.* Cambridge, Mass.: Harvard University Press, 1957.

Zborowski, Mark, and Herzog, Elizabeth. *Life is with People: The Culture of the Shtetel.* New York: Schocken Books, 1962 (first published, 1952).

POVERTY AND SLUMS: THE RECENT PAST

Abbott, Edith, assisted by Sophonisba P. Breckinridge. *The Tenements of Chicago, 1908-1935.* Chicago: University of Chicago Press, 1936.

Addams, Jane. *Twenty Years at Hull House.* New York: Macmillan, 1911.

Beames, Thomas. *The Rookeries of London: Past, Present, and Prospective.* London: Thomas Bosworth, 1850.

Booth, Charles. *On the City: Physical Pattern and Social Structure, Selected Writings,* ed. Harold W. Pfautz. Chicago: University of Chicago, 1967.

——ed. *Life and Labour of the People in London,* 3d ed. 17 vols. London: Macmillan, 1902-1903.

Bremner, Robert H. *From the Depths: The Discovery of Poverty in the United States.* New York: N.Y.U. Press, 1956.

Brody, David. *Steelworkers in America: The Nonunion Era.* Cambridge, Mass.: Harvard University Press, 1960.

Byington, Margaret F. *Homestead: The Households of a Mill Town.* Volume V of the Pittsburgh Survey. New York: Charities Publication Committee, 1910.

Chadwick, Edwin. *The Sanitary Condition of the Labouring Population of Great Britain.* Edinburgh: Edinburgh University Press, 1965 (first published 1842).

DeForest, Robert W., and Veiller, Lawrence, eds. *The Tenement House Problem, Including the Report of the New York State Tenement House Commission of 1900.* 2 vols. New York: Macmillan, 1903.

Dinneen, Joseph F. *Ward Eight.* New York: Harper, 1936.

Douglas, Paul. *Real Wages in the United States, 1890–1926.* Boston: Houghton Mifflin, 1930.

Engels, Frederick. *The Condition of the Working Class in England,* trans. and ed. W. O. Henderson and W. H. Chaloner. Oxford: Basil Blackwell, 1958 (first published in German, 1845).

Fitch, John A. *The Steel Workers.* Volume IV of the Pittsburgh Survey. New York: Charities Publication Committee, 1911.

Ford, James, with the collaboration of Katherine Morrow and George N. Thompson. *Slums and Housing, With Special Reference to New York City.* 2 vols. Cambridge, Mass.: Harvard University Press, 1936.

Glaab, Charles N., and Brown, A. Theodore, *A History of Urban America.* New York: Macmillan, 1967.

Hole, James. *The Homes of the Working Classes: With Suggestions for their Improvements.* London: Longmans, Green and Co., 1866.

Hunter, Robert. *Poverty.* New York: Macmillan, 1904.

Kellogg, Paul U., ed. *Wage-Earning Pittsburgh.* Volume VI of the Pittsburgh Survey. New York: Survey Associates, 1914.

——*The Pittsburgh Survey: Civic Frontage.* Volume 1 of the Pittsburgh Survey. New York: Survey Associates, 1914.

Kenngott, George F. *The Record of a City: A Social Survey of Lowell, Mass.* New York: Macmillan, 1912.

Lieberson, Stanley. *Ethnic Patterns in American Cities.* New York: Free Press of Glencoe, 1963.

Massachusetts Council of Churches, *Boston's West End: A Study of Church and Community.* Boston: Massachusetts Council of Churches, 1949.

Mayhew, Henry. *Selections from London Labour and the London Poor.* London: Oxford University Press, 1965. Selections taken from the definitive edition of *London Labour and the London Poor,* 1861–1862.

McKelvey, Blake. *The Urbanization of America, 1860–1915.* New Brunswick, N.J.: Rutgers University Press, 1963.

Nelli, Humbert S. *Italians in Chicago 1880–1930: A Study of Ethnic Mobility.* New York: Oxford, 1970.

Osofsky, Gilbert. *Harlem: The Making of a Ghetto.* New York: Harper and Row, 1966.

Park, Robert E. *The Immigrant Press and Its Control.* New York: Harper, 1922.

Reynolds, Marcus T. *The Housing of the Poor in American Cities.* Baltimore: American Economic Association, 1893.

Riis, Jacob A. *How the Other Half Lives: Studies Among the Tenements of New York.* New York: Sagamore Press, 1957 (first published 1890).

Rowntree, B. Seebohm. *Poverty: A Study of Town Life.* London: Longmans, Green and Co., 1922 (first published 1901).

Ward, David, *Cities and Immigrants: A Geography of Changes in Nineteenth Century America.* New York: Oxford University Press, 1971.

Warner, Sam Bass, Jr. *The Private City: Philadelphia in Three Periods of Its Growth.* Philadelphia: University of Pennsylvania Press, 1968.

——*Streetcar Suburbs: The Process of Growth in Boston, 1870-1900.* Cambridge, Mass.: Harvard and MIT Press, 1962.

——and Burke, Colin B. "Cultural Change and the Ghetto," *Journal of Contemporary History,* 4 (1969), 173-187.

Weber, Adna Ferrin. *The Growth of Cities in the Nineteenth Century.* Ithaca: Cornell University Press, 1899.

Whitehill, Walter Muir. *Boston: A Topographical History,* 2d ed. Cambridge, Mass.: Harvard University Press, 1968 (first edition 1959).

Wirth, Louis. *The Ghetto.* Chicago: University of Chicago Press, 1928.

Woods, Robert A., ed. *Americans in Process: A Settlement Study.* Boston: Houghton Mifflin, 1902.

——*The City Wilderness.* Boston: Houghton Mifflin, 1898.

Worthington, Thomas Locke. *The Dwellings of the Poor and Weekly Wage Earners In and Around Towns.* New York: Scribner, 1893.

Wright, Carroll D. *The Slums of Baltimore, Chicago, New York and Philadelphia.* Seventh Special Report of the Commissioner of Labor. Washington, D.C.: Government Printing Office, 1894.

RESIDENTIAL PATTERNS, SOCIAL AFFILIATIONS, FAMILY

Abrams, Charles. *The Future of Housing.* New York: Harper, 1946.

Adams, Bert N. "Occupational Position, Mobility, and the Kin of Orientation," *American Sociological Review,* 32 (1967), 364-377.

Allport, Gordon W., Bruner, Jerome S., and Jahndorf, E. M. "Personality Under Social Catastrophe," *Character and Personality,* 10 (1941), 1-22.

Anderson, R. T., and Anderson, Barbara Gallatin. "Voluntary Associations and Urbanization: A Diachronic Analysis," *American Journal of Sociology,* 65 (November 1959), 265-273.

Angell, Robert C. *The Family Encounters the Depression.* New York: Charles Scribner's Sons, 1936.

Ash, Joan. *Living in a Slum: A Study of People in a Central Slum Clearance Area in Oldham.* London: Ministry of Housing and Local Government, Sociological Research Section, undated (mineographed).

Axelrod, Morris. "Urban Structure and Social Participation," *American Sociological Review,* 21 (February 1956), 13-18.

Back, Kurt W. *Slums, Projects, and People: Social Psychological Problems of Relocation in Puerto Rico.* Durham, N.C.: Duke University Press, 1962.

Bell, Robert R. *Premarital Sex in a Changing Society.* Englewood Cliffs, N.J.: Prentice-Hall, 1966.

Bell, Wendell, and Boat, Marion D. "Urban Neighborhoods and Informal Social Relations," *American Journal of Sociology,* 62 (1957), 391–398.

——and Force, Maryanne T. "Urban Neighborhood Types and Participation in Formal Associations," *American Sociological Review,* 21 (1956), 25–34.

Bernert, Eleanor H., and Ikle, Ted C. "Evacuation and the Cohesion of Urban Groups," *American Journal of Sociology,* 58 (1952), 133–138.

Billingsley, Andrew. *Black Families in White America.* Englewood Cliffs, N.J.: Prentice-Hall, 1968.

Blood, Robert O., Jr. "The Husband-Wife Relationship," in Ivan F. Nye and Lois Wladis Hoffman, eds., *The Employed Mother in America.* Chicago: Rand McNally, 1963.

——and Hamblin, Robert L. "The Effect of the Wife's Employment on the Family Power Structure," *Social Force,* 36 (1958), 348–352.

——and Wolfe, Donald M. *Husbands and Wives: The Dynamics of Married Living.* Glencoe, Ill.: The Free Press, 1960.

Boston Housing Authority, *West End Project Report: A Preliminary Redevelopment Study of the West End of Boston.* Boston: Boston Housing Authority, 1953.

Bogue, Donald J. *Skid Row in American Cities.* Chicago: Community and Family Study Center (University of Chicago), 1963.

Bott, Elizabeth. *Family and Social Network.* London: Tavistock Publications, 1957.

Bracey, Howard E. *Neighbours: Subdivision Life in England and the United States.* Baton Rouge: Louisiana State University, 1964.

Branch, Melville, Jr. *Urban Planning and Public Opinion: National Survey Research Investigation.* Princeton: Bureau of Urban Research, 1942.

Bronfenbrenner, Urie. "Socialization and Social Class Through Time and Space," in Eleanor E. Maccoby, Theodore M. Newcomb, and Eugene L. Hartley, eds., *Readings in Social Psychology,* 3d ed. New York: Holt, 1958.

Burgess, Ernest W., and Locke, Harvey J. *The Family.* New York: American Book Co., 1945.

Caplow, Theodore, and Forman, Robert. "Neighborhood Interaction in a Homogeneous Community," *American Sociological Review,* 15 (1950), 357–366.

——Stryker, Sheldon, and Wallace, Samuel E. *The Urban Ambience: A Study of San Juan, Puerto Rico.* Totowa, N.J.: Bedminster Press, 1964.

Chombard de Lauwe, Pierre. *La vie quotidienne des familles ouvrières,* Paris Centre National de la Recherche Scientifique, 1956.

Clark, S. D. *The Suburban Society.* Toronto: University of Toronto Press, 1966.

Cohen, Albert, and Hodges, Harold M. "Characteristics of the Lower-Blue-Collar-Class," *Social Problems*, 10 (1963), 303–334.

Davis, Allison, and Havighurst, Robert J. "Social Class and Color Differences In Child Rearing," *American Sociological Review*, 18 (1946), 142–149.

——*Father of the Man*. Boston: Houghton, Mifflin, 1947.

Dobriner, William M. *Class in Suburbia*. Englewood Cliffs, N.J.: Prentice-Hall, 1963.

Dore, R. P. *City Life in Japan: A Study of a Tokyo Ward*. Berkeley: University of California Press, 1967.

Drake, St. Clair, and Cayton, Horace R. *Black Metropolis: A Study of Negro Life in a Northern City*. New York: Harcourt, Brace, 1945.

Duncan, Otis Dudley and Duncan, Beverly. *The Negro Population of Chicago: A Study of Racial Succession*. Chicago: University of Chicago Press, 1957.

——"Residential Distribution and Occupational Stratification," *American Journal of Sociology*, 60 (1955), 493–503.

Elias, Norbert, and Scotson, John L. *The Established and the Outsiders: A Sociological Enquiry Into Community Problems*. London: Frank Cass, 1965.

Fava, Sylvia Fleis. "Contrasts in Neighboring: New York City and a Suburban County," in William M. Dobriner, ed., *The Suburban Community*. New York: G. P. Putnam's, 1958.

Fellin, Phillip, and Litwak, Eugene. "Neighborhood Cohesion Under Conditions of Mobility," *American Sociological Review*, 28 (1963), 364–376.

Ferguson, Thomas, and Pettigrew, Mary G. "A Study of 388 Families Living in Old Slum Houses," *Glasgow Medical Journal*, 35 (1954), 169–182.

——"A Study of 718 Slum Families Rehoused for Upwards of Ten Years," *Glasgow Medical Journal*, 35 (1954), 183–201.

Festinger, L., Schacter, S., and Back, K. *Social Pressures in Informal Groups: A Study of Human Factors in Housing*. New York: Harper, 1950.

Firey, Walter. *Land Use in Central Boston*. Cambridge, Mass.: Harvard University Press, 1947.

——"Sentiment and Symbolism as Ecological Variables," *American Sociological Review*, 10 (1945), 140–148.

Fitzgerald, Ellen Waldron. "The Marital Relationship and Adaptation to Forced Residential Change." Ph.D. dissertation, Harvard University, 1967.

Foley, Donald L. "The Use of Local Facilities in a Metropolis," *American Journal of Sociology*, 56 (1950), 238–246.

Foote, Nelson N., et al. *Housing Choices and Housing Constraints*. New York: McGraw Hill, 1960.

Freedman, Ronald. "Migration Differentials in the City as a Whole," in

Paul K. Hatt and Albert J. Reiss, Jr., eds., *Reader in Urban Sociology.* Glencoe, Ill.: Free Press, 1951.

Fried, Marc. "Grieving for a Lost Home," in Leonard J. Duhl, ed., *The Urban Condition.* New York: Basic Books, 1963.

——"Transitional Functions of Working-Class Communities: Implications for Forced Relocation," in Mildred B. Kantor, ed., *Mobility and Mental Health.* Springfield, Ill.: C. C. Thomas, 1965.

——and Gleicher, Peggy. "Some Sources of Residential Satisfaction in an Urban Slum," *Journal of American Institute of Planners,* 27 (1961), 305–315.

——and Levin, Joan. "Some Social Functions of the Urban Slum," in B. J. Frieden and R. Morris, eds., *Urban Planning and Social Policy.* New York: Basic Books, 1968.

Frieden, Bernard J. *The Future of Old Neighborhoods: Rebuilding for a Changing Population.* Cambridge, Mass.: M.I.T. Press, 1964.

——"Housing and National Urban Goals: Old Policies and New Realities," in James Q. Wilson, ed., *The Metropolitan Enigma: Inquiries Into the Nature and Dimensions of America's Urban Crisis,* 2d Report. Cambridge, Mass.: Harvard University Press, 1968.

——and Newman, JoAnn. "Home Ownership for the Poor?" *Transaction,* 7 (October 1970), 47–53.

Frieden, Elaine. *Housing Preferences of Older People.* Boston: United Community Services of Metropolitan Boston, 1959.

——*Housing Preferences of Older People: Follow-up Study No. 2.* Boston: United Community Services of Metropolitan Boston, 1962.

——"Social Differences and Their Consequences for Housing the Aged," *Journal of the American Institute of Planners,* 26 (May 1960), no. 2.

Gans, Herbert. *The Levittowners.* New York: Vintage Books, 1967.

——*The Urban Villagers.* Glencoe, Ill.: Free Press, 1962.

——"Urbanism and Suburbanism as Ways of Life," in Arnold M. Rose, ed., *Human Behavior and Social Processes.* New York: Houghton Mifflin, 1962.

Gleicher, Peggy. "Some Aspects of Social Affiliations Among Women in an Urban Slum." Master's thesis, Northeastern University, Boston, Mass., 1965.

Glick, Paul C. *American Families.* New York: Wiley, 1957.

Goode, Erich. "Social Class and Church Participation," *American Journal of Sociology,* 72 (1966), 102–111.

Goode, William J. "Marital Satisfaction and Instability: A Cross-Cultural Analysis of Divorce Rates," *International Social Science Journal,* 14 (1962), 507–526.

——"The Theoretical Importance of Love," *American Sociological Review,* 24 (1959), 38–47.

Greer, Scott. "Urbanization Reconsidered: A Comparative Study of Local Areas in a Metropolis," *American Sociological Review,* 21 (1956), 19–25.

——and Kube, Ella. "Urbanism and Social Structure: A Los Angeles Study," in Marvin B. Sussman, ed., *Community Structure and Analysis.* New York: Crowell, 1959.

Hall, Edward T. *The Hidden Dimension.* Garden City, N.Y.: Doubleday, 1966.

——*The Silent Language.* Garden City, N.Y.: Doubleday, 1959.

Hartman, Chester. "The Housing of Relocated Families," *Journal of American Institute of Planners,* 30 (1964), 113–131.

——"Social Determinants of Housing Satisfaction and Housing Choice: Boston's West End." Ph.D. dissertation, Harvard University, 1967.

——"Social Values and Housing Orientations," *Journal of Social Issues,* 19 (1963), 113–131.

Hausknecht, Murray. *The Joiners.* New York: Bedminster Press, 1962.

Heer, David M. "The Marital Status of Second-Generation Americans," *American Sociological Review,* 26 (1961), 233–241.

——"The Measurement and Bases of Family Power: An Overview," *Marriage and Family Living,* 25 (1963), 133–139.

Herbst, P. F. "Family Living—Patterns of Interaction," in O. A. Oeser and S. B. Hammond, eds., *Social Structure and Personality in a City.* London: Routledge and Kegan Paul, 1954.

Hill, Reuben. *Families Under Stress.* New York: Harper and Bros., 1949.

——"Generic Features of Families Under Stress," *Social Casework,* 39 (1958), 139–150.

——and Konig, René, eds. *Families in East and West: Socialization Process and Kinship Ties.* The Hague: Mouton, 1970.

Hoggart, Richard. *The Uses of Literacy: Changing Patterns in English Mass Culture.* Fairlawn, N.J.: Essential Books, Inc., 1957.

Hole, Vere. "Social Effects of Planned Rehousing," *Town Planning Review,* 30 (1959), 161–173.

Homans, George C. *The Human Group.* New York: Harcourt, 1950.

——"Social Behavior as Exchange," *American Journal of Sociology,* 62 (1958), 597–606.

Jackson, Brian. *Working Class Community: Some General Notions Raised by a Series of Studies in Northern England.* New York: Praeger, 1968.

Janowitz, Morris. *The Community Press in an Urban Setting: The Social Elements of Urbanism,* 2d ed. Chicago: University of Chicago Press, 1967.

Jennings, Hilda. *Societies in the Making: A Study of Development and Redevelopment Within a County Borough.* London: Routledge and Kegan Paul, 1962.

Kates, R. W., and Wohlwill, J. F., issue eds. *Journal of Social Issues,* 22 (1966), no. 4 ("Man's Response to the Physical Environment.")

Keller, Suzanne. *The Urban Neighborhood.* New York: Random House, 1968.

Kenkel, William F. "Observational Studies of Husband-Wife Interaction in Family Decision-Making," in Marvin B. Sussman, ed., *Sourcebook in Marriage and the Family,* 2d ed. Boston: Houghton Mifflin, 1963.

Kerr, Madeline. *The People of Ship Street.* London: Routledge and Kegan Paul, 1958.

Kinsey, Alfred C., et al. *Sexual Behavior in the Human Female.* Philadelphia: W. B. Saunders, 1953.

——Pomeroy, Wardell, and Martin, Clyde. *Sexual Behavior in the Human Male.* Philadelphia: W. B. Saunders, 1948.

Kjellberg, Ernst, and Saflund, Gosta. *Greek and Roman Art: 3000 B.C. to A.D. 550,* trans. Peter Fraser. New York: Thomas Y. Crowell, 1968.

Kohn, Melvin L. "Social Class and Parent-Child Relationships: An Interpretation," *American Journal of Sociology,* 68 (1963), 471–480.

——and Carroll, Eleanor E. "Social Class and the Allocation of Parental Responsibilities," *Sociometry,* 23 (1960), 372–392.

Komarovsky, Mirra. *The Unemployed Man and His Family.* New York: The Dryden Press, 1940.

——*Blue-Collar Marriage.* New York: Random House, 1962 and 1964.

——"Class Differences in Family Decision-Making on Expenditures," in Nelson N. Foote, ed., *Household Decision-Making.* New York: New York University Press, 1961.

——"The Voluntary Associations of Urban Dwellers," *American Sociological Review,* 11 (December 1946), 686–698.

Konig, René. "Family and Authority: The German Father in 1955," *Sociological Review,* 5 (1957), 77–78.

Kuper, Leo, et al. *Living in Towns.* London: Cresset Press, 1953.

Lang, Olga. *Chinese Family and Society.* New Haven: Yale University Press, 1946.

Laumann, Edward O. *Prestige and Association in an Urban Community: An Analysis of an Urban Stratification System.* New York: Bobbs-Merrill, 1966.

——and Guttman, Louis. "The Relative Associational Contiguity of Occupations in an Urban Setting," *American Sociological Review,* 31 (1966), 169–178.

Lavanburg Foundation, Fred L. *What Happened to 386 Families Who Were Compelled to Vacate Their Slum Dwellings to Make Way for a Large Housing Project.* New York: Fred L. Lavanburg Foundation, 1933.

Leach, E. R. *Political Systems of Highland Burma: A Study of Kachin Social Structure.* Boston: Beacon Press, 1954.

Liebow, Elliot. *Tally's Corner: A Study of Negro Streetcorner Men.* Boston: Little, Brown, 1967.

Littman, Richard A., Moore, Robert C. A., and Pierce-Jones, John. "Social-Class Differences in Child Rearing: A Third Community for Comparison with Chicago and Newton," *American Sociological Review,* 22 (1957), 694–704.

Litwak, Eugene. "Geographic Mobility and Extended Family Cohesion," *American Sociological Review,* 25 (1960), 385–394.

——"Occupational Mobility and Extended Family Cohesion," *American Sociological Review,* 25 (1960), 9–21.

——"Voluntary Associations and Neighborhood Cohesion," *American Sociological Review,* 25 (1960), 258–271.

Lopata, Helena Znaniecki. "The Function of Voluntary Associations in an Ethnic Community: 'Polonia,' " in Ernest W. Burgess and Donald Bogue, *Contributions to Urban Sociology*. Chicago: University of Chicago Press, 1964.

Lynd, Robert S., and Lynd, Helen Merrell. *Middletown: A Study in Contemporary American Culture*. New York: Harcourt, Brace, 1929.

——*Middletown in Transition: A Study in Cultural Conflicts*. New York: Harcourt, Brace, 1937.

MacDonald, John S., and MacDonald, Leatrice. "Chain Migration, Ethnic Neighborhood Formation, and Social Networks," *Milbank Memorial Fund Quarterly*, 42 (1964), 82–97.

——"Urbanization, Ethnic Groups, and Social Segmentation," *Social Research*, 29 (1962), 433–448.

Malone, Charles A., Pavenstedt, Eleanor, Mattick, Else, Bandler, Louise S., Stein, Maurice, R., and Mintz, Norbett L. *The Drifters: Children of Disorganized Lower-Class Families*. Boston: Little, Brown, 1967.

McKenzie, Roderick Duncan. *The Neighborhood: A Study of Local Life in the City of Columbus, Ohio*. Chicago: University of Chicago Press, 1923.

McKinley, Donald G. *Social Class and Family Life*. Glencoe, Ill.: Free Press, 1964.

Merton, Robert K. "The Social Psychology of Housing," in Wayne Dennis, ed., *Current Trends in Social Psychology*. Pittsburgh: University of Pittsburgh Press, 1948, pp. 163–215.

Michel, Andrée. "La famille urbaine et la parenté en France," in Reuben Hill and René Konig, *Families in East and West: Socialization Process and Kinship Ties*. Paris: Mouton, 1970.

Miller, Daniel, and Swanson, Guy R. *The Changing American Parent: A Study in the Detroit Area*. New York: John Wiley and Sons, 1958.

Minuchin, Salvador, Braulio, Montalvo, Guerney, Bernard G., Jr., Rosman, Bernice L., and Schumer, Florence. *Families of the Slums: An Exploration of Their Structure and Treatment*. New York: Basic Books, 1967.

Mitchell, G. Duncan, and Lupton, Thomas. "The Liverpool Estate," in E. I. Black and T. S. Simey, eds., *Neighborhood and Community: An Enquiry into Social Relationships on Housing Estates in Liverpool and Sheffield*. Liverpool: University Press of Liverpool, 1954.

Mogey, John M. "Changes in Family Life Experienced by English Workers Moving From Slums to Housing Estates," *Marriage and Family Living*, 17 (1955), 123–128.

——*Family and Neighbourhood: Two Studies in Oxford*. London: Oxford University Press, 1956.

Morris, Robert N., and Mogey, John. *The Sociology of Housing: Studies at Berinsfield*. London: Routledge and Kegan Paul, 1965.

Montague, Joel B., Jr. *Class and Nationality: English and American Studies*. New Haven: College and University Press, 1963.

Neighbourhood and Community: An Enquiry into Social Relationships on Housing Estates in Liverpool and Sheffield. Liverpool: University Press of Liverpool, 1954.

Nye, Ivan. "Marital Interaction," in Ivan F. Nye and Lois Wladis Hoffman, eds., *The Employed Mother in America*. Chicago: Rand McNally, 1963.

Oeser, O. A., and Hammond, S. B. *Social Structure and Personality in a City*. London: Routledge and Kegan Paul, 1954.

Park, Robert E., Burgess, Ernest W., and McKenzie, Roderick D. *The City*. Chicago: University of Chicago Press, 1925.

Parker, Seymour, and Kleiner, Robert. *Mental Illness in the Urban Negro Community*. New York: Free Press, 1966.

Parsons, Talcott. "The Social Structure of the Family," in Ruth Nanda Anshen, ed., *The Family: Its Function and Destiny*. New York: Harper, 1949.

——*The Social System*. Glencoe, Ill.: Free Press, 1951.

——and Bales, Robert F. *Family: Socialization and Interaction Process*. Glencoe, Ill.: Free Press, 1955.

Pfeil, Elisabeth. "The Pattern of Neighbouring Relations in Dortmund-Nordstadt," in R. E. Pahl, ed., *Readings in Urban Sociology*. Oxford: Pergamon Press, 1968.

Pineo, Peter C. "Disenchantment in the Later Years of Marriage," *Marriage and Family Living*, 23 (1961), 3–11.

Psathas, George. "Ethnicity, Social Class and Adolescent Independence from Parental Control," *American Sociological Review*, 22 (1957), 415–423.

Rabban, Meyer. "Sex-Role Identification in Young Children in Diverse Social Groups," *Genetic Psychological Monograph*, 42 (1950), 81–158.

Rainwater, Lee. *Family Design*. Chicago: Aldine Publishing Co., 1965.

——"Fear and the House-as-Haven in the Lower Class," *Journal of American Institute of Planners*, 32 (1966), 23–31.

——"Marital Sexuality in Four Cultures of Poverty," *Journal of Marriage and the Family*, 26 (1964), 216–232. (Also: Jerold Heiss, ed., *Family Roles and Interaction*. Chicago: Rand McNally, 1968).

——Coleman, Richard P., and Handel, Gerald. *Workingman's Wife*. New York: Oceana Publications, 1959.

——and Weinstein, Karol Kane. *And the Poor Get Children: Sex, Contraception, and Family Planning in the Working Class*. Chicago: Quadrangle Books, 1960.

Rapoport, Robert, and Rapoport, Rhona. "Work and Family in Contemporary Society," *American Sociological Review*, 30 (1965), 381–394.

Reid, Margaret G. *Housing and Income*. Chicago: University of Chicago Press, 1962.

Rex, J. A. "The Sociology of a Zone of Transition," in R. E. Pahl, ed., *Readings in Urban Sociology*. Oxford: Pergamon Press, 1968.

Riessman, Frank. *The Culturally Deprived Child*. New York: Harper and Bros., 1962.

Rosser, Colin, and Harris, Christopher. *The Family and Social Change: A Study of Family and Kinship in a South Wales Town*. London: Routledge and Kegan Paul, 1965.

Rossi, Peter H. "Residence and Locality: Social Psychological Indicators of Community Living" (mimeographed, 1970).

——*Why Families Move.* New York: Free Press of Glencoe, 1955.

Roth, Julius, and Peck, Robert F. "Social Class and Social Mobility Factors Related to Marital Adjustment," *American Sociological Review,* 16 (1951), 478–487.

Safa, Helen Icken. "From Shanty Town to Public Housing: A Comparison of Family Structure in Two Urban Neighborhoods in Puerto Rico," *Caribbean Studies,* 4 (1964), 3–12.

——"The Social Isolation of the Urban Poor," in Irwin Deutscher and Elizabeth J. Thompson, eds., *Among the People.* New York: Basic Books, 1968.

Schermer Associates, George. *More Than Shelter: Social Needs in Low- and Moderate-Income Housing.* Prepared for the National Commission on Urban Problems. Washington, D.C.: Government Printing Office, 1968.

Scheuch, Erwin K. "Family Cohesion in Leisure Time," *Evolution of the Forms and Needs of Leisure.* Hamburg: UNESCO Institute for Education, 1962.

Schorr, Alvin L. *Slums and Social Insecurity.* Research Report No. 1, Social Security Administration. Washington, D.C.: Government Printing Office, 1963.

Sears, Robert R., Maccoby, Eleanor E., and Levin, Harry. *Patterns of Child Rearing.* Evanston, Ill.: Row, Peterson, 1957.

Seeley, John R. "The Slum: Its Nature, Use, and Users," *Journal of American Institute of Planners,* 25 (1959), 7–14.

Shryock, Henry S., Jr. *Population Mobility Within the United States.* Chicago: Community and Family Study Center (University of Chicago), 1964.

Simmel, Georg. "The Metropolis and Mental Life," in Kurt H. Wolff, ed. and trans., *The Sociology of Georg Simmel.* New York: Free Press, 1950.

Smith, David Horton. "Correcting for Social Desirability Response Sets in Opinion-Attitude Survey Research," *Public Opinion Quarterly,* 31 (1967), 87–94.

Sommer, Robert. *Personal Space: The Behavioral Basis of Design.* Englewood Cliffs, N.J.: Prentice-Hall, 1969.

Stacey, Margaret. *Tradition and Change: A Study of Banbury.* London: Oxford University Press, 1960.

Sternlieb, George. *The Tenement Landlord.* New Brunswick, N.J.: Urban Studies Center, Rutgers University, 1966.

Strodtbeck, Fred L. "Family Interaction, Values and Achievement," in David C. McClelland, Alfred L. Baldwin, Urie Bronfenbrenner, and Fred L. Strodtbeck, *Talent and Society: New Perspectives in the Identification of Talent.* Princeton: D. Van Nostrand, 1958.

Sussman, Marvin B. *Community Structure and Analysis.* New York: Thomas Crowell and Co., 1959.

——"The Help Pattern in the Middle-Class Family," *American Sociological Review,* 18 (1953), 22–28.

——"The Isolated Nuclear Family: Fact or Fiction," in Marvin B. Sussman, ed., *Sourcebook in Marriage and the Family,* 2d ed. Boston: Houghton Mifflin, 1963.

Suttles, Gerald D. *The Social Order of the Slum: Ethnicity and Territory in the Inner City.* Chicago: University of Chicago Press, 1968.

Sweetser, Frank L., Jr. "A New Emphasis for Neighborhood Research," *American Sociological Review,* 7 (1942), 525-533.

Taeuber, Karl E., and Taeuber, Alma F. *Negroes in Cities: Residential Segregation and Neighborhood Change.* Chicago: Aldine Publishing, 1965.

Taube, Gerald, and Levin, Jack. "Public Housing as Neighborhood: The Effect of Local and Nonlocal Participation," *Social Science Quarterly,* 52 (1971), 534-542.

Tilly, Charles. "Metropolitan Boston's Social Structure," in Metropolitan Area Planning Council, Commonwealth of Massachusetts, *Social Structure and Human Problems in the Boston Metropolitan Area,* 1965.

——"Occupational Rank and Grade of Residence in a Metropolis," *American Journal of Sociology,* 67 (1961), 323-330.

——and Brown, C. Harold. "On Uprooting, Kinship, and the Auspices of Migration," *International Journal of Comparative Sociology,* 8 (1967), 139-164.

Tönnies, Ferdinand. *Community and Society.* East Lansing, Mich.: Michigan State University Press, 1957.

Townsend, Peter. *The Family Life of Old People: An Inquiry in East London.* London: Routledge and Kegan Paul, 1957.

Vereker, Charles, and Mays, John Barron, with the assistance of Elizabeth Gittus and Maurice Broady. *Urban Redevelopment and Social Change: A Study of Social Conditions in Central Liverpool,* 1955-56. Liverpool: Liverpool University Press, 1961.

Warner, W. Lloyd, and Srole, Leo. *The Social Systems of American Ethnic Groups.* New Haven: Yale University Press, 1945.

White, Martha Sturm. "Social Class, Child-Rearing Practices and Child Behavior," *American Sociological Review,* 22 (1957), 704-712.

Whyte, William Foote. "A Slum Sex Code," *American Journal of Sociology,* 49 (1943), 24-31.

——"Social Organization in the Slums," *American Sociological Review,* 8 (1943), 34-39.

——*Street Corner Society: The Social Structure of an Italian Slum.* Chicago: University of Chicago Press, 1943.

Wilkening, Eugene A. "Joint Decision-Making in Farm Families," *American Sociological Review,* 23 (1958), 182-192.

Willmott, Peter. *The Evolution of a Community: A Study of Dagenham After Forty Years.* London: Routledge and Kegan Paul, 1963.

——and Young, Michael. *Family and Class in a London Suburb.* London: Routledge and Kegan Paul, 1960.

Wilson, Robert L. "Livability of the City: Attitudes and Urban Development," in F. Stuart Chapin, Jr., and Shirley F. Weiss, eds., *Urban Growth Dynamics in a Regional Cluster of Cities.* New York: Wiley, 1962.

Wirth, Louis. "Urbanism as a Way of Life," *American Journal of Sociology,* 44 (1938), 1–24.

Wolgast, Elizabeth H. "Economic Decisions in the Family," *Journal of Marketing,* 23 (1958), 151–158.

Wood, Robert C. *Suburbia: Its People and Their Politics.* Boston: Houghton Mifflin, 1959.

Wright, Charles R., and Hyman, Herbert. "Voluntary Association Memberships of American Adults: Evidence from National Sample Survey," *American Sociological Review,* 23 (1958), 284–294.

Yang, Martin C. *A Chinese Village: Taitou, Shantung Province.* New York: Columbia University Press, 1945.

Young, Michael, and Willmott, Peter. *Family and Kinship in East London.* London: Routledge and Kegan Paul, 1957.

Zelditch, Morris, Jr. "Role Differentiation in the Nuclear Family: A Comparative Study," in Talcott Parsons and Robert F. Bales, eds., *Family: Socialization and Interaction Process.* Glencoe, Ill.: Free Press, 1955.

Zilbach, Joan J. "Family Development," in Judd Marmor, ed., *Modern Psychoanalysis.* New York: Basic Books, 1968.

——"Crisis in Chronic Problem Families," in Guido Belsasso, ed., *Psychiatric Care of the Poor.* Boston: Little, Brown, 1971.

Zimmer, Basil G. "Participation of Migrants in Urban Structures," *American Sociological Review,* 20 (1955), 218–224.

——and Hawley, Amos H. "The Significance of Membership in Associations," *American Journal of Sociology,* 65 (September 1959), 196–201.

Zola, Irving Kenneth. "Observations on Gambling in a Lower-Class Setting," *Social Problems,* 10 (1963), 353–361.

Zorbaugh, Harvey Warren. *The Gold Coast and the Slum: A Sociological Study of Chicago's Near North Side.* Chicago: University of Chicago Press, 1929.

Zweig, Ferdynand. *The British Worker.* Harmondsworth, Middlesex: Penguin Books, 1952.

WORK EXPERIENCES, SOCIAL ATTITUDES, AND PERSONALITY

Adorno, Theodore W., Frenkel-Brunswik, Else, Levinson, Daniel J., and Sanford, R. Nevitt. *The Authoritarian Personality.* New York: Harper, 1950.

Allen, Vernon L. "Personality Correlates of Poverty," in Vernon L. Allen, ed., *Psychological Factors in Poverty.* Chicago: Markham Publishing Co., 1970.

Allport, Gordon W. "Attitudes," in Carl Murchison, ed., *A Handbook of Social Psychology.* Worcester, Mass.: Clark University Press, 1935.

——*The Nature of Prejudice.* Cambridge, Mass.: Addison-Wesley, 1954.

Argyris, Chris. *Interpersonal Competence and Organizational Effectiveness.* Homewood, Ill.: Dorsey Press, 1962.

Aronfreed, Justin M. *Conduct and Conscience: The Socialization of Internalized Control Over Behavior.* New York: Academic Press, 1968.

—— "The Nature, Variety, and Social Patterning of Moral Responses to Transgression," *Journal of Abnormal and Social Psychology,* 63 (1961), 223–240.

Bakke, E. Wight. *Citizens Without Work.* New Haven: Yale University Press, 1940.

Bancroft, Gertrude. *The American Labor Force: Its Growth and Changing Composition.* New York: John Wiley, 1958.

—— and Garfinkle, Stuart. "Job Mobility in 1961," *Monthly Labor Review,* Special Labor Force Report (August 1963).

Bartlett, F. C. *Remembering.* Cambridge: Cambridge University Press, 1932.

Bendix, Reinhard. "Compliant Behavior and Individual Personality," *American Journal of Sociology,* 58 (1952), 292–303.

—— *Work and Authority in Industry.* New York: Wiley, 1956.

Blau, Peter M. "Cooperation and Competition in a Bureaucracy," *American Journal of Sociology,* 59 (1954), 530–535.

—— *The Dynamics of Bureaucracy.* Chicago: University of Chicago Press, 1955.

—— "Social Mobility and Interpersonal Relations," *American Sociological Review,* 21 (1956), 290–295.

Blauner, Robert. *Alienation and Freedom: The Factory Worker and His Industry.* Chicago: University of Chicago Press, 1964.

Bradney, Pamela. "Quasi-familial Relationships in Industry," *Human Relations,* 10 (1957), 271–278.

Caplow, Theodore. *The Sociology of Work.* Minneapolis: University of Minnesota Press, 1954.

Chinoy, Ely. *Automobile Workers and the American Dream.* New York: Doubleday, 1955.

Christie, Richard, and Jahoda, Marie, eds. *Studies in the Scope and Method of "The Authoritarian Personality."* Glencoe, Ill.: Free Press, 1954.

Crandell, Dewitt L., and Dohrenwend, Bruce P. "Some Relations Among Psychiatric Symptoms, Organic Illness, and Social Class," *American Journal of Psychiatry,* 123 (1967), 1527–1538.

DeVries, Egbert. *Man in Rapid Social Change.* Garden City, N.Y.: Doubleday, 1961.

Dornbusch, Sanford M., and Heer, David M. "The Evaluation of Work by Females, 1940–1950," *American Journal of Sociology,* 63 (1957), 27–30.

Douvan, Elizabeth. "Social Status and Success Striving," *Journal of Abnormal and Social Psychology,* 52 (1956), 219–223.

—— and Adelson, Joseph. "The Psychodynamics of Social Mobility in Adolescent Boys," *Journal of Abnormal and Social Psychology,* 56 (1958), 31–44.

Dubin, Robert. "Industrial Workers' Worlds: A Study of the 'Central Life Interests' of Industrial Workers," *Social Problems*, 3 (1956), 131–142.

Duffy, N. F. "Occupational Status, Job Satisfaction and Levels of Aspiration," *British Journal of Sociology*, 11 (1960), 348–355.

Durkheim, Emile. *On the Division of Labor in Society*, trans. George Simpson. New York: Macmillan, 1933.

Dynes, Russell R., Clarke, Alfred C., and Dinitz, Simon. "Levels of Occupational Aspiration: Some Aspects of Family Experience as a Variable," *American Sociological Review*, 21 (1956), 212–215.

Erikson, Erik Homburger. "Ego Development and Historical Change," *The Psychoanalytic Study of the Child*, 2 (1946), 359–396.

Etzioni, Amitai. *Modern Organizations*. Englewood Cliffs, N.J.: Prentice-Hall, 1964.

Form, William H., and Geschwender, James A. "Social Reference Basis of Job Satisfaction: The Case of Manual Workers," *American Sociological Review*, 27 (1962), 228–237.

Form, William H., and Rytina, Joan. "Ideological Beliefs on the Distribution of Power in the United States," *American Sociological Review*, 34 (1969), 19–30.

Freedman, Sanford J. "Perceptual Changes in Sensory Deprivation: Suggestions for a Conative Theory," *Journal of Nervous and Mental Disorders*, 132 (1961), 17–21.

Freud, Sigmund. *Civilization and Its Discontents* (1930), *Complete Psychological Works of Sigmund Freud*. Standard Edition, vol. XXI. London: Hogarth Press, 1961.

Fried, Marc. "The Role of Work in a Mobile Society," in Sam B. Warner, Jr., ed., *Planning for a Nation of Cities*. Cambridge, Mass.: M.I.T. Press, 1966.

——"Social Problems and Psychopathology," in Henry Wechsler, Leonard Solomon, and Bernard Kramer, *Social Psychology and Mental Health*. New York: Holt, Rinehart and Winston, 1970.

Friedman, Eugene A., and Havighurst, Robert J., with William H. Harlan, Janet Bower, Dolores C. Gruen, Ralph R. Ireland, and Ethel Hanas. *The Meaning of Work and Retirement*. Chicago: University of Chicago Press, 1954.

Friedmann, Georges. *The Anatomy of Work*. New York: The Free Press of Glencoe, 1961.

Fromm, Erich. *Escape From Freedom*. New York: Rinehart and Co., 1941.

Goldthorpe, John H., Lockwood, David, Bechhofer, Frank, and Platt, Jennifer. *The Affluent Worker: Industrial Attitudes and Behavior*. Cambridge: Cambridge University Press, 1968.

——*The Affluent Worker in the Class Structure*. Cambride: Cambridge University Press, 1969.

Gottesman, I. I. "Biogenetics of Race and Class," in Martin Deutsch, Irwin Katz, and Arthur R. Jensen, eds., *Social Class, Race, and Psychological Development*. New York: Holt, Rinehart and Winston, 1968.

Gouldner, Alvin W., and Petersen, Richard A. *Notes on Technology and the Moral Order*. Indianapolis: Bobbs-Merrill, 1962.

Gurin, Gerald, Veroff, Joseph, and Feld, Sheila. *Americans View Their Mental Health: A Nationwide Interview Survey*. New York: Basic Books, 1960.

Hardin, E. "Full Employment and Workers' Education," *Monthly Labor Review,* 90 (1967), 21–25.

Heer, David M. "Dominance and the Working Wife," *Social Forces,* 36 (1958), 341–347.

Held, Richard. "Exposure-History as a Factor in Maintaining Stability of Perception and Coordination," *Journal of Nervous and Mental Disorders,* 132 (1961), 26–32.

——and Freedman, Sanford J. "Plasticity in Human Sensorimotor Control," *Science,* 142 (1963), 455–462.

Henry, Andrew F., and Short, James F., Jr. *Suicide and Homicide.* Glencoe, Ill.: Free Press, 1954.

Henry, William E. "The Business Executive: The Psychodynamics of a Social Role," *American Journal of Sociology,* 54 (1949), 286–291.

Hoffman, Lois Wladis. "The Decision to Work," in F. Ivan Nye and Lois W. Hoffman, *The Employed Mother in America.* Chicago: Rand McNally, 1963.

——"Effects of Maternal Employment on the Child," *Child Development,* 32 (1961), 187–197.

Hoffman, Martin. "Psychiatry, Nature, and Science," *American Journal of Psychiatry,* 117 (1960), 205–210.

Horton, John E., and Thompson, Wayne E. "Powerlessness and Political Negativism: A Study of Defeated Local Referendums," *American Journal of Sociology,* 67 (1962), 485–493.

Hyman, Herbert H. "The Value Systems of Different Classes: A Social Psychological Contribution to the Analysis of Stratification," in Reinhard Bendix and Seymour Lipset, eds., *Class, Status and Power: A Reader in Social Stratification.* Glencoe, Ill.: Free Press, 1953.

——and Singer, Eleanor, eds. *Readings in Reference Group Theory and Research.* New York: Free Press, 1968.

Inkeles, Alex. "Industrial Man: The Relation of Status to Experience, Perception, and Value," *American Journal of Sociology,* 66 (1960), 1–31.

——"Personality and Social Structure," in Robert K. Merton, Leonard Broom, Leonard S. Cottrell, Jr., eds., *Sociology Today: Problems and Prospects.* New York: Basic Books, 1959.

——"Sociology and Psychology," in Sigmund Koch, ed., *Psychology: A Study of Science.* New York: McGraw-Hill, 1963.

——and Levinson, Daniel J. "National Character: The Study of Modal Personality and Sociocultural Systems," in Gardner Lindzey, ed., *Handbook of Social Psychology.* Cambridge, Mass.: Addison-Wesley, 1954.

Jaques, Elliot. *The Changing Culture of a Factory.* London: Tavistock Publications, 1951.

Jensen, Arthur R. "Patterns of Mental Ability and Socioeconomic Status," *Proceedings of the National Academy of Sciences,* 60 (1968), 1330–1337.

Jephcott, Agnes P., Seear, Nancy, and Smith, John H. *Married Women Working*. London: George Allen and Unwin, Ltd., 1962.

Kahl, Joseph A. "Some Measurements of Achievement Orientation," *American Journal of Sociology*, 70 (1965), 669–681.

Kahn, Robert L., Wolfe, Donald M., Quinn, Robert P., and Snoek, J. Diedrick, in collaboration with Robert A. Rosenthal. *Organizational Stress: Studies in Role Conflict and Ambiguity*. New York: John Wiley, 1964.

Katz, Daniel, and Kahn, Robert L. *The Social Psychology of Organizations*. New York: John Wiley, 1966.

——and Stotland, Ezra. "A Preliminary Statement to a Theory of Attitude Structure and Change," in Sigmund Koch, ed., *Psychology: A Study of a Science, Volume 3. Formulations of the Person and the Social Context*. New York: McGraw-Hill, 1959.

Kelman, Herbert C. "Compliance, Identification and Internalization: Three Processes of Attitude Change," *Journal of Conflict Resolution*, 2 (1958), 51–60.

——"Processes of Opinion Change," *Public Opinion Quarterly*, 25 (1961), 57–78.

Killingsworth, Charles C. "Unemployment in the United States," in William Haber, ed., *Labor in a Changing America*. New York: Basic Books, 1966.

Kirscht, John P., and Dillehay, Ronald C. *Dimensions of Authoritarianism: A Review of Research and Theory*. Lexington, Ky.: University of Kentucky Press, 1967.

Knupfer, Genevieve. "Portrait of the Underdog," *Public Opinion Quarterly*, 11 (1947), 103–114.

Kohn, Melvin L. "Social Class and Parental Values," *American Journal of Sociology*, 64 (1959), 337–351.

——*Class and Conformity: A Study in Values*. Homewood, Ill.: Dorsey Press, 1969.

Kornhauser, Arthur. *Mental Health of the Industrial Worker*. New York: John Wiley, 1965.

Lafitte, Paul. *Social Structure and Personality in the Factory*. New York: Macmillan, 1958.

Leggett, John C. *Class, Race, and Labor: Working-Class Consciousness in Detroit*. New York: Oxford University Press, 1968.

Levin, Joan. "Social Status Ambiguity and Residential Relocation." Ph.D. dissertation, Harvard University, 1963.

Levitan, Sar A., ed. *Blue-Collar Workers: A Symposium on Middle America*. New York: McGraw-Hill, 1971.

——"The Poor in the Work Force," in Task Force on Economic Growth and Opportunity (Third Report), *The Disadvantaged Poor: Education and Employment*. Washington, D.C.: United States Chamber of Commerce, 1966.

Lindemann, Erich. "Psycho-Social Factors as Stressor Agents," in J. M. Tanner, ed., *Stress and Psychiatric Disorder*. Oxford: Blackwell Scientific Publishers, Ltd., 1960.

——"Symptomatology and Management of Acute Grief," *American Journal of Psychiatry,* 101 (1944), 141–148.

Lipset, Seymour M. *Political Man: The Social Basis of Politics.* Garden City, N.Y.: Doubleday, 1960.

Lipsitz, Lewis. "Working-Class Authoritarianism: A Re-evaluation," *American Sociological Review,* 30 (1965), 103–109.

MacKinnon, William J., and Centers, Richard. "Authoritarianism and Urban Stratification," *American Journal of Sociology,* 61 (1956), 610–620.

Mayo, Elton. *The Human Problems of an Industrial Civilization.* Boston: Harvard University Graduate School of Business Administration, 1946.

McClelland, David C. *The Achieving Society.* Princeton: Van Nostrand, 1961.

——and Atkinson, John W. *The Achievement Motive.* New York: Appleton Century Crofts, 1953.

McGuire, William J. "The Nature of Attitudes and Attitude Change," in *Handbook of Social Psychology,* 2d ed., III, 136–314. Reading, Mass.: Addison and Wesley, 1968.

McKendrick, Neil. "Josiah Wedgwood and Factory Discipline" in David S. Landes, ed., *The Rise of Capitalism.* New York: Macmillan, 1966.

McKenzie, Robert, and Silver, Allan. *Angels in Marble: Working-Class Conservatives in Urban England.* Chicago: University of Chicago Press, 1968.

Merton, Robert K. "The Machine, the Worker, and the Engineer," *Science,* 105 (1947), 79–84.

Miller, S. M., and Riessman, Frank. "Are Workers Middle Class?" *Dissent,* 8 (1961), 507–513.

Moore, Wilbert E., and Feldman, Arnold S. *Labor Commitment and Social Change in Developing Areas.* New York: Social Science Research Council, 1960.

Morse, Nancy C., and Weiss, R. S. "The Function and Meaning of Work and the Job," *American Sociological Review,* 20 (1955), 191–198.

Myrdal, Alva, and Klein, Viola. *Women's Two Roles: Home and Work.* London: Routledge and Kegan Paul, 1956.

Myrdal, Gunnar, with Richard Sterner and Arnold Rose. *An American Dilemma: The Negro Problem and Modern Democracy.* New York: Harper, 1944.

Nary, Edwina M. "Some Aspects of the Occupational Role Among Women in a Urban Slum." Master's thesis, Northeastern University, Boston, Mass., 1965.

Neugarten, Bernice L. "Kansas City Study of Adult Life," in Irma Gross, ed., *Potentialities of Women in the Middle Years.* East Lansing: Michigan State University Press, 1956.

Newcomb, Theodore M. *Personality and Social Change: Attitude Formation in a Student Community.* New York: Holt, 1957.

Parsons, Talcott, and Shils, Edward. "Values, Motives, and Systems of Action," in Parsons and Shils, eds., *Toward a General Theory of Action.* Cambridge, Mass.: Harvard University Press, 1951.

Pearlin, Leonard I., and Kohn, Melvin C. "Social Class, Occupation, and Parental Values: A Cross-National Survey, *American Sociological Review,* 31 (1966), 466–479.

Perrella, Vera. "Women and the Labor Force," *Monthly Labor Review,* 91 (1968), 1–12.

Photiadis, John D., and Biggar, Jeanne. "Religiosity, Education, and Ethnic Distance," *American Journal of Sociology,* 67 (1962), 666–672.

Purcell, Theodore V. *Blue-Collar Man: Patterns of Dual Allegiance in Industry.* Cambridge, Mass.: Harvard University Press, 1960.

Rainwater, Lee. "Work and Identity in the Lower Class," in Sam B. Warner, Jr., ed., *Planning For a Nation of Cities.* Cambridge, Mass.: M.I.T. Press, 1966.

Redl, Fritz, and Wineman, David. *Children Who Hate.* Glencoe, Ill.: Free Press, 1951.

Riesen, Austin H. "Stimulation as a Requirement for Growth and Function in Behavioral Development," in D. W. Fiske and D. T. Maddi, *Functions of Varied Experience.* Homewood, Ill.: Dorsey Press, 1961, pp. 57–80.

——"Studying Perceptual Development Using the Technique of Sensory Deprivation," *Journal of Nervous and Mental Diseases,* 132 (1961), 21–25.

Riesman, David, Glazer, Nathan, and Denney, Ruel. *The Lonely Crowd.* New Haven: Yale University Press, 1950.

Rodman, Hyman. "The Lower-Class Value Stretch," *Social Forces,* 42 (1963), 205–215.

Roethlisberger, Frederick J., and Dickson, William J. *Management and the Worker.* Cambridge, Mass.: Harvard University Press, 1939.

Rokeach, Milton. *Beliefs, Attitudes, and Values: A Theory of Organization and Change.* San Francisco: Jossey-Bass, 1968.

——*The Open and Closed Mind: Investigation into the Nature of Belief Systems and Personality Systems.* New York: Basic Books, 1960.

Rosen, Bernard C. "The Achievement Syndrome: A Psychocultural Dimension of Social Stratification," *American Sociological Review,* 21 (1956), 203–211.

Rossi, Alice. "Equality Between the Sexes: An Immodest Proposal," *Daedalus* (Spring 1964), 607–652.

Runciman, W. G. *Relative Deprivation and Social Justice: A Study of Attitudes to Social Inequality in Twentieth Century England.* Berkeley and Los Angeles: University of California Press, 1966.

Saben, Samuel. "Geographic Mobility and Employment Status, March 1962–March 1963," *Monthly Labor Review,* 87 (1964), 873–881.

Sarbin, Theodore. "Notes on the Transformation of Social Identity," in Leigh M. Roberts et al., eds., *Comprehensive Mental Health: The Challenge of Evaluation.* Madison: University of Wisconsin Press, 1968.

Schein, Edgar H., and Bennis, Warren G. *Personal and Organizational Change Through Group Methods.* New York: John Wiley, 1965.

Seeman, Melvin. "On the Personal Consequences of Alienation in Work," *American Sociological Review,* 32 (1967), 273–283.

Shannon, Lyle W. "The Economic Absorption and Cultural Integration of In-migrant Workers: Characteristics of the Individual Versus the Nature of the System," in Eugene B. Brody, ed., *Behavior in New Environments: Adaptation of Migrant Populations.* Beverly Hills: Sage Publications, 1969.

Silletoe, Alan. *Saturday Night and Sunday Morning.* New York: Alfred Knopf, 1959.

Sobol, Marion G. "Commitment to Work," in F. Ivan Nye, and Lois W. Hoffman, *The Employed Mother in America.* Chicago: Rand McNally, 1963.

Spinley, B. M. *The Deprived and the Privileged: Personality Development in English Society.* London: Routledge and Kegan Paul, 1953.

Srole, Leo. "Social Integration and Certain Corrolaries: An Exploratory Study," *American Sociological Review,* 21 (1956), 709–716.

Stember, Charles H. *Education and Attitude Change: The Effect of Schooling on Prejudice Against Minority Groups.* New York: Institute of Human Relations Press, 1961.

Stephenson, Richard M. "Mobility Orientation and Stratification of 1,000 Ninth Graders," *American Sociological Review,* 22 (1957), 204–212.

Stodolsky, Susan S., and Lesser, Gerald, eds. "Learning Patterns in the Disadvantaged," *Harvard Educational Review,* 37 (1967), 546–593.

Stolz, Lois Meek. "Effects of Maternal Employment on Children: Evidence from Research," *Child Development,* 31 (1960), 749–782.

Stouffer, Samuel A., et al. *The American Soldier: Studies in Social Psychology in World War II.* 4 vols. Princeton: Princeton University Press, 1949.

Straus, Murray. "Deferred Gratification, Social Class, and the Achievement Syndrome," *American Sociological Review,* 27 (1962), 326–335.

Swados, Harvey. *On The Line.* Boston: Little, Brown, 1957.

Tajfel, Henri. "Cognitive Aspects of Prejudice," *Journal of Social Issues,* 25 (1969), 79–98.

Thompson, Barbara, and Finlayson, Angela. "Married Women Who Work in Early Motherhood," *British Journal of Sociology,* 14 (1963), 150–168.

Trist, Erich L., and Bamforth, Kenneth W. "Some Social and Psychological Consequences of the Long-Wall Method of Coal-Getting," *Human Relations,* 4 (1951), 3–38.

Walker, Charles R., and Guest, Robert H. *The Man on the Assembly Line.* Cambridge, Mass.: Harvard University Press, 1952.

Weiss, Robert S., and Samelson, Nancy M. "Social Roles of American Women: Their Contribution to a Sense of Usefulness and Importance," *Marriage and Family Living,* 20 (1958), 358–366.

Whyte, William Foote, ed. *Industry and Society.* New York: McGraw-Hill, 1946.

Wicker, Allan W. "Attitudes versus Actions: The Relationship of Verbal and Overt Behavioral Responses to Attitude Objects," *Journal of Social Issues,* 25 (1969), 41–78.

Williams, Robin M., Jr., with John P. Dean and Edward A. Suchman. *Strangers Next Door: Ethnic Relations in American Communities.* Englewood Cliffs, N.J.: Prentice-Hall, 1964.

Wilson, James Q., and Banfield, Edward C. "Public Regardingness as a Value Premise in Voting Behavior," *American Political Science Review,* 4 (1964), 876–887.

Worthy, James C., "Factors Influencing Employee Morale," *Harvard Business Review,* 28 (1950), 61–73.

Zigler, Edward, and deLabry, Jacques. "Concept-Switching in Middle-Class, Lower-Class, and Retarded Children," *Journal of Abnormal and Social Psychology,* 65 (1962), 267–273.

STRUCTURE AND DYNAMICS OF SOCIAL CLASS SYSTEMS

Abegglen, James C. "Personality Factors in Social Mobility: A Study of Occupationally Mobile Businessmen," *Journal of Genetic Psychology,* 58 (1958), 101–159.

Agger, Robert E., Goldrich, Daniel, and Swanson, Bert E. *The Rulers and the Ruled: Political Power and Impotence in American Communities.* New York: John Wiley, 1964.

Allingham, John D. "Class Regression: An Aspect of the Social Stratification Process," *American Sociological Review,* 32 (1967), 443–449.

Aron, Raymond. "Social Class, Political Class, Ruling Class," in Reinhard Bendix and Seymour Martin Lipset, *Class, Status and Power, Second Edition.* New York: Free Press, 1966.

Baltzell, E. Digby. *Philadelphia Gentlemen: The Making of a National Upper Class.* New York: Free Press, 1958.

Banfield, Edward C. *The Unheavenly City: The Nature and Future of Our Urban Crisis.* Boston: Little, Brown, 1968.

Barber, Bernard. *Social Stratification.* New York: Harcourt, Brace and Co., 1957.

Barnard, Chester I. *The Functions of the Executive.* Cambridge, Mass.: Harvard University Press, 1938.

Becker, Howard S. "Schools and Systems of Stratification," in A. H. Halsey, Jean Floud, and C. Arnold Anderson, eds., *Education, Economy, and Society.* New York: Free Press, 1961.

Bendix, Reinhard, and Lipset, Seymour Martin, eds. *Class, Status, and Power: Social Stratification in Comparative Perspective,* 2d ed. New York: Free Press, 1966.

Benoit-Smullyan, Emile. "Status, Status Types, and Status Interrelations," *American Sociological Review,* 9 (1944), 151–161.

Bernstein, Basil. "Social Class and Linguistic Development: A Theory of Social Learning," in A. H. Halsey, Jean Floud, and C. Arnold Anderson, eds., *Education, Economy and Society.* New York: Free Press, 1961.

Bieri, James, and Lobeck, Robin. "Self-Concept Differences in Relation to Identification, Religion and Social Class," *Journal of Abnormal and Social Psychology,* 62 (1961), 94–98.

Birnbaum, Norman. *The Crisis of Industrial Society*. New York: Oxford University Press, 1969.

Blau, Peter M., and Duncan, Otis Dudley. *The American Occupational Structure*. New York: John Wiley, 1967.

Bloom, Richard, Whiteman, Martin, and Deutsch, Martin. "Race and Social Class as Separate Factors Related to Social Environment," *American Journal of Sociology*, 70 (1965), 471–476.

Blum, Zahava D., and Rossi, Peter H. "Social Class Research and Images of the Poor: A Bibliographic Review," in Daniel P. Moynihan, ed., *On Understanding Poverty: Perspectives from the Social Sciences*. New York: Basic Books, 1968.

Bottomore, T. B. *Classes in Modern Society*. New York: Pantheon Books, 1966.

Broom, Leonard, Jones, F. Lancaster, and Zubrzycki, Jerzy. "Social Stratification in Australia," in J. A. Jackson, ed., *Social Stratification*. Cambridge: Cambridge University Press, 1968.

Brunner, Edmund deS., and Wayland, Sloan. "Occupation, Labor Force Status and Education," *Journal of Educational Sociology*, 32 (1958), 8–20.

Caplovitz, David. *The Poor Pay More: Consumer Practices of Low-Income Families*. New York: The Free Press of Glencoe, 1963.

Caro, Francis G., and Pihlblad, C. Terence. "Social Class, Formal Education, and Social Mobility," *Sociology and Social Research*, 48 (1964), 428–439.

Centers, Richard. *The Psychology of Social Classes: A Study of Class Consciousness*. Princeton: Princeton University Press, 1949.

Clark, Terry N., ed. *Community Structure and Decision-Making: Comparative Analyses*. San Francisco: Chandler Publishing, 1968.

Cohen, Wilbur J. "The Elimination of Poverty: A Primary Goal of Public Policy," in George H. Dunne, ed., *Poverty in Plenty*. New York: P. J. Kenedy, 1964.

Cole, G. D. H. *Studies in Class Structure*. London: Routledge and Kegan Paul, 1955.

Coleman, James S., and Campbell, Ernest Q., Hobson, Carol J., McPartland, James, Mood, Alexander M., Weinfeld, Frederick D., and York, Robert L. *Equality of Educational Opportunity*. Washington, D.C.: Government Printing Office, 1966.

Conference on Economic Progress. *Poverty and Deprivation in the United States: The Plight of Two-Fifths of a Nation*. The Keyserling Report. Washington, D.C.: Conference on Economic Progress, 1962.

Coser, Rose Laub. "Authority and Decision-Making in a Hospital," *American Sociological Review*, 23 (1958), 56–63.

Crain, Robert L., and Rossi, Peter H. "Comparative Community Studies with Large N's," *American Statistical Association Proceedings of the Social Statistics Section*, 1968, pp. 72–80.

Dahl, Robert A. *Who Governs? Democracy and Power in an American City*. New Haven: Yale University Press, 1961.

Dahrendorf, Ralf. *Class and Class Conflict in Industrial Society.* Stanford: Stanford University Press, 1959 (first published in German, 1957).

Davis, Kingsley A. "A Conceptual Analysis of Stratification," *American Sociological Review,* 7 (1942), 309–321.

——"Reply," *American Sociological Review,* 18 (1953), 394–397.

——and Moore, Wilbert E. "Some Principles of Stratification," *American Sociological Review,* 10 (1945), 387–397.

Deutsch, Martin P. "The Disadvantaged Child and the Learning Process," in A. Harry Passow, ed., *Education in Depressed Areas.* New York: Bureau of Publications, Teachers College, 1963.

——"Social Class in Language Development," *American Journal of Orthopsychiatry,* 35 (1965), 78–88.

——Katz, Irwin, Jensen, Arthur R., eds. *Social Class, Race, and Psychological Development.* New York: Holt, Rinehart and Winston, 1968.

Domhoff, G. William. *Who Rules America?* Englewood Cliffs, N.J.: Prentice-Hall, 1967.

Dunne, George H. *Poverty in Plenty.* New York: P. J. Kenedy, 1964.

Eckstein, Otto. "Another View of Unemployment," in William Haber, ed., *Labor in a Changing America.* New York: Basic Books, 1966.

Eisenstadt, S. N. "Prestige, Participation and Strata Formation," in J. A. Jackson, ed., *Social Stratification.* Cambridge: Cambridge University Press, 1968.

Empey, LaMar T. "Social Class and Occupational Aspiration: A Comparison of Absolute and Relative Measurement," *American Sociological Review,* 21 (1946), 703–709.

Engels, Frederick. "Socialism: Utopian and Scientific (1877)," in Karl Marx and Frederick Engels, *Selected Works,* Volume II. Moscow: Foreign Languages Publishing House, 1962.

Farber, Bernard. "Social Class and Intelligence," *Social Forces,* 44 (1965), 215–225.

Form, William. "Status Stratification in a Planned Community," *American Sociological Review,* 10 (1945), 605–613.

Fried, Marc et al. *A Study of Demographic and Social Determinants of Functional Achievement in a Negro Population.* Final Report to Office of Economic Opportunity, Division of Research and Plans, Washington, D.C., 1971.

Furstenberg, Friedrich. "Structural Changes in the Working Class: A Situational Study of Workers in the Western German Chemical Industry," in J. A. Jackson, ed., *Social Stratification.* Cambridge: Cambridge University Press, 1968.

Gans, Herbert. "Culture and Class in the Study of Poverty: An Approach to Anti-Poverty Research," in Daniel P. Moynihan, ed., *On Understanding Poverty: Perspectives from the Social Sciences.* New York: Basic Books, 1969.

Gerth, Hans, and Mills, C. Wright, trans. *From Max Weber: Essays in Sociology.* New York: Oxford University Press, 1946.

Glass, D. V., ed. *Social Mobility in Britain.* Glencoe, Ill.: Free Press, 1954.

Glick, Paul C., and Miller, Herman P. "Educational Level and Potential Income," *American Sociological Review*, 21 (1956), 307–312.

Goldstein, Sidney. "Migration and Occupational Mobility in Morristown, Pennsylvania," *American Sociological Review*, 20 (1955), 402–448.

Goldthorpe, John H. "Social Stratification in Industrial Society," in Paul Halmos, ed., *The Development of Industrial Society*, The Sociological Review, Monograph No. 8, 1964.

Hagen, E. E. *On the Theory of Social Change*. Homewood, Ill.: The Dorsey Press, 1962.

Haggstrom, Warren C. "The Power of the Poor," in Frank Riessman, Jerome Cohen, and Arthur Pearl, eds., *Mental Health of the Poor*. New York: Free Press of Glencoe, 1964.

Halbwachs, Maurice. *The Psychology of Social Class*, trans. Claire Delavenay. London: William Heinemann, 1958 (originally *Esquisse d'une psychologie des classes sociales*, Paris: Riviere, 1955).

Haley, Bernard F. "Changes in the Distribution of Income in the United States," in James G. Scoville, ed., *Perspectives on Poverty and Income Distribution*. Lexington, Mass.: D. C. Heath, 1971.

Hamilton, Richard. "The Income Difference Between Skilled and White Collar Workers," *British Journal of Sociology*, 14 (1963), 363–373.

——"The Marginal Middle Class: A Reconsideration," *American Sociological Review*, 31 (1966), 192–199.

Harrington, Michael. *The Other America: Poverty in the United States*. New York: MacMillan, 1962.

——"Poverty and Politics," in George H. Dunne, ed., *Poverty in Plenty*. New York: P. J. Kenedy, 1964.

Hatt, Paul K. "Stratification in the Mass Society," *American Sociological Review*, 15 (1950), 216–222.

Hess, Robert D. "The Transmission of Cognitive Strategies in Poor Families: The Socialization of Apathy and Under-Achievement," in Vernon L. Allen, ed., *Psychological Factors in Poverty*. Chicago: Markham Publishing Co., 1970.

Hodge, Robert W., Treiman, Donald J., and Rossi, Peter H. "A Comparative Study of Occupational Prestige," in Reinhard Bendix and Seymour Martin Lipset, eds. *Class, Status and Power*, 2d ed. New York: Free Press, 1966.

Hodges, Harold M., Jr. "Social Stratification in a Metropolitan Complex," in Robert Gutman and David Popenoe, eds., *Neighborhood, City and Metropolis*. New York: Random House, 1970.

Hunt, James McV. *Intelligence and Experience*. New York: Ronald Press, 1961.

Hunter, Floyd. *Community Power Structure*. Chapel Hill: University of North Carolina Press, 1953.

Huxley, Aldous. *Brave New World*. New York: Harper, 1932.

Hyman, Herbert H. "The Psychology of Status," *Archives of Psychology*, 38 (1942), no. 269.

Inkeles, Alex, and Rossi, Peter H. "National Comparisons of Occupational Prestige," *American Journal of Sociology,* 61 (1956), 329–339.

Jackson, Elton F. "Status Consistency and Symptoms of Stress," *American Sociological Review,* 27 (1962), 469–480.

——and Burke, Peter. "Status and Symptoms of Stress: Additive and Interaction Effects," *American Sociological Review,* 30 (1965), 556–564.

——and Crockett, Harry J., Jr. "Occupational Mobility in the United States," *American Sociological Review,* 29 (1964), 5–15.

Janowitz, Morris. "Some Consequences of Social Mobility in the United States," *Transactions of the Third World Congress of Sociology,* 3 (1956), 191–201.

Jensen, Arthur R. "How Much Can We Boost IQ and Scholastic Achievement?" *Harvard Educational Review,* 39 (1969), 1–123.

Johnston, Denis F., and Hamel, Harvey R. "Educational Attainment of Workers in March 1965," *Monthly Labor Review,* 89 (1966), 250–257.

Kahl, Joseph A. *The American Class Structure.* New York: Rinehart and Co., 1957.

Kalish, Carol B. "A Portrait of the Unemployed," *Monthly Labor Review,* 89 (1966), 7–14.

Katz, Irwin. "A New Approach to the Study of School Motivation in Minority Group Children," in Vernon L. Allen, ed., *Psychological Factors in Poverty.* Chicago: Markham Publishing Co., 1970.

Keller, Suzanne. *Beyond the Ruling Class: Strategic Elites in Modern Society.* New York: Random House, 1963.

Keyserling, Leon H. "Key Questions on the Poverty Problem, " in George H. Dunne, ed., *Poverty in Plenty.* New York: P. J. Kenedy, 1964.

——*Poverty and Deprivation in the United States: The Plight of Two-Fifths of a Nation.* Washington, D.C.: Conference on Economic Progress, 1962.

——*Progress or Poverty: The U.S. at the Crossroads.* Washington, D.C.: Conference on Economic Progress, 1964.

Kolko, Gabriel. *Wealth and Power in America: An Analysis of Social Class and Income Distribution.* New York: Praeger, 1962.

Kornhauser, William. " 'Power Elite' or 'Veto Groups'?" in Reinhard Bendix, and Seymour Martin Lipset, eds., *Class, Status and Power,* 2d ed. New York: Free Press, 1966.

Lampman, Robert J. *The Low Income Population and Economic Growth.* Study Paper No. 12, Joint Economic Committee, U.S. Congress. Washington, D.C.: Government Printing Office, 1959.

——"Population Change and Poverty Reduction, 1947–75," in Lee Fishman, ed., *Poverty Amid Affluence.* New Haven: Yale University Press, 1966.

Lassiter, Roy L. "The Association of Income and Education for Males by Region, Race, and Age," *Southern Economics Journal,* 32 (1965), 15–22.

Lebergott, Stanley. "Labor Force and Employment Trends," in Eleanor
    Bernert Sheldon and Wilbert E. Moore, eds., *Indicators of Social
    Change: Concepts and Measurements.* New York: Russell Sage, 1968.
——*Manpower in Economic Growth: The American Record Since 1800.*
    New York: McGraw-Hill, 1964.
Lenski, Gerhard. *Power and Privilege: A Theory of Social Stratification.*
    New York: McGraw-Hill, 1966.
Lesser, G., Fifer, G., and Clark, D. "Mental Abilities of Children from
    Different Social Class and Cultural Groups," *Society for Research in
    Child Development,* 30 (1965), 1–115.
Levine, Robert A. "Rethinking our Social Strategies," *The Public Interest*
    (Winter 1968).
Lipset, Seymour Martin. "Social Mobility and Urbanization," *Rural
    Sociology,* 20 (1955), 220–228.
——and Bendix, Reinhard. *Social Mobility in Industrial Society.* Berkeley
    and Los Angeles: University of California Press, 1967 (paperback; first
    published 1959).
Lundberg, Ferdinand. *The Rich and The Super-Rich: A Study in the Power
    of Money Today.* New York: Lyle Stuart, 1968.
Marris, Robin, and Wood, Adrian, eds. *The Corporate Economy: Growth,
    Competition and Innovative Potential.* Cambridge, Mass.: Harvard
    University Press, 1971.
Marshall, T. H. *Class, Citizenship and Social Development.* Garden City,
    N.Y.: Doubleday (Anchor Books), 1965 (first published 1963 as
    Sociology at the Crossroads).
Marx, Karl. *Critique of the Gotha Programme,* in Karl Marx and Frederick
    Engels, *Selected Works,* Volume II. Moscow: Foreign Languages
    Publishing House, 1962.
——*The Eighteenth Brumaire of Louis Bonaparte,* in Karl Marx and
    Frederick Engels, *Selected Works,* Volume I. Moscow: Foreign
    Languages Publishing House, 1962.
——and Engels, Frederick. *The German Ideology* (Parts 1 and 111), trans.
    R. Pascal. New York: International Publishers, 1947.
——and Engels, Frederick. *Manifesto of the Communist Party,* in Karl
    Marx and Frederick Engels, *Selected Works,* Volume I. Moscow:
    Foreign Languages Publishing House, 1858.
Matza, David. "The Disreputable Poor," in Reinhard Bendix and Seymour
    Martin Lipset, eds., *Class, Status and Power,* 2d ed. New York: Free
    Press, 1966.
Mayer, Kurt B. *Class and Society,* rev. ed. New York: Random House, 1955.
——"Social Stratification in Two Equalitarian Societies: Australia and the
    United States," *Social Research,* 5 (1964), 435–465.
Merton, Robert K. *Social Theory and Social Structure,* rev. ed. Glencoe,
    Ill.: Free Press, 1957.
——and Rossi, Alice S. "Contributions to the Theory of Reference Group
    Behavior," in Robert K. Merton, *Social Theory and Social Structure,*
    rev. ed. Glencoe, Ill.: Free Press, 1957.

Miller, Herman P. *Income Distribution in the United States.* A 1960 Census
Monograph. Washington, D.C.: Government Printing Office, 1966.

Miller, S. M. "The American Lower Class: A Typological Approach," *Social
Research,* 31 (1964), 1–22.

——"Comparative Social Mobility: A Trend Report and Bilbiography,"
Current Sociology, 9 (1960), 1–89.

——"Poverty in an International Context" (mimeographed), Convenor's
Paper for Working Group on Poverty, *World Congress of Sociology.*
Evian, France: September 1966 (November 1966).

——and Harrison, Ira E. "Types of Dropouts: The Unemployables," in
Arthur B. Shostak and William Gomberg, eds., *Blue-Collar World:
Studies of the American Workers.* Englewood Cliffs, N.J.: Prentice-Hall,
1964.

——and Riessman, Frank. *Social Class and Social Policy.* New York: Basic
Books, 1968.

——"The Working Class Subculture: A New View," *Social Problems,* 9
(1961), 86–97.

Miller, Walter B. "Lower Class Culture as a Generating Milieu of Gang
Delinquency," *Journal of Social Issues,* 14 (1958), 5–19.

Mills, C. Wright. *The Power Elite.* New York: Oxford University Press,
1956.

——*White Collar: The American Middle Classes.* New York: Oxford
University Press, 1951.

Morgan, James N., David, Martin H., Cohen, Wilbur J., and Brazer, Harvey
E. *Income and Welfare in the United States.* New York: McGraw-Hill,
1962.

Mueller, Eva, and Schmiedeskamp, Jay. *Persistent Unemployment.*
Kalamazoo, Mich.: Upjohn Institute for Employment Research, 1962.

Murdock, George P. *Social Structure.* New York: Macmillan, 1949.

Orshansky, Mollie. "Counting the Poor: Another Look at the Poverty
Profile," *Social Security Bulletin* (January 1965), 3–29.

Orwell, George. *Nineteen Eighty-Four.* New York: Harcourt, Brace, 1949.

Osofsky, Gilbert. "The Enduring Ghetto," *Journal of American History,*
55 (1968), 243–255.

Ossowski, Stanislaw. *Class Structure in the Social Consciousness,* trans.
Sheila Patterson. New York: Free Press, 1963 (originally published in
Poland, 1958).

Parsons, Talcott. "An Analytical Approach to the Theory of Social Stratification," *American Journal of Sociology,* 45 (1940), 841–862.

——"A Revised Analytical Approach to the Theory of Social Stratification,"
in Bendix and Lipset, eds., *Class, Status and Power.* Glencoe, Ill.: Free
Press, 1953.

——"On the Concept of Political Power," in Reinhard Bendix and
Seymour Martin Lipset, eds., *Class, Status, and Power: Social Stratification in Comparative Perspective,* 2d ed. New York: Free Press, 1966.

——"The School Class as a Social System: Some of Its Functions in American Society," *Harvard Educational Review,* 29 (1959), 297–318.

Pettigrew, Thomas F. *Profile of the Negro American.* Princeton: Van Nostrand, 1964.

Presthus, Robert. *Men At The Top: A Study in Community Power.* New York: Oxford University Press, 1964.

Rainwater, Lee. *Behind Ghetto Walls: Black Families in a Federal Slum.* Chicago: Aldine Publishing Co., 1970.

——"Crucible of Identity: The Negro Lower Class Family," *Daedalus* (Winter 1966), 172–216.

——"The Problem of Lower-Class Culture and Poverty-War Strategy," in Daniel P. Moynihan, ed. *On Understanding Poverty: Perspectives from the Social Sciences.* New York: Basic Books, 1969.

Rogoff, Natalie. *Recent Trends in Occupational Mobility.* Glencoe, Ill.: Free Press, 1953.

Rosenfeld, Eva. "Social Stratification in a 'Classless' Society," *American Sociological Review,* 16 (1951), 766–774.

Ryan, William. *Blaming the Victim.* New York: Pantheon Books, 1971.

Schmid, Calvin F., and Nobbe, Charles E. "Socioeconomic Differentials Among Nonwhite Races," *American Sociological Review,* 30 (1965), 909–922.

Schorr, Alvin L. "The Nonculture of Poverty." *American Journal of Orthopsychiatry,* 34 (1964), 907–912.

——*Poor Kids: A Report on Children in Poverty.* New York: Basic Books, 1966.

Schumpeter, Joseph. *Imperialism and Social Classes.* New York: Augustus M. Kelley, 1951.

Sewall, William H., Haller, Archie O., and Straus, Murray A. "Social Status and Educational and Occupational Aspirations," *American Sociological Review,* 22 (1957), 67–73.

Sexton, Patricia Cayo. *Education and Income: Inequalities of Opportunity in Our Public Schools.* New York: Viking Press, 1961.

Shils, Edward. "Deference," in J. A. Jackson, ed., *Social Stratification.* Cambridge: Cambridge University Press, 1968.

Shostak, Arthur B., and Gomberg, William, eds. *Blue Collar World: Studies of the American Worker.* Englewood Cliffs, N.J.: Prentice-Hall, 1964.

——*New Perspective on Poverty.* Englewood Cliffs, N.J.: Prentice-Hall, 1965.

Sibley, Eldridge. "Some Demographic Clues to Stratification," *American Sociological Review,* 7 (1942), 322–330.

Simpson, George. "Class Analysis: What Class is Not," *American Sociological Review,* 4 (1939), 827–835.

Sjoberg, Gideon. "Are Social Classes in America Becoming More Rigid?" *American Sociological Review,* 16 (1951), 775–783.

Soarès, Glaucio Ary Dillon. "Economic Development and Class Structure," in Reinhard Bendix and Seymour Martin Lipset, eds., *Class, Status, and*

Power: Social Stratification in Comparative Perspective, 2d ed. New York: Free Press, 1966.

Sorokin, Pitirim A. "What is a Social Class?" *Journal of Legal and Political Sociology,* 4 (1947), 5–28.

Spady, William G. "Educational Mobility and Access: Growth and Paradoxes," *American Journal of Sociology,* 73 (1967), 273–286.

Spengler, Joseph J. "Changes in Income Distribution and Social Stratification," *American Journal of Sociology,* 59 (1953), 247–259.

Stein, Robert L. "Work History, Attitudes, and Income of the Unemployed," *Monthly Labor Review,* 86 (1963), 1405–1413.

Stryker, Perrin. *The Character of the Executive: Eleven Studies in Managerial Qualities.* New York: Harper, 1960.

Surace, Samuel J. *Ideology, Economic Change, and the Working Classes: The Case of Italy.* Berkeley and Los Angeles: University of California Press, 1966.

Svalastoga, Kaare. *Prestige, Class and Mobility.* Copenhagen: Gyldenal, 1959.

Swanstrom, Thomas E. "Out-of-School Youth, February 1963-Part 11," *Monthly Labor Review,* 87 (1964), 1416–1424.

Tawney, R. H. *Equality.* London: George Allen and Unwin, 1931.

Thernstrom, Stephan. *Poverty and Progress: Social Mobility in a Nineteenth Century City.* Cambridge: Harvard University Press, 1964.

Thurow, Lester C. "The Causes of Poverty," *Quarterly Journal of Economics,* 81 (1967), 39–57.

——and Lucas, Robert E. B. *The American Distribution of Income: A Structural Problem.* Washington, D.C.: Government Printing Office, 1972.

Titmuss, Richard M. *Income Distribution and Social Change.* Toronto: University of Toronto Press, 1962.

Townsend, Peter. "The Meaning of Poverty," *British Journal of Sociology,* 13 (1962), 210–227.

Trevor-Roper, H. R. "Karl Marx and the Study of History," in H. R. Trevor-Roper, *Men and Events,* New York: Harper, 1957.

Tumin, Melvin M. "Some Principles of Stratification: A Critical Analysis," *American Sociological Review,* 18 (1953), 387–394.

U.S. Bureau of the Census. "Negro Population: March, 1965," *Current Population Reports.* Washington, D.C.: Government Printing Office, 1966.

——*Statistical Abstract of the United States: 1967,* 88th ed. Washington, D.C.: Government Printing Office, 1967.

——"Trends in Social and Economic Conditions in Metropolitan Areas," *Current Population Reports.* Washington, D.C.: Government Printing Office, 1959.

Warner, W. Lloyd, and Abegglen, James C. *Occupational Mobility in American Business and Industry, 1928–1952.* St. Paul: University of Minnesota Press, 1955.

——and Lunt, Paul S. *The Status System of A Modern Community,* New Haven: Yale University Press, 1942.

——with Meeker, Marchia, and Eells, Kenneth. *Social Class in America: A Manual of Procedure for the Measurement of Social Status.* Chicago: Science Research Associates, 1949.

Weber, Max. "Capitalism and Rural Society in Germany," in H. H. Gerth and C. Wright Mills, eds., *From Max Weber: Essays in Sociology.* New York: Oxford, 1946.

——*The Theory of Social and Economic Organization,* trans. A. M. Henderson and T. Parson. Glencoe, Ill.: Free Press, 1947.

Wesolowski, Wlodzimierz, and Slomczynski, Kazimierz. "Social Stratification in Polish Cities," in J. A. Jackson, ed. *Social Stratification.* Cambridge: Cambridge University Press, 1968.

Wickersham, Edward D. *Detroit's Insured Unemployed and Employable Welfare Recipients.* Kalamazoo, Mich.: Upjohn Institute for Employment Research, 1963.

Wilensky, Harold L. "Class, Class Conspicuousness, and American Workers," in William Haber, ed., *Labor in a Changing America.* New York: Basic Books, 1966.

Wiley, Norbert F. "The Ethnic Mobility Trap and Stratification Theory," *Social Problems,* 15 (1967), 147–159.

Woodworth, Robert S., and Marquis, Donald G. *Psychology,* 5th ed. New York: Henry Holt and Co., 1947.

Wrong, Dennis H. "The Functional Theory of Stratification: Some Neglected Considerations," *American Sociological Review,* 24 (1959), 772–782.

——"Social Inequality Without Social Stratification," *Canadian Review of Sociology and Anthropology,* 1 (1964), 5–16.

Yasuda, Saburo. "A Methodological Inquiry Into Social Mobility," *American Sociological Review,* 29 (1964), 16–23.

Young, Michael. *The Rise of the Meritocracy: 1870–2033: The New Elite of Our Social Revolution.* New York: Random House, 1959.

Zaniewski, Romuald. *L'Origine du proletariat Romain et contemporain.* Louvain: Editions Nauwelaerts, 1957.

Notes

PROLOGUE: THE WEST END AND THE WORLD OF WORKING-CLASS PEOPLE

1. In a subsequent volume, *Adaptation to Social Change: Relocation and Transition,* we will study the effects of forced residential relocation on the lives and adjustments of this working-class community.

2. A separate volume, on which work is currently in progress, will be devoted to problems and problem subgroups and is entitled *Deprivation and Pathology in Working-Class Life.*

3. The postrelocation interviews also included some prerelocation information for women who had previously been unavailable for interview. The total female sample for whom either prerelocation or postrelocation or both interviews are available is 552. Both prerelocation and postrelocation interviews are available for 335 women. There are also 334 interviews with male heads of household.

CHAPTER 1: CONTINUITIES IN WORKING-CLASS EXPERIENCE

1. For evidence concerning cross-national similarities in class structure see Broom et al., 1968; Furstenberg, 1968; Glass, 1954; Goldthorpe, 1964; Hodge, Treiman, and Rossi, 1966; Inkeles, 1960; Inkeles and Rossi, 1956; Lipset and Bendix, 1959; Mayer, 1964; S. M. Miller, 1960; Pearlin and Kohn, 1966; Soarés, 1966; Wesolowski and Slomczynski, 1968.

2. Thernstrom (1964) has shown that the rates of upward social mobility over nearly a century have remained fairly constant. Estimates of recent rates of upward social mobility and of the slightly lower rates of downward social mobility can be found in Lipset and Bendix, 1959; S. M. Miller, 1960; and Blau and Duncan, 1967.

3. For the relevant references to the literature on working-class history see the Bibliography section on Historical Background of Modern Social Class Structure. Specific references will be given in notes only for points that require documentation.

4. There are divergent views among historians about each major historical epoch we have discussed. The differences are perhaps least reconcilable concerning the industrial revolution, its eighteenth century antecedents, and its consequences.

5. The literature on the peasantries of Europe and on the conditions that led to emigration to the United States is vast and many references to these issues can be found in the Bibliography section on Peasantries and the Conditions of Migration. Several disparate studies have proved of special value in clarifying the framework for this discussion. For the changing social conditions of nineteenth century European peasants, Handlin's composite portrait (1951) is invaluable, as is the more detailed examination of the situation in Italy by Foerster (1919). Warriner's analysis of different forms of peasant agricultural organization (1939) and Wolf's theoretical clarification of economic organization in peasant life from a larger social structural viewpoint (1966) are important and quite unusual works.

CHAPTER 2: ETHNIC ORIGINS OF WORKING-CLASS COMMUNITIES

1. There is considerable variation in the calculations of immigration due to different sources of data, estimates, and corrections. The first census of the United States was taken in 1790 and the first immigration statistics were recorded in 1819. Prior to 1790, estimates of immigration or of foreign born are based on the most meager evidence. The major sources used for these figures are: Carpenter, 1927; Hansen, 1940; Hutchinson, 1956; Rubin, 1958; U.S. Census Bureau, 1965; U.S. Immigration Commission, 1911; Willcox, 1931; and Wittke, 1964.

2. U.S. Immigration Commission, 1911. On the basis of careful calculations from several sources, Joseph (1914) concluded that approximately 1,562,800 Jews migrated to the United States between 1881 and 1910.

3. The detailed literature on emigration from various countries is enormous but of variable quality. For the major sources see the Bibliography section on Peasantries and the Conditions of Migration.

4. Most migratory movements are selective of those migrants with educational and occupational levels higher than the average for the populations from which they come. However, a recent study of migrants from rural Mexico to Monterrey, Mexico shows a gradual shift from highly selective patterns of "pioneer" migration to those more typical of "mass" migration in which the distribution of migrants approximated the characteristics of the origin population (Browning and Feindt, 1969).

5. Close to this view in their emphases on social and psychological factors that gave particularly destructive force to economic impoverishment are the works of Arensberg and Kimball (1948), Eisenstadt (1954), Handlin (1951), and Thomas and Znaniecki (1918). Hagen (1962), Polanyi (1944), and Schumpeter (1951), adopt a similar orientation in dealing with related problems of economic development.

6. The literature on the nineteenth and early twentieth century slums is vast and almost painfully repetitious in its catalog of abominations. A view of these slum conditions can be obtained from the major works listed in the Bibliography under Poverty and Slums: The Recent Past.

7. Erickson (1957) presents the most systematic examination of the

conflict between organized labor and the immigrants. American industry maintained an excess supply of unskilled, immigrant labor to depress wages and to fight the unionization movement. More than any other factor, this produced intense antagonism in American labor toward immigration. Industry, on the other hand, opposed such restriction until the early 1920s when enormous prosperity diminished the fear of increased wage demands. For the Boston Brahmin opposition to immigration see Solomon, 1956.

8. DeForest and Veiller (1903) quote extensively from this early report of the Association for Improving the Condition of the Poor, published in 1853.

9. Despite the delicacy of the descriptive efforts in many studies, they are nauseating indictments of an era and its antisocial orientation. The studies from different decades also reveal the incredibly slow and meager progress that occurred. See Bibliography section on Poverty and Slums: The Recent Past.

10. A comparison of the reports for different periods in New York or of Handlin (1941) and Woods (1902) for the North End and West End of Boston indicate that most of the improvements in slum housing occurred during the latter part of the nineteenth century. The extensive use of pictures and photographs in many reports suggests that relatively little further improvement had taken place between the beginning and the middle of the twentieth century. The housing presented as the very worst examples of slum dwellings in New York around 1900 or in Pittsburgh around 1908 are hardly worse than many of the physical structures in the West End in 1958 and in many other slum areas in 1972. However, housing densities have certainly diminished and the proportion of such housing in the total housing stock has decreased (Frieden, 1964).

11. This, in itself, is a fascinating chapter of human intolerance, a chapter that is not yet concluded since its force is evident in contemporary forms of racism. Even Engels (1845), whose explicit ideology stressed the environmental sources of degradation among the lower classes, could not resist quite devastating descriptions of the Irish in England. Riis (1890) and Woods (1902) realized that a gradual process of assimilation occurred, but their comments about the most recent immigrant groups suggest profound pessimism about the continuity of this pattern. Hunter (1904), progressive critic of societal forces that maintained the condition of the poor and the immigrant, believed that the immigrants of the late nineteenth century, Italians, Jews, and Slavs, were of distinctly inferior hereditary stock and that to allow their intermarriage with native white Americans, by virtue of allowing their entrance into the United States, was virtually a form of race suicide.

12. The factual data for analyzing assimilation and changes in occupational distribution of immigrants and their children leaves much to be desired. Many of the studies of immigration and of immigrants, however, provide a coherent picture of the experience of different ethnic groups. Several other sources provide additional data concerning the processes of

immigrant achievement: Blau and Duncan, 1967; Bogardus, 1928; Carpenter, 1927; Fried, 1969; Glazer and Moynihan, 1963; Gordon, 1964; Lieberson, 1963; Nelli, 1970; Schmid and Nobbe, 1965; Thernstrom, 1964; Thomas, 1954.

13. See particularly: Ferguson and Pettigrew, 1954b; Firey, 1947; Fried, 1963; Fried and Gleicher, 1961; Gans, 1962; Hartman, 1963; Hoggart, 1957; Hole, 1866; Jennings, 1962; Mogey, 1956; Park and Miller, 1921; Riis, 1890; Willmott and Young, 1960.

14. The evidence is substantial that migrants have a difficult adjustment even under relatively benign conditions. Thus, the adaptation of Jewish immigrants to Israel, many ideologically committed to Zionism, produced many short-term and long-term casualties (Eisenstadt, 1954; Shuval, 1963; Weinberg, 1961). The tolerance of the social system toward newcomers is clearly one differentiating factor determining ease of adjustment (Murphy, 1965, 1959; Shannon, 1969; Shannon and Shannon, 1967). Differences in social class, ethnicity, and prior urban experience are individual variables that seem to influence ease of adjustment considerably.

15. Because conceptions of the slum so often include human debility and social disorganization and pathology, the term has occasionally been rejected as a proper designation for stable, working-class districts, Gans (1962a) and Hunter (1904), a half century apart, both take this position. The term is used here in a narrower sense to describe an area of deteriorated housing inhabited by low status people. The specific characteristics of the populations living in such areas are empirical questions to be investigated.

16. Abrams (1946) provides a detailed typology of slum areas including these among his many distinctions. Seeley (1959) provides a useful categorization of different types of residents of slum areas. Matza (1966) unifies a diversity of types in his resurrection of the Shavian distinction of the disreputable poor from the respectable working class but tends to perpetuate conventional stereotypes in stressing pathological characteristics without relating individual processes to larger social system dynamics. Marx's conception of the *lumpenproletariat* had an equally moralistic and equally demeaning connotation.

17. Most of the literature on immigration discusses the phenomenon of chain migration as a major mechanism of monetary, occupational, or social assistance for low status immigrants from friends, relatives, and former neighbors who had migrated earlier. For different populations compare Brown et al. (1963) and Schwarzweller (1963) on Appalachian Mountain families, Fried (1969, 1971) on blacks, Kosa (1956), on Hungarians, and MacDonald and MacDonald (1962, 1964) on Italians. Tilly and Brown (1967) substantiate the impression that kin contacts are particularly prevalent and perhaps most crucial for migrants of low status from rural areas.

18. Autobiographies, informal documents, and a few studies indicate both the relative ease of provisional acceptance in working-class slum areas which overrode ethnic distinctions and the antipathies which engendered

strain and, occasionally, persisting antagonisms. The history of ethnic conflict, of delinquency and teenage gang warfare in adjacent ethnic areas, and of ethnic riots reveal the most intense forms of working-class ethnic exclusiveness. Overt conflict, however, seems to occur mainly during the height of transition and of threats to existing stability and proprietary achievement (Glazer and Moynihan, 1963; Handlin, 1959; Elias and Scotson, 1965; Jackson, 1968; Suttles, 1968). It is too soon to determine whether the recent "invasion" of low-rent slum areas by Negroes, Puerto Ricans, and Mexicans will similarly give way to integrated working-class areas. The resistance of older white working-class communities is great, but there is some evidence of scattered areas of integration which have been successful.

19. Seeley (1959) provides a systematic delineation of the major types of slum residents and the reasons for their local residence. He estimates that considerably more than half of them are there by virtue of temporary or permanent economic and social necessity.

20. Gans (1962a), Suttles (1968), Whyte (1943), and Zola (1963) report illicit activities in areas that are predominantly Italian. But Liebow (1967) refers to similar phenomena in a lower-class Negro area and Jackson (1968) discusses almost identical activities in English working-class districts. W. Miller (1958) maintains that illicit behavior is an integral feature of lower-class culture and is far more widespread than is ordinarily realized. Minor forms of illegal behavior are almost certainly endemic, although they tend to be accepted rather than approved by slum residents.

CHAPTER 3: THE POPULATION OF THE WEST END

1. For additional descriptive material about the physical changes in the West End and some of the associated social changes see Firey, 1947; Gans, 1962; Handlin, 1941; Hartman, 1967; Massachusetts Council of Churches, 1949; Warner, 1962; Whitehill, 1968; Woods, 1902.

2. There are no detailed natural histories of urban, ethnic slums although Osofsky (1966) provides the broad outlines of such a history for Harlem in New York. The scattered evidence, however, suggests that, while there were undoubtedly ethnic concentrations, successive waves of migration resulted in mixed distributions of ethnic groups. Concentrated areas of Negro settlement existed for a very long time, but many of the ethnic slums around the turn of the century also included a Negro population. At a micro-level there was greater ethnic segregation and, even at the turn of the century, the Italian, Jewish, Slavic, Negro, or Irish blocks could often be distinguished from one another. For a critique of conceptions of the ethnically homogeneous ghetto as the major residential pattern in American immigrant life see Warner and Burke, 1969.

3. These figures are drawn from Hartman, 1967, and the redevelopment project report of the Boston Housing Authority, March 1953.

4. In order to estimate the rates and characteristics of movement in and out of the West End during the years between the first announcement of

redevelopment in 1952 and the time of prerelocation interviewing in 1958, a 20 percent sample of houses in the West End was randomly selected and the characteristics of the people living in these houses determined from the Police Listings in the city of Boston. These Police Listings record the names of all adults living in all buildings (as of January 1) each year with some supplementary information about the residents (for example, age, occupation). All references to recent changes in population characteristics are based on this sample which was collected, coded, and analyzed by Margaret Mayr, a member of the research staff. The population in 1958 given above is based on an extrapolation from these data, although the Boston Redevelopment Authority, calculating the population only for the somewhat narrower relocation area, estimated the population in 1958 as 7,500.

5. Most of the studies which provide detailed information about ethnic distributions within slum areas suggest the pattern of neighborhood heterogeneity and smaller-scale concentrations (Byington, 1910; Kenngott, 1912; McKenzie, 1923; Riis, 1890; Suttles, 1968; Warner and Srole, 1945; Woods, 1898, 1902; Zorbaugh, 1929). Apart from the high levels of segregation of Negroes, at least during the period 1930–1960, and possibly for Jews during the first or second decade of this century (Lieberson, 1963; Taeuber and Taeuber, 1965; Wirth, 1928), there are only a few recorded instances of relatively large, homogeneous areas (Firey, 1947; Whyte, 1943; Wood, 1955). Osofsky (1968) indicates that during earlier periods, the residential concentration of Negroes was similar to that described for other ethnic groups, with segregation on a micro-scale and heterogeneity within larger areas. See also Warner and Burke (1969) on exaggerated impressions of ethnic homogeneity in residence.

6. A more accurate comparison of marital status requires age adjustments or age controls. This estimate allows only a gross comparison of the level of frequency of female-based households. In the United States among all white families 10 percent and among all black families 23 percent had a female head (U.S. Bureau of the Census, 1959). Certainly there is a sharp gradient by income, but even comparing lower income groups the West End figure remains high.

7. Comparing these data with Lampman's (1959) national estimates and using Lampman's criteria, we find that the West End with 22 percent was higher than the country as a whole with a total of 19 percent of the population living below the poverty line. In view of the fact that total population calculations include people over sixty-five years of age, and rates of poverty increase considerably at this age level, the West End figure would have to be adjusted upward for a more precise comparison.

8. Few studies of working-class residential slums provide sufficiently detailed breakdowns for all of these variables to make precise comparisons of demographic and social characteristics useful. Some descriptive material for comparable communities in the United States can be found in Lavanburg Foundation, 1933; McConnel, 1942; McKenzie, 1923; W. Miller, 1958; Seeley, 1959; Suttles, 1968; Whyte, 1943; Wood, 1955; Zorbaugh, 1929.

CHAPTER 4: RESIDENTIAL EXPERIENCES AND ORIENTATIONS

1. The use of multistoried apartment dwellings for the lower classes is evidently ancient. Excavations reveal them in the late Roman Empire (Kjellberg and Saflund, 1968). Many buildings, not unlike tenements, that date from the Middle Ages are still visible in smaller Italian and French cities. Descriptions of London, Glasgow, Paris, and other European cities indicate that such buildings were used to house working-class people over many centuries.

2. Whether this pattern of street occupancy is due to the attraction of public places for social interaction or to the effort to escape from poor housing, as Schorr (1963) suggests, cannot be conclusively answered. A striking instance that reveals the cultural and social significance of public places for low status people, however, was reported by a Chilean psychiatrist. He told about public housing in Santiago in which the government-provided furniture had been moved out of the living rooms into the common halls so that social interaction could take place within a larger collectivity. While localism in social relationships is not limited to working-class people, it rarely reaches this level of commitment in other classes. For the literature on social class and national variations in localism, see the section in the Bibliography on Residential Patterns, Social Affiliations, Family.

3. If we include vacant apartments, there were 3,600 dwelling units in the renewal area of the West End.

4. Relatively few studies report details of housing, making comparison difficult. However, analysis of reports on slum housing suggests that (a) West End apartments were somewhat larger, on the average, than those in other slum areas, and (b) there has been minimal change in the number of rooms per family in slum housing over many decades. Compared to the 1950 census data for other tenement areas in the city of Boston, the sheer level of dilapidation in the West End was relatively low. Thus 78 percent of the dwelling units in the North End were either dilipidated or without private bath, and several other slum areas (largely those with higher proportions of rooming houses) had rates of 50 percent or more. While the criteria for dilapidation employed in the late nineteenth century were undoubtedly more extreme, Woods (1902) reports only 13 percent of West End dwellings in poor condition from a late nineteenth century investigation of housing.

5. The ratings were done by the interviewers after the interview was completed. There may have been some "halo" effect due to the quality of the apartment or to the sympathetic characteristics of many of the respondents. The original checklist used by the interviewers contained five possible ratings for buildings and five equivalent ratings for dwelling units. For purposes of tabulation and analysis, these were collapsed into three categories by combining "excellent" and "good," leaving the rating "fair" intact, and combining "poor" and "very poor."

6. The ratings for the dwelling units classified as "poor" and "very poor" combine to correspond with the U.S. Census Bureau category "dilapidated."

Our figures show considerable agreement with the 1950 block statistics for the West End in the United States Census of Housing. According to this census, 20 percent of all dwelling units were dilapidated or lacked a private bath. Our figures for 1957–1958, which show that 26 percent of the dwelling units were in poor or very poor condition, present only a small discrepancy that is readily accounted for by the additional deterioration of the intervening years.

7. Prejudices about the effectiveness of lower-class residents as tenants have been widely displaced, in recent decades, from white ethnic groups to blacks who are frequently charged with destructive housing behavior. Recent data from the Boston black ghetto indicate, however, that precisely the same phenomenon that affected West End housing operates there. The quality of apartments is markedly superior to the quality of the buildings. See Fried et al, 1971.

8. The housing quality index is a summation of five housing characteristics: quality and repair of the building, quality and repair of the apartment, general appearance of the apartment and its decoration, age and quality of apartment furnishings, all interviewer ratings, and household density or number of persons per room (respondent information). Since approximately one-third of the respondents were interviewed shortly *after* they had left the West End and many of the components are based on interviewer observations, the analyses with this index use only two-thirds of the sample. An alternative index, excluding interviewer ratings, was developed which is moderately highly correlated with the primary index of housing quality ($r = .589$). Despite variations in the levels of relationships, the findings by both measures are regularly similar. Moreover, there are no striking differences between those who had moved at this time and those interviewed in their West End homes. Since the measure based on interviewer ratings, however, has greater face validity, we have based our conclusions and presentation on that index.

9. The family per capita income variable was based on total family income divided by the number of members in the household. The groupings were derived from Lampman (1959) for distinguishing people living below the minimum and those living at a marginal economic level or a comfortable level. In the light of Keyserling's (1964) and Orshansky's (1965) similar analyses, the criteria used by Lampman were relatively conservative in defining the level of poverty.

10. We shall not ordinarily report tests of significance in presenting tables but shall emphasize percentage differences which approximate statistically significant levels. Occasionally, in order to stress a particular point or to distinguish several relationships which are otherwise not as clear, we shall refer to X^2 results to aid in such discriminations. For the relationship between per capita income and housing quality, $X^2 = 32.0$, d.f. $= 4$, p $< .001$. For a fuller discussion of methodological and technical questions see the Methodological Note at the end of the volume.

11. The strength of this relationship may be exaggerated because of overlapping components: household density is one of five components in the housing quality index and is itself calculated as the number of rooms divided by the number of persons in the household. In view of the stability of this finding, however, with many different controls and its replication with individual components of the housing index (excluding household density), the overlap cannot entirely account for the association.

12. The zero-order correlation coefficients for the relationships between housing quality and marital satisfaction, severity of alcoholism, marital values, and social problems, respectively, are: .27, .25, .17, and .34. The composite index of social problems includes: per capita income, employment status of husband and wife, health, marital status, and marital satisfaction.

13. This finding is based on a stepwise, multiple regression in which the index of social problems alone accounts for 11 percent of the variance in housing quality. The first ten variables that cumulatively account for 37 percent of the variance are: social problems, number of children in the household, number of dwellings in past ten years, values regarding marriage, homeownership, ethnic derogation status, severity of alcoholism, household orientation to children, frequency of family interaction, and ego efficacy. The absence of a specific social class indicator is due to the interrelationships of social class and many of these variables, although, as is evident from controlled tables, social class remains a significant but often complex influence on housing quality. For a discussion of the procedures used in the regression analyses see the Methodological Note.

14. Reid is critical of the conclusion that there is a strong association between income and housing (Reid, 1962). Her own examination of data, however, is based on mean rentals by census tract, an index that is a statistical artifact misrepresenting the variability of rents within so large a unit as a census tract.

15. See Branch, 1942; Foote et al., 1960; Wilson, 1962.

16. Numerous studies describe the intense involvement of working-class people with their residential areas. See Bibliography sections on Poverty and Slums: The Recent Past and on Residential Patterns, Social Affiliations, Family. Observations for earlier periods can be found in Firey (1945), Hole (1866), Riis (1890), and Warner (1968). Studies of suburbs indicate that commitment is not unique for working-class people (Gans, 1967; Willmott and Young, 1960; and Wilson, 1962). The data on class differences in residential stability, although complex, indicate greater mobility with increasing occupational status and, most particularly, this holds for inter-community moves (Shryock, 1964).

17. We have introduced this new term, ethnospansive, to stress the fact that the absence of discriminatory attitudes is not merely a low level of ethnocentricity but is itself a positive orientation.

18. See Frieden (1946) for a discussion of the filtering down process. Rex

(1968) provides an excellent theoretical discussion of competition and conflict in the housing market. Persisting problems of housing for low income families are described in Schermer Associates, 1968.

19. For comparative data which reveal widespread similarities see Ash, undated; Back, 1962; Chombard de Lauwe, 1956; Jennings, 1962; Kerr, 1958; Mogey, 1956; Seeley, 1959; Suttles, 1968; Willmott, 1963; and Young and Willmott, 1957.

20. Hartman (1967) examined this issue by case analysis and determined that many instances of excessively high or low densities could be traced to the desire to remain in the West End in spite of a lack of housing to meet altered household needs such as increased or decreased household size. Three-quarters of the subsample he examined had remained in the same apartment despite the marriage and departure of children, the birth of children, or divorce and separation.

21. The measure of apartment satisfaction is a composite index based on several indicators of expressed satisfaction or dissatisfaction, and on scalings of sources of satisfaction and dissatisfaction with the apartment. The residential satisfaction measure is similarly a composite index consisting of five different expressions of general or specific feelings about and sources of satisfaction and dissatisfaction with the area.

22. The full-scale, stepwise multiple regression with apartment satisfaction as the dependent variable and excluding residential satisfaction from entering the equation (in order to determine the component influences more clearly) accounts for only 25 percent of the variance at the end of thirteen steps. In addition to the variables given above, these include: household orientation to child (partly influenced by number of children), rural-urban background, intergenerational mobility, length of West End residence, social mobility orientation, marital status, employment status scale, ego efficacy, and community shopping preferences. In view of the correlations it is evident that some of these variables enter the regression equation only because of their strength among low status people and have little real consequence for people of higher status.

23. In stressing the concordance in studies of working-class communities, we must note the absence of systematic comparative investigations of class differences. Willmott and Young, however, comparing a working-class slum and a middle-class suburb concluded that the similarity in surface involvement hid a profound difference in intensity of commitment to the neighborhood (Young and Willmott, 1957; Willmott and Young, 1960). But Rossi's study of residential moves (1955) and Caplow, Stryker, and Wallace's study in Puerto Rico (1964) suggest greater investment in the residential area among middle class than among lower class people. Rainwater (1966) stresses the fear of the neighborhood among many people living in a predominantly black, low income, public housing project.

24. For numerous reasons, the findings about people in middle and higher status positions can least readily be generalized beyond the West End.

25. Bracey (1964), Gans (1969), Kuper (1953), Wood (1959). There are

occasional fragments of evidence suggesting that, even in suburban life, or in housing developments, people oriented to stable working-class life engage more fully in local social interaction than do people from other origins (Neighborhood and Community, 1954; Vereker and Mays, 1961; Willmott and Young, 1960). On the basis of several studies in different kinds of communities, Willmott (1963) observed that, even in the spread out suburban development at Dagenham with relatively few local resources available, working-class tenants developed a neighborhood life more similar to that in a working-class slum in London than to the pattern of a middle-class suburb.

26. The stepwise multiple regression on residential satisfaction accounts for 31 percent of the variance in satisfaction through seven factors: local resource use (20 percent), apartment satisfaction, length of West End residence, social mobility orientation, severity of alcoholism, household size, and residential ethnocentricity. As with apartment satisfaction, however, the variation in determinants among people in different social class positions and the complex interactions with social class mean that a simple, stepwise regression cannot fully reveal all of the relevant determinants.

27. The variable ego efficacy, which we shall refer to frequently, is derived from the coded responses to incomplete sentences which, in turn, were factor analyzed. It refers to the ability to control or master difficulties and problems.

28. Willmott (1963) makes a similar observation. Demographic studies (Goldstein, 1955; Land, 1969; Taeuber, 1961) have indicated that the longer a person lives in a place, the less likely he is to move. Interestingly enough, this generalization does not hold as clearly for home owners as for renters (Browning and Feindt, 1969; Speare, 1970).

29. This sample was selected, interviewed, and analyzed by Dr. Joan Levin Ecklein. The sample was drawn from Police Lists for the relocation area for two successive years (1952 and 1953). Since they were interviewed in 1963, they had all been living outside the West End for ten years or more at the time of interview.

30. For a more detailed discussion and analysis of the attitudes of West Enders toward public housing see Hartman (1963, 1967). Schermer Associates (1968) indicate that similar attitudes toward current public housing in the United States are widespread.

31. A stepwise multiple regression on housing aspirations reveals that a little more than 30 percent of the total variance is accounted for by six partly overlapping variables: socioeconomic status potential (a global variable based on factor analysis emphasizing those measures like age, marital status, ethnicity, education, and other determinants of social class position), household size, social mobility orientation, marital status, ideological conservatism, and global socioeconomic status (another global variable which was a first principle component in a factor analysis and includes measures that reflect current social class position, for example, per capita income, occupation, employment status, education). A similar

stepwise regression, omitting these global and overlapping indices, reveals a similar array of individual determinants of housing aspirations and accounts for a similar proportion of the variance.

CHAPTER 5: WORKING-CLASS COMMUNITY LIFE AND SOCIAL RELATIONSHIPS

1. Festinger, Schacter, and Back (1950) were among the first to demonstrate the importance of propinquity for social relationships within a "segregated" housing development, in this case a student veterans' housing project. Similarly, several studies of suburban life provide clear images of extensive, local social interaction (Clark, 1966; Gans, 1967; Wood, 1959), and the importance of localism appears to increase along an urban-suburban gradient with social class held constant (Fava, 1958; Greer, 1956; Greer and Kube, 1959). Upper-class forms of localism are less adequately reported and appear to be more segmented and more formally organized around local clubs and resources (Baltzell, 1958; Zorbaugh, 1929).

2. Back, 1962; Cohen and Hodges, 1963; Hodges, 1970; Jackson, 1968; Jennings, 1962; McKenzie, 1923; W. Miller, 1958; Mogey, 1956; Safa, 1968; Seeley, 1959; Whyte, 1943a; Young and Willmott, 1957; Zorbaugh, 1929. To say that many studies of working-class communities have come to similar conclusions should not be taken to imply that there are not several studies that present contradictory evidence. A number of studies of middle-class, suburban communities also provide evidence of high frequencies of local preference. See especially Bracey, 1964; Festinger, Schacter, and Back, 1950; Foote et al., 1960; Gans, 1967; Greer, 1956; Greer and Kube, 1959; Willmott and Young, 1960.

3. The zero-order correlations for each of these variables with the index of residential satisfaction are, respectively, .247, .258, and .190. The meaning of ethnic embeddedness, which will be discussed subsequently, is the relationship between an individual's own ethnic identity and the relative frequency of that ethnic group living in the local area.

4. For some of the more systematic evidence see Anderson and Anderson, 1959; Axelrod, 1956; Bell and Force, 1956; Etzioni, 1964; Goode, 1966; Hausknecht, 1962; Komarovsky, 1946; Wright and Hyman, 1958; Zimmer and Hawley, 1959.

5. The data reported by Caplovitz (1963) indicate a much smaller proportion of low income consumers who used credit for small purchases. But the entire point of his analysis was to reveal the dilemmas of consumer behavior among people whose neighborhood lives had been disrupted by rebuilding and renewal. There is little doubt that the patterns we are describing depend on long-term stability in the local area both of the population as a whole and of the storekeepers themselves.

6. For a similar description of local shopping in a working-class area and its social functions see Jennings, 1962. Jennings also points out that the use of the local English pub was a particularly happy circumstance since the wives knew where they could reach their husbands when they wanted

them and the bartender kept a watchful eye on his clients. Young and Willmott (1957) also describe similar patterns.

7. A stepwise multiple regression on family use of formal facilities reveals that almost 28 percent of the variance is accounted for by length of residence alone. A set of other indices of neighborhood involvement (closeness of neighbor relations, local residence of parents, use of consumer services) and of more idiosyncratic working-class patterns (expressiveness of anger) or problems (severity of alcoholism) add up to 42 percent of the variance explained.

8. It is striking that in the stepwise regressions on discrete local behavior patterns, only the use of formal facilities shows a modest proportion of the variance explained and that largely by length of residence. By contrast, only 16 percent of the variance is explained for use of consumer services and the use of formal facilities is the single, major explanatory variable. A stepwise, multiple regression was also done with a composite measure based on several different forms of local usage as the dependent variable. For this measure, 43 percent of the variance is accounted for by four variables: area of West End known, length of residence, standard of living, and social anxiety.

9. This interpretation, which we shall document more fully as we proceed, can only be proffered in view of the large number of alternative hypotheses we could test and reject in this study. It should be emphasized that this interpretation resulted from the data analysis and was not a prior expectation. This interpretation, in turn, led to a series of hypothesis tests that, within the limits of cross-sectional data, tended to confirm it.

10. Merton (1948) initially distinguished between locals and cosmopolitans. He was not primarily concerned with class differences in local-cosmopolitan orientations, but a review of community data suggests that class and class origins are perhaps among the most significant determinants of these differences. Thus, in middle-class suburban communities with a high degree of localism, the residents show, at the same time, highly cosmopolitan orientations and behavior (Foley, 1950; Greer and Kube, 1959). It is primarily working-class locals who are exclusively local. Rossi (1970) has observed, with a similar implication, that localism and cosmopolitanism should not be regarded as the poles of a single dimension but are rather two separate dimensions.

11. There is a conventional impression that black communities differ from white ethnic working-class communities like the West End in the frequency of local interpersonal contact. For many reasons including the forced residential choices blacks have to make due to discrimination, levels of interpersonal involvement are lower, but a large proportion of blacks in Boston (42 percent) find their neighborhoods desirable mainly because of interpersonal relationships. The consequences of forced choice show up in the moderately large number who find the local population disagreeable. See Fried et al., 1971.

12. Much of the working-class community literature refers to the dominance of kinship although (a) it is evident that the specific references are

almost invariably to kin no more distant than siblings, parents, and married children, and (b) there has been little data for distinguishing the *relative* importance of kin, friends, and neighbors. For an earlier discussion of social relationships in the West End see Gleicher, 1965. For similar findings about the range of relevant kinship ties in a middle-class urban sample see Firth, Hubert, and Forge, 1970.

13. Although the large-scale migration of blacks to Boston occurred more than thirty years after the Italian migration became a trickle, similar factors obtain for blacks in Boston. For young black adults living in metropolitan Boston, 75 percent had relatives in the Boston area and 41 percent of these had relatives living in the same neighborhood in which they themselves lived. The extent of the local community cannot be directly compared for blacks in Boston and for West Enders but the similarity in proportions (57 percent in the West End; 41 percent for blacks distributed throughout metropolitan Boston) of kin living in the local area is self-evident. See Fried et al., 1971.

14. The attribution of primacy to kinship in social organization derives from anthropological investigations, particularly among nonliterate people. However, more attention has been devoted to the structure of kinship than to its influence on actual relationships in daily life. Contiguity may also be focal even in tribal societies in accounting for some of the peculiarities of so-called kinship terminology. For a reanalysis of Trobriand kinship terminology which points up difficulties entailed by Malinowski's failure to observe the importance of contiguity in his stress on kinship see Leach (1954). Pitt-Rivers (1961) uses a similar formulation in discussing the absence of major kinship links in a Spanish peasant pueblo.

15. It is fascinating that working-class people in urban areas of England and the United States show a closer similarity in this regard than do working-class and middle-class people in urban communities in England (see Willmott, 1963; Willmott and Young, 1960; and Young and Willmott, 1957).

16. Although the importance of the mother-daughter relationship in the working class has been frequently noted, Young and Willmott (1957) and Jennings (1962) have given it particular emphasis in a manner that corresponds quite closely to the manifest ties people had in the West End.

17. These studies leave a gap in our understanding since they do not clarify the closeness or intensity of these relationships in different social classes. The criterion for kinship interaction in most of the studies is so low that it allows the inclusion of quite peripheral contact. While a low level of contact reveals little difference by social class and is widespread, a more severe criterion would establish the variation or consistency in close ties. See Litwak, 1960a, 1960b; Sussman, 1953, 1959, 1963. In France, Michel (1970) found greater frequency of kin contact among professionals than among working-class people but used no controls for availability of kin although class variations in geographical mobility might account for the results.

18. The index of frequency of family interaction is a summation of the

separate measures for frequency of contact with parents, with siblings, and with married children. Since few people had both parents and married children available, the high frequency group includes those who had a great deal of contact with *either* their own parents *or* their married children and with siblings. The more comprehensive measure of kin involvement is based on this index of frequency of family interaction, a second index of interaction with and local availability of kin, plans to move near relatives, the number of kin listed among the five closest people, and the comparative sense of closeness to relatives versus friends.

19. To simplify the following discussion, attention will be devoted primarily to the controlled correlations for kin involvement (Appendix table 5.2). However, the data for kin involvement and for frequency of family interaction are so similar that we can justifiably extend the discussion to either aspect of relationships with close kin.

20. Liebow (1967) and Rainwater (1970) found sporadic and tenuous, but personally important, social interaction patterns among blacks in the lowest social status positions. Fried et al. (1971) discovered that, in a random sample of blacks in Boston, there is a curvilinear pattern with local social affiliations most important for stable, working-class people and of less importance at lower and higher statuses. Working-class areas in a middle-class suburb did not show as high a level of localism as the working-class community in East London (Willmott and Young, 1960), but Willmott (1963) found neighboring quite important on a working-class estate. Mitchell and Lupton (1954) found inexplicable differences in neighboring behavior and attitudes among three different blocks in the same working-class housing estate. Within the same buildings of a German working-class apartment house suburb Pfeil (1968) found that neighboring and desires for privacy conflict with one another but both are important. Sweetser (1942) found a high degree of low-level neighboring on a middle-class block. But Morris and Mogey (1965) claim that respectable working-class people have more widespread neighborly relations than do those in the middle class.

21. Festinger, Schacter, and Back (1950) show the effect of physical structure on social relationships with beautiful, experimental clarity. See also Caplow and Forman (1950); Kuper (1953); Merton (1948).

22. In almost every one of the separate regression equations on each variable representing different forms of local behavior, closeness of neighbor relations was a significant component. Closeness of neighbor relations was the only variable that played so omnipresent a part in accounting for diverse forms of localism.

23. For data suggesting that residents of public housing who had *both* local and nonlocal commitments were more highly satisfied with the local area than any other subgroup see Taube and Levin, 1972.

24. In the regression analyses, a little more than 30 percent of the variance in kin closeness and in frequency of family interaction is accounted for by a small number of variables. But virtually none of the other forms of localism enter these equations (except for organizational partici-

pation which accounts for only .07 percent of the variance in kin closeness). On the other hand, as we have indicated on several occasions, the use of formal facilities, the use of consumer services, the preference for communal shopping, local organizational participation, and closeness to neighbors are all strongly interwoven with one another and several of these variables enter each of the regression equations in accounting for each of these discrete forms of localism. Neither kinship closeness nor frequency of family interactions enters, within the prescribed criteria, to account for any of the above forms of local behavior.

25. Local resource use was deliberately omitted from the regression to highlight the more specific characteristics influencing community role satisfaction. However, since it bears the highest correlation with such satisfaction (r = .623), it would inevitably have entered the regression equation first with the largest proportion of the variance explained.

26. This is a matter of considerable importance since the evident curvilinear relationship accounts for two issues: (1) it clarifies the relatively low order of correlation we have ordinarily found between occupational status and community behavior which runs counter to other observations of differences associated with social class position, and (2) it provides evidence that other studies, which have found relatively high levels of localism, friendship, and kinship affiliation in middle-class subgroups and lower levels in working-class subgroups, may have failed to pick up this curvilinear relationship due to reliance on correlational techniques (and their derivatives). In tabular analysis or analysis of variance, too highly aggregated a definition of class groups would similarly obscure the curvilinearity.

CHAPTER 6: FAMILY ROLES AND RELATIONSHIPS

1. Michel (1970) observes that French working-class men participate *more* actively in household tasks than those of higher status but this is the only report of such a pattern.

2. The age-grouping in these data may obliterate some of the finer differences which show a curvilinear pattern in age at first marriage for the American population as a whole (Glick, 1957).

3. For the classical study of the companionate, middle-class family see Burgess and Locke, 1945. See also Parsons, 1949.

4. Komarovsky (1964) and Rainwater and Weinstein (1960) have made a particular point of the conflict engendered by these differences in the responsiveness to one another and in needs for affection displayed by working-class men and women. This problem may arise in different forms in the middle class as well.

5. Rainwater and Weinstein (1960) find the same contrast in conceptions of spouses between working-class men and women.

6. Materials for assessing life-cycle changes in marital values or behavior in different social classes are difficult to find. We use these data on age differences to estimate some of the changes that may take place, but they

must be viewed with some caution. It is quite reasonable to assume that people of higher status, particularly with increasing age, who differed markedly from the typical working-class population of the West End would have more readily moved out. The lack of comparative data makes it impossible to assess this.

7. The embeddedness of families among kin and neighbors in the pre-industrial community and family isolation in industrial society have both undoubtedly been overstated. The formulation by Parsons (1949, 1951; Parsons and Bales, 1955) of the functional necessity for separation of the nuclear family from kinship dependency has been challenged on the basis of data indicating that kinship ties are not so attenuated as we might have believed (Litwak, 1960a, 1960b; Sussman, 1953, 1959, 1963). The data, however, do not vitiate the basic proposition of family autonomy beyond pointing out that modest contact among parents, children, and siblings persists in modern societies (see also Firth, Hubert, and Forge, 1970). For recent discussions of this issue in comparative perspective see Hill and König, 1970.

8. We have adapted Bott's (1957) terms, segregated and joint conjugal role relations, to take account of the fact that shared participation by husband and wife in various marital role relationships may occur in several ways including separate but equal and interchangeable activities or those that are carried out together between the partners.

9. Lower status men often participate more actively in the household than they say men ought to do. Kenkel (1963) has also found little effect of ideology on family household decision-making and Hoffman (1960) found modest effects.

10. Blood and Wolfe, 1960; Heer, 1963; Komarovsky, 1964; and McKinley, 1964 have all generalized from limited indicators of husband-wife functioning to interpretations of differential power. Herbst (1954) and Strodtbeck (1958) use broader criteria but their generalizations to discussions of power remain questionable. Kenkel (1963) and Hoffman (1960) avoid some of the dangers of assuming that decision-making alone reflects power or dominance.

11. Virtually all of the studies, with the exception of Herbst (1954) report this finding: Blood and Wolfe, 1960; Bott, 1957; Komarovsky, 1963, 1964; Konig, 1957; Lang, 1946; McKinley, 1964; Mogey, 1955; Rainwater, 1965; Scheuch, 1962. Higher levels of joint marital functioning in the household and fewer class differences seem to obtain in rural than in urban areas (see Lang, 1946; Wilkening, 1958). For a fuller discussion of these differences in household functioning see Fitzgerald, 1967.

12. Data on blacks in Boston (Fried et al., 1971) reveal a very similar set of social class differences in household participation by husbands and wives. For other data on class differences in household roles see Blood and Wolfe (1960), Komarovsky (1963, 1964), Rainwater and Weinstein (1960).

13. Relevant data or observations on this point can be found in several studies: Arensberg and Kimball, 1948; Blood and Wolfe, 1960; Fitzgerald,

1967; Hoggart, 1957; Kerr, 1958; Komarovsky, 1961; Neugarten, 1956; Townsend, 1957; Wolgast, 1958; Yang, 1945; Young and Willmott, 1957.

14. There is a marked difference in the X^2 at each age level: for those twenty to thirty-four, $X^2 = 18.2$, $P < .01$; for thirty-five to forty-nine, $X^2 = 8.4$, $P < .05$; for those fifty and over, $X^2 = 2.1$ (N.S.).

15. The total variance explained, excluding other marital role relationships from a stepwise multiple regression, is only 18 percent for the household functional role relationship. On the other hand, the intercorrelations among different marital role relationships along the dimension of segregation-sharing are very considerable, ranging between .179 for conflict resolution patterns and household role relationship to .450 for the correlation between the sociability and companionship role relationships. Clearly we can speak of a general dimension of segregation-sharing to which we shall return in subsequent discussion.

16. For studies of family roles in response to crises see Angell, 1936; Bakke, 1940; Hill, 1949, 1958; Komarovsky, 1940.

17. Most of this evidence concerning household role allocation, other than the frequency of family interaction, negates Bott's hypothesis of the link between closeknit networks and segregated marital role relationships. However, there is supporting data for this hypothesis in a different form, as we shall see in considering marital satisfaction.

18. Blum and Rossi (1968) summarize many of the child-rearing studies of class differences. The major investigations of class differences in child-rearing are Davis and Havighurst (1946), Littman et al, (1957). Sears, Maccoby, and Levin (1957), and White (1957). Several other studies, however, provide additional information about different classes or parent-child relationships in the working class: Aronfreed (1968), Bronfenbrenner (1959), Jackson and Marsden (1966), Malone et al. (1967), Minuchin et al. (1967), McKinley (1964), Miller and Swanson (1958), Rainwater (1970), Redl and Wineman (1951), Riessman (1962), Spinley (1953), Willmott (1969). The work of Kohn and his collaborators on class differences in child-rearing values is also germane: Kohn, 1959, 1963, 1969; Kohn and Carroll, 1960; Pearlin and Kohn, 1966. The West End data on child-rearing orientations are drawn from the postrelocation interviews since these questions had to be omitted from the prerelocation interviews due to the length of the schedule. There are also systematic and unsystematic observations, but this was not a central area of inquiry in the West End.

19. If we consider only the measure of authoritarian child-rearing orientations and its correlations with age for men and women of different social class status, we find a pattern consistent with the relationships for other variables. The correlations between age and child-rearing authoritarianism for women, going from moderately high to very low social class status are: .47, −.07, .03; for men: .24, .01, −.09.

20. In the precarious situation of interviewing in a crisis and in a community in which many husbands were reluctant to allow their wives to be interviewed, we decided that wisdom rather than valor was demanded and did not include direct questions about sex.

21. See particularly Bell, 1966; Kinsey et al., 1948; Kinsey et al., 1953; Komarovsky, 1964; Rainwater, 1968; Rainwater and Weinstein, 1960; Whyte, 1943.

22. Pineo (1961) studied a narrower age range and found only the diminution in joint sociability with age or age of children. For comparable ages, these findings are similar to Pineo's.

23. We are considering only the health of the women in this analysis, but the data reveal that the health of the husband had equivalent effects.

24. We were initially taken with Bott's (1957) hypothesis that segregated marital role relationships are associated with extensive closeknit network ties. While segregation in each marital role relationship is linked to social class differences, segregation in conjugal roles is minimally associated with any form of closeknit network pattern except for occasional manifestations of such an association in the lowest status group.

25. The zero-order correlation between the sociable role relationship in marriage and the companionship role relationship in marriage is .450. Blood and Wolfe (1960) also emphasize the importance of joint sociability and this is implicit or explicit in many of the studies of middle-class marital life.

26. Little more of the sociable role relationship in marriage is accounted for by the stepwise multiple regression on that variable than with the household role relationship. Altogether 24 percent of the variance was explained by ten variables including many of those we have discussed. The most important of these, on the basis of the proportion of variance explained, are: severity of alcoholism (wife or husband), per capita income, expressiveness of anger, household role relationship, health status, kinship involvement, employment status of husband and wife, housing quality, social class status, and self-evaluation as wife.

27. See Burgess and Locke (1945). For excellent descriptive materials on class differences in companionship, within a narrow range of social class, see Komarovsky (1964) and Rainwater and Weinstein (1960).

28. The distinction often made between expressive and instrumental roles in structural-functional analysis (Parsons and Bales, 1955) and given particular emphasis in the analysis of the family by Zelditch (1955) confounds social functions and psychological transactions. All role relationships include and virtually require for effective performance both instrumental and expressive components. But roles and role relationships lose all meaning unless they are conceptualized primarily in instrumental terms. Greater attention to role relationships, as dynamic components of social behavior, rather than to roles, as the structural base of role relationships allows for the clarification of expressive components in characterizing instrumentally-oriented interaction patterns.

29. We must again recall that there is the possibility that higher status people who maintained companionship roles in marriage into later phases of the life cycle gradually moved out of the West End. Alternatively, the sense of relative economic or social deprivation that led to continued residence in a working-class area beyond youth may have entailed imped-

iments to marital companionship for people who wanted to live in a higher status neighborhood.

30. Some small proportion of the families at the lowest class level may represent what Minuchin et al. (1967) refer to as *enmeshment*, the close intertwining of familial roles and relationships for purposes of security that results in a loss of role differentiation to the point of ineffectiveness. A similar phenomenon is referred to by Zilbach (1968) involving a complete redefinition of the roles of various household members which may free husband and wife for a companionate relationship since they no longer treat one another as spouses in other respects.

31. Nye (1963) finds that the employment of the wife makes less difference in marital adjustment among higher than among lower status families, a result that is concordant with these data although it deals with somewhat different variables. For analyses of wife's employment on other aspects of marriage see Blood, 1963; Blood and Hamblin, 1958; Blood and Wolfe, 1960; Heer, 1958; Hoffman, 1963; Nye, 1963.

32. These observations are based on several different stepwise multiple regression analyses with marital companionship as the dependent variable. If we exclude some of the highly intercorrelated marital relationship variables, we account for 21 percent of the variance in marital companionship. When we include these as well as other variables, 34 percent of the variance in marital companionship is explained.

33. As with other marital roles, we find these data contradict the hypothesis that segregated marital roles are associated with closeknit network relationships (Bott, 1957).

34. See Goode (1959) for the different ways in which different societies structure the love relationship.

35. Apart from Komarovsky's (1964) study of working-class marriage and Rainwater's work dealing with several aspects of working-class family life (Rainwater, 1968; Rainwater, 1970; Rainwater, Coleman, and Handel, 1959; Rainwater and Weinstein, 1960), there are few studies that deal explicitly with marital satisfaction in working-class families. McKinley (1964) concerns himself primarily with parent-child relationships in different social classes. Minuchin et al. (1967) and Malone et al. (1967) focus mainly on problem families. Several other studies (Blood and Wolfe, 1960; Cohen and Hodges, 1963; Drake and Cayton, 1945; Gans, 1962; Goode, 1962; Gurin et al., 1960; Liebow, 1967; Miller, 1964; Roth and Peck, 1951) present useful information concerning white or black working-class families or class differences in aspects of family life.

36. Social class differences for self-evaluations of marital satisfaction were greater than those to be found with a composite index based on self-evaluations supplemented by ratings of more descriptive responses about the marital relationship. The two other questions providing these descriptive data were: "What are the nicest features of your marriage?" and "What are the worst features of your marriage?" Since we would anticipate that biased ratings would be more distorting for lower than for higher status respondents, the source of this difference remains unclear. It may well be

that higher status respondents overstated their marital satisfication or that lower status respondents understated it.

37. Although there are data on marital satisfaction for both male and female respondents, the data from the women is more complete. Thus, most of the analysis presented refers to female respondents. The similarities in relationships that could be compared, however, and the high correlation between marital satisfaction of husbands and wives suggests that these findings generally apply to the men as well.

38. If we include marital companionship in the regression on marital satisfaction, it alone accounts for 46 percent of the variance explained and the total variance explained rises to 60 percent. But even if we exclude this because of the possibility of some contamination between these indices, we explain 43 percent of the variance; and the first five variables that enter the stepwise multiple regression are all intrafamilial factors: marital sociability, conflict resolution patterns, household size, level of conflict between husband and wife, and household role relationship. These five variables explain 38 percent of the variance.

39. It is important to note here, particularly in view of the variables involved, that selective factors in continued residence in the West End among people of higher status may account for these empirical relationships among the high status subgroup.

40. We have already referred to some of the data on crisis that suggests marked alterations resulting from such long-term stress, although, at the same time, it indicates that effective family functioning can be a bulwark against such effects. Zilbach (1971) adds another dimension in discussing the ways in which some chronic problem families virtually live from crisis to crisis and, at times, maintain their integrity around these crises. In a different work, Zilbach (1968) presents a developmental family framework that clarifies the changes that may be introduced by new family issues for which a prior set of family arrangements may not be adaptive

41. For discussions of marital relationships among black families, particularly in lower social class positions see Billingsley, 1968; Fried et al., 1971; Liebow, 1967; and Rainwater, 1968, 1970. Our knowledge about black families, especially those in stable working-class or middle-class positions, however, remains distressingly meager.

42. See Fried et al., 1971; Rainwater, 1968. While many of the component indices differ, the findings based on tabular analysis and regression analysis of the determinants of life satisfaction are quite similar in the West End and in a black population in Boston (Fried et al., 1971).

CHAPTER 7: WORK EXPERIENCES AND WORK ORIENTATION

1. This measure is derived directly from Lampman's calculations (1959). Since our data were precoded in ranges of twenty-five dollars, these figures lose some precision. According to subsequent analyses (Keyserling, 1962; Keyserling, 1964; Orshansky, 1965), Lampman's estimates were viewed as conservative. Moreover, the West End figures exclude people over sixty-

five years of age for whom the rates are highest in national calculations. Thus, the rates of poverty in the West End were higher than is indicated by these data.

2. The national unemployment rate for married men for the period 1958-1959, comparable to the prerelocation West End rate, was 5.1 percent. Since we did not use a strict labor force definition, our figures may overestimate or underestimate unemployment but could do so, at best, by a slight amount. Indeed, even with a narrower definition of unemployment that is possible with the postrelocation data (9.9 percent), the figures are substantially above the national average, which was 4.6 percent for married men in 1961 when most of the interviews were done.

3. Fully 25 percent of the variance in education was accounted for by parental socioeconomic status alone in a stepwise multiple regression. With the addition of age and several other variables, the explained variance reached 40 percent.

4. These results conform with those of other studies of occupational mobility, although there are variations in precise quantitative conclusions. In this instance, 28 percent of the variance in male occupational status was accounted for by parental social class status.

5. It is unlikely that the low rate of occupational achievement among the Italians was merely a consequence of selective out-migration since Italians were the dominant ethnic group and represented a wider distribution of statuses than any other ethnic group. Other evidence, moreover, supports the delay in achieving parity with the occupational status of the American population among Italians in this country (Blau and Duncan, 1967; Lieberson, 1963).

6. Almost certainly occupational aspirations are both cause and effect. In a recent study of blacks, in which early childhood aspirations were distinguished from current aspirations, these were highly intercorrelated and childhood aspirations had considerable influence on adult educational and occupational achievement (Fried et al., 1971). It is reasonable to make the assumption that a similar phenomenon operated in the West End, although we do not have the date to verify it. Presumably, childhood aspirations influence both adult aspirations and adult achievements but, in turn, adult achievements have some subsequent influence on further aspirations.

7. Goldthorpe et al. (1969) point out that this was one of the areas in which the "affluent workers" they studied were explicitly encouraged to move up by management but that, in view of the meager opportunities and the meager payoff for greater investment, few were interested in taking advantage of the possibility of becoming foremen.

8. The stepwise regression on prerelocation (1958) per capita income reveals that eight variables cumulatively explain only 9 percent of the variance. These include education, employment stability, psychological orientations, and parental relationships. However, in view of the very different patterns of poverty associated with differences in marital status and life-cycle position, the stepwise regression is not an adequate procedure

for locating the determinants of poverty without the use of dummy variables. For a fuller analysis of poverty and unemployment in the West End, see the volume *Deprivation and Conflict in Working-Class Life* (Fried, in preparation). Data on blacks in Boston give only somewhat greater importance to stable, structural factors and similarly reveal that incomes and employment status are more effectively accounted for by situational forces beyond the control of the individual (Fried et al., 1971).

9. There is a substantial shift into and out of poverty annually in the nation as a whole even given relatively stable economic conditions (Levitan, 1966).

10. For a discussion of the reorganization of work in modern industry see Friedmann, 1961. An analysis of the ways in which a number of different industries have organized both automated and nonautomated labor and the personal consequences of these organizational patterns is given by Blauner, 1964. The psychological justification for a new conception of labor involving greater decision-making power has been a major theme in the work of numerous psychologists and sociologists of industrial organization (Argyris, 1962; Jaques, 1951; Katz and Kahn, 1966; Schein and Bennis, 1965; Trist and Bamforth, 1951; Walker and Guest, 1952).

11. For studies of patterns and problems in work roles see Barnard, 1938; Form and Geschwender, 1962; Goldthorpe et al., 1969; Bendix, 1956; Blau, 1954, 1955; Bradney, 1957; Chinoy, 1955; Coser, 1958; Homans, 1950; Merton, 1957; Moore and Feldman, 1960; Worthy, 1950.

12. For efforts to understand the problem of morale as an organizational issue see Mayo, 1946, and Roethlisberger and Dickson, 1939. But these influential studies never approached the conception of total reorganization of work rules and industrial processes that more recent investigations have done (see note 10). See also Homans, 1950, 1958; and Whyte, 1946.

13. A sign of change and, nonetheless, an indication of the importance of routinization for maintaining the interchangeability of laborers is evident in a special news release entitled "Young Workers Disrupt Key G.M. Plant": "Production on the world's fastest assembly line . . . has been seriously disrupted by mostly young workers who say they are being asked to work too hard and too fast to be able to turn out quality automobiles . . . The struggle has raised a wider issue of how management can deal with a young worker who is determined to have a say as to how a job should be performed and is not so easily moved by management threats that there are plenty of others waiting in line if he does not want to do the job" (*New York Times*, January 23, 1972, p. 1).

14. Kornhauser (1965) found little difference by occupational status in concern over job security. Apart from the differences in the indices, security in the Detroit factories seems to have been more homogeneous for all occupational statuses. Duffy (1960) found security to be the single most important criterion of job satisfaction among highly skilled Australian workers.

15. There is some disagreement in the literature concerning class differences in job satisfaction. Lafitte (1958) and Wilensky (1966) found

few differences in job satisfaction associated with differences in occupational status while Inkeles (1960) and Kornhauser (1965) found distinct decreases in satisfaction as a function of lower occupational positions. See also Friedmann and Havighurst, 1954.

16. Gurin et al. (1960) emphasize this distinction between ego satisfactions and extrinsic satisfactions as a major discriminating factor at different occupational status levels. Morse and Weiss (1955), Kornhauser (1965), and Duffy (1960) have observed similar differences associated with occupational position. See also Kahn et al., 1964; Seeman, 1967.

17. Blauner (1964) and Walker and Guest (1952) have observed that, particularly in the routinization of the assembly line but more widely in working-class jobs, men will occasionally disrupt a routine simply in order to be able to deal with the challenge of broken equipment or some other task dilemma that requires more innovation than their usual tasks.

18. For a view of the functions of executive roles and of the personalities of people in executive positions see Barnard, 1938; Henry, 1949; Stryker, 1960; Warner and Abegglen, 1955. There have been remarkably few similar studies of professionals from the vantage point of personal investments and rewards.

19. It would be difficult to generalize mobility findings from a working-class slum to the population as a whole. However, these rates are remarkably similar to those for the United States given by Lipset and Bendix (1959) and by S. M. Miller (1960).

20. See Dornbusch and Heer, 1957; Goode, 1962; Hoffman, 1961; Jephcott, Seear, and Smith, 1962; Komarovsky, 1964; Myrdal and Klein, 1956; Rossi, 1964; Sobol, 1963; Stoltz, 1960; Thompson and Finlayson, 1963; Weiss and Samelson, 1958.

21. For a more detailed analysis of employment among women in the West End see Nary, 1965.

22. The stepwise regression on education reveals that 41 percent of the variance in education is explained by only four variables: parental socioeconomic status (20 percent), age (14 percent), assimilation status (4 percent), and ego efficacy (3 percent). Similarly, with occupation as the dependent variable, education alone explains 25 percent of the variance, and parental socioeconomic status, the second strongest independent variable, accounts for an additional 3 percent of the variance.

CHAPTER 8: SOURCES OF WORKING-CLASS ATTITUDES AND VALUES

1. E. G. Wilson and Banfield (1964) represent the first view; Form and Rytina (1969) represent the latter.

2. While views about the political authoritarianism of blue-collar workers have been widely discussed, Lipset (1960) provided one of the more substantial formulations of this proposition. Form and Rytina (1969), Lipsitz (1965), and Miller and Riessman (1968) have rejected this view. Williams (1964) points up variations in ethnic attitudes of people in

different social classes depending on the group that is perceived as a threat in a given place or at a specific time.

3. Wilensky (1966) and Wrong (1961) have stressed the demise of the working class mainly on the grounds of the lack of working-class self-consciousness. Goldthorpe et al. (1968, 1969) and Leggett (1968) have presented evidence opposed to this view, supporting the earlier views of Centers (1949). A recent volume of studies (Levitan, 1971) itself reveals the many contrasting views about working-class attitudes.

4. See Pettigrew (1964) and the two issues of *Daedalus* (Fall and Winter 1965) entitled "The Negro American."

5. The original materials gave sparse attention to attitudinal data. Thus there are important gaps in depicting ethnic, religious, or political attitudes in the West End, although we have used a variety of responses to recapture many of these in indices and indicators.

6. The zero-order correlation between ethnic involvement and assimilation status is .537.

7. There are distinct differences between more recent immigrants, who arrived after many eastern and southern European countries had achieved major advances in industrialization and in education, and earlier immigrants from the same countries of origin. For this reason, in particular, findings on ethnic groups from more recent data (for example, Blau and Duncan, 1967) cannot be generalized to account for occupational status and mobility among former immigrant populations in the United States.

8. Hyman, 1942; Hyman and Singer, 1968; Merton and Rossi, 1957; Newcomb, 1957; Stouffer et al., 1949.

9. Religious commitment is an index of the level of involvement with religion consisting of a summation of two component items: frequency of church attendance and subjective importance of religion.

10. One difference between ethnic involvement and religious commitment was that people who had a high degree of religious commitment showed a higher level of role satisfaction in major interpersonal and social relationships regardless of social class position, an association that did not hold for ethnic involvement.

11. One of the earlier comprehensive considerations of prejudice was Allport's (1954) investigation of the nature of discriminatory processes. Adorno and his collaborators (1950) linked prejudice to a vast range of orientations and beliefs of "the authoritarian personality." See also Bartlett, 1932; Kelman, 1958, 1961; Rokeach, 1960, 1968; Stember, 1961; Tajfel, 1969; and Williams, 1964.

12. The zero-order correlation between ethnic involvement and residential ethnocentricity (feelings about ethnic similarities and ethnic differences in residential areas) is .405. Although we do not have a measure of ethnic involvement for the West End men and have only their postrelocation residential ethnocentricity, the zero-order correlation between wife's level of ethnic involvement and husband's residential ethnocentricity was even higher (r = .451).

13. Few studies of ethnic communities provide comparative data.

McConnel (1942) points out that in New Haven ethnic fragmentations in working-class, multiethnic communities were minimal and Warner and Srole (1945) imply a merging of ethnic diversities into a common multiethnic working-class subculture. Suttles (1968) emphasizes ethnic conflict, but most of his examples of conflict deal with blacks who were recently inmigrant into the community (the relative importance of blackness, recency, or tenancy in public housing is unspecified); he notes, however, the tendency of Italian and Mexican-American teenagers to form overlapping clusters. Whether more or less tolerant than other ethnically diverse communities, it is evident that the West End was hardly unique in its ethnospansiveness.

14. The importance of economic threat and of marginal positions has often been discussed in dealing with high levels of prejudice. Horton and Thompson (1962) present an excellent analysis of the effects of powerlessness on a diffuse feeling of threat that is easily converted into (displaced) prejudices.

15. Most people in working-class positions in the West End would undoubtedly fall into what some have called the "traditional" working class. But studies that have been done, both in England and in the United States in very recent years as well as in previous decades, document the observation that most working-class people, including the new "affluent workers," define themselves as working class or by some other term that is virtually synonymous with this (Centers, 1949; Goldthorpe et al., 1968; Kornhauser, 1965; Leggett, 1968; MacKinnon and Centers, 1956; Runciman, 1966; Willmott, 1963).

16. Many analyses of political involvement have indicated lower levels of sophistication among lower status people and less awareness of the issues that directly affect their lives. Several analyses (Centers, 1949; Form and Rytina, 1969; Goldthorpe et al., 1968, 1969; and Leggett, 1968) provide evidence that while working-class people tend to be relatively inert as a political force for many reasons, their views more realistically appraise the situation than is often recognized.

17. These items are based on Srole's anomie scale (Srole, 1956).

18. Kohn, 1969; Williams, 1964; Kirscht and Dillehay, 1967; Rokeach, 1960, 1968.

19. Aronfreed, 1961, 1968; Davis and Havighurst, 1946; White, 1957; Kohn, 1963; Littman et al., 1957; McKinley, 1964; Sears, Maccoby, and Levin, 1957.

20. Social conformity is a composite index based on three items: a preference for security or innovation, the importance of propriety in a situation of husband-wife conflict, and the willingness to accede to group pressure in a strike that an individual does not support.

21. See especially the work of Kohn (Kohn 1959, 1963, 1969; Kohn and Carroll, 1960; Pearlin and Kohn, 1966).

22. For a useful review of the large literature on authoritarianism see Kirscht and Dillehay (1967). Christie and Jahoda (1954) provide an early and extensive volume of criticism. Photiadis and Biggar (1962) present

evidence suggesting the spurious nature of extensive intercorrelations among attitudes in the realm of authoritarianism.

23. Less extreme than the very small proportion of workers who ordinarily support radical right leaders but theoretically and practically more important is working-class support for stable, conservative parties. In the United States, there appears to be a larger working-class vote for conservative presidential candidates than one would predict from prior surveys of political party support. A study of working-class conservatism in England (McKenzie and Silver, 1968) indicates that the practical positions of working-class conservatives are deviant from the mass of working men who support Labour, but their underlying views are similar to those who vote for the Labour Party.

CHAPTER 9: PERSONALITY AND SOCIAL BEHAVIOR IN WORKING-CLASS LIFE

1. Bendix, 1952; Erikson, 1946; Freud, 1930; Fried, 1970; Fromm, 1941; Gouldner and Petersen, 1962; Henry and Short, 1954; Inkeles, 1959, 1963; Inkeles and Levinson, 1954; McClelland, 1961; Parsons, 1951; Riesman et al., 1950; Sarbin, 1968.

2. On the profound personal importance of sociability see Cohen and Hodges, 1963; Gans, 1962; Hoggart, 1957; Miller, 1958; Minuchin et al. (1967); Rainwater, 1966; Whyte, 1943; and Young and Willmott, 1957. The significance of conformity has been more systematically studied by Kohn and others (Hess, 1970; Kerr, 1958; Kohn, 1959, 1963, 1969; Kohn and Carroll, 1960; Pearlin and Kohn, 1966). The opposite end of the social class scale has also been discussed in a number of studies on the importance of independence among higher status people, particularly those in decision-making positions (Abegglen, 1958; Barnard, 1938; Henry, 1949; Stryker, 1960; Warner and Abegglen, 1955).

3. Since the data on personality for the West End sample are more adequate for the women than for the men, most of the analyses will be based on information about women. Comparisons with the men have been made, and the patterns of relationship are generally quite similar. Most of the analyses are based on incomplete sentences, frequently in the form of composite indices of personality based on factor analyses of coded responses.

4. Miller and Riessman (1961) have discussed the central importance of stability and security in working-class life. Liebow (1967), Minuchin et al. (1967), Rainwater (1966), and Redl and Wineman (1951) have shown how the conditions that make stability and security impossible for working-class people, particularly those in the lowest status positions, often lead to alternative choices of excitement, expressive life styles, and the rejection of potential sources of security as unreliable. Miller (1958) has also described the importance of excitement in lower-class life but regards it as a primary cultural characteristic.

5. Aronfreed, 1961, 1968; Davis and Havighurst, 1946; Hess, 1970; Katz, 1970; Kohn, 1969; McKinley, 1964; Sears, Maccoby, and Levin, 1957.

6. A lowered sense of self-esteem among children and adults of low status has been reported in a number of studies: Allen, 1970; Bieri and Lobeck, 1961; Coleman et al., 1966; Douvan and Adelson, 1958; Haggstrom, 1964; Katz, 1970; Kerr, 1958; Rainwater, Coleman, and Handel, 1959.

7. In the classical, psychoanalytic model, depressive character structure reflects the inadequate internalization of rewarding (and loved) objects and arises as clinical depression when external sources of support are withdrawn. The adequate internalization of loving and loved objects, on the other hand, is the basic condition for self-esteem.

8. See Blau (1956) for a discussion of social mobility and interpersonal difficulties. For similar materials concerning status consistency see Jackson, 1962; Jackson and Burke, 1965; Levin, 1963. However, particularly in view of the relationships between interpersonal dependency and attributes of localism among women of high status (see below), there are undoubtedly selective factors of residence that led to high interpersonal dependency among women who had been upwardly mobile and wanted to live in the West End.

9. We have already described the index of social anxiety and its components. Although we have called this personality trait social anxiety to indicate its multidimensional character, the anxiety components are not limited to social interaction. Social anxiety-relaxation implies more general differences in free-floating anxiety as opposed to relatively relaxed confrontation in impersonal situations as well as in interpersonal relationships.

10. The index involved, interpersonal isolation-integration, is based on a large number of indicators of local and nonlocal social relationships. Thus, it includes data based on neighbors and kin and local friends as well as information about other friendships and social interaction outside the West End.

11. The health status index combines a summary of twelve items in a medical systems review of physical symptoms and severity and coded data on the severity of recent illnesses. The psychoneurotic index is based on a factor-analyzed set of familiar, psychomotor symptoms (originally from the Cornell Medical Index) with a factor pattern almost identical to that obtained by Gurin et al. (1960) and suggested, on other grounds, by Crandell and Dohrenwend (1967). The social problems index is a combination of subindices concerning difficulties in finances, employment, marriage, and discrepancy between health status and medical contact. For a more detailed discussion and analysis of these indices see *Deprivation and Pathology in Working-Class Life* (Fried, in process).

12. We have frequently raised the question of the degree to which the class differences we find might be distortions due to selective in-migration or selective out-migration. The fact that these personality findings correspond so well with other studies of randomly sampled populations gives particular strength to generalizations to wider populations. While the low levels of ego efficacy among low status people might be affected by selective out-migration, the high levels of ego efficacy among the high

status people are hardly what one would expect from selective in-migration.

13. The index of ego efficacy itself is composed of five different sub-indices, each derived from sentence completion responses and the composite produced by a varimax rotation of a factor matrix. The five subindices are: blame orientation, mastery, depression-optimism, affect intensity, stereotypy. For the men, similar components were not available, but an equivalent index of ego control based on indicators of competitiveness, determination, sense of achievement, and importance of success provides a basis for the analysis of ego strengths.

CHAPTER 10: WORKING-CLASS LIFE AND THE STRUCTURE OF SOCIAL CLASS

1. These views have initially been developed to account for the patterns among the lowest status populations and some of the theoretical difficulties stem from this limited focus. For the culturalist position, see Lewis, 1959, 1961, 1966; and W. Miller, 1958. For the environmentalist position, see Harrington, 1962, 1964; and Schorr, 1963, 1964, 1966.

2. It is patently evident, of course, that public opinion does not so readily grant either the societal causation of deprivation or the social responsibility for its amelioration. For a fuller discussion of some of the problems and difficulties that are particularly disruptive among low status populations see *Deprivation and Pathology in Working-Class Life* (Fried, in preparation).

3. For some of the extensive literature on inequalities in industrial societies, see Bibliography section on Structure and Dynamics of Social Class Systems.

4. See particularly Barber, 1957; K. Davis, 1942, 1953; Davis and Moore, 1945; Parsons, 1940, 1953.

5. Sjoberg, 1951; Wrong, 1959.

6. Wilensky, 1966; Wrong, 1961.

7. Although distinctions of ranks and statuses have been described throughout history, the term "class" itself came into use only during the late eighteenth century (Ossowski, 1963; Williams, 1960). The extensive use of the term by Marx and Engels cast subsequent analysis of social class phenomena into a framework they had defined (see Trevor-Roper, 1957).

8. The careful differentiation of classes is elaborated in Engels (1874) and is the basis for analysis by Marx (1852) in contrast to the class formulations devoted to purely revolutionary objectives in Marx and Engels (1848). For discussions of class consciousness, see Bendix and Lipset, 1966; Bottomore, 1966; Marx and Engels, 1846; and Ossowski, 1963.

9. Engels referred to the polarization of classes quite early (1845) and it recurs repeatedly in his writing (1877), in the work of Marx (1852, 1875), and in their joint works (1846, 1848). Aron (1966) criticizes their exclusive derivation of political power from economic forces and Keller (1963) elaborates this point. Dahrendorf (1957) discusses the range of

Marx-Engels propositions and modifies some of their variables for class analysis.

10. Such exaggerated contrasts are evident in the work of T. H. Marshall (1963). Despite many insights about stratification, his historical analyses are misleading. He overlooks the flexibility in legal definitions of the Middle Ages and the vast changes in legal status that occurred. He fails to note the economic and occupational distinctions that modified the legal categories of feudal societies. For the modern period, his analysis of citizenship as equalization is overstated since, in a functional sense, the prerogatives of citizenship are hierarchically ranked and differentially allocated depending on other social class attributes and do not simply represent a new and equivalent status for all.

11. There are only a small number of comparative studies of social class or mobility and these indicate that, despite numerous differences in precise measures, the similarities are impressive: Lipset and Bendix, 1959; S. M. Miller, 1960; Soarès, 1966. To these can be added the more discrete studies revealing many fundamental similarities in class structure and mobility: Blau and Duncan, 1967; Broom et al., 1968; Furstenberg, 1968; Glass, 1954; Mayer, 1964; Svalastoga, 1959; Wesolowski and Slomczynski, 1968. For further comparative studies, see the Bibliography section on Structure and Dynamics of Social Class Systems.

12. These categories or dimensions derive from Weber's analysis of social stratification (Gerth and Mills, 1946; Weber, 1947). In recent years, Weber's categories have been invoked with increasing frequency as the complexity and interaction of hierarchies has become more evident in modern societies. See particularly S. M. Miller, 1966, and Runciman, 1966.

13. Parson's (1966) theoretical analysis of the concept of power provides a valuable basis for the analysis of the legal-political dimension of stratification in parallel with the economic-occupational dimension.

14. Polanyi (1944) argues cogently the view that only with the industrial revolution did a society develop in which economic considerations triumphed over all other factors in decisions about the organization of society. But there are preliterate, preindustrial, and industrial societies in which economic (and/or occupational) factors have decisive significance. Moreover, noneconomic variables also have great importance in industrial societies. See Dunne, 1964; Lipset and Bendix, 1959; Marshall, 1963b; Morgan et al., 1962; Ossowski, 1963.

15. B. Moore (1966) points out that the political organization of industrial societies has been quite various and bears the stamp of the forms of transition from preindustrial societies. The same may be said for the interrelationships of legal-political, economic-occupational, and social-psychological dimensions of stratification. Extreme contrasts are provided by the early development of an economic-occupational patriciate in Holland and Italy, the convergence and interchange between political and economic control in England, and the monolithic control of all forms of social position by the Junker aristocracy of Prussia.

16. For a parallel view of the significance of psychological factors see

S. M. Miller and Riessman, 1968. See also Eisenstadt (1968) and Shils (1968).

17. The major contribution to this understanding resulted from the work of W. Lloyd Warner and his colleagues (see especially Warner and Lunt, 1942; Warner, Meeker, Eells, 1949; and Warner and Srole, 1945). Although they referred to their primary variable as social class, the central reference was social acceptance, and, thus, is comparable to what is more often conceived as the dimension of prestige or social status. Lynd and Lynd (1929, 1937) had already remarked on the importance of status distinctions in local communities and subsequent work on "typical" American communities further confirmed the observations of the Warner group.

18. An interesting variant sometimes occurs when a low status minority gains control of a sphere of opportunities or rewards like public service occupations (police, firemen, streetcleaners) or of gambling, prostitution, or drugs. The monopoly of these rewards helps to raise the economic level of many members of that minority, but since the activity is generally limited or derogated, it also serves to reinforce discrimination and impediments to further mobility. This paradox comes close to an ethnic mobility trap in which the few available avenues of achievement may create more severe long-run limitations (Wiley, 1967).

19. Much attention has been devoted to the problem of oligarchic elitist trends in American government at national (Domhoff, 1967; Mills, 1956) and local (Agger, Goldrich, and Swanson, 1964; Crain and Rossi, 1968; Hunter, 1953; Presthus, 1964) levels. A diversity of elites is some assurance of continued competition which, in turn, provides guarantees against monolithic amalgamations of power (Clark, 1968; Dahl, 1961; Kornhauser, 1966). Nonetheless, free competition and free enterprise are threatened and limited by the economic and political advantages of congealed and amalgamated power and control and our society has discovered no mechanism for dealing with this problem other than legislation that is necessarily weak in order to avoid serious interference with reasonable forms of enterprise.

20. Goldthorpe, 1964; H. Miller, 1966; Kolko, 1962; Titmuss, 1962. For a contrasting view see Spengler, 1953.

21. Since the top income category is $15,000 and over, it has no known upper limit and can only be represented by an approximate peaking over several income categories. This representation, however, is almost certainly conservative and understates the income categories covered by the top incomes.

22. See Bancroft, 1958, and Perrella, 1968. The proportions are highest in the range of husbands' incomes from approximately $4,000 to $7,000 per year, swelling the total family incomes in the middle and upper middle parts of the distribution.

23. The most thorough and complete analysis of this problem is presented by H. Miller (1966), although the problem has been quite extensively studied by economists. Kolko (1962) argues that no substantial changes have taken place in income distribution in the United States since

1910. While his position has been attacked as inadequately founded, his arguments have not been demonstrably disproved. Thus, we must at least give this view the credence of a reasonable if unsubstantiated analysis.

24. All of the loss, represented by the drop in shares of the national income from 54 to 43 percent, shown for the top 20 percent were actually sustained only by the top 5 percent and the remaining 15 percent of this top quintile actually had the largest rise in shares of the national income of any segment of the income distribution. We should also observe that the 1929 figures for the two lowest quintiles in 1929 are "assumed" since all we know is that the total of the two lowest quintiles is 13 percent (H. Miller, 1966). If it were the case that the lowest quintile had received 5 percent of the national income in 1929, an entirely plausible assumption, the degree of stability in the lowest income segment would be even more striking. Haley (1971), using the same data but calculating Gini ratios concludes that there has been some equalization of incomes. Quite apart from the very small differences in Gini ratios for different years during this period, the apparent equalization is produced by the large drop in income shares of the top 5 percent.

25. Kahl's attempt to tease apart some of the differences in effect of different components of mobility opportunities presents the logic of such analyses (Kahl, 1957).

26. A number of studies of social class and mobility also consider immigration or in-migration to cities as a determinant of mobility for natives. That is, the influx of low status migrants is seen as a force which pushes low status natives into higher positions since the lower positions can now be occupied by lower status migrants (Blau and Duncan, 1967; Kahl, 1957). In principle, this is conceivable if it leads to economic expansion and technological change producing more jobs at higher levels which can be filled by natives. In practice, however, immigration usually results from prior economic expansion and the immigrant most often fills those jobs already being vacated by natives who are moving into higher occupational positions.

27. Lipset and Bendix (1959) stress the similarities among industrial nations and S. M. Miller (1960) emphasizes the variations within a larger context of very gross similarity. It is difficult to assess these slightly divergent views. However, the similarities among industrial nations in mobility rates from manual to nonmanual occupations seem greater than Miller's conclusion implies. His tables indicate that approximately three-quarters of the reports give upward mobility rates within the narrow range of 20 to 30 percent (Miller, 1960, table 1, p. 30).

28. Blau and Duncan, 1967; Goldstein, 1955; Jackson and Crockett, 1964; Lipset and Bendix, 1959; Rogoff, 1953; Thernstrom, 1964.

29. Lipset and Bendix, 1959. S. M. Miller's (1960) more detailed break-downs cannot be so simply summarized but his calculations for the United States agree roughly with those of Lipset and Bendix. Jackson and Crockett (1964) give a similar ratio but lower rates in both directions.

30. Abegglen, 1958; Warner and Abegglen, 1955. See also Blau, 1956; Dynes, Clarke, and Dinitz, 1956; and Janowitz, 1956.

31. Glass, 1954; Rogoff, 1953. For more recent applications see Blau and Duncan, 1967; Jackson and Crockett, 1964; S. M. Miller, 1960. For a critical analysis of the measure see Yasuda, 1964.

32. See Blau and Duncan (1967) and Bottomore's discussion of mobility (Glass, 1954). These reports provide some justification for the notion of distinctive social class structures rather than of simple occupational hierarchies. Laumann and Guttman (1966) find similar evidence of broad class structures in their analysis of social interaction patterns.

33. Bancroft and Garfinkle, 1963; Eckstein, 1966; Hardin, 1967; Johnston and Hamel, 1966; Keyserling, 1964; Mueller and Schmiedeskamp, 1962.

34. Blau and Duncan, 1967; Brunner and Wayland, 1958; Glass, 1954; Sexton, 1961; Sibley, 1942. See particularly the study by Spady, 1967, which demonstrates that the gap between men from high status and low status backgrounds in completing college has been increasing over time.

35. For supporting analyses see the Bibliography section on Structure and Dynamics of Social Class Systems.

36. These relationships and differentials can be ascertained by comparing the occupations or incomes of different categories of educational attainment separately for different parental social class positions, different ethnic-racial groups, or different assimilation statuses. See Blau and Duncan, 1967; Glick and Miller, 1956; Lassiter, 1965; Mayer, 1955; H. Miller, 1966; Schmid and Nobbe, 1965.

37. For judicious summaries of these views see Hunt, 1961; Woodworth and Marquis, 1947. The history of efforts to apply conceptions of inherited intelligence to justify anti-black racism brought some of the theoretical defects and methodological misconceptions more fully to the fore. For a review of this literature see Pettigrew, 1964. A recent report by Jensen, 1969, returns to the genetic interpretation of racial differences in intelligence but ignores the evidence of history in the similar misconceptions applied to other ethnic groups at earlier periods (see Boody, 1926; Kirkpatrick, 1926). Some of Jensen's earlier data reports (1968), on which his interpretations were based, have passed relatively unnoticed but contain methodological errors that preclude any substantive conclusion since the dimensions of class and color are contaminated within his samples. See also the more recent work of Lesser et al. (1965) and Stodolsky and Lesser (1967) which show that ethnic differences account for variations in the kinds of skills but social class differences within each ethnic group account for most of the variation in level of ability.

38. Freedman, 1961; Held, 1961; Held and Freedman, 1963; Hunt, 1961; Riesen, 1961a, 1961b.

39. Bloom, Whiteman, and Deutsch, 1965; Caro and Pihlblad, 1964; Empey, 1946; Glass, 1954; Sewall, Haller, and Straus, 1957. Numerous studies point to the divergence between freely-formed aspirations or values

and reality-bound expectations or motivation. See Caro and Pihlblad, 1964; Empey, 1947; Rosen, 1956; Stephenson, 1957.

40. Although the proportions of the population in poverty, if poverty is defined in the same income terms for different years, have declined considerably since 1929, the rate of decline has been slower than is warranted by the rate of growth of the national income. For discussions of poverty see Cohen, 1964; Conference on Economic Progress, 1962; Keyserling, 1964a, 1964b; Lampman, 1959, 1966; Morgan et al., 1962; Townsend, 1962; U.S. Bureau of the Census, 1967.

41. Bancroft and Garfinkle, 1963; Eckstein, 1966; Johnston and Hamel, 1966; Kalish, 1966; Killingsworth, 1966; Morgan et al., 1962; Mueller and Schmiedeskamp, 1962; Saben, 1964; Stein, 1963; Wickersham, 1963.

42. For a stark suggestion about functional inequalities in a merit system see Young, 1959. Huxley (1932) and Orwell (1949) carry the idea of stabilizing functional inequalities a few steps further. Less fanciful interpretations of the limits of inequality are given by the contrasting views of Spengler, 1953, and Wrong, 1961; and by Tawney, 1931, and Tumin, 1953.

43. See K. Davis, 1953; Form, 1945; Rosenfeld, 1951, for some of the impediments to maintaining classless systems.

44. See Domhoff, 1967; Lundberg, 1968; Marris and Wood, 1971.

Index

405

DATE DUE

4/17/65			
FE 4 '85			
GAYLORD			PRINTED IN U.S.A.